Praise for *Beyond Common Sense*

"Incrementally, chapter by chapter, this world-class collection of scholars and researchers upends our common-sense understandings of human prejudice and the law's ability to control it. Yet, just as importantly, it brings to the fore a vastly deeper understanding of these issues. It is more than a state-of-the-art collection; it is a classic collection that, for a long time, will be indispensable to discussions of prejudice and the law, as well as the relationship between science and the public good."

Claude M. Steele, Stanford University

"The legal system is also a system of perception, emotion, interpersonal relations, and judgment. It is thus crucial that lawyers, social scientists, and indeed the broader public understand its psychological dimensions. This volume assembles key examples of the recent strides psychologists have made in understanding courtroom processes and the psychosocial dimensions that shape how law works in a variety of settings from workplaces to the media. It will be a vital resource for both professionals and students."

Craig Calhoun, President, Social Science Research Council

"This collection is a gem! It unmasks the fallacies on race and gender that pass for 'common sense' so skillfully that it is hard to read without shouting 'Aha!'"

Nancy Cantor, Chancellor and President, Syracuse University

"This is a timely and extremely interesting analysis of the many ways in which psychological science can contribute to a more accurate understanding of various psychological issues often raised in legal proceedings. This book will be useful, and a very good read, for the general public as well as the psychological and legal communities."

Sharon S. Brehm, Indiana University Bloomington,
President of the American Psychological Association (2007)

"This book is an indispensable guide—for scholars and practitioners alike—to the psychological science of the legal system. Its pages are filled with important, hard-won lessons that we can turn to our advantage or ignore at our peril."

Daniel Gilbert, Harvard University

To my sons, Alex and Jake, who show me the power of intuition every day, and to my wife, Susan, who lovingly reminds me of the power of law.

EB

To my children, Geoff, Lydia, and Vanessa – who demonstrate that families happen by choice, not just by law – and to my husband, Doug, who devotedly goes beyond common knowledge in his work and in our lives.

STF

Beyond Common Sense

Psychological Science in the Courtroom

Edited by
Eugene Borgida and Susan T. Fiske

© 2008 by Blackwell Publishing Ltd

BLACKWELL PUBLISHING
350 Main Street, Malden, MA 02148-5020, USA
9600 Garsington Road, Oxford OX4 2DQ, UK
550 Swanston Street, Carlton, Victoria 3053, Australia

The right of Eugene Borgida and Susan T. Fiske to be identified as the authors of the editorial material in this work has been asserted in accordance with the UK Copyright, Designs, and Patents Act 1988.

First published 2008 by Blackwell Publishing Ltd

1   2008

Library of Congress Cataloging-in-Publication Data

Beyond common sense : psychological science in the courtroom / edited by Eugene Borgida and Susan T. Fiske.
    p. cm.
  Includes bibliographical references and index.
  ISBN 978-1-4051-4573-2 (hardcover : alk. paper) — ISBN 978-1-4051-4574-9 (pbk. : alk. paper) 1. Forensic psychology—United States. 2. Justice, Administration of—Psychological aspects—United States. 3. Discrimination in justice administration—Psychological aspects—United States. 4. Discrimination—United States. 5. Physical-appearance-based bias. I. Borgida, Eugene. II. Fiske, Susan T.
  KF8922.B49 2008
  614′.1—dc22
                                                                          2007019834

A catalogue record for this title is available from the British Library.

Set in 10.5 on 12.5 pt Galliard
by SNP Best-set Typesetter Ltd., Hong Kong
Printed and bound in Singapore
by C.O.S. Printers Pte Ltd

The publisher's policy is to use permanent paper from mills that operate a sustainable forestry policy, and which has been manufactured from pulp processed using acid-free and elementary chlorine-free practices. Furthermore, the publisher ensures that the text paper and cover board used have met acceptable environmental accreditation standards.

For further information on
Blackwell Publishing, visit our website at
www.blackwellpublishing.com

Contents

Notes on Contributors

Craig A. Anderson, Distinguished Professor of Psychology at Iowa State University, is a leader in human aggression theory and media violence research. He is widely regarded as the foremost expert on the effects of exposure to violent video games. His research on aggression, media violence, depression, and social judgment has had a profound influence on psychological research and theory and on modern society. He is coauthor of *Violent Video Game Effects on Children and Adolescents: Theory, Research, and Public Policy* (2007, Oxford University Press). His tireless efforts to educate public policy-makers and the general public have earned him recognition as one of the most influential and respected social psychologists in the world.

Mahzarin R. Banaji is the Richard Clarke Cabot Professor of Social Ethics in the Department of Psychology at Harvard University, and the Carol K. Pforzheimer Professor at the Radcliffe Institute for Advanced Study. Her BA is from Nizam College in India and her PhD from Ohio State University. She held a postdoctoral fellowship at the University of Washington and previously taught at Yale University where she was Reuben Post Halleck Professor of Psychology. She is the author of numerous articles and book chapters, and the recipient of awards such as a James McKeen Cattell Fund Award, and fellowships from the Guggenheim and Rockefeller Foundations. Banaji studies human thinking and feeling as it unfolds in social context.

R. Richard Banks is Professor of Law and Justin M. Roach, Jr. Faculty Scholar at Stanford Law School. Professor Banks has written and lectured extensively, especially in the area of race and the law. Much of his scholarly work has concerned the structure of conceptions of racial discrimination. Relevant articles include "Beyond profiling: Race, policing, and the drug war," *Stanford Law Review, 56* (2003), "Racial profiling and antiterrorism efforts," *Cornell Law Review, 89* (2004), and "Race-based suspect selection and color blind equal protection doctrine and discourse," *UCLA Law Review, 48* (2001).

Margaret A. Berger is the Suzanne J. and Norman Miles Professor of Law at Brooklyn Law School in New York, where she teaches evidence, civil procedure, and courses on the interaction of science and the law. She is the coauthor of *Weinstein's Evidence*, and has authored chapters in both editions of the Federal Judicial Center's *Reference Manual on Scientific Evidence*, as well as many articles on issues relating to science in the courtroom. She currently serves on the National Academies of Science Committee on Law, Science and Technology. Professor Berger is a graduate of Radcliffe College and Columbia University School of Law.

Eugene Borgida is Professor of Psychology and Law, Adjunct Professor of Political Science, and Morse-Alumni Distinguished Professor of Psychology at the University of Minnesota. He was the Fesler-Lampert Chair in Urban and Regional Affairs at the University of Minnesota, 2002–2003. He received his BA with High Honors in Psychology and Sociology from Wesleyan University, and his PhD in Social Psychology from the University of Michigan. He has written on social cognition, attitudes and persuasion, political psychology, and on the use of psychological science in court. Borgida has served as an expert witness in a number of class action and single-plaintiff sex discrimination cases.

Margaret Bull Kovera is Professor of Psychology and former Director of the Forensic Psychology PhD Program at John Jay College of Criminal Justice and the City University of New York. She is a Fellow of the American Psychological Association and has received the 2000 Saleem Shah Award for Early Career Achievement in Psychology and Law and the 2004 Outstanding Teacher and Mentor in Psychology and Law Award from the American Psychology-Law Society (AP-LS). She is the President-elect of AP-LS. For the past decade, she has had continuous funding from the National Science Foundation for her research on jury decision-making and eyewitness identification.

Linda L. Collinsworth, Assistant Professor of Psychology at Millikin University, was recently named the John C. Griswold Distinguished Professor of Behavioral Sciences. She is a graduate of the University of Illinois, Urbana/Champaign. She has done extensive work in the area of sexual harassment, having participated in the evaluation of over 100 plaintiffs in sexual harassment litigation. Dr Collinsworth was graduate research fellow with the Department of Defense Manpower Data Center assisting with their studies of sexual harassment in the military. In addition, she was a member of the research team that examined gender bias in the Federal courts managed by the 8th Circuit.

Faye J. Crosby is Professor of Psychology at the University of California, Santa Cruz. A social psychologist specializing in issues of social justice, she has written, cowritten, edited, or coedited 14 books and over 150 articles and chapters. Crosby is the recipient of numerous awards including the Carolyn Wood Sherif Award (bestowed by Division 35 of the APA), the Lewin Award (bestowed by the Society for the Psychological Study of Social Issues), and an honorary doctorate from Ball State University. Crosby's most recent book, published by Yale University Press, is *Affirmative Action is Dead; Long Live Affirmative Action*. Crosby also writes about and attempts to put into practice good mentoring.

Shari Seidman Diamond (JD, University of Chicago; PhD, Social Psychology, Northwestern University) is Howard J. Trienens Professor of Law and Professor of Psychology at Northwestern University and Senior Research Fellow at the American Bar Foundation. A leading empirical researcher on the jury process and legal decision-making, she has published extensively in both law reviews (e.g., *Stanford, Virginia, University of Chicago*) and behavioral science journals (e.g., *American Psychologist, Law & Society Review, Law and Human Behavior*). She has practiced law (Sidley & Austin), been Editor of the *Law & Society Review*, served as President of the American Psychology-Law Society, and received the 1991 APA Award for Distinguished Research Contributions in Public Policy. She has testified as an expert in American and Canadian courts on juries, trademarks, and deceptive advertising.

John F. Dovidio (MA, PhD in Social Psychology from the University of Delaware) is currently Professor of Psychology at Yale University. Dr Dovidio is Editor of the *Journal of Personality and Social Psychology – Interpersonal Relations and Group Processes*, and he was previously Editor of *Personality and Social Psychology Bulletin*. His research interests are in stereotyping, prejudice, and discrimination; social power and nonverbal communication; and altruism and helping. He received SPSSI's Gordon Allport Intergroup Relations Prize in 1985, 1998, and 2001 for his research on intergroup relations and the Kurt Lewin Award in 2004.

Alice H. Eagly is Professor of Psychology, James Padilla Chair of Arts and Sciences, and Faculty Fellow in the Institute for Policy Research at Northwestern University. Her interests include the study of gender, attitudes, prejudice, and stereotypes. She has written or edited several books and numerous journal articles and chapters in edited books. Her awards include the Distinguished Scientist Award of the Society for Experimental Social Psychology, the Donald Campbell Award for Distinguished Contribution to Social Psychology, and the Carolyn Wood Sherif Award of the Society for the Psychology of Women for contributions a scholar, teacher, mentor, and leader.

Jennifer L. Eberhardt is currently an Associate Professor of Psychology at Stanford University. She received her PhD in Psychology from Harvard University. Before going to Stanford she held a joint faculty position at Yale University in Psychology and in African & African American Studies. Professor Eberhardt's primary research interests include racial stereotyping, prejudice, and discrimination. In her most recent work, she examines how the stereotypic association of Black Americans with criminality can influence visual perception, attention, and memory. She has explored this topic with the lay public as well as with police officers from a variety of law enforcement agencies.

Phoebe C. Ellsworth is the Frank Murphy Distinguished University Professor of Psychology and Law at the University of Michigan. She received her AB from Harvard and her PhD in Social Psychology from Stanford. Her research interests include death penalty attitudes, jury behavior, social science methodology and the use of social science in law, and the relationship between cognition and emotion. She is a fellow of the American Academy of Arts and Sciences, and is on the board of directors of the Death Penalty Information Center.

David L. Faigman is Distinguished Professor of Law, University of California, Hastings College of the Law. He writes extensively on the law's use of science. He is the author of *Laboratory of Justice: The Supreme Court's 200-Year Struggle to Integrate Science and the Law* and *Legal Alchemy: The Use and Misuse of Science in the Law*. He is also coauthor of the four-volume treatise, *Modern Scientific Evidence:*

The Law and Science of Expert Testimony (with Kaye, Saks, Sanders, & Cheng). Professor Faigman was a member of the National Academies of Science panel that investigated the scientific validity of polygraphs.

Susan T. Fiske is Professor of Psychology, Princeton University (PhD, Harvard University). Her research investigates emotional prejudices (pity, contempt, envy, and pride) at cultural, interpersonal, and neural levels, and she has expert-witnessed in gender discrimination cases. She authored *Social Cognition* (1984, 1991, 2007, each with Taylor) and *Social Beings: A Core Motives Approach to Social Psychology* (2004). Among her editing projects are the *Annual Review of Psychology* (with Schacter & Kazdin) and the *Handbook of Social Psychology* (with Gilbert & Lindzey). She was elected President of the American Psychological Society and member of the American Academy of Arts and Sciences.

Louise F. Fitzgerald is Professor of Psychology and Women's Studies at the University of Illinois at Urbana-Champaign. She received her BA in Psychology from the University of Maryland and her PhD in Psychology from the Ohio State University (1979). She is one of the leading social science experts in the U.S. on the topic of sexual harassment in education and the workplace, which she was among the first to study in a scientific manner. She is the author of more than 75 scholarly articles, chapters, and monographs and has coauthored three books on the topic of women and work. She was the social science consultant to Professor Anita Hill's legal team during the confirmation hearings of U.S. Supreme Court Justice Clarence Thomas, and serves extensively as a behavioral science consultant and expert witness. Most recently, she was appointed senior social science consultant to the U.S. Eighth Circuit's Taskforce on Gender Fairness in the Courts. In recognition of her contributions, she was the 2003 recipient of the American Psychological Association's Public Interest Award for Distinguished Contributions to Research in Public Policy.

Maryanne Garry is a Reader in Psychology at Victoria University of Wellington in New Zealand. She received her PhD in 1993 from the University of Connecticut. Her research examines factors that contribute to or help reduce false memories, such as doctored photographs, real photographs, or placebos, and has appeared in numerous journals and books. She is a member of the Executive Board for the Society of Applied Research in Memory and Cognition, and she has been an expert witness in several countries, commenting on the reliability of human memory.

Douglas A. Gentile is a developmental psychologist, and is Assistant Professor of Psychology at Iowa State University and the Director of Research for the National Institute on Media and the Family. As the director of the Media Research Lab at Iowa State University, he is one of the country's leading researchers of media's impacts on children and adults (both positive and negative). Dr Gentile has authored numerous studies and is the editor of the recent book *Media Violence and Children: A Complete Guide for Parents and Professionals* (2003, Praeger) and coauthor of the upcoming book, *Violent Video Game Effects on Children and Adolescents: Theory, Research, and Public Policy* (2007, Oxford University Press). His research has been reported on National Public Radio's *Morning Edition*, NBC's *Today Show*, in the *New York Times, Washington Post, Los Angeles Times,* and *USA Today.* He received his doctorate in child psychology from the Institute of Child Development at the University of Minnesota.

Peter Glick (AB, Oberlin College, 1979; PhD, University of Minnesota, 1984) is a Fellow of the American Psychological Association and the Association for Psychological Science. His work on ambivalent sexism (with Susan T. Fiske) was recognized with the 1995 Gordon W. Allport Prize for best paper on intergroup relations. This theory and related empirical work challenge conventional views of prejudice as an antipathy by showing how "benevolent sexism" (subjectively positive, but patronizing, attitudes toward women) as well as hostile sexism is related to gender inequality.

Sarah M. Greathouse received her MS in Legal Psychology from Florida International University and is currently working on her PhD in Psychology at the City University of New York. To date, her research has focused on issues relevant to jury decision-making and eyewitness identification and has been funded by the Society for the Psychological Study of Social Issues and the American Psychology-Law Society. She serves as the editorial assistant for *Law and Human Behavior,* the official journal of the American Psychology-Law Society.

Samuel R. Gross, Professor of Law at the University of Michigan, teaches and studies criminal procedure, the law of evidence, and the use of social science in law. His published work has focused on the death penalty, racial profiling, false convictions and exonerations, the use of expert witnesses in litigation, and the relationship between pretrial negotiations and trial outcomes.

Barbara A. Gutek holds the Eller Chair in Women and Leadership and is a Professor in the Department of Management and Organizations, Eller College of Management, University of Arizona. She is the author of over 100 books and articles, including some of the first research articles on sexual harassment, published in the early to mid-1980s. In 1994 Gutek received two awards from the American Psychological Association: the Division 35 Heritage Award for a "substantial and outstanding body of research on women and gender" and the Committee on Women in Psychology Award as a "Distinguished Leader for Women in Psychology." She also received an award from the Academy of Management's Women in Management Division, the Sage Scholarship Award, in 1994. She was President of the Society for the Psychological Study of Social Issues in 1996–1997.

Lisa E. Hasel is an Iowa State University PhD student. She is the 2006 Psi Chi/APS Albert Bandura Graduate Research Award winner for her research on face composites. This research, published in *Law and Human Behavior*, shows that composites created by eyewitnesses in multiple-witness cases can be improved by morphing. A 2004 summa cum laude BA graduate of Tufts University, she graduated with the highest thesis honors. Lisa became the first Social Psychology Research Fellow at the Innocence Project in New York City in the Fall of 2006. She expects to complete her PhD at Iowa State University in 2008.

Harlene Hayne is the Head of the Psychology Department and the Director of the Early Learning Project at the University of Otago in Dunedin, New Zealand. She received her PhD from Rutgers University and was a Postdoctoral Fellow at Princeton University. Hayne is an Associate Editor of *Psychological Review* and she serves on the editorial boards of *Developmental Psychology*, *Journal of Experimental Child Psychology*, *Infancy*, and *Infant Behavior and Development*. She is a Fellow of the Royal Society of New Zealand, and the past recipient of the American Psychological Foundation's Robert L. Fantz Award for Excellence in Infancy Research.

Michelle C. Haynes received her PhD in Social Psychology from New York University in 2006. She is currently an Assistant Professor as

University of Massachusetts Lowell. Her research examines stereotyping processes in organizationally relevant contexts.

Madeline E. Heilman is Professor of Psychology at New York University. For over 20 years she was Coordinator of the Industrial/Organizational Psychology program, which is now part of the Social Psychology program. After receiving her PhD from Columbia University, she joined the faculty at Yale's School of Organization and Management and was a Visiting Professor at Columbia University's Graduate School of Business. A Fellow of SIOP, APA, and APS, she currently serves on the editorial boards of the *Journal of Applied Psychology* and the *Academy of Management Review*. Her research has focused on sex bias in work settings, the dynamics of stereotyping, and the unintended consequences of preferential selection processes.

William G. Iacono is a Distinguished McKnight University Professor at the University of Minnesota. He has served as a consultant regarding lie detection for the U.S. Congress Office of Technology Assessment, the CIA, the Joint Security Commission of the Clinton Administration, the Department of Defense, and the State of Minnesota Task Force for the Treatment of Sex Offenders. He has testified in state and federal courts regarding the scientific status of lie detection, voice stress analysis, and "brain fingerprinting" on over 30 occasions; he has also testified before elected representatives, including the U.S. Senate, about legislation regarding applications of lie detector tests.

Saul M. Kassin is Distinguished Professor of Psychology at John Jay College of Criminal Justice. Kassin's research focuses on police interrogations and confessions and their impact on juries. He also studies the psychology of eyewitness testimony, including its general acceptance in the scientific community. He is a Fellow of APA and APS, has testified as an expert witness in state, federal, and military courts, lectures frequently to judges, lawyers, law-enforcement groups, and psychologists, and has appeared as a consultant for several national and syndicated news programs. He has authored the textbooks *Psychology* and *Social Psychology* and has coauthored and edited a number of scholarly books, including: *Confessions in the Courtroom, The Psychology of Evidence and Trial Procedure*, and *The American Jury on Trial: Psychological Perspectives*.

Anne M. Koenig is a graduate student in Social Psychology at Northwestern University, working with Alice Eagly. She received an MS from Northwestern University and a BS from Iowa State University. Her research interests include prejudice, stereotypes, and gender issues. She is especially interested in the influence of nontraditional gender behaviors on perceivers' impressions. Along these lines, her dissertation research examines the main tenets of role congruity theory of prejudice.

Linda Hamilton Krieger is a Professor of Law at the University of California, Berkeley School of Law (Boalt Hall), where she teaches employment discrimination law, civil procedure, and antidiscrimination law and policy. After graduating from Stanford University (BA, Psychology, 1975) and New York University School of Law (JD, 1978), Krieger practiced law in San Francisco, where she litigated employment discrimination cases at the trial and appellate court levels. Before joining the Boalt faculty in 1996, Professor Krieger taught at the Stanford Law School and was a Research Fellow at the Stanford Center on Conflict and Negotiation. Since joining the Boalt Hall faculty she has served as a Bunting Fellow at the Radcliffe Institute for Advanced Study at Harvard University (2004–2005) and as a Visiting Professor at the Harvard Law School (2006–2007). Her major writings include "The content of our categories: A cognitive bias approach to discrimination and equal employment opportunity" (*Stanford Law Review*, 1995), "Civil rights perestroika: Intergroup relations after affirmative action" (*California Law Review* 1998), *Backlash Against the ADA: Reinterpreting Disability Rights* (University of Michigan Press, 2003), and "Behavioral realism in employment discrimination law" (with S. T. Fiske, *California Law Review*, 2006).

Frank J. Landy holds the title of Emeritus Professor of Psychology at Penn State University. In his 26-year career at Penn State, he conducted field research and published widely in areas related to industrial and organizational psychology. In 1989 Landy was elected President of the Society for Industrial and Organization Psychology (Division 14 of the APA). Throughout his career he has been an active consultant to business and industry, concentrating on issues related to employment decision-making. Currently the CEO of the Landy Litigation Support Group, he devotes most of his professional time to advising parties to litigation on issues related to employment discrimination.

Elizabeth F. Loftus is Distinguished Professor at the University of California, Irvine. She holds faculty positions in both Criminology,

Law, and Society and in Psychology and Social Behavior. She received her PhD in Psychology from Stanford University. Since then she has published 20 books and over 400 scientific articles. Loftus's research of the last 30 years has focused on the malleability of human memory. She has been recognized for this research with five honorary doctorates and election to the National Academy of Sciences and the American Philosophical Society. She is past President of the Association for Psychological Science, the Western Psychological Association, and the American Psychology-Law Society.

Todd D. Nelson is the Gemperle Foundation Distinguished Professor of Psychology at California State University, Stanislaus. He received his PhD in Social Psychology from Michigan State University in 1996. In addition to several chapters and empirical articles, he has published a textbook on prejudice, edited a book on ageism, and was Editor of a 2005 *Journal of Social Issues* issue on ageism. His research examines the effect of ageism on older adults.

Julie E. Phelan is a Javits Fellow and PhD candidate in Social Psychology at Rutgers University in New Brunswick, New Jersey. She graduated from Lafayette College in Easton, Pennsylvania with a BA in Psychology and a BA in Art. Her research interests include intergroup relations, implicit social cognition, and gender prejudice.

Lee Ross is the Stanford Federated Credit Union Professor of Psychology at Stanford University, where he has taught since receiving his PhD from Columbia University in 1969. The author of two influential books (*Human Inference* and *The Person and the Situation*) with Richard Nisbett and many articles on biases in judgment and decision-making, Ross has more recently focused his work on sources of intergroup misunderstanding and conflict, and barriers to dispute resolution. He has also published research on death penalty attitudes, strategies for overcoming stereotype threat, and other topics relevant to psychology and law, and been a frequent trial consultant in tort cases.

Laurie A. Rudman (PhD in Psychology from the University of Minnesota) is an Associate Professor of Psychology at Rutgers University in New Brunswick, New Jersey. Her research interests are social cognition and intergroup relations with a focus on implicit attitudes and beliefs. The author of over 40 professional publications, she is currently Associate Editor of *Personality and Social Psychology Bulletin*. Her honors and awards include a National Research Service Award

(National Institutes of Health), and (with Eugene Borgida) the Gordon Allport Prize for the best paper on intergroup relations, given annually by the Society for the Psychological Study of Social Issues.

Gary L. Wells is Distinguished Professor at Iowa State University and Director of Social Science at the AJS Institute of Forensic Science and Public Policy in Greensboro, NC. He is a 1977 PhD (Social Psychology) from Ohio State. He has over 150 publications and his research on eyewitness identification has appeared regularly in top journals in psychology. His findings have been incorporated into policies and practices in many legal jurisdictions across the U.S. and Canada. Wells received the Distinguished Contributions to Psychology and Law Award from the American Psychology-Law Society in 2001 and was President of the Society in 2005–2006.

Foreword: The Moral Obligation to be Intelligent

John Erskine, founder of Columbia University's core curriculum in the 1920s, wrote an essay with the title I admiringly filch[1] in which he poses this question:

> If a wise man would ask, what are the modern virtues? and should answer his own question . . . what virtues would he name? . . . When the wise man brings his list of our genuine admirations, will intelligence be one of them? We might seem to be well within the old ideal of modesty if we claimed the virtue of intelligence. But before we claim the virtue, are we convinced that it is a virtue?

Throughout the essay, Erskine bemoans the English and American lack of faith in intelligence as a virtue, contrasting it with the special place accorded instead to goodness as a virtue. Although he sees some bucking of this trend (for example, "we do not insist that the more saintly of two surgeons shall operate on us for appendicitis"), Erskine's thesis remains that intelligence is not given its due in Anglo-Saxon tradition.

To be clear, neither Erskine nor I use the term intelligence to mean a general mental faculty – tapped by how fast I can type (I can type very fast) or whip through multiple choice questions (we did not do multiple choice in India) – that nineteenth- and many twentieth-century psychologists called intelligence. Instead, what I mean, with the benefit of the writings of Robert Sternberg and Howard Gardner, and what Erskine meant even without, is a broad set of competencies, skills, and knowledge.

---

[1] The same title was used for a collection of Lionel Trilling's essays, edited by Leon Wieseltier (Farrar, Strauss, & Giroux, 2000).

In the introduction to a collection entitled *American Character and Other Essays*, Erskine defends criticism leveled against the central thesis of the essay in question: "I still feel that the essay says clearly what I meant – that to be as intelligent as we can is a moral obligation – that intelligence is one of the talents for the use of which we shall be called to account – *that if we haven't exhausted every opportunity to know whether what we are doing is right, it will be no excuse for us to say that we meant well*" (emphasis mine).

Speaking to Phi Beta Kappa at Amherst College, he said that "to know is to achieve virtue . . . Between this rising host that follow intelligence [speaking of immigrants], and the old camp that put their trust in a stout heart, a firm will, and a strong hand, the fight is on. Our college men will be in the thick of it. If they do not take sides, they will at least be battered in the scuffle. At this moment they are readily divided into those who wish to be men – whatever that means – and those who wish to be intelligent men, and those who, unconscious of blasphemy or humor, prefer not to be intelligent, but to do the will of God."

Perhaps more so than in Erskine's time, today we recognize the importance of being intelligent rather than merely earnest. But I hazard that even today we still separate intelligence from goodness of heart; we not only assume the two to be divorced, we continue to place value on the latter. We expect our judges and jurors, lawyers and prosecutors, and other guardians of the law to strive to be good, to be as pure of heart as humanly possible. We do not set the same standards of intelligence and competence, asking as intently: What do they know, and knowing what they know, are they fit to judge?

As a science of the mind has grown, any simple separation between intelligence and goodness has become untenable, as has the privileging of either. More so than ever, to be good requires intelligence about matters that our predecessors, even those here just yesterday, not only did not know but could not know. So the standards of what it means for *us* to be intelligent are indeed higher, and one reason they are legitimately higher is the vibrant presence of the mind and behavioral sciences. At every turn, the data from these sciences teach us something about ourselves so new, or challenge a view of ourselves that is so appealing (and so wrong), that it is not possible – unless one is despairingly lacking in curiosity (if not goodness itself!) – to ignore the evidence.

If a proper offering of justice is a public purpose then a justice system that is not constantly striving and evolving in its use of new knowledge is in trouble. To avoid it, what can we know, to start with?

Modern psychology provides at least two clear messages: Our minds and behavior are fallible; our minds and behavior are malleable.

First the bad news: There are known and established limits on the human ability to introspect and know, limits on the ability to compute and assess, limits placed on us by the situations of our existence, by the experiences we have, by the fact that our brains and minds evolved in the ways in which they did. I have argued that the bounds on rationality, the very ones that keep us from being smart also keep us from being good. And to avoid the problem of having to define what is good, I have used as the gold standard each person's own conscious report of their preferences, beliefs, and values. If obvious deviance from our own statements of what is good and virtuous is brought to light, we are faced with a question that should be a primary motivator in the law: What are we willing to do, given our drifting from our own goals of fair and just treatment?

A striking example of "we are what we see" is Craig Anderson's review of the effects of viewing aggression on producing aggression. The length and breadth of that work is a persuasive sampling of our bounded rationality – that we mimic even unwanted aspects of our environment because of the laws of learning, because the stuff is out there. We mimic it whether we intend to or not. Why is it that science has put all the nails in the coffin of this problem but nobody is willing to perform the last rites? Most likely, it is because the message from the evidence on the effects of viewing aggression runs up against the First Amendment. But even somebody like myself, a First Amendment fanatic, believes that nowhere is there better expertise than among the great legal minds of this country to work out the issues raised by this robust body of science. If hate speech is something we have attempted to tackle alongside the First Amendment, why not this?

From study after study pointing to the bounds on our ability to be who we would like to be, in a thousand different ways, the pillar of twentieth-century social psychology was erected to show that good people can be bad – and just as bad as bad people! If this insight alone could be incorporated into the way the law intuits about humans and their situations, we will have catapulted ourselves into a place radically different than the primitive assumptions that show up in our thinking about the few bad apples in Enron, the bad Americans of Abu Ghraib that we cannot seem to shake off.

The good news comes from observations that we are flexible, sensitive to context and adapting to changing demands. As just one example, Susan Fiske has shown that although social groups dictate how we look at individuals, we see people as individuals rather than as members of social groups – if knowledge about their groups becomes irrelevant to the task at hand.

We change our behavior – actively, by placing ourselves at tables where the food tastes like nothing we've eaten before. First we spit it out, then we become addicted. Likewise, first we might shy away or fight, but if the stakes change we are equally naturally able to cooperate and help. We also change our minds, or rather our minds are changed. Ellsworth and Gross's analysis of radical shifts in attitude toward capital punishment is worth scrutiny not just because of what it says about that blemish but also for what it says about the very concept of attitude. So this remarkable flexibility is also a part of what we have discovered about what it means to be human. Attitudes, preferences, beliefs, values and the behaviors that reflect them are not fixed even though they may appear that way, perhaps because the world they reflect is relatively stable.

In both – understanding the limits and the capacities of humans in the context of social relationships, social groups, and social institutions – lies the stuff of what the law must be intelligent about. To be intelligent means many things of course. For the present purpose, I will underscore that intelligence is knowing how to weigh the evidence that flies in the face of steadfast assumptions. It means to know when causality can be inferred and not, to know when the weight of correlational evidence must be taken seriously, to know that a replication is worth much more than a single demonstration, to know that when new methods divulge strange truths about us and our brethren, it may be the theory that has to go. The moral obligation to be intelligent requires that we keep abreast of discoveries that require old views to be bagged and put out on the curb for recycling – every week.

Eugene Borgida and Susan Fiske have breathed life into Erskine's idea that we are morally obliged to be intelligent. They understand that although this requirement should be everywhere, it is so much more urgent where decisions carry the authority of the law, where decisions wield justice, where the difference between suffering and happiness lies in the power given to a few and chosen to defend the many and less chosen.

As my own conversations with judges and lawyers have grown, I have been filled with admiration for their ability to understand large and obscure areas of knowledge required for every case before them, only to learn entirely new domains required by the next one. But let me push here a bit. To understand, for example, the technicalities of the Challenger disaster in order to assign legal responsibility, is one thing. It is quite another to develop a feeling for the tectonic movements of a science so as to be ready to anticipate and cope with the big breaks when they occur. It is this latter form of education that Borgida and Fiske's volume offers.

The research presented in this book shows what the mind and behavioral sciences have discovered about perception, memory, judgment, and decision-making, about discrimination generally, and more specifically about racial profiling, harassment, and capital punishment. But these papers do more than tackle a set of topics. As a totality they also reveal a way of knowing, a unique type of expertise that has developed iteratively about human nature and social circumstances that stands ready to be absorbed into the bones of the law.

Treat this book as a sanctuary in which to allow the mind to change its view of itself. Reading it, I was struck by the strength of the experimental evidence in some cases, the strength of the integration and argument in others, and above all the singular message it offers up: Common sense may be plenty common, but it is not always sense.

The building blocks of concepts that the law fundamentally deals with – mental states and social structures – are the topics of this volume, and in them lies much of what we are morally obliged to be intelligent about.

Mahzarin R. Banaji
Cambridge, MA

Acknowledgments

Even common sense acknowledges that it "takes a village" to success-fully launch any multifaceted project, and ours was no exception. We thank Kay Deaux and Lee Ross, who encouraged the book in its formative stages. Christine Cardone, Executive Editor for Psychology at Wiley-Blackwell, supported and coaxed us from the beginning, and then championed our project as it developed. Sarah Coleman at Wiley-Blackwell impressively facilitated the completed project, and Joanna Pyke lived up to her advance billing as a skilled and astute copy editor. At our local editorial offices, many thanks go to the superb research assistance of Margy Pickering and Lauren Christiansen in the Psychol-ogy Department at the University of Minnesota, and to Mary Rumsey, legal reference librarian extraordinaire at the University of Minnesota Law Library. They checked, organized, discussed, and corrected. Any remaining errors, of course, are not their fault but doubtless ours. Because of all their great effort on our behalf, the volume that you have before you is a much better book.

Introduction

Eugene Borgida and Susan T. Fiske

The trouble with people is not that they don't know, but that they know so much that ain't so.

Josh Billings (1874)

One significant value of much social science research is that it makes clearer what we only dimly perceive, if we perceive it at all. It is not surprising to hear people say about many psychological findings that, "of course, we knew this all along." Yet, very often, what we thought we knew all along is not quite correct or, more importantly, not quite correct in substantial detail.

Faigman, Kaye, Saks, and Sanders (2005)

What people think they know about human behavior "that ain't so" or perhaps "not quite correct in substantial detail" is fundamentally what this edited volume investigates. To be sure, people rely on their common sense and use "flawed" intuition (Krieger, 2004; Krieger & Fiske, 2006) to interpret many significant contemporary issues – from the promise of biotechnology (Silver, 2006) to why ordinary people torture enemy combatants (Fiske, Harris, & Cuddy, 2004) or make false confessions (Kassin, 2005), even to the lively debate between proponents of evolutionary theory and intelligent design. For example, according to Lilienfeld (2006): "The foremost obstacle standing in the way of the public's acceptance of evolutionary theory is not a dearth of common sense. Instead, it is the public's erroneous belief that common sense is a dependable guide to evaluating the natural world" (p. 48).

The timely scientific contributions and analytic commentaries in this volume directly confront common sense and intuitive beliefs about human behavior. Across the board, the scientific chapters address whether insights from psychological science challenge and even contradict intuitive understandings about stereotyping, prejudice, and discrimination, but – significantly – also in about a dozen other behavioral domains that intersect with various legal system processes (e.g., eyewitness identification, repressed memories, polygraph testing, affirmative action, and others). Indeed, various chapters reveal a substantive "disconnect" between lay conceptions of human behavior and the pertinent scientific data base (also see Krieger & Fiske, 2006).

The Impetus for this Project

In large part, the idea for this collection came from the lively "crossfire" debate that took place at the 2004 annual meeting of the Association for Psychological Science (APS) during an invited symposium on "Psychology and the law: Stereotypes and discrimination." Industrial-organizational psychologist Frank Landy chaired the session, and the participants included both coauthors of this book, Lee Jussim (Psychology, Rutgers University), Barbara Gutek (Management and Psychology, University of Arizona), and employment discrimination attorney, David Copus (then with Jones, Day, Reavis & Pogue and now Of Counsel with Ogletree Deakins). In large part, the debate revolved around a set of controversial issues:

- To what extent does a body of scientific research advance our thinking about human behavior beyond common sense and common knowledge?
- Does scientific knowledge in a particular field of inquiry have to be "perfect" in order to play a role in educating fact finders (whether juror or judge)?
- Do inconsistencies or disagreements in a particular field of science mean that the field's contributions (i.e., areas of agreement or scientific consensus) should be dismissed as inapplicable to the legal questions at hand?
- Is the external validity or generalizability of experimental laboratory research so inferentially constrained that scientific findings based on such an approach should be inadmissible in litigation contexts?
- Do scientists become "advocates" and "activists" the moment they decide to serve as expert witnesses in litigation, as some have

claimed (Mitchell & Tetlock, in press)? Different scientific fields have struggled with these same questions in policy as well as legal contexts (Kaiser, 2000). Many climate scientists, for example, seem to be persuaded that the scientific database supports limits on the emission of heat-trapping or "greenhouse" gases to stem the adverse effects of global warming. But there is also considerable debate among climate scientists as to whether scientists should be policy advocates (offering "policy prescriptive statements") or science educators who offer "policy-relevant statements" and leave the policy decision-making to governmental agencies (Revkin, 2007).

Evidentiary Standards and Issues

While these and related issues were vigorously debated at the APS symposium with regard to the use of gender stereotyping research in single plaintiff and class action sex discrimination litigation, we were struck by the extent to which most of these issues had surfaced at other "intersections" between the law and the psychological or social sciences over the past two decades. In many but not all instances, these issues played out in the context of proferred expert scientific testimony and the evidentiary "gate-keeping responsibility" of trial court judges (Faigman & Monahan, 2005; Sales & Shuman, 2005; Sanders, Diamond, & Vidmar, 2002). Under the U.S. Supreme Court precedent established in 1993 with *Daubert v. Merrell Dow Pharmaceuticals, Inc.* (reiterated and extended in two other Supreme Court cases that comprise the "*Daubert* trilogy" – *General Electric Co. v. Joiner*, 1997, and *Kumho Tire Ltd. v. Carmichael*, 1999), trial court judges must determine whether the basis for the opinion (i.e., the methods used to evaluate the empirical basis for the opinion before the court) is more likely than not valid and reliable, and whether the proferred expert opinion is relevant. In addition, *Kumho* held that all types of expert testimony, whether clinical or experimental, are subject to this judicial gate-keeping role in federal courts, and that appellate courts should be inclined to defer to admissibility rulings made at the trial court level.

The Federal Rules of Evidence (2004) and most state evidence codes have been amended to reflect this gate-keeping role for judges. Federal Rule 702, more so than any other rule of evidence, exemplifies the influence of *Daubert* and its progeny. Rule 702 essentially codified the *Daubert* "gatekeeper" requirement and highlights the complex set of issues that arise when trial judges have to make admissibility decisions about psychological (or any other type of) scientific evidence:

> If scientific, technical, or other specialized knowledge will assist the trier of fact to understand the evidence or to determine a fact in issue, a witness qualified as an expert by knowledge, skill, experience, training, or education, may testify thereto in the form of an opinion or otherwise, if (1) the testimony is based upon sufficient facts or data; (2) the testimony is the product of reliable principles and methods; and (3) the witness has applied the principles and methods reliably to the facts of the case.

What are the practical implications? First, different types of knowledge are subject to the scrutiny of *Daubert* requirements (scientific, technical, and other specialized knowledge). Second, a witness must be qualified "by knowledge, skill, experience, training, or education" to offer an expert opinion. Third, the particular expert opinion must "assist the trier of fact to understand the evidence or to determine a fact in issue." This aspect of Rule 702 calls attention to one core question we raised earlier: Does the body of scientific research that is the foundation for the expert's opinion advance our thinking about human behavior beyond a common-sense understanding? If so, then the expert opinion is helpful to the fact finder. The fourth aspect of Rule 702 requires that the expert opinion be based on "sufficient facts or data" and be the "product of reliable principles and methods." Do the principles and methods on which the opinion is based pass the *Daubert* test of validity? Is the method adequate and sufficient to support the opinion proffered to the court?

Finally, Rule 702 emphasizes that a qualified witness may offer an opinion if "the witness has applied the principles and methods reliably to the facts of the case." If the expert opinion is admissible, then it must be relevant to some fact in dispute in a particular case; the methodological basis for the expert evidence must support or "fit" the proffered opinion. In *United States v. I. Lewis Libby*, 05–394 (D.D.C. 2006), for example, former chief of staff for Vice President Dick Cheney, Lewis Libby, adopted a "false memory defense" in his obstruction of justice trial related to the alleged disclosure of covert CIA agent Valerie Plame. The motion to admit expert testimony on behalf of Libby's defense from two prominent psychologists who specialize in memory and eyewitness behavior was denied on the basis of the "fit" criterion from *Daubert*. While the proferred testimony met the *scientific status* standard, DC District Court Judge Walton ruled that the testimony would not assist the jury in understanding the evidence and facts at issue in the case.

In most instances, the expert provides fact finders with general information, and the fact finders must apply the general information to the particulars of the case at hand. A *social framework analysis*, for example, uses general conclusions from tested, reliable, and peer-reviewed social science research and applies them to the case (Borgida, Hunt, & Kim, 2005; Faigman & Monahan, 2005; Fiske & Borgida, 1999; Monahan & Walker, 2002). It assesses *general causation* in a research area, in order to inform fact finders about more *specific causation* issues associated with a particular case. General causation concerns whether causality between two factors exists at all. For example, an expert who testifies that smoking can cause lung cancer is addressing general causation because the testimony is designed to establish that the phenomenon occurs. Specific causation, in contrast, refers to whether the phenomenon of interest occurred in a particular context. It refers to whether causality between two factors actually did exist in the case at hand. In our smoking and lung cancer example, an expert who testifies that smoking a particular brand of cigarettes caused a specific patient's lung cancer is addressing specific causation.

This distinction between general causation and specific causation, which surfaces in several of the science chapters and commentaries in this volume, represents a significant challenge to both psychological and social scientists and legal gatekeepers. At the crux of the matter is whether research on general causation is relevant and admissible in a given case *in the absence of* proof of specific causation (Faigman & Monahan, 2005). Will courts permit testimony on the general without specific proof of the particulars? Importantly, in non-medical causation cases (e.g., *Daubert* involved a medical case where the question was whether a morning sickness drug caused birth defects), a psychological scientist who can validly describe a general phenomenon may not have the wherewithal scientifically to claim that it is more likely than not that an individual case is an instance of that general phenomenon. In other words, some research domains may be well represented with considerable quality research at the general level without any testimony conveying inferences about specific causation. Nevertheless, expert opinion at the level of specific causation remains a pressure point in this legal context. As Faigman (1999) observed, legal and scientific thinking about scientific evidence differ considerably: "While science attempts to discover the universals hiding among the particulars, trial courts attempt to discover the particulars hiding among the universals" (p. 69).

Taking Stock: Psychological Science in the Courtroom

The *Daubert* trilogy framework, as just discussed, most certainly represents a consensus framework for taking stock of scientific opinions proffered in court. We suggest that this approach also constitutes a useful framework for taking stock of psychological science in other legal and social policy contexts as well. From the outset of this project, we presumed that researchers could be quite capable of addressing in a non-partisan manner what psychological science has to offer about a particular area of research (e.g., areas of agreement and areas of disagreement) and whether (or not) the scientific database advances our understanding of a given "slice" of human behavior beyond what is accessible to common sense and intuitive understandings. In fact, this was precisely our "charge" to the 14 prominent social scientists and their colleagues who have contributed science chapters to Parts I and II of this volume. We also asked these scientists to address a related question if it was pertinent to their area of research: Is the research in their domain of expertise scientifically "mature" enough, and sufficiently generalizable to the legal issues at hand, that expert opinion would potentially assist fact finders?

We then identified seven commentators, five of whom are highly respected authorities on different issues at the law and social science intersection, and two senior and highly respected psychological scientists who individually have had considerable research *and* litigation experience, to provide brief commentaries on these 14 science chapters. We asked them to focus on whether, and to what extent, some or all of these 14 "exemplars" advance our understanding of the common set of legal and scientific evidence issues that undergird this project. Commentators were specifically asked for their perspective on the legal, policy, and/or scientific significance of some or all of the research areas presented in Parts I and II of this volume; they were not asked to provide more narrow, peer-review "critiques" of each contribution.

What Lies Ahead

The 14 science chapters were not randomly selected from some larger population of "relevant" research topics in psychological science. To the contrary, we selected 14 topics that have already emerged as among the most significant and controversial legal and social policy questions in contemporary society. From the outset of this project, we suspected that the general framework just presented, based on evidentiary standards in the law, could be usefully applied to thinking about these diverse domains of empirical research. We had every reason to believe that our roster of scientists and legal scholars would ultimately provide us (and you!) with the "data" to evaluate the utility of this approach. Part I presents seven science chapters on stereotyping, prejudice, and discrimination in the context of race, age, and gender. Part II presents seven chapters about psychological science on other processes in the legal system.

Across both sets of science chapters, virtually all of the issues embedded in our evidentiary framework emerge. First, to varying degrees, the science chapters directly assess scientific status in the pertinent field and the extent of (and where relevant, the lack of) scientific consensus. Patterns of findings that are peer reviewed, robust, and established via multiple methods are identified. Some scientific domains are more "mature" than others and have been "in business" for a longer time (e.g., research on eyewitness identification discussed in the Wells and Hasel chapter); others are relatively new, less well-developed, but progressing and generating potentially important scientific insights (e.g., research described in Nelson's chapter on the "young science of prejudice against older adults"). Still others, like the Anderson and Gentile chapter on media violence, review the "unequivocal scientific evidence" in the context of a general public and media industry that seems to believe (for various reasons discussed in the chapter) that the science is equivocal. The accuracy of polygraph exams, for example, has been scientifically challenged by independent review panels at the National Research Council and the National Academy of Science, yet, as Iacono's chapter discusses, the widespread use of the polygraph continues in government agencies and elsewhere, and does not appear to diminish in forensic settings either.

Relatedly, challenges to internal and external validity are discussed in several of the science chapters. For example, the external validity critique of "artificial work" paradigms (vs. "real world" paradigms) that Landy discusses in his commentary applies to a few of the chapters on stereotyping, prejudice, and discrimination. The chapters by Eagly and Koenig, and especially by Heilman and Haynes, address this critique head on in the context of research on gender prejudice and stereotyping and gender bias in performance appraisals. And the legal commentaries by Berger and by Diamond contribute further insights into how to think about the generalizability of experimental research in the context of eyewitness identification and false confessions.

Besides taking stock of the psychological science via the *Daubert* test of scientific validity, all of the science chapters address the relationship between the pertinent body of scientific knowledge and common sense or common knowledge. In her legal commentary, using a few of these chapters to make the case, Krieger dissects common-sense psychological theories that work their way into legal rules and discrimination jurisprudence. As with Krieger's chapter, those by Banks, Eberhardt, and Ross, Ellsworth and Gross, Wells and Hasel, Kassin, and Kovera and Greathouse point out that various legal system actors, including trial level and appellate judges who are deciding issues of law, are prone to relying on "flawed" intuitive theories when thinking about matters of legal doctrine. Lay jurors are certainly prone to this way of thinking, but the argument here is that judges also rely on ad hoc, intuitive theories when thinking about social science evidence on the death penalty, the psychology of false confessions, eyewitness identification issues, and remedying the effects of pretrial publicity. Importantly, no *Daubert*-type criteria can evaluate these embedded lay psychological theories. As Krieger notes, this state of affairs is hugely problematic: ". . . There is a whole judicial world out there in the nation's courtrooms, where judges are doing psychology, much of it demonstrably bad psychology, and weaving it, unscrutinized, into the law." Krieger, and other contributors to this volume, share the view that extant empirical research holds the promise to help shape various legal doctrines in "more behaviorally realistic ways."

Strikingly, many of the science chapters in this volume exhume culturally entrenched common-sense beliefs that influence judgments about a wide swath of legally relevant behavior. *In each instance*, the science reported in the chapter is at odds with or undermines these common-sense beliefs. Fitzgerald and Collinsworth use as a case in point the scientifically established failure of plaintiffs in sexual harassment cases to lodge formal complaints about the harassment. Loftus, Garry, and Hayne, in their chapter on repressed and recovered memory, take on the widely held but empirically unsupported beliefs about repression and false memories. For example, they suggest that "claims for its validity are more a matter of clinical faith than of scientific reality."

The gap between science and common sense also appears in the research literatures on eyewitness identification (Wells & Hasel, chapter 8) and false confessions (Kassin, chapter 10). Lay fact finders are not sufficiently well informed in either realm. Wells and Hasel, in fact, suggest that the legal system itself – not just lay fact finders – may not understand what psychological science has to offer about eyewitness identification. Kassin also addresses this disconnect between the science and common sense, making the case that the psychology of false confessions is profoundly counterintuitive: "Generalized common sense leads us to trust confessions, a behavior that breaches self-interest in a profound way (most people believe they would never confess to a crime they did not commit and they cannot imagine the circumstances under which anyone would do so)" (p. 23).

This disconnect between a science-based understanding and what Banks' legal commentary in chapter 20 refers to as "prevailing common-sense understandings" is perhaps most acute in the science chapters on stereotyping, prejudice, and discrimination. For example, in their chapter Banks, Eberhardt, and Ross focus on unintentional (vs. purposeful, intentional) discrimination as it currently exists under antidiscrimination law, and conclude on the basis of several areas of research that race remains salient and consequential in the context of criminal justice decision-making and policy. "Race matters," they suggest; research, not common sense, strongly implies that discrimination is a matter of context, and discriminatory actions are influenced by the particular contexts and settings in which decisions are made.

Crosby and Dovidio also focus on how much the conceptualization of discrimination implicit in the law is at odds with the dynamics of discrimination as revealed by contemporary empirical research in social psychology. More specifically, they discuss how affirmative action in the U.S. challenges commonly held assumptions about the dynamics of discrimination (i.e., the focus on intentional discrimination) and in fact aligns with what social psychologists know about implicit biases. Affirmative action policy, as their chapter suggests, is a social and legal policy that actually was designed to address subtle forms of discrimination: "In short, one way to conceive of affirmative action policy is to see it as having recognized the implausibility of the emphasis on conscious intent, an emphasis that is embedded in the common knowledge of American jurisprudence, and then crafting a plan of action that is more congruent with the current, research-based understanding of implicit bias" (p. 16).

Similarly, Eagly and Koenig suggest that science and common sense part ways when trying to understand the nature of gender prejudice. They suggest that "context is paramount" when understanding gender prejudice. Contrary to "prevailing common-sense understandings," prejudice is not simply the expression of inaccurate and negative attitudes toward a particular group, and members of a majority group, not just members of minority groups, can be targets of prejudice. For example, drawing on the social psychological science that examines role-congruity theory (Eagly, 2004; Eagly & Diekman, 2005; Eagly & Karau, 2002), Eagly and Koenig argue that people can be prejudiced toward any social group when the group's stereotype activates conflicts with the characteristics necessary to enact the social roles they are trying to occupy. Extant science on gender stereotyping, reviewed by Rudman, Glick, and Phelan, reveals the empirical complexity that contradicts two beliefs grounded in common knowledge: a) that individuating information about a person necessarily thwarts stereotypical judgments (and sex discrimination), and b) that favorable beliefs about women – positive female stereotypes – are beneficial to them; instead, the empirical evidence suggests that these favorable beliefs may actually harm women by undermining their credibility and prestige.

Thus, as all of the science chapters in this volume indicate, common sense, intuitive psychological "theories" about human behavior, abound inside and outside the courtroom. The truly significant question in all of these clashes between psychological science, on the one hand, and common sense, on the other, is (as Krieger articulates in her commentary) therefore whether different types of jurisprudence and social policy will be based on unchecked, ad hoc, and implicit psychological understandings, as is currently the case, or whether advances in psychological and social sciences will explicitly inform legal theories and policy.

The answers to this question, and other important evidentiary concerns also raised in this volume, are "cutting-edge" matters within psychological science and legal scholarship circles. That these concerns are now before us, in both the scientific and legal communities, not to mention in society at large, could not come at a more propitious time for the social and behavioral sciences. These sciences are being challenged strenuously and the scope of their contributions is being questioned by funding agencies and politicians alike. What is so apparent from the volume you hold in your hands is that people's perceptions of this body of scientific knowledge are deeply influenced by common-sense lay theories that are out of synch with the realities of scientific evidence.

We hope that the project represented in this book can inform a civil dialogue about this conflict, and generate new research agendas. We hope that you will decide, as we have, that the science chapters and commentaries address the "weight" of the evidence regarding the added value of psychological science in legal and policy contexts. Whether this work and these perspectives will ultimately lead to substantive changes remains to be seen. Stay tuned.

REFERENCES

Billings, Josh (Henry W. Shaw) (1874). *Everybody's friend, or: Josh Billings' encyclopedia & proverbial philosophy of wit & humor.* American Publishing Co.

Borgida, E., Hunt, C., & Kim, A. (2005). On the use of gender stereotyping in sex discrimination litigation. *Journal of Law and Policy, 13*(2), 613–628.

Daubert v. Merrell Dow Pharmaceuticals, Inc., 509 U.S. 579 (1993).

Eagly, A. H. (2004). Prejudice: Toward a more inclusive definition. In A. H. Eagly, R. M. Baron, & V. L. Hamilton (Eds.), *The social psychology of group identity and social conflict: Theory, application, and practice* (pp. 45–64). Washington, DC: APA Books.

Eagly, A. H., & Diekman, A. B. (2005). What is the problem? Prejudice as an attitude-in-context. In J. F. Dovidio, P. Glick, & L. Rudman (Eds.), *Reflecting on the nature of prejudice*: Fifty years after Allport (pp. 19–35). Malden, MA: Blackwell.

Eagly, A. H., & Karau, S. J. (2002). Role congruity theory of prejudice toward female leaders. *Psychological Review, 109,* 573–598.

Faigman, D. L. (1999). *Legal alchemy: The use and misuse of science in the law.* W. H. Freeman.

Faigman, D. L., Kaye, D. H., Saks, M. J., & Sanders, J. (Eds.) (2005). *Modern scientific evidence: The law and science of expert testimony.* (2005–2006 ed., Vol. 2, pp. 567–620). Eagan, MN: Thomson West.

Faigman, D. L., & Monahan, J. (2005). Psychological evidence at the dawn of the law's scientific age. *Annual Review of Psychology, 56,* 631–659.

Federal Rules of Evidence (2004, December 31). Washington, DC: U.S. Government Printing Office.

Fiske, S. T., & Borgida, E. (1999). Social framework analysis as expert testimony in sexual harassment suits. In S. Estreicher (Ed.), *Sexual Harassment in the Workplace* (pp. 575–83). Boston: Kluwer Law.

Fiske, S. T., Harris, L. T., & Cuddy, A. J. C. (2004). Policy Forum: Why ordinary people torture enemy prisoners. *Science, 306,* 1482–1483.

General Electric Co. v. Joiner, 522 U.S. 136 (1997).

Kaiser, J. (2000). Taking a stand: Ecologists on a mission to save the world. *Science, 287*(5456), 1188–1192.

Kassin, S. M. (2005). On the psychology of confessions: *Does* innocence *put* innocents *at risk? American Psychologist, 60*(3), 215–228.

Krieger, L. H. (2004). The intuitive psychologist behind the bench: Models of gender bias in social psychology and employment discrimination law. *Journal of Social Issues, 60*(4), 835–848.

Krieger, L. H., & Fiske, S. T. (2006). Behavioral realism in employment discrimination law: Implicit bias and disparate treatment. *California Law Review, 94,* 997–1062.

Kumho Tire Ltd. v. Carmichael, 526 U.S. 137 (1999).

Lilienfeld, S. O. (2006). Why scientists shouldn't be surprised by the popularity of intelligent design: Perspectives from psychology. *Skeptical Inquirer, 30*(3), 46–49.

Mitchell G., & Tetlock, P. E. (in press). Antidiscrimination law and the perils of mindreading. *The Ohio State Law Review.*

Monahan, J., & Walker, L. (2002). *Social science in law: cases and materials* (5th ed.). Westbury, NY: Foundation.

Revkin, A. C. (2007, February 6). Melding science and diplomacy to run a global climate review. *New York Times.*

Sales, B. D., & Shuman, D. W. (2005). *Experts in court: Reconciling law, science, and professional knowledge.* Washington, DC: American Psychological Association.

Sanders, J., Diamond, S. S., & Vidmar, N. (2002). Legal perceptions of science and expert knowledge. *Psychology, Public Policy, and Law, 8,* 139–53.

Silver, L. M. (2006). *Challenging nature: The clash of science and spirituality at the new frontiers of life.* Ecco/Harper Collins.

Part I

Psychological Science on Stereotyping, Prejudice, and Discrimination

1

Race, Crime, and Antidiscrimination

R. Richard Banks, Jennifer L. Eberhardt, and Lee Ross

Introduction

Well into the twentieth century, racism was an accepted and fundamental aspect of many of our social institutions. Then, in the course
of a few decades, American society came to view racial discrimination
and the overt expression of racist sentiments as morally repugnant.
The Supreme Court, Congress, and innumerable state and local legislatures prohibited discrimination in a wide array of settings. These
reforms aimed to secure racial minorities equal treatment in housing,
in the workplace, in the marketplace, and in the courts.

One consequence of the momentous changes during this period
was the ascendance of the antidiscrimination principle, which, at its
core, prohibits adverse treatment of individuals on the basis of their
race. The antidiscrimination principle has achieved broad acceptance
and popular legitimacy in American society. It is a principle that constitutional and statutory law alike embrace. Today, in marked contrast
to earlier eras, both conservatives and liberals join in condemning racial
discrimination. Indeed, leaders of the Civil Rights Movement who
once were excoriated as dangerous agitators and agents of civil unrest
(and sometimes jailed for that reason), now are universally honored.

Yet there is ongoing debate about racial discrimination in contemporary society. The persistence of significant racial disparities in
education, employment, income, and health, for example, has fueled
disagreement about the extent and nature of discrimination currently
faced by racial minority group members. Social psychological research
has played a prominent role in this debate, largely by shifting the focus
from the sorts of deliberate, animus-driven forms of discrimination that
are clearly proscribed by law, to subtler, less conscious, and less hostile
manifestations of racial bias whose legal status and social significance

are far less clear. Indeed, a great deal of social psychological research focuses on bias among individuals who genuinely believe themselves to be racially unbiased and in fact would be distressed to find out that their behavior indicates otherwise (Dovidio & Gaertner, 1986; Eberhardt & Fiske, 1998; Fiske, 1998; Greenwald & Banaji, 1995). This research demonstrates that, notwithstanding the legal and moral condemnation of discrimination and overt bias, negative racial stereotypes remain psychologically salient to virtually all Americans. Moreover, racial discrimination can be documented both inside and outside of the laboratory, and may well shape the experiences of many racial minorities.

These issues are especially salient in the criminal justice system. Overtly race-based laws and sentencing schemes are now nonexistent. Moreover, state actors in the criminal justice system who once staunchly defended racially biased practices now insist that they are affording equal treatment to all. Since the 1980s, however, racial disparities in rates of incarceration have become *more*, rather than less, pronounced. Aggregate increases in incarceration, coupled with growing disparities, have resulted in staggering and unprecedented levels of incarceration for Black men in particular (see Banks, 2003). A study by the Bureau of Justice Statistics found that in 2001 nearly 17% of Black men were currently or previously imprisoned, that Black men are more than five times as likely as White men to enter prison, and that Black women are six times as likely as White women to enter prison, and nearly as likely as White *men* to do so (Bonczar, 2003). The central role of the war on drugs in contributing to such racial disparities has been well established (Mauer, 1999; Meares, 1998; Tonry, 1995). Social scientists also point to a host of socioeconomic factors, including poverty, educational attainment, unemployment, family structure, and neighborhood influences.

This chapter considers some social psychological research that bears on the question of racial discrimination in the decision-making of law enforcement officers, judges, and juries. We make two claims. First, race remains a psychologically and socially salient characteristic that often influences people's perception, judgment, and decision-making. Contrary to any assumption that the criminal justice system has become color blind, the research we review leaves little doubt that race can influence decision-making in the domain of criminal justice. Second, thorny policy questions arise when the findings of the social psychological research are considered in light of substantial, and troubling, racial differences in the likelihood of criminal victimization, criminal offending, and incarceration.

This chapter is structured as follows. First, we present some specific research findings that bear on the issue of unintentional racial discrimination in the criminal justice system. Then we discuss the implications of unintentional discrimination for antidiscrimination law. Finally, we situate the findings of the social psychological research in the context of real-world crime statistics and describe some of the conceptual and practical policy questions that arise.

The Research

In this section, we examine social psychological studies relevant to controversies regarding decision-makers' use of race in stops and arrests, decisions to shoot, and harshness of sentencing.

Racial profiling

During the late 1990s, controversy about the racial profiling of African American and Latino motorists prompted changes in law enforcement policies. Law enforcement agencies and government officials now routinely and publicly disavow racial profiling in ordinary policing, including drug law enforcement. Many states and local jurisdictions have prohibited racial profiling, and the Bush Administration has, for the most part, banned its use by federal law enforcement agencies. Racial profiling nevertheless remains of particular interest in the context of this chapter. Well-entrenched beliefs and practices might be expected to survive in spite of legal prohibitions. The stereotype of African American criminality would certainly qualify as well entrenched, and might promote racial profiling.

In a recent series of studies, Eberhardt, Goff, Purdie, and Davies (2004) examined the psychological association between race and criminality. In one study they exposed police officers to a set of either Black faces or White faces and asked simply, "Who looks criminal?" The results of this study not only confirmed the existence of the relevant stereotype, but also showed the importance of a factor widely recognized in minority communities but too often ignored in research on race—racial *prototypicality*. Police officers not only viewed more Black faces than White faces as criminal, they viewed those Black faces rated as most stereotypically or prototypically Black (e.g., those faces with wide noses, thick lips, or dark skin) as the most criminal of all.

Eberhardt and colleagues (2004) also conducted studies to examine how the stereotypic association between African Americans and criminality might operate in the context of racial profiling. Specifically, they asked whether prompting people to think about crime makes them more likely to visually attend to or focus on Black people. Eberhardt et al. prompted half of the students participating in the study to think about crime by subjecting them to a "subliminal priming" procedure that involved a brief presentation of line drawings of objects associated with violent crime (e.g., guns, handcuffs, and knives). These participants, all of whom were White, were exposed to the crime images so quickly that they were not able to consciously recognize them. The other half of the participants, who were in the control condition, were subliminally exposed to a "dummy" image that consisted of jumbled patches from each crime-relevant line drawing. Next, all of the participants were shown a Black face and a White face simultaneously.

As predicted, the participants who had been primed to think about crime looked at the Black face more than did those participants in the control condition. Moreover, Eberhardt et al. found that explicit prejudice did not moderate this selective attention to Black faces. Students who scored low on measures of explicit prejudice were just as likely as higher scoring participants to attend disproportionately to the Black face when they were primed to think about crime. The researchers suggested that this visual bias may be due to implicit associations between Blacks and crime – associations that are automatic, unintentional, and frequently beyond the individual's control.

Such associations between race and criminality are not limited to college students. Eberhardt et al. conducted a similar study with police officers and found the same pattern of results. They exposed police officers to words associated with violent crime (e.g., apprehend, capture, arrest, shoot) rather than visual images. Officers who were primed to think of apprehending, capturing, arresting, and shooting were visually drawn to the Black face. Near the end of the study, officers were presented with a Black photo lineup and a White photo lineup and asked to indicate the two faces they saw earlier in the study. Officers who had been prompted to think of violent crime recalled seeing a Black face that appeared more stereotypically Black than the face they actually had seen. The same priming, however, produced no systematic pattern of memory errors when the task involved identification of White faces.

The decision to "shoot" a "suspect"

Perhaps the most volatile charges of racial bias in law enforcement arise from police officers' use of lethal force against African American or

Latino suspects. Beyond the much publicized cases of Rodney King and Amadou Diallo and scores of other more mundane cases reported in short articles in our daily newspapers, there is the sobering statistic that African Americans are four times more likely than Whites to die during, or as a result of, an encounter with a law enforcement officer (Brown & Langan, 2001).

Anecdotal and statistical evidence of this sort has led a number of social psychological researchers to examine the potential influence of race on research participants' decisions about whether to "shoot" a potential "suspect" (Correll, Park, Judd, & Wittenbrink, 2002; Greenwald, Oakes, & Hoffman 2003; Plant & Peruche, 2005). These studies typically use a videogame simulation in which study participants are presented with a series of images of Black or White men who are either "armed" (e.g., holding a gun) or "unarmed" (e.g., holding a harmless object such as a wallet or cell phone) and instructed to shoot only if the man in the image is armed. Once again, the results of such studies attest to the potential consequences of racial stereotypes that associate Black people with threats of violence. Participants made the fastest and most accurate decisions when deciding whether to shoot *armed Black* men and *un*armed *White* men (e.g., see Correll et al, 2002). More specifically, the decision to shoot an armed target was made more quickly and accurately if that target happened to be African American rather than White, and the decision not to shoot an unarmed target was made more quickly and accurately if the target happened to be White rather than African American.

The shooting behavior studies – some of which have been conducted not only with university undergraduates and community members but with police officers as well – provide powerful evidence that racial stereotypes create associations and expectations that may play a role in the sort of split-second decisions that may literally be a matter of life or death for police officers and suspects alike. Two additional findings are worth noting. First, none of the shooting behavior studies found any relationship between standard paper-and-pencil measures of individual racial bias and performance in the shooting task. Second, and perhaps even more surprisingly, researchers found no difference in shooting behavior as a function of the participant's race. In studies that examined the behavior of both Black and White participants, both types of participants were quicker in correctly deciding to shoot when the target was Black and in deciding not to shoot when the target was White (Correll et al., 2002).

Sentencing decisions

Racial disparities in sentencing, particularly capital sentencing, have long fueled substantial popular and scholarly debate. For most of our history, the debate was stoked by evidence of particular harshness in the penalties meted out to Blacks convicted of killing Whites, or to Black males convicted of raping or assaulting White women (Cole, 1999; Kennedy, 1997). Some researchers continue to find evidence that Black defendants are more likely to receive a death sentence than White defendants (e.g., Baldus, Woodworth, Zuckerman, Weiner, & Broffitt, 1998). The more robust finding, however, pertains to the race of the victim rather than the race of the perpetrator: Killers of White victims are more likely to be sentenced to death than are killers of Black victims. This finding, which holds even after researchers do their best to statistically control for a wide variety of nonracial factors that may influence sentencing, has been characterized by the U.S. General Accounting Office (1990) as "remarkably consistent across data sets, states, data collection methods, and analytic techniques" (p. 5).

Racial stereotypes may nonetheless play a significant role in determining which individual defendants receive the death penalty. One recent study has examined whether a stereotypically Black appearance increases the likelihood that a defendant will be sentenced to death. In this study, Eberhardt, Davies, Purdie-Vaughns, and Johnson (2006) presented the photographs of convicted African American defendants eligible to receive the death penalty in Philadelphia between 1979 and 1999 to study participants who were unaware that the photographs depicted convicted murders. The participants were asked to rate the racial stereotypicality of each face. Among African American defendants convicted of murdering a White victim, the findings were dramatic. Whereas 58% of those defendants rated as highly stereotypically Black had been sentenced to death, only 24% of those defendants low in racial stereotypicality were sentenced to death. This stereotypicality effect was statistically significant even after controlling for defendant attractiveness and various other nonracial factors likely to influence sentencing, including aggravating and mitigating circumstances, heinousness of crime, defendant socioeconomic status, and victim socioeconomic status.

In a similar study Blair, Judd, and Chapleau (2004) used sentencing data from Florida to examine the relationship between sentence length and the Afrocentric features of White and Black defendants. Importantly, study participants were asked to rate the Afrocentricity of each defendant's features relative to other members of the defendant's racial group. (In other words, participants were asked to compare White defendants to other Whites, and Black defendants to other Blacks. Thus, overall rating of Afrocentric features was the same across groups, despite the fact that Black defendants, as a group, would obviously have more Afrocentric features than White defendants.) Although Black and White defendants, in the aggregate, received comparable sentences when controlling for defendant criminal history, as predicted, the investigators found that when Black and White defendants were considered jointly, Afrocentric features were associated with longer sentences. The association between Afrocentric features and harshness of treatment is provocative, and may constitute further evidence of the pervasive influence of race-related stereotypes.

Other investigators have employed a subtler methodology to examine this relationship between stereotypes and sentencing. In two studies by Graham and Lowery (2004) – one with police officers and the other with juvenile probation officers – participants were first subliminally primed with either words related to African Americans (e.g., minority, Harlem, basketball) or race-neutral words (e.g., jealousy, accident, pleasure). The participants were then presented with a short vignette describing a crime against a person or property in which the cause of the crime was left ambiguous and the race of the alleged perpetrator was not specified. Finally, the participants were asked to rate the alleged perpetrator's character traits (e.g., maturity level, violent disposition) and to indicate an appropriate punishment.

In each of these studies, participants primed with race-related words proved more likely to attribute negative traits to the alleged offender and, accordingly, to recommend harsher sanctions for that offender – even though they were never asked to guess the offender's race (Graham & Lowery, 2004). The investigators concluded that "at least some of [the racial disparities in the juvenile justice system] might be due to the unconscious racial stereotypes of those who determine the fate of offending youth." Interestingly, these investigators, like many others who use related methodologies, found no statistically significant association between individual participants' explicit racial attitudes and the effect of the racial prime on their responses.

The findings reviewed above counter any assumption that discrimination is a relic of the past. The research clearly documents the continuing role of race in perception and decision-making, notwithstanding the adoption of the antidiscrimination principle and the moral condemnation of racial bias.

However, the studies identify a different species of discrimination than that which is most familiar to the lay public. The conventional view is that racial discrimination is overt, conscious, intentional, controlled, and categorical. It is assumed that people who discriminate know they are doing so, and indeed intend to do so. Such discrimination is also thought to reflect beliefs about, and attitudes toward, an entire group. In sum, the thought of racial discrimination may often conjure an image of the old-fashioned racist, the sheriff blocking the door to the schoolhouse, for example, because, he says, Negroes are inferior and cannot be permitted to attend school with Whites. This prototypical image of discrimination developed partly as a reflection of the sort of bias and discrimination characteristic of the Jim Crow era. During much of that period, views that would today be regarded as horribly misguided and indefensible were then openly expressed and endorsed. It was the effort to overthrow that form of discrimination that gave rise to the antidiscrimination principle. Thus, it is unsurprising that contemporary lay theories of discrimination continue to draw upon the dominant forms of racial bias from the era during which the antidiscrimination principle arose.

In contrast to the conventional understanding of discrimination, the sort of bias and discrimination captured by the studies we review is unconscious, unintentional, automatic, and sensitive to within-group distinctions. In the shooting studies, for example, there was no evidence that individual differences in shooting behavior could be explained on the basis of individual differences in levels of conscious bias. The same disjunction between behavior and conscious bias arose in the racial profiling studies. The sentencing studies used real-world data to show the extent to which the judges and jurors attend to intragroup distinctions in making sentencing decisions. And, finally, where the conventional account centers on the unreconstructed racist, the studies we review center on the decision-making of individuals who would likely profess, and genuinely believe themselves, to be racially unbiased both in their views and in their intentions. Nevertheless, the evidence shows that race shapes their perceptions and judgments.

The accumulation of social psychological evidence concerning unintentional discrimination has prompted a number of legal scholars to examine the applicability of antidiscrimination law to such discrimination. Our goal in the next section is to briefly describe the implications of unintentional discrimination for antidiscrimination law.

The Law

We begin by noting the increasingly common view that antidiscrimination law currently prohibits only intentional discrimination. Some commentators have concluded that evidence of unintentional discriminaton therefore calls for a reformation of antidiscrimination doctrine. This view is mistaken. Yet the belief that the antidiscrimination doctrine exempts unintentional discrimination is easy to understand. In the Supreme Court's 1976 decision in *Washington v. Davis*, the Court seemed to conclude that a claim of racial discrimination in violation of the Equal Protection Clause of the Constitution requires a finding of discriminatory intent. The Court stated that "a *purpose* to discriminate must be present." During the next few years, the Supreme Court twice reiterated the so-called intent requirement, stating forthrightly that "Proof of racially discriminatory intent or purpose is required to show a violation of the Equal Protection Clause." Lower federal courts have generally followed the lead of the Supreme Court, speaking of discrimination as intentional, or as the result of a discriminatory purpose.

The Supreme Court's decision in *Washington v. Davis*, though, need not be read as exempting from prohibition racial discrimination that is prompted by unconscious bias. Consider the facts of the case. Unsuccessful Black applicants for employment as police officers in the District of Columbia argued that the personnel test employed to select officers violated the equal protection clause, largely because four times as many Blacks as Whites failed the exam. In deciding this case, the Court had to articulate a standard for evaluating a policy that did not facially distinguish on the basis of race. One possibility was that a formally race neutral policy would violate the Equal Protection Clause if it disproportionately burdens historically disadvantaged racial minorities without sufficient justification. This was the disparate impact standard that had been embraced by the lower court in *Washington v. Davis*, and recently incorporated by the Supreme Court into the federal statute prohibiting employment discrimination. *Washington v. Davis* presented the question of whether the same standard should apply to a claim of racial discrimination in violation of the Constitution. The Supreme Court said "no." A facially neutral policy could be characterized as illegal discrimination under the federal statute on the basis of its disparate impact, the Court said, but a constitutional challenge to a facially neutral policy required a finding of discriminatory intent.

The Supreme Court drew upon the discriminatory intent/discriminatory purpose language, then, to distinguish the constitutional standard from the disparate impact standard that had been adopted in the statutory context, not to distinguish intentional discrimination and conscious from an intentional discrimination and unconscious bias. The Court said, in effect, that invalidation of a facially neutral practice as discriminatory requires not only a disparate impact, but also a discriminatory intent. In neither *Washington v. Davis* nor subsequent cases did the Court say anything about unconscious bias or unintentional discrimination. The Supreme Court, of course, has never stated that discrimination is permissible if it is the unintentional result of unconscious bias. Nor is it obvious that there is any persuasive reason to exempt unintentional discrimination from the nondiscrimination mandate.[1]

Nevertheless, the Court has tended to speak in terms of discriminatory intent or purpose, a choice of terminology that reflects the conventional lay understanding of discrimination as conscious and intended. In this view, when people are treated differently on account of race, it is because the decision-maker has consciously and intentionally done so.

This widespread view of discrimination as conscious and intentional may cause judges and juries not to find discrimination where in fact they should. One might reasonably expect that conventional understanding to shape the inferences that one would be willing to draw from ambiguous evidence. If one believes that most discrimination is conscious and intentional, then in the absence of evidence of conscious ill will or intent to discriminate, one might be likely to conclude that no discrimination occurred. Similarly, if one accepts as genuine the assertion by an alleged discriminator that he did not intend to discriminate, then one likewise would conclude that no discrimination occurred. If judges and juries assume that discrimination is necessarily conscious and intentional, then they may often overlook, much less remedy, discrimination that is unintentional. Further, employers and other institutional actors will wrongly conclude that discrimination will not occur in their organization as long as everyone genuinely commits to the view that racial discrimination is impermissible and immoral. If discrimination is the product of unconscious processes over which

---

[1]   Of course, this is not to say that there is never a reason to distinguish between the two, as they may raise different remedial questions, and may be associated with different levels of moral condemnation.

people have little control, then the desire not to discriminate, by itself, would be insufficient to end discrimination.

The realization that much discrimination may be unintentional, however, does not necessarily resolve the difficult choices that antidiscrimination law confronts. In the case of interpersonal decisions or policies that are formally race-neutral, it will often be extraordinarily difficult to decide whether discrimination occurred. Consider *Washington v. Davis*. The police department had continued to use a personnel test that failed many times more Blacks than Whites even though the test had never been shown to predict performance as a police officer. On the other hand, the same department had also undertaken vigorous affirmative action efforts to recruit more Black officers and diversify the force. Given the ambiguity of the facts, could one confidently conclude that the department's selection of the test reflected a discriminatory purpose.

Determining whether a facially neutral policy or practice is discriminatory entails uncertainty. Absolute accuracy in identifying discrimination is impossible, even more so if discrimination is sometimes unintentional. Thus, antidiscrimination law must balance the tradeoff between leaving some discrimination unremedied and characterizing a challenged decision as discriminatory when, in fact, it was not. An accurate understanding of the social psychology of discrimination may be an important component of this calculus, but the recognition of unintentional discrimination does not dictate how the balance should be set.

One could require strong evidence that a particular decision was discriminatory. Such a standard would be satisfied by evidence that someone intended to discriminate or harbored conscious ill will toward a particular racial group. Such a high standard, however, would capture only the most obvious cases of discrimination, and would leave undetected instances of subtle, unintentional discrimination. But a more capacious approach attentive to the possibility of unintentional discrimination would have problems as well. It might incline judges and juries to impose liability not only in more cases where discrimination occurred, but also in more cases where, in fact, no discrimination occurred. The choice between these two approaches requires a legal determination, a means of balancing the risks of error. That determination is one with respect to which a variety of considerations may be relevant. It is not simply a matter of accurately understanding discrimination.

In sum, the recognition of unintentional discrimination does not call for any major reformation of antidiscrimination doctrine, but it does highlight the error of assuming that discrimination is necessarily conscious and intentional. It is important to recognize that discrimination may occur in the absence of conscious intent or ill will. However, that recognition cannot, by itself, determine the appropriate legal standard.

The Policy

Antidiscrimination law must not only balance the risks of error, it must also give content to the ideal of equal treatment that is at the heart of antidiscrimination law. Efforts to enforce the nondiscrimination mandate in the domain of criminal justice confront the difficult substantive question of how to implement the equal treatment principle. This dilemma is not a consequence of unintentional discrimination, but it can be well illustrated or dramatized with the findings of the social psychological research that we have reviewed.

The social psychological research is premised on there being no differences between Blacks and Whites, other than race. Experimental studies achieve their power and persuasiveness by controlling for every variable other than race. This approach allows researchers to isolate the significance of race. In the shooting studies, for example, it seems sensible to explain differences in participants' shooting behavior in terms of their responses to a suspect's race, because the suspects were identical in every way other than race.

The assumption that Blacks and Whites differ only in terms of race, however, does not extend readily to the social world. There are substantial differences between Blacks and Whites, in addition to race. What it means to say that racial inequality is deep and pervasive is that Blacks and Whites are not, to put it in terms of legal jargon, similarly situated in the social world. Race as people encounter it in the social world is unlike race as people encounter it in the laboratory. In the laboratory, race is the only thing that differs, as individuals are presumed to be otherwise identical. In the social world, in contrast, the difference of race is coupled with all sorts of other differences. This is especially true in the domain of criminal justice, where Blacks and Whites differ with respect to the likelihood of being a victim of crime, a perpetrator of crime, and being incarcerated. These differences are substantial and consequential.

The differences associated with race complicate the questions that arise at the intersection of race and crime. If groups differ along all sorts of dimensions other than race, then the policy-maker, as we will show, is presented with choices that cannot be resolved simply by a decision to eliminate discrimination. The policy questions, in our view, should not be reduced to, and cannot be adequately resolved by, the goal of elimination of discrimination. Conversely, the desire to eliminate discrimination should not be permitted to obscure the need for analysis of the race-related costs and benefits of particular policy choices.

In what follows, we consider some of the policy choices that arise when the research findings are situated in a real-world context.

The decision to shoot a suspect

The findings of the shooting behavior studies are sobering, and resonant with instances in which unarmed Black men have been shot by law enforcement officers. The arresting findings of these studies should not cause us to bypass, however, the difficult policy questions that the studies also highlight. Recall a principal finding of the shooting studies: that participants mistakenly "shot" unarmed Black suspects more often than unarmed White suspects, and failed to "shoot" armed White suspects more often than armed Black ones. While such findings offer strong evidence of racial discrimination, it is less clear how that discrimination should be eliminated. Was the problem that participants did shoot *un*armed Black suspects, or that they did *not* shoot armed White suspects? This is an important question.

A simple understanding of the antidiscrimination principle would be that race should play no role in decision-making. In the social settings that law enforcement officers and criminal suspects occupy, however, the idea of a race blind criterion against which deviations could be measured is nonsensical. Everyone has a race, and in a face-to-face social interaction, each party is aware of the other's race. It is difficult even to conceive of how police would behave if they (and criminal suspects) did not notice race, or, less outrageously, if race played no role in their decision-making.

One might say then simply that Black and White suspects should be treated identically. In what manner, though, should we attempt to achieve that goal? Should we train officers to delay a fraction of a second more when confronted with a Black suspect to make sure that he is actually armed before shooting? Or should we train officers to delay a fraction of a second less when confronted with a potentially dangerous White suspect? Either remedy, ironically, requires that the officer be trained to notice rather than to disregard the suspect's race.

Shoot/no shoot decisions entail tradeoffs that are perhaps most readily addressed in terms of signal-detection theory and the two types of errors classically dealt with in that theory (Green & Swets, 1966). In the present case one error would be to *shoot* an *un*armed suspect; the other would be *not* to shoot an *armed* suspect. To restate the findings of the shooter studies in signal-detection terms, one would say that participants made more errors of the first type in the case of

Black suspects, and more errors of the second type in the case of White suspects. In other words, there seemed to be a different tolerance for each type of error with Black suspects compared to White suspects.

To say that the tolerance for each type of error should be the same for Black as for White suspects does not indicate which shooting threshold is preferable. Again, should Black suspects be treated as White suspects are treated, or should White suspects be treated as Black suspects are treated? Typically, there is a tradeoff between the two types of errors, with the relative frequency of each type of error dependent on the decision-maker's requisite threshold of certainty that the suspect is armed before discharging his weapon. In particular, fewer shootings of unarmed suspects would be achievable only at the cost of more failures to shoot armed suspects, which would result in more dead police officers (assuming that armed suspects would sometimes use those weapons) and more dangerous felons remaining at large. Conversely, more shootings of armed suspects who might otherwise harm officers and endanger the community would be achievable only at the cost of more shootings of innocent citizens in that community. To balance the possibilities of these different types of errors, one would need to associate a cost with each type of error. The goal would be to train officers so as to minimize the aggregate costs (or, put differently, to maximize the expected aggregate benefits) of their shooting behavior.

One might reasonably conclude that however the balance is struck between protecting the lives of unarmed suspects on one hand, and the lives of officers and other community members on the other, the shooting threshold should be precisely the same for Black and White suspects. But that seemingly reasonable conclusion raises another question: What if the adoption of an identical shooting threshold for all suspects did *not* result in the lowest possible aggregate error? In other words, what if officers made more mistakes when they treated Black and White suspects identically? In the shooting behavior studies, where there is no association between race of a suspect and the likelihood that a suspect is armed, the use of the same certainty threshold would result in identical outcomes with Black and White suspects. In actual police–citizen encounters, however, Black and White suspects may differ in the likelihood of being armed, and/or in the likelihood of using their weapons to avoid arrest. Data compiled by the Bureau of Justice Statistics reveal that Blacks are dramatically overrepresented not only as victims of police violence, but as perpetrators of violence against police officers as well (Brown & Langan, 2001). Indeed, while data show that Blacks are five times as likely as Whites to be killed by the police, data also show that Blacks are five times as likely as Whites to kill a police officer (Brown & Langan, 2001).

If race is probabilistically useful in deciding whether to take the risk of shooting versus not shooting a suspect, then a dilemma arises. The shooting behavior that minimizes the total errors for both Black and White suspects may be behavior that takes into account the suspect's race. Should suspects be treated "the same" even if that means more errors would result? There will often be a tension between the ideal of race blind treatment and other values that also animate the commitment to nondiscrimination. Although we have illustrated this tension using studies that show differences in "shooting" error rates based on the race of the suspect, the analysis is not limited to that sort of example. Rather, the dilemma potentially arises whenever race is associated with relevant, though difficult to observe, characteristics. Again, our purpose here is neither to prescribe policy nor to suggest what weight should be given to different, competing, desiderata. (As an aside, however, it would surely be reasonable on many grounds to undertake the relevant cost-benefit analysis and decisions with heavy input from the community at risk – especially insofar as the crime in question is largely Black on Black or White on White.) Instead, we simply reiterate that a careful consideration of outcomes will inevitably be an important factor in any designation or identification of a nondiscriminatory baseline.

Sentencing

The same sort of dilemma that arises with respect to shooting behavior is also apparent when we consider the sentencing studies. More specifically, changes in policy designed to eliminate a sentencing disparity based on the race of the victim would create or exacerbate a sentencing disparity based on the race of the defendant. The statistics that highlight this tradeoff are the ones noted earlier suggesting that killers of Whites were more likely to be sentenced to death than were killers of Blacks (for a review, see Baldus et al., 1998 or U.S. General Accounting Office, 1990). Such racial disparity in sentencing suggests a lack of race-blindness on the part of judges and/or juries, and even more disturbingly a tendency for the decision-makers in question to value the lives of White victims more highly than the lives of Black victims (Kennedy, 1997). Yet, once again, there is the question of how to remedy the racial disparity. Increase death sentences for killers of Black victims or decrease death sentences for killers of White victims?

The fact that most capital sentencing cases concern intraracial rather than interracial murders exacerbates the problem. In particular, there is no decision-rule or sentencing threshold that could simultaneously eliminate sentencing disparities based on race of the victim without introducing disparities involving the race of the defendant. Eliminating the race-of-victim disparity – either by executing more murderers of Blacks or by executing fewer murderers of Whites – would necessarily create a race-of-defendant disparity.

The studies conducted by Eberhardt et al. (2006) and Blair et al. (2004), which linked harshness of sentencing to perceived racial prototypicality, raise less familiar but perhaps no less troubling questions, one normative, the other empirical. Should steps be taken to somehow remedy that form of discrimination? And if so, what might the consequences be of taking those steps? The first question is whether such *intra*group disparities in sentencing violate antidiscrimination norms, even when there is no *inter*group disparity. While the legal issue is one about which scholars might disagree, there can be little doubt that the findings in question reflect the impact of the very racial stereotypes, associations, and biases that antidiscrimination laws are presumably designed to address. The second question is whether measures that somehow addressed such stereotypicality discrimination in intragroup sentencing could produce or exacerbate disparities in *intergroup* outcomes.

As with race-of-defendant and race-of-victim disparities, eliminating such stereotypicality discrimination in sentencing could produce a racial disparity in *inter*group outcomes, thereby presumably violating the antidiscrimination principle. Recall the finding by Eberhardt et al. that racial stereotypicality influenced the likelihood of being sentenced to death for Black murderers of White victims, but not for Black murderers of Black victims (Eberhardt et al., 2006). This finding suggests that eliminating the stereotypicality disparity in sentencing – through the imposition of more death sentences for low stereotypicality defendants, for example – would produce an even stronger sentencing disparity with respect to murders of White victims in comparison to Black victims. The findings by Blair et al. (2004) linking the presence of stereotypically Black features in *White* perpetrators to disproportionately harsh treatment further complicate these issues. Should *White* defendants really enjoy constitutional protection against sentencing biases that are based on their personal appearance, or more particularly, that are based on the degree to which their appearance somehow triggers stereotypic associations that more typically burden the everyday experiences of *Black* citizens in general and Black defendants in particular?

Racial profiling

While only criminal defendants bear the brunt of discrimination in sentencing, and confrontations with police officers who must decide whether to shoot are fortunately (for all concerned) rare, decisions that officers make about whether to stop or search individuals who arouse their suspicion of wrongdoing are far from rare, and may especially burden minority group members. The application of the antidiscrimination principle to such decisions again raises difficult issues of remedy.

If rates of criminality for all groups or for all neighborhoods (which may of course differ in their racial composition) were similar, the standard for evenhandedness or racial fairness would be obvious. One would look for evidence of different frequencies of stops-searches, and/or for differences in the proportions of stops that failed to yield evidence of wrongdoing. But if rates of overall criminal behavior, or rates of particular types of criminal behavior, differ across groups, then a decision to eliminate racial disparities in stop-search rates would again create other types of undesirable disparities. More specifically, law enforcement officers would be obliged either to subject innocent members of the lower crime-rate group to a greater likelihood of an unwarranted stop than innocent members of the higher crime-rate group, or to allow more guilty members of the higher crime-rate group to escape detection and punishment than similarly guilty members of the lower crime-rate group.

Attempts to provide evenhanded treatment in terms of frequency of stop-searches can introduce treatment disparities in another way as well. If apprehension of the guilty reduces crime in a given neighborhood, then disparities in the apprehension of the guilty would, given high rates of intraracial crime, translate into racial disparities in the protection from crime provided to the relevant communities at large (Farmer & Terrell, 2001). It is not possible to simultaneously eliminate racial disparities in the likelihood of investigation of the innocent, the apprehension of the guilty, and the law enforcement protection provided for communities (Alschuler, 2002). In any case, analysts would be obliged to at least consider and compare the relative costs and benefits of any particular tradeoff (Banks, 2003).

Conclusion

In this chapter, we have reviewed some recent social psychological research regarding racial discrimination in the criminal justice system.

The research documents, persuasively in our view, the continued psychological salience of race, with respect to criminal justice in particular. The studies we reviewed found evidence of the influence of race on perception, judgment, and decision-making even among individuals who regard themselves as racially unbiased. These important findings rebut any facile assumption that the criminal justice system has become color blind.

When these findings are considered in light of differences across racial groups in criminal victimization, criminal wrongdoing, and incarceration, however, some difficult policy questions arise. Such policy questions extend beyond, and should not be reduced to, the goal of eliminating discrimination. Ultimately, the design of optimal social policy with respect to race and criminal justice system depends on a weighing of individual rights against the common good, both for particular groups and for society as a whole. One goal of such a policy calculus should be to create both the perception and reality of racial fairness.

REFERENCES

Alschuler, A. W. (2002). Racial profiling and the Constitution. *University of Chicago Legal Forum, 163*, 223–269.

Baldus, D. C., Woodworth, G., Zuckerman, D., Weiner, N. A., & Broffitt, B. (1998). Racial discrimination and the death penalty in the post-Furman era: An empirical and legal overview, with recent findings from Philadelphia. *Cornell Law Review, 83*, 1638–1770.

Banks, R. R. (2003). Beyond profiling: Race, policing, and the drug war, *Stanford Law Review, 56*, 571–603.

Blair, I. V., Judd, C. M., & Chapleau, K. M. (2004). The influence of Afrocentric facial features in criminal sentencing. *Psychological Science, 15*, 674–679.

Bonczar, T. P. (2003). Prevalence of imprisonment in the U.S. population, 1974–2001. *U.S. Department of Justice*. Washington, DC.

Brown v Board of Education, 347 U.S. 483 (1954).

Brown, J., & Langan, P. A. (2001). Policing and homicide, 1976–98: Justifiable homicide by police, police officers murdered by felons. *Bureau of Justice Statistics*.

Cole, D. (1999). *No equal justice: Race and class in the American criminal justice system*. New York: New Press.

Correll, J., Park, B., Judd, C. M., & Wittenbrink, B. W. (2002). The police officers dilemma: Using ethnicity to disambiguate potentially threatening individuals. *Journal of Personality and Social Psychology, 83*, 1314–1329.

Dovidio, J. F., & Gaertner, S. L. (Eds.) (1986). *Prejudice, discrimination and racism.* San Diego, CA: Academic Press.

Eberhardt, J. L., Davies, P. G., Purdie-Vaughns, V. J., & Johnson, S. L. (2006). Lookingdeathworthy: Perceived stereotypicality of Black defendants predicts capital-sentencing outcomes. *Psychological Science, 17,* 384–387.

Eberhardt, J. L. & Fiske, S. T. (Eds.) (1998). *Confronting racism: The problem and the response.* Thousand Oaks, CA: Sage Publications.

Eberhardt, J. L., Goff, P. A., Purdie, J. A., & Davies, P. G. (2004). Seeing Black: Race, crime, and visual processing. *Journal of Personality and Social Psychology, 87,* 876–893.

Farmer, A., & Terrell, D. (2001). Crime versus justice: Is there a trade-off? *Journal of Law and Economics, 44,* 345–366.

Fiske, S. T. (1998). Stereotyping, prejudice, and discrimination. In D. T. Gilbert, S. T. Fiske, & G. Lindzey (Eds.), *Handbook of social psychology* (4th ed., pp. 357–411). New York: McGraw-Hill.

Graham, S., & Lowery, B. S. (2004). Priming unconscious racial stereotypes about adolescent offenders. *Law & Human Behavior, 28,* 483–504.

Green, D. M., & Swets, J. A. (1966). *Signal detection theory and psychophysics.* Oxford, England. Wiley.

Greenwald, A. G., & Banaji, M. R. (1995). Implicit social cognition: Attitudes, self-esteem, and stereotypes. *Psychological Review, 102,* 4–27.

Greenwald, A. G., Oakes, M. A., & Hoffman, H. (2003). Targets of discrimination: Effects of race on responses to weapons holders. *Journal of Experimental Social Psychology, 39,* 399–405.

Kennedy, R. (1997). *Race, crime, and the law.* New York: Pantheon Books.

Mauer, M. (1999). The crisis of the young African American male and the criminal justice system. *U.S. Commission on Civil Rights.*

Meares, T. L. (1998). Social organization and drug law enforcement. *American Criminal Law Review, 35,* 191–227.

Plant, A. E., & Peruche, M. B. (2005). The consequences of race for police officers' responses to criminal suspects. *Psychological Science, 16,* 180–183.

Tonry, M. (1995). *Malign neglect: Race, crime, and punishment in America.*

U.S. General Accounting Office (1990). *Death penalty sentencing: Research indicates pattern of racial disparities.* Washington, DC: Author. *Washington v. Davis,* 426 U.S. 229 (1976).

2

Discrimination in America and Legal Strategies for Reducing It

Faye J. Crosby and John F. Dovidio

As every American school child knows, in the United States it is against the law to discriminate. Individuals and organizations found to act in a discriminatory manner are subject to legal sanctions as well as to social disapproval. Since the passage of the Civil Rights legislation in 1964, women and people of color have – in theory – been protected against discrimination.

To say that one can bring a suit against an individual or organization on the grounds that one has been discriminated against is to assume that the parties involved, including the courts, have some understanding of what constitutes discrimination. When rendering of a legal decision that discrimination does or does not exist in a specific instance, legal decision-makers often rely on their conceptions about what constitutes discrimination. How judges and juries think about discrimination determines whether they will find that discrimination exists.

We believe that some aspects of the conceptualization of discrimination implicit in contemporary judicial law are at variance with the dynamics of discrimination that have been revealed through systematic research in social psychology (Kang & Banaji, 2006; Smith & Crosby, in press). Specifically, judicial law currently envisions hostile intent as an essential part of discrimination. American jurisprudence has traditionally, and does currently, also see discrimination in terms of discrete episodes rather than in terms of the slow accumulation of disadvantage by some (e.g., people of color, White women) and the complementary accumulation of advantages by others (e.g., White men). Such is the "common knowledge" of contemporary American law as it relates to equal opportunity and to discrimination.

In contrast to the jurisprudence surrounding "equal opportunity law" are the regulations that govern affirmative action in employment. Brought into being by a series of executive orders, affirmative action in employment is a proactive system that does not share all the assumptions made by the more common reactive system of lawsuits. Indeed, in many ways affirmative action operates in a way that is distinct from many aspects of the American legal system.

Our chapter is organized into three parts. In the first part, we outline what social psychologists know about the dynamics of discrimination. We illustrate the processes and mechanisms by focusing on Whites' orientations toward Blacks, which has been a primary stimulus for antidiscrimination legislation in the United States. Our review in this section reveals the limitations of conceiving of discrimination as occurring primarily through hostile intent and suggests the importance of a proactive policy for combating contemporary forms of discrimination. The second part of our chapter presents the basics of affirmative action. A commonly misunderstood and often disliked system, affirmative action in employment operates in ways that challenge commonly held assumptions about the dynamics of discrimination and that are concordant with what social psychologists know about discrimination. The final part of our chapter suggests some ways in which we can all benefit by attempts to foster dialogue between legal experts and social psychologists.

Conceptions of Prejudice and Discrimination and the Law

Over the past 40 years, principles of equality and justice have been increasingly endorsed by more and more White Americans (Schuman, Steeh, Bobo, & Krysan, 1997). Overt expressions of prejudice in the United States have declined significantly. As Bobo (2001) concluded in his review of trends in racial attitudes, "The single clearest trend in studies of racial attitudes has involved a steady and sweeping movement toward general endorsement of the principles of racial equality and integration" (p. 269). Nevertheless, at the same time racial disparities in fundamental aspects of life, such as income and health persist, and in some spheres of life are increasing (Blank, 2001). Moreover, discrimination has been identified as a critical element creating and sustaining these disparities (Elvira & Zatzick, 2002; Smedley, Stith, & Nelson, 2003).

One explanation for the discrepancy between the decline in overt racial prejudice and the persistence of racial disparities is that the nature of prejudice and its expression in discrimination has changed over time. New forms of prejudice have emerged. Theories such as aversive racism (Dovidio & Gaertner, 2004), modern racism (McConahay, 1986), symbolic racism (Sears, Henry, & Kosterman, 2000), and subtle prejudice (Pettigrew & Meertens, 1995) all share one basic contention: it is that although most White Americans *consciously* endorse egalitarian principles and sincerely believe that they are not prejudiced, they continue to harbor, often *unconsciously*, negative feelings and beliefs toward Blacks and other people of color. Despite the dramatic decrease in explicit (self-reported) prejudice, the vast majority of White Americans retain relatively negative unconscious associations with Blacks (Blair, 2001).

The existence of conscious egalitarian values coupled with unacknowledged negative feelings and beliefs produces systematic patterns of interracial behavior and discrimination. Specifically, in contrast to the direct and overt pattern of discrimination exhibited by traditionally prejudiced people, the expression of discrimination by Whites who exhibit contemporary racism is more complex and influenced by a number of factors. One key element is the nature of the situation. From the perspective of aversive racism (Dovidio & Gaertner, 2004), because aversive racists consciously recognize and endorse egalitarian values and because they truly aspire to be nonprejudiced, they will *not* discriminate in situations with strong social norms when discrimination would be obvious to others and to themselves. However, the unconscious negative feelings and beliefs that aversive racists also possess will produce discrimination in situations in which normative guidelines are weak or when negative actions toward a Black person can be justified or rationalized on the basis of some factor other than race. Support for this pattern of outcomes has been obtained across studies involving a wide variety of actions, including helping and juror decision-making (Crosby, Bromley, & Saxe, 1980; Dovidio & Gaertner, 2004; Gaertner & Dovidio, 1986).

We note that other forms of contemporary racial biases, such as *modern racism* (McConahay, 1986) and *symbolic racism* (Sears et al., 2000) also hypothesize a conflict between the denial of personal prejudice and underlying unconscious negative feelings and beliefs. However, whereas modern and symbolic racism theories focus on the ideology and actions of conservatives, the aversive racism framework emphasizes biases among people who are politically liberal and who openly endorse nonprejudiced beliefs, but whose *unconscious* negative feelings get expressed in subtle, indirect, and rationalizable ways (Nail, Harton, & Decker, 2003).

Recently, Saucier, Miller, and Doucet (2005) reviewed experiments of Whites' helping behavior over the past 40 years, specifically testing implications of the aversive racism framework. Across 31 different studies, Saucier et al. found "that less help was offered to Blacks relative to Whites when helpers had more attributional cues available for rationalizing the failure to help with reasons having nothing to do with race" (p. 10). Moreover, the pattern of discrimination against Blacks remained stable over time. Saucier et al. summarized: "The results of this meta-analysis generally supported the predictions for aversive racism theory" (p. 13). They concluded: "Is racism still a problem in our society? . . . Racism and expression of discrimination against Blacks can and will exist as long as individuals harbor negativity toward Blacks at the implicit level" (p. 14).

Aversive racism, for instance, has been shown to affect how Whites make personnel decisions about White and Black candidates. In one study of hiring decisions (Dovidio & Gaertner, 2000), White college students evaluated a Black or White candidate who had credentials that were systematically manipulated to represent very strong, moderate, or very weak qualifications for the position. Consistent with the aversive racism framework, when the candidates' credentials clearly qualified them for the position (strong qualifications) or the credentials clearly were not appropriate (weak qualifications), there was no discrimination against the Black candidate. However, when candidates' qualifications for the position were less obvious and the appropriate decision was more ambiguous (moderate qualifications), White participants recommended the Black candidate significantly less often than the White candidate with exactly the same credentials. Moreover, when Dovidio and Gaertner compared the responses of participants in 1989 and 1999, the pattern of subtle discrimination in selection decisions remained essentially unchanged despite a drop in overt expressions of prejudice, measured by a self-report scale.

Subsequent research illuminates the processes operating to justify this type of discrimination against Blacks. In a study by Hodson, Dovidio, and Gaertner (2002), White participants were asked to help make admissions decisions for their university about a Black or White applicant who had uniformly strong, uniformly weak, or mixed credentials. In the Uniformly Strong Credentials condition, the applicant had high college-board scores and excellent high school grades; in the Uniformly Weak Credentials condition, the applicant had low college-board scores by the university standards and very modest high school grades. In the Mixed Credentials condition, the applicant had high college-board scores and very modest high school grades *or* low college-board scores and excellent high school grades.

Conceptually replicating the findings of Dovidio and Gaertner (2000), discrimination against Black applicants occurred only in the Mixed Qualifications condition, and primarily among participants who had some evidence of negative feelings toward Blacks in general (see also Brief, Dietz, Cohen, Pugh, & Vaslow, 2000). In addition, providing a rationalization for their decisions, there were systematic differences as a function of race in how these participants weighed the credentials of applicants with mixed credentials. For Black applicants, White participants gave the weaker dimension (college-board scores or grades) greater weight in their decisions, whereas for White applicants they assigned the stronger of the qualifications more weight. Additionally, people may often shift their emphasis of the importance of different types of credentials in ways that permit discrimination while maintaining a belief in the objective basis of the decision (Uhlmann & Cohen, 2005).

Subtle bias can also adversely affect interracial interactions as well. Whites may successfully exert control over their most overt communications, but their unconscious biases (i.e., implicit attitudes) often produce subtle nonverbal cues of tension (e.g., high rates of eye blinking) and aversion (e.g., low levels of eye contact) in interactions with Blacks (Dovidio, Kawakami, Johnson, Johnson, & Howard, 1997). The negativity amplifies Black disadvantage in two ways. First, Whites in general, and particularly those who harbor unconscious biases, find interracial situations to be cognitively demanding, presumably because they are working hard to suppress their biases (Richeson & Shelton, 2003). Second, even when negative cues are subtle, as with nonverbal behavior, they can shape the behaviors of Black interlocutors, leading them to behave in less favorable and competent ways than Whites (Word, Zanna, & Cooper, 1974). Again, without ill intention or recognition of the role of bias by Whites, Blacks at this stage of the employment process – when the opportunity is ostensibly equal – will still be susceptible to subtle bias and tend to fare worse than Whites.

As this line of research illustrates, the existence of contemporary forms of racism, such as aversive racism, has three fundamental implications for truly fair employment practices and their enforcement through the law. Current antidiscrimination laws include, as noted earlier, hostile intent as an essential element of discrimination, and successful prosecution requires evidence demonstrating that race was the primary determinant of the negative treatment. However, theory and research on contemporary forms of racism reveal, first, that discrimination often currently happens *without conscious intent*, and in fact frequently occurs among people who truly believe that they are nonprejudiced. Psychology has found that people typically overestimate how much their own and others' actions are governed by intention and vastly underestimate how much behavior occurs without conscious guidance. Furthermore, after people have engaged in behaviors they tend to infer their intentions from their actions (Wilson, 2002). Thus, good intentions are not sufficient for protecting Whites from discriminating against members of minority groups.

Second, with contemporary forms of racism, discrimination against Blacks and other minority groups typically does not occur blatantly. Instead, it is manifested primarily when it can be justified or rationalized by other, ostensibly nonrace-related, elements in the situation. One consequence is that people may discriminate on racial grounds without acknowledging racial bias. Because people generally embrace explanations for their actions that present them in the most favorable light, they often feel that they understand the reasons for their action while, in fact, they fail to recognize the true motivation for their behavior (Wilson, 2002). Another consequence is that, because contemporary racism operates mainly in combination with these factors, it is also typically difficult and often impossible for others, including the legal system, to isolate race as *the* primary basis for a particular individual's negative action toward a Black person or member of another minority group.

Third, expressions of contemporary racism by Whites can often produce disparate outcomes for Whites and Blacks in ways other than direct negative treatment of Blacks. Giving Whites an extra benefit of the doubt (e.g., by dismissing negative qualities, as in the Hodson et al., 2002, experiment) or providing Whites with assistance even when there is ample justification not to help (Saucier et al., 2005) can offer systematic advantages to Whites relative to Blacks. Nevertheless, because the treatment of Blacks still conforms to the established guidelines in the situation, discrimination *against* Blacks – in its legal definition – has not occurred. At the experiential level, people are generally cognizant and responsive to the concrete consequences, and thus may avoid actions that blatantly harm members of another group. They are less likely to perceive and consider the impact of a failure to act, for example the failure to help a Black person as much as if he or she were White.

Contemporary research on prejudice and discrimination shows why the principled support of equal opportunity does not necessarily translate into equality in practice. By demonstrating how even well-meaning Whites who genuinely endorse egalitarian values may discriminate against Blacks and other minorities, current research in the social sciences takes us beyond common knowledge about the dynamics and consequences of racism. By documenting how, like a virus that has mutated, contemporary racism has evolved in such a way as to perpetuate racial disparities without producing unlawful behavior, current research calls attention to the limitations of intuition – even when the intuition exists in the minds of legal scholars and practitioners.

Although we have developed our argument with respect to White–Black relations, which has been the defining form of race relations throughout the history of the United States, other empirical evidence indicates that the principles of subtle bias also translate into discrimination against Latinos (Dovidio, Gaertner, Anastasio, & Sanitioso, 1992) and even into contemporary sexism (Swim, Aikin, Hall, & Hunter, 1995).

Because subtle, contemporary forms of biases can have such diverse adverse effects on members of traditionally disadvantaged groups without conscious ill intentions and without blatant negative actions, policies that provide simply equal opportunity are not sufficient for addressing and reducing unfair social disparities. Subtle biases, which are difficult to recognize and may not be illegal under current definitions of discrimination, may in fact be reinforcing the status quo by emphasizing (and often unintentionally creating) justifications for inequity. The unconscious nature of contemporary bias and its multiple subtle effects make this type of bias difficult to identify conclusively in a single instance. Thus, an alternative approach for policy to promote justice is to focus on systematic patterns in disparities of aggregated *outcomes*, not on the motivations or intentions of particular individuals. Affirmative action is one such policy.

Affirmative Action

One remedy for discrimination that does not assume conscious hostility or even intentionality on the part of hegemonic individuals or organizations is affirmative action, which remains a highly controversial policy. After describing the origins of affirmative action and its current instantiation, we explain how the policy can address subtle forms of discrimination. We then provide evidence relating to the effectiveness of affirmative action for reducing disparities based on gender, race, and ethnicity.

Over 40 years ago President Lyndon Johnson signed Executive Order 11246 and created the system that has come today to be known as affirmative action. The term "affirmative action" had been used earlier by Presidents Franklin Roosevelt and John Kennedy, but Johnson was the first to set into place an entire system. The policy was designed to work in concert with other programs like Head Start to help the United States move toward Johnson's vision of "The Great Society."

Executive Order 11246 mandates that any organization above a minimum size (currently, 50 employees) wishing to have a contact above a minimum amount (currently, $50,000) with the federal government needs to be "an affirmative action employer." Organizations that wish not to be affirmative action employers are not forced to seek or hold contracts; indeed, so long as an organization does not actively and overtly discriminate against individuals on the basis of their gender, ethnic designation, country of origin, and so on, the organization is free to behave in whatever way it wishes – so long as it does not try to obtain money from the federal government in exchange for goods or services.

The federal regulations that accompany the executive order spell out what it means to be an affirmative action employer. An affirmative action employer is one that has an affirmative action plan. This plan essentially entails two steps. The first step involves using approved techniques to detect evidence of potential discrimination; if there is such evidence, the second step concerns making a good faith effort to reduce or eliminate the discrimination.

With respect to the first step, federal regulations identify "protected classes" of people along two dimensions (and only two dimensions): gender and ethnicity. Women constitute one protected class because sex discrimination has historically been a problem in the United States. On the dimension of ethnicity, people who self-identify as African American, Latino or Hispanic American, Native American, and Asian American are all considered to be part of the protected classification. To monitor for evidence of potential discrimination, affirmative action employers delineate the types of jobs in the organization (e.g., clerical, managerial) and then, using census and other data on the availability pools, estimate the proportionate representations that members of the different protected classes would be expected to occupy in each type of job. The employers then compare their actual representations of women, African Americans, Latinos, Native Americans, and Asian Americans with the expected numbers based on the data on the availability of appropriately qualified individuals in each group.

If this analysis reveals that members of the protected classes are represented at proportions lower than what was projected by availability pools, the second step of the plan involves defining the good faith efforts that will be pursued to address imbalances. The firm could not fire present employees in its quest for balance, but it could set goals, linked to general or specific dates. A variety of options are open to firms. For example, the firm could open a program that retrained its clerical employees so that they could become technicians. It could require that any opening for a technical job be advertised widely in print and over the web and not just advertised by word of mouth. It could also require that all hiring committees for technical jobs include at least one ethnic minority employee and that all hiring committees submit a report stating the applicants and reasons for not hiring them. The firm could even implement a system by which a minority person would be hired as long as he or she (a) met the stated qualifications for the job and (b) was among the top candidates for the job (say, among the top three or five).

What happens to a firm that finds in the first (self-monitoring) step of the affirmative action program that it has a problem and that then is unsuccessful in reducing the problem? As long as the plans for reducing imbalance are sensible and the firm is making a genuine effort to follow them, absolutely nothing happens to the firm. No punitive actions are taken. Indeed, even when firms are found to be willfully attempting to subvert the process of becoming less discriminatory, it is rare that severe sanctions are applied. The most severe sanction is to forbid the firm from receiving federal contracts, and this sanction occurs only a few times each decade (Crosby et al., 2003).

Besides its political advantages of devising a system that was voluntary (so long as a business did not want to do business with the federal government or was not part of the federal government) and which was based much more on incentives than punishments (Crosby, 2004), President Johnson's system of affirmative action also addressed many of the issues related to the operation of contemporary, subtle forms of racism. First, hostile intent was not assumed. The stimulus for remedial action was the recognition of a discrepancy between the firm's actual representations of members of protected classes in different positions in the company relative to what would be expected given the general availability of appropriately qualified members of these groups; not inflammatory or wrong-minded statements. Second, recognition of the statistical disparities was sufficient to initiate action, regardless of other justifications or rationalizations that could be posed to explain these discrepancies. The rules were clear and set up in advance; they could not be changed when imbalances were perceived. Third, because the system was outcome based, it avoided having to rely on existing legal definitions of discriminatory intent that adversely affects members of disadvantaged groups. It seems as if President Johnson was astute from a psychological as well as a political perspective.

Johnson's plan seemed to work so well that his successor, President Richard Nixon, added to it. In 1969 Nixon signed Executive Order 11458. EO 11458 established a system for government procurements that was in some ways fashioned on the employment system created by Johnson and that in some ways grew out of the Small Business Act of 1953. The Small Business Act had introduced the idea of setting aside a percentage of contract dollars for entities with certain properties, such as being small. EO 11458 created the Office of Minorities Business Enterprises and required that a proportion of government procurement dollars go to minority-owned businesses. Both the Public Works Employment Act of 1977 and Public Law N. 95–507 further endorsed the practice of set-aside programs through which minority-owned businesses could enter into procurement contracts. In 1988 the Women's Business Ownership Act extended the concept of set-asides to women. In recent years, set-aside programs have faded in prominence. Because of difficulties in justifying the particular proportion of resources set aside, President Clinton eliminated several set-aside procurement programs in the military and elsewhere. Through a series of decisions including *Adarand Constructors v. Pena* (1995), the Supreme Court has severely curtailed the operation of set-aside programs.

Effectiveness of affirmative action

Given what we have described about the dynamics of discrimination, we would expect proactive practices like affirmative action to be more effective than the kinds of reactive practices that are typical in American law because the proactive policies capitalize on how people actually think, feel, and act. No form of affirmative action assumes that hostility is a necessary ingredient for discrimination. No form of affirmative action relies on those who have been wronged to come forward on their own behalf or even to know that they have been wronged. No form of affirmative action presumes that discrimination is always dramatic or episodic; and all forms implicitly acknowledge that tiny injustices and imbalances can accumulate to become major problems. Especially for the kind of affirmative action mandated by Executive Order 11246, the policy enlists someone to make it their job to monitor how well practices are working and thus avoids the inferential problems that arise when one relies on casual, anecdotal, or unsystematic evidence

(Crosby, Iyer, Clayton, & Downing, 2003). In short, one way to conceive of affirmative action policy is to see it as having recognized the implausibility of the emphasis on conscious intent, an emphasis that is embedded in the common knowledge of American jurisprudence, and then crafting a plan of action that is more congruent with the current, research-based understanding of implicit bias.

The question thus becomes: How effective have the various forms of affirmative action proven to be? The answer in brief is: very. Looking at affirmative action in employment, it is possible to gauge the effectiveness of EO 11246 in three ways; and all three ways tell the same story.

One strategy used by some social scientists is to compare the federal government with other employers. Such comparisons show that slow but steady progress has been made by African Americans, Latinos, and women (of all ethnic groups) since 1965 when affirmative action was created (Reskin, 1998). One study showed, for example, that the number of African American managers and professionals in the employ of the federal government rose 200% from 1970 to 1980 while the number of White managers and professionals rose only 29% (Konrad & Linnehan, 1995a, b). In 1970, five years after the inauguration of affirmative action in the federal government, college-educated African American men had ten times more chance of working as a manager in a public sector job than in a job in the for-profit sector (Smith, 1976).

A second strategy used by scholars to gauge the success of EO 11246 is to compare hiring and employment patterns of federal contractors, on the one hand, and nonfederal contractors on the other. Adjusting for market sector (e.g., manufacturing or retail), the figures show that federal contractors have hired, retained, and promoted more women and people of color than comparable companies that are not federal contractors (see Crosby, 2004, for a review). One study looked at over 40,000 firms in 1966 and 1970, and found that federal contractors had a much greater chance than other firms of moving from an all-White work force to an integrated work force (Ashenfelter & Heckman, 1976).

The final strategy for gauging the effectiveness of affirmative action in employment is to conduct surveys in which employees identify their employers as either having or not having affirmative action programs. One such study found that 33% of the employees who worked for a firm that was not an affirmative action employer declared that no African Americans worked at their companies while only 7% of those working for affirmative action employers said the same (Herring &

Collins, 1995). The same investigators found that people of color earned more at affirmative action companies than at other companies. Other researchers demonstrated that the advantages that White men typically enjoy in likelihood of being hired were significantly diminished in organizations with affirmative action programs (Holzer & Neumark, 1999).

Similar to the effectiveness of EO 11246 is the effectiveness of the procurement program started by President Nixon. Although such programs are no longer widely utilized, studies by economists have documented their success. Typical is a study conducted by the Urban Institute. The study looked at 58 cities around the nation that did or did not have in place targeted procurement programs. In the cities without such programs, minority owned businesses captured only 45% of the market share that one would expect strictly on the basis of the proportion of contractors who were minority. In contrast, for cities with procurement programs, minority-owned businesses received 57% of the expected market share (Larson, 1999).

In higher education, too, vigorous affirmative action programs have resulted in more students of color at colleges and universities (Bowen & Bok, 1998). A detailed study of a major law school also documented the increase in ethnic minority matriculants and graduates as a result of race-sensitive admissions policies (Lempert, Chambers, & Adams, 2000a, b). A recent, much-noticed article by law professor Richard Sander (2004) claims that race-sensitive admissions plans have outlived their effectiveness for law school and now contribute to a shortage of African Americans who graduate from law school and also pass the bar; however, a number of authorities (Ayres & Brooks, in press; Chambers, Clydesdale, Kidder, & Lempert, in press; Wilkins, in press) have questioned Sander's assumptions, methods, and conclusions. Thus, despite its apparent effectiveness, affirmative action remains a contentious issue in the academy, in public discourse, and in the courts.

Attitudes toward affirmative action

Whereas the majority of Americans vehemently dislike discrimination, only a minority of Americans strongly support affirmative action as a way to reduce discrimination – despite its apparent effectiveness (Crosby, 2004). As might be expected, support for affirmative action is stronger among women than men and stronger among ethnic minorities than among White Americans (Crosby, Iyer, & Sincharoen, 2006). Similarly, support for "soft" forms of affirmative action such as outreach is stronger than support for "hard" forms such as using ethnicity as a tie-breaking factor when deciding which of two equally qualified candidates to hire or to admit to university (Kravitz & Klineberg, 2000, 2004).

Many explanations have been proposed for why Americans are not more unwavering in their support of affirmative action. Each of these has received some empirical support. One set of explanations for the tepid support for affirmative action is that the policy is misunderstood in terms of both its consequences and how it operates. People do not seem to be well educated about the effectiveness of affirmative action programs for reducing disparities. In addition, if they are, they tend to discount it with other beliefs. There is, for example, a widespread belief that affirmative action engenders self-doubt among its direct beneficiaries and hostility among White people. This assumption is basically incorrect. Although this may occur under some specific circumstances (such as when a female candidate believes her selection was based solely on gender), a very substantial empirical literature shows neither self-doubt nor hostility generally arising among recipients as a result of affirmative action (Crosby, 2004, Chapter 4).

Several studies have also demonstrated the poor understanding that many people, even highly educated people, have of how affirmative action operates (see Crosby, 2004, for a review). A substantial proportion of people think of affirmative action as selection primarily based on social category membership (e.g., race or sex), *rather than* selection based on merit. The more citizens think of affirmative action as category-based instead of merit-based, the more they oppose the policy (Golden, Hinkle, & Crosby, 2001). Americans seem uncomfortable with strategies that call attention to people's group identities (Ozawa, Crosby, & Crosby, 1996) and tend to value solutions to social problems like so called "equal opportunity" that emphasize the individual and ignore or minimize attention group membership.

Another reason why Americans might have a negative reaction to affirmative action is that they have a strong affinity for simple justice (e.g., the dictum that one should treat all people the same). Affirmative action is a relatively complex solution to a complex problem – addressing disparities due to contemporary as well as old-fashioned forms of bias. People who seriously engage with issues of social justice may, for example, ponder the myriad imprecise ways to assess merit; but most Americans seem to want to shy away from sophisticated analyses of justice (Crosby, 2004).

Although there can be truly principled objections to affirmative action that do not involve personal prejudice, there is also evidence that blatant and subtle forms of prejudice contribute directly and indirectly to opposition to affirmative action. With respect to overt expressions of prejudice, dozens of studies demonstrate that opposition to affirmative action is reliably associated with racism and sexism (see Crosby et al., 2006, for a review). In addition, consistent with the operation of contemporary biases, racism and sexism may operate indirectly by leading people to adopt an ostensibly nonrace-related justification for opposing affirmative action, such as the belief that it has negative psychological consequences on the beneficiaries or that it violates principles of fairness, *because* they have negative feelings toward the groups that will benefit from the program For example, White Americans are more likely to see affirmative action as violating principles of fairness when the beneficiaries are Blacks than people with disabilities (Dovidio & Gaertner, 1996). Thus, subtle bias as well as overt racism and sexism can contribute to "misunderstandings" that produce negative attitudes toward affirmative action. Not coincidentally, these factors, which contribute to the social disparities that affirmative action is designed to address, also contribute to the opposition that people have toward the program that can effectively reduce these disparities. Again, these biases do not have to be intentional to have significant consequences for equality in America.

Law and Psychology: Coming into Alignment

We understand that professionals in the areas of the law, public policy, and social psychology share the same basic ideals of justice and fairness; our common goal is a just society. Although the principles that underlie affirmative action are sound and appropriate for combating both blatant and subtle forms of discrimination, social conditions, social attitudes, and legal perspectives change over time. Policies as critical as affirmative action operate in this changing environment, and thus to continue to ensure that they achieve their goal the effectiveness of different implementation strategies need to be reviewed periodically. The coordination of psychological and legal perspectives is critical in this process. The challenge, then, is how to align laws based on precedent and legal procedures that are meticulous and rigorous with rapidly evolving social forces, such as subtle discrimination, that perpetuate social injustice.

To bring social science knowledge and the law into greater alignment, social psychologists need to understand better at which places subtle bias could operate within the legal process. With greater understanding of the complexities of the system, social psychologists might be able to work more effectively with legal scholars and the courts to address discrimination structurally with laws and policies that combat it in its subtle as well as blatant forms. Certainly, there are a number of prominent legal scholars (e.g., Krieger, 1998) and social psychological researchers who bridge the two fields. Journals are devoted to understanding law and social behavior. Nevertheless, still the most common role of social psychologists in the area of antidiscrimination law is as expert witnesses in particular cases. Certainly, this work has had some impact, including at the level of the Supreme Court (Fiske, Bersoff, Borgida, Deaux, & Heilman, 1991). However, rather than becoming involved primarily in individual and isolated cases, with appropriate knowledge of the legal process and the opportunity social psychology and the law can become powerful allies in developing structural antidiscrimination laws that are necessary for achieving a truly just society.

Nevertheless, social psychologists should not realistically anticipate that the legal system will accept their advice uncritically and or embrace the assistance of social psychologists immediately. As Krieger and Fiske (2006) have explained, the scientific process and legal process reflect very different perspectives. The scientific process is one of successive approximations to knowledge, with empirical progress and theoretical development scaffolding on previous work. Science is a process that values change, as new theories challenge and improve upon existing theories. In contrast, jurisprudence is based on precedent and stability. Krieger and Fiske explain:

> In empirical psychology, as in all science, theory emendation represents the hallmark of success. In jurisprudence, on the other hand, theory change, unaccompanied by legislation or constitutional amendment, threatens subjective conceptions of the courts' legitimacy. For this reason, once a particular model of human behavior becomes embedded in legal doctrine, judges may go to great lengths to avoid having to modify it. (p. 49)

As specified in the Supreme Court's decision in *Daubert v. Merrell Dow Pharmaceuticals, Inc.* (1993), psychological theory may be considered in legal cases when it meets certain high standards: (a) thorough empirical testing; (b) peer review and publication; (c) widespread acceptance within the scientific community; and (d) a known and acceptable error rate. Nevertheless, even then it may not be readily accepted within the legal system. Krieger and Fiske estimate that the time lag between scientific acceptance and legal acceptance is at least five years.

Moreover, the courts may be particularly resistant to accepting social psychological research and theory related to contemporary bias and discrimination because of the nature of the changes required. In particular, social psychological evidence of subtle bias suggests that the legal system should de-emphasize the role of conscious intention as a critical condition for proving discrimination. In addition, another potential way to achieve justice and equality is for legal and public policy to define discrimination in terms of unfair consequences rather than unfair intentions and motivation to discriminate. Practically, this is obviously difficult to do on a case-by-case basis, but it can be done at an aggregated level. Whereas discrimination is difficult to discern when information is presented in particular cases sequentially, it is much more obvious when data are aggregated over time and people (Crosby, Clayton, Alksnis, & Hemker, 1986). These ideas, focusing on disparate outcomes by collecting and examining aggregated data, are the essence of affirmative action.

There are other obstacles to legal acceptance, as well. The emphasis on unconscious processes in discrimination is at odds with the common experience of people, as "intuitive psychologists," that they understand why they do what they do (Wilson, 2002). Thus, the psychological argument about unconscious influences is fundamentally at odds with the common experiences and everyday understandings of judges and legislators (Krieger, 2004). Also, the fact that discrimination very often occurs when the action can be justified on nonracial grounds does not fit well with the way the court currently conceives of motivating factors. Specifically, reasons proffered to explain the actions are typically judged to be either a *true reason* or a *phony reason*. A phony reason is typically interpreted as a cover-up or purposeful misrepresentation of the true reason. Current psychological research demonstrates that people who are discriminating may genuinely believe that they behaved on the basis of nonracial factors when race is actually the primary causal agent. Thus, the reason they present for their action is neither entirely true nor phony, the court's dichotomy. Promoting such principles of social psychology that are at such odds with judges' common experience and the court's common practice may elicit more than the normal reluctance of the legal system, perhaps producing active resistance and backlash.

Given the subtle nature of contemporary bias, the role of unconscious processes, and way discrimination can often be justified on nonracial grounds, it is not surprising that acts that may systematically disadvantage minorities often go unrecognized as formal discrimination. In addition, the fact that the explanations in current social psychological theory are inconsistent with common knowledge and current legal perspectives make the courts reluctant to redefine the laws to directly combat this subtle bias. Thus, it is particularly important for individuals and organizations to take responsibility for ensuring fair outcomes for all groups. This is the essence of affirmative action. The core of affirmative action in employment involves self-monitoring on the part of federal contractors. In education, too, organizations determine their goals on the basis of systematically collected data. Although not well loved in opinion polls, affirmative action has been a highly effective policy. The reason for its effectiveness lies in the match, on the one hand, between human behavior and, on the other, the legal mechanisms established by affirmative action as it, like other aspects of American law, seeks to reduce discrimination.

REFERENCES

Adarand Constructors, Inc. v. Pena, 115 S. Ct. 2097 (1995).

Ashenfelter, O., & Heckman, J. (1976). Measuring the effect of an antidiscrimination program. In J. Blum & O. Ashenfelter (Eds.), *Evaluating the labor market effects of social programs* (pp. 47–89). Princeton, NJ: Princeton University Press.

Ayres, I., & Brooks, R. (in press). Does affirmative action reduce the number of Black lawyers? *Stanford Law Review.*

Blair, I. V. (2001). Implicit stereotypes and prejudice. In G. B. Moskowitz (Ed.), *Cognitive social psychology: The Princeton Symposium on the Legacy and Future of Social Cognition* (pp. 359–374). Mahwah, NJ: Erlbaum.

Blank, R. M. (2001). An overview of trends in social and economic well-being, by race. In N. J. Smelser, W. J. Wilson, & F. Mitchell, F. (Eds.), *Racial trends and their consequences* (Vol. 1, pp. 21–39). Washington, DC: National Academy Press.

Bobo, L. (2001). Racial attitudes and relations at the close of the twentieth century. In N. J. Smelser, W. J. Wilson, & F. Mitchell, F. (Eds.), *Racial trends and their consequences* (Vol. 1, pp. 264–301). Washington, DC: National Academy Press.

Bowen, W. G., & Bok, D. (1998). *The shape of the river: Long-term consequences of considering race in college and university admissions.* Princeton, NJ: Princeton University Press.

Brief, A. P., Dietz, J., Cohen, R. R., Pugh, S. D., & Vaslow, J. B. (2000). Just doing business: Modern racism and obedience to authority as explanations for employment discrimination. *Organizational Behavior and Human Decision Processes, 81,* 72–97.

Chambers, D. L., Clydesdale, T. T., Kidder, W. C., & Lempert, R. O. (in press). The real impact of eliminating affirmative action in American law schools: An empirical critique of Richard Sander's study. *Stanford Law Review.*

Crosby, F. J. (2004). *Affirmative action is dead; long live affirmative action.* New Haven, CT: Yale University Press.

Crosby, F., Bromley, S., & Saxe, L. (1980). Recent unobtrusive studies of black and white discrimination and prejudice: A literature review. *Psychological Bulletin, 87,* 546–563.

Crosby, F., Clayton, S., Alksnis, O., & Hemker, K. (1986). Cognitive biases in perception of discrimination. *Sex Roles, 14,* 637–646.

Crosby, F.J., Iyer, A., Clayton, S., & Downing, R. (2003). Affirmative action: Psychological data and the policy debates. *American Psychologist, 58,* 93–115.

Crosby, F. J., Iyer, A., & Sincharoen, S. (2006). Understanding affirmative action. *Annual Review of Psychology, 57,* 585–611.

Daubert v. Merrell Dow Pharmaceuticals, Inc., 509 U.S. 579 (1993).

Dovidio, J. F., & Gaertner, S. L. (1996). Affirmative action, unintentional racial biases, and intergroup relations. *Journal of Social Issues, 52*(4), 51–75.

Dovidio, J. F., & Gaertner, S. L. (2000). Aversive racism and selection decisions: 1989 and 1999. *Psychological Science, 11,* 319–323.

Dovidio, J. F., & Gaertner, S. L. (2004). Aversive racism. In M. P. Zanna (Ed.), *Advances in experimental social psychology* (Vol. 36, pp. 1–51). San Diego, CA: Academic Press.

Dovidio, J. F., Gaertner, S. L., Anastasio, P. A., & Sanitioso, R. (1992). Cognitive and motivational bases of bias: The implications of aversive racism for attitudes toward Hispanics. In S. Knouse, P. Rosenfeld, & A. Culbertson (Eds.), *Hispanics in the workplace* (pp. 75–106). Newbury Park, CA: Sage.

Dovidio, J. F., Kawakami, K., Johnson, C., Johnson, B., & Howard, A. (1997). On the nature of prejudice: Automatic and controlled process. *Journal of Experimental Social Psychology, 33,* 510–540.

Elvira, M. M., & Zatzick, C. D. (2002). Who's displaced first? The role of race in layoff decisions. *Industrial Relations, 41,* 329–361.

Fiske, S. T., Bersoff, D. N., Borgida, E., Deaux, K, & Heilman, M. E. (1991). Social science research on trial: Use of sex stereotyping research in Price Waterhouse v. Hopkins. *American Psychologist, 46,* 1049–1060.

Gaertner, S. L., & Dovidio, J. F. (1986). The aversive form of racism. In J. F. Dovidio & S. L. Gaertner (Eds.), *Prejudice, discrimination, and racism* (pp. 61–89). Orlando, FL: Academic Press.

Golden, H., Hinkle S., & Crosby, F. J. (2001). Reactions to affirmative action: Substance and semantics. *Journal of Applied Social Psychology, 31,* 73–88.

Herring, C., & Collins, S. M. (1995). Retreat from opportunity? The case of affirmative action. In M. P. Smith & J. R. Feagin (Eds.), *The bubbling cauldron: Race, ethnicity, and the urban crisis* (pp. 163–181). Minneapolis, MN: University of Minnesota Press.

Hodson, G., Dovidio, J. F., & Gaertner, S. L. (2002). Processes in racial discrimination: Differential weighting of conflicting information. *Personality and Social Psychology Bulletin, 28,* 460–471.

Holzer, H. J., & Neumark, D. (1999). *Assessing affirmative action.* Cambridge, MA: National Bureau of Economic Research.

Kang, J., & Banaji, M.R. (2006). Fair measures: A behavioral realist revision of "affirmative action." *The California Law Review, 94*(4), 1063–1118.

Konrad, A. M., & Linnehan, F. (1995a). Formalized HRM structures: Coordinating equal employment opportunity or concealing organizational practices? *Academy of Management Journal, 38,* 787–820.

Konrad, A. M., & Linnehan, F. (1995b). Race and sex differences in line managers' reactions to equal employment opportunity and affirmative action interventions. *Group and Organizational Management, 20,* 409–439.

Kravitz, D. A., & Klineberg, S. L. (2000). Reactions to two versions of affirmative action among Whites, Blacks, and Hispanics. *Journal of Applied Psychology, 85,* 597–612.

Kravitz, D. A., & Klineberg, S. L. (2004). Predicting affirmative action attitudes: Interactions of the effects of individual differences with the strength of the affirmative action plan. In N. DiTomaso & C. Post (Eds.), *Research in the Sociology of Work, Vol. 14: Diversity in the Work Force* (pp. 107–130). Amsterdam: Elsevier.

Krieger, L. H. (1998). Civil rights Perestroika: Intergroup relations after affirmative action. *California Law Review, 86,* 1254–1333.

Krieger, L. H. (2004). The intuitive psychologist behind the bench: Models of gender bias in social psychology and employment discrimination law. *Journal of Social Issues, 60,* 835–848.

Krieger, L. H., & Fiske, S. T. (2006). Behavioral realism in employment discrimination law: Implicit bias and disparate treatment. *California Law Review.* (in press).

Larson, T. (1999). Affirmative action programs for minority- and women-owned businesses. In P. Ong (Ed.), *The impacts of affirmative action: Policies and consequences in California* (pp.133–169). Walnut Creek, CA: Altamira Press.

Lempert, R. O., Chambers, D. L., & Adams, T. K. (2000a). Michigan's minority graduates in practice: The river runs through law school. *Law and Social Inquiry, 25,* 395–505.

Lempert, R. O., Chambers, D. L., & Adams, T. K. (2000b). Law school affirmative action: An empirical study of Michigan's minority graduates in practice: Answers to methodological queries. *Law and Social Inquiry, 25,* 585–597.

McConahay, J. B. (1986). Modern racism, ambivalence, and the modern racism scale. In J. F. Dovidio & S. L. Gaertner (Eds.), *Prejudice, discrimination, and racism* (pp. 91–125). Orlando, FL: Academic Press.

Nail, P. R., Harton, H. C., & Decker, B. P. (2003) Political orientation and modern versus aversive racism: Tests of Dovidio and Gaertner's (1998) Integrated Model. Journal of Personality and Social Psychology, 84, 754–770.

Ozawa, K., Crosby, M., & Crosby, F. J. (1996). Individualism and resistance to affirmative action: A comparison of Japanese and American samples. *Journal of Applied Social Psychology, 26,* 1138–1152.

Pettigrew, T. F., & Meertens, R. W. (1995). Subtle and blatant prejudice in Western Europe. *European Journal of Social Psychology, 25,* 57–76.

Reskin, B. F. (1998). *The realities of affirmative action in employment.* Washington, DC: American Sociological Association.

Richeson, J., & Shelton, J. N. (2003). When prejudice does not pay: Effects of interracial contact on executive function. *Psychological Science, 14,* 287–290.

Sander, R. H. (2004). A systemic analysis of affirmative action in American law schools. *Stanford Law Review, 57,* 367–483.

Saucier, D. A., Miller, C. T., & Doucet, N. (2005). Differences in helping Whites and Blacks: A meta-analysis. *Personality and Social Psychology Review, 9,* 2–16.

Schuman, H., Steeh, C., Bobo, L., & Krysan, M. (1997). *Racial attitudes in America: Trends and interpretations.* Cambridge, MA: Harvard University Press.

Sears, D. O., Henry, P. J., & Kosterman, R. (2000). Egalitarian values and contemporary racial politics. In D. O. Sears, J. Sidanius, & L. Bobo (Eds.), *Racialized politics: The debate about racism in America* (pp. 75–117). Chicago, IL: University of Chicago Press.

Smedley, B. D., Stith, A. Y., & Nelson, A. R. (Eds.) (2003). *Unequal treatment: Confronting racial and ethnic disparities in health care.* Washington, DC: National Academy Press.

Smith, A. E., & Crosby, F. J. (in press). From Kansas to Michigan: The path from desegregation to diversity. In G. Adams, N. Branscomb, & M. Bernat (Eds.), *Brown at 50.* Washington, DC: Psychological Press.

Smith, S. P. (1976). Government wage differentials by sex. *Journal of Human Resources, 11,* 185–199.

Swim, J. K., Aikin, K., Hall, W. S., & Hunter, B. A. (1995). Sexism and racism: Old-fashioned and modern prejudices. *Journal of Personality and Social Psychology, 68,* 199–214.

Uhlmann, E. L., & Cohen, G. L. (2005). Constructed criterion: Redefining merit to justify discrimination. *Psychological Science, 16,* 474–480.

Wilkins, D. B. (in press). A systematic response to systemic disadvantage: A response to Sander. *Stanford Law Review.*

Wilson, T. D. (2002). *Strangers to ourselves: Discovering the adaptive unconscious.* Cambridge, MA: Belknap Press.

Word, C. O., Zanna, M.P., & Cooper, J. (1974). The nonverbal mediation of self-fulfilling prophecies in interracial interaction. *Journal of Experimental Social Psychology, 10,* 109–120.

3

The Young Science of Prejudice Against Older Adults: Established Answers and Open Questions About Ageism

Todd D. Nelson

In a field that has only been in existence for about 36 years,[1] research on age prejudice has revealed many robust findings, a few counterintuitive results, and it has left open a number of unanswered questions. The purpose of this chapter is to highlight the major findings in ageism research, the unexpected discoveries, and to point future researchers to issues that still require investigation. The field is growing, as more and more researchers are sensing the theoretical and practical need for empirical attention devoted to a problem that affects millions of older adults. As we begin to shed light on the causes and consequences of age prejudice, we can start to devise ways to reduce age stereotyping, thereby enhancing the quality of life for all older adults. This chapter will explore the state of the literature on ageism, and address the following questions: How does what we know so far compare to common knowledge about aging and ageism? How can research on ageism inform those in the legal system? Is the state of the research literature on ageism sufficiently mature to inform lawyers, judges, and policy-makers?

Assumptions vs. Research Evidence

People tend to hold a number of stereotypes about older individuals, and they also tend to endorse a great many myths about aging (Nelson, 2002). For example, it is often believed that older people are cognitively

---

[1]   I mark the beginning of research on ageism with the coining of the term "age-ism" by Butler (1969).

slower, sexless, unable or unwilling to change, less intelligent, weaker, physically slower, stubborn, negative, conservative, and dependent (Bytheway, 1995; Cuddy & Fiske, 2002; Lehr, 1983; Thornton, 2002). As with any stereotype about a given group, there will always be some people in that group for whom the stereotypes are accurate. Below, we will explore the assumptions that underlie stereotypes about older people, and discuss how research has taken us beyond common sense in our understanding of age prejudice.

Ageism Exists

If you were to ask someone, "Do you have negative feelings about your grandmother, or your older boss, or the elderly woman who works at the flower store?" they would likely reply, "Of course not! Those people are dear, dear people in my life. I have nothing but affection for them." If that same person were to be asked, "Do you think all old people are poor drivers, or that, generally, older people are grumpy?" you would be more likely to get answers that endorse the aging stereotypes you just expressed. This mixed message we get from people about their attitudes toward older people had perplexed researchers for a while. Starting with early research by Tuckman and Lorge (1953), which showed that people have negative attitudes toward aging and elderly people, and continuing to the present day, researchers have found evidence that age prejudice exists in the U.S. (Falk & Falk, 1997; Kite & Wagner, 2002; Palmore, 1982). Other researchers have uncovered evidence that suggests that the attitudes of young people toward older adults are no more negative than they are toward any other group (Bell, 1992; Crocket & Hummert, 1987; Lutsky, 1980). Which assertion are we to believe? A closer inspection of the methodologies of these studies sheds light on the reasons for the divergent findings. When people are asked about their attitudes toward "older people," the image that is evoked is a negative stereo-type about an older person. However, when one is asked to evaluate a specific older person (coworker, boss, friend, for example), fewer examples of old-age related stereotypes come to mind, and the attitude is much more likely to be positive (Crockett & Hummert, 1987).

Origin of Ageism

Cultural views

Anyone who has been exposed to U.S. culture, even peripherally, quickly learns that the U.S. has a cultural bias in favor of youth.

Movies, television, magazines, and advertisers who support those media all cater to the youngest demographic in our population. Why this focus on youth? Largely, I will argue, it stems from our fear of aging. In the U.S., we have a tremendous anxiety about the aging process, and death (Nelson, 2002). Old age is stereotypically perceived as a negative time, whereupon the older person suffers declines in physical attributes, mental acuity, loss of identity (retirement from job), loss of respect from society, and increasing dependence on others (Kite & Wagner, 2002). Americans enjoy their individuality, and feelings of control over what happens with their own bodies. Aging and death are seen as out of our control, and that produces feelings of fear and anxiety. Along with no perceived control over the aging process (and eventual death), many Americans also view death as the end of their self. The belief that one's self has a fixed ending is also quite anxiety-provoking. Contrast this with those who believe that they have a spirit that lives on (either in Heaven, Nirvana, or some other spiritual place, or via reincarnation), and these individuals tend to have a different view on their life. Life is just one phase of an eternal journey that they have been on. They believe that they will continue this journey indefinitely. These individuals view aging in much the same way as those in traditional Eastern cultures. In Eastern cultures, the self, life, and death are all interconnected within the person. Death, in this view, is not something that is feared. Rather, it is seen as a welcome relief from life's travails. Death is seen as a passage to a different spiritual existence, where one can join his/her elders (Butler, Lewis, & Sunderland, 1991). Traditional Eastern cultures, as a result, have had little or no anxiety about death, and aging (Levy & Langer, 1994). In fact, they viewed older adults with much reverence. Older persons were given special status and power in their society.

Times are changing in Eastern cultures, however, and so are attitudes toward older persons. As these cultures become more modernized, and feel the influence of Western cultures, capitalism, and individualistic values, they begin to feel less obligated to maintain traditions of filial piety (motivation, emotion, and intergenerational reciprocity in support of one's elderly parents; Ng, 2002; Williams, Ota, Giles, Pierson, Gallois, Ng, Lim, et al., 1997). Ng (2002) suggests that it is an exaggeration to say that Eastern cultures revere their elders, while Western cultures abandon them. Rather, research indicates that there is quite a degree of variability in Eastern attitudes toward older adults (Williams, et al., 1997). Williams et al. (1997) found that Koreans had the most positive attitudes toward their elders, while Chinese persons surveyed expressed a much more negative attitude.

Japanese people appear to be experts at masking their derision for older persons. Koyano (1989) found a big distinction between *tatemae* (how one ought to behave and feel) and *hone* (how one actually behaves and feels). On the surface, for many Japanese, is a mask of respecting and honoring elders, while just below the mask lies a dismissal of elders as silly.

Terror management theory

An interesting theory that parsimoniously explains one way that ageism can arise is "terror management theory" (TMT; Greenberg, Pyszczynski, & Solomon, 1986; Pyszczynski, Greenberg, Solomon, Arndt, & Schimel, 2004; Solomon, Greenberg, & Pyszczynski, 1991). According to TMT, culture and religion are creations that give order and meaning to our existence, and these protect us from frightening thoughts of our own mortality, and the seeming random nature of life. Self-esteem is derived from believing that one has a place and purpose in the world. Thus, according to TMT, self-esteem serves as a buffer against anxiety associated with thoughts of one's mortality.

According to TMT, because older people are a reminder of our impending mortality, people in the U.S. tend to associate negative feelings with (and ascribe negative qualities to) older adults. The anxiety and fear that are associated with death lead young people to blame older people for their plight – getting older. In so doing, they can deny the thought that they too will grow old (and die). By blaming the older person, stereotyping him/her, and treating elders with pity, anger, irritation, or patronizing speech, younger people are able to trick themselves into believing that they will not eventually die. This derogation of older people only serves to create a perpetual cycle of ever-increasing prejudice against older persons. The more negatively younger people treat older persons, the weaker and more negatively older people are perceived, and the increasingly negative way older people appear, in turn only increases the anxiety young people have about death, and this amplifies their tendency to act in ageist ways toward older people (Martens, Goldenberg, & Greenberg, 2005). Much empirical evidence (Martens, Greenberg, Schimel, & Landau, 2004; Martens, et al., 2005) and theoretical evidence (Greenberg, Schimel, & Martens, 2002) supports the utility of this theory as it is applied toward our understanding of the origins of ageism.

Ageism is Institutionalized

Prejudice against older adults remains one of the most socially condoned, institutionalized forms of prejudice in the U.S. (Nelson, 2006; Nelson, 2002). While much research has been devoted to understanding the causes and effects of prejudice against people based on their race or gender, comparatively little empirical attention has been devoted to understanding why some cultures (and the U.S. in particular) have such a negative view of aging and older people (Nelson, 2005). Perhaps one reason why it has gone relatively "under the radar" of researchers is that age prejudice is so institutionalized. Why is this the case?

One likely reason: fear. As discussed earlier, old age is something we fear because it is associated with death. We fear the loss of freedom that may accompany old age (e.g., caring for ourselves, being able to drive, financial freedom). We want to deny the possibility that "it" (old age, mortality) will happen to us. One way to deny that possibility is to "blame the victim" (the older adult) for their predicament. These fears are the primary motive for the marginalization of older people via age stereotypes and prejudice (Greenberg et al., 2002; Nelson, 2005).

How institutionalized is ageism today? Walk into any greeting card store, and enter the section on birthday cards (excluding children's birthdays). One common message is communicated, no matter which card you pick up: Sorry to hear you are another year older. Birthdays are seen as a slide downward, toward failing health, failing mental acumen, and death, and they certainly are not occasions to celebrate. A popular line of birthday "gag" gifts has a theme of "over the hill" attached to various items, from black balloons, to a plastic gravestone(!). The message is clear: Aging is bad, and we make fun of people who are getting older. Another indicator of how entrenched ageism is in U.S. culture can be found in the drive to hide physical signs of aging. A recent survey by the National Consumer's League (2004) found that 90 million Americans each year (and that is likely a conservative estimate) purchase products or undergo medical procedures to hide the physical indicators of their age. Why are people willing to spend so much money, and undergo unnecessary, risky medical procedures to hide physical signs of aging? Society tells us that aging is bad.

People are Automatically Ageist

Because some features of a person are more likely to be readily noticed in social perception, those variables are more likely to be used as bases for social categorization. Much research supports the idea that we tend to consistently categorize people upon three dimensions – race, age, and gender – when we are perceiving others (Brewer, 1988; Fiske & Neuberg, 1990). Because these dimensions tend to be activated rather automatically, researchers refer to them as "basic" or "primitive" categories (Hamilton & Sherman, 1994). A review of the research also suggests that, as a result of the automatic activation of these categories in social perception, beliefs about category-related target characteristics (i.e., stereotypes) are also automatically activated (Montepare & Zebrowitz, 1998). In one particularly compelling demonstration, Perdue and Gurtman (1990) found that when younger persons are primed with the word "old" they are faster to subsequently recognize negative trait words, and slower to recognize positive trait words. Conversely, when they are primed with the word "young", they are faster to later recognize positive trait words, and slower to recognize negative trait words.

In another demonstration of the automatic influence of ageist attitudes, Nosek, Banaji and Greenwald (2002) reported data collected from the Implicit Association Test (IAT; Greenwald, McGhee, & Schwartz, 1998) on what can be referred to as "implicit ageism." The IAT measures implicit attitudes (like ageist beliefs, or stereotypical associations between category and characteristics). Implicit attitudes are "introspectively unidentified (or inaccurately identified) traces of past experience that mediate favorable or unfavorable feeling, thought, or action toward social objects" (Greenwald & Banaji, 1995, p. 5).

The IAT requires the respondent to learn various associations between categories and characteristics (e.g., Bad/White Good/Black, and Bad/Black Good/White). Response latencies are measured to assess the degree to which the pairings are easier or more difficult for the participant to identify correctly (for that pairing run). To the degree that participants are faster at a particular pairing, and with a particular category, results would indicate that the participant "has a preference for" that category (or pairing).

Based on the results of 68,144 tests that were submitted via a web demonstration site for the IAT, Nosek et al. (2002) found that the older the respondents, the more positive their explicit attitudes toward older people were. The main finding was that regardless of the age of the respondents, they had significantly negative implicit attitudes toward older persons. These data, coupled with the priming study by Perdue and Gurtman (1990), provide support for the notion that people have strong negative beliefs associated with older persons, and these attitudes operate without conscious awareness to influence our conscious thought, behavior, and feelings toward older people. It is difficult, but not impossible, to break these strong biases in social perception. With enough motivation, one can focus on relearning a default association of a more positive series of characteristics with the category "older person" (or at least a "stop rule" to cut short any stereotypes from influencing behavior upon activation of the category) (Monteith, Zuwerink, & Devine, 1994).

Young People Have Mixed Feelings About Older People

Fiske and her colleagues (1999, 2002) developed the stereotype content model (SCM), which suggests that there are two critical dimensions of stereotypes: warmth and competence. Stereotypes associated with a group on each of these intersecting dimensions gives a richer picture of the group's status in society, and the typical stereotypes associated with the group. Fiske and her colleagues found that many groups are stereotyped as high on one dimension, but low on another. This appears to be the case with views of elderly people. Data indicate that older people tend to be perceived as incompetent, but warm (Cuddy & Fiske, 2002; Cuddy, Norton, & Fiske, 2005). They are also viewed as physically and cognitively inferior, but socially acute. Overall, however, these data suggest that younger people tend to pity older adults (Cuddy et al., 2005).

We Talk to Older People Differently

Age stereotypes lead people to behave differently toward older persons. Because the stereotypes portray an image of one who is in declining physical health, and who increasingly has problems with memory or sharp mental processing, people will then assume the older person cannot understand, or do for themselves what must be done to take care of themselves (Nelson, 2002). Work by Caporael and her colleagues (Caporael, 1981; Caporael & Culbertson, 1986; Caporael, Lukaszewski, & Culbertson, 1983) has shown that people tend to speak to older people in a couple of ways. In "overaccommodation," younger persons are overly polite, use an exaggerated speech intonation, and speak in simple sentences (using simple words). In "baby talk," younger persons speak using a simplified speech register, using a higher pitch, louder voice, and exaggerated intonation. Caporael et al. (1983) found that this type of baby talk was undistinguishable from actual "baby talk" (the way adults exaggerate their words and voice pitch to babies).

Old Age Does Not Strip Away Self-esteem

Stereotypes about older adults also suggest that older adults have lower self-esteem, and have more dour dispositions than younger persons. However, some research shows that older people have higher self-esteem than high school students (Cottrell & Atchley, 1969). Both Atchley (1982) and Snyder (1987) note that when one is older one has a more solid self-concept, which acts as a good buffer against life's stressors. However, one's self-esteem and mood can take a hit if one loses independence and control over one's environment, and in the event that one's physical capacities decline.

Only Some Older Persons Dislike Ageist Treatment

Caporael et al. (1983) found that some older people actually prefer to be spoken to in much the same manner as an adult communicates with a child. Specifically, those older adults who had lower functional abilities found such speech to convey a soothing, nurturing quality. Giles and his colleagues (1994) found, however, that older persons who have higher cognitive and social functioning view baby talk as disrespectful and humiliating.

Some more light may be shed on these interesting findings with data that I obtained (Nelson, 2004). I sent surveys to over 3,300 older adults in California, asking them whether they had ever experienced age prejudice or discrimination, and how they reacted to it. Data from the 852 returned surveys indicated a major difference in the way older adults responded to the survey, depending on their age. Neugarten (1974) said that those adults aged 55–74 really view themselves differently, as young, than those aged 75 and older. Neugarten found that many of these "young-old" adults still had older parents living, and they tended to view "old age" (and stereotypes, and health and mental failings associated with age) as something associated with their parent's generation. Those older than 75 (whom Neugarten called the "old-old") were less likely to have this perspective (because no one was older than them, the term "old people" *must* be in reference to them). Nelson's data indicated that the old-old individuals did not perceive any age discrimination or prejudice in their daily lives. They also reported that if they were the victim of ageist behavior, it would not bother them. However, the "young-old" reported that they *had* experienced ageism, and that when it occured, it made them *very upset*. These results may reflect a desire of the old-old to protect their self-esteem by denying that they are part of a stigmatized group. The reaction of the young-old to ageism (of being upset) also may suggest that the young-old want to delay as much as possible their entry into the old-old group, because they fear how they will be treated (as stigmatized persons).

Ageism is Found Even in Helping Professions

It is an unfortunate truth that ageism even persists among those whose job it is to help older persons (Troll & Schlossberg, 1971). Research has found that some physicians and other health care professionals tend to regard older patients through age stereotypes, such that the older patient is more likely to be viewed as "depressing, senile, untreatable, or rigid" (Reyes-Ortiz, 1997, p. 831). To medical students, working with older patients is not typically viewed as desirable, because older patients present with health concerns that are believed to be less amenable to treatment, though there is often little basis for that assumption other than a stereotype about aging and health issues (Madey & Gomez, 2003).

Mental health professionals are just as likely to harbor ageist beliefs as their physician counterparts (Garfinkel, 1975). Kastenbaum (1964) refers to the "reluctant therapist" in addressing this issue. These therapists tend to shun older clients because they believe that older people often do not have any serious psychological issues that merit therapy, and that they are just lonely and want to exploit the therapist as a captive listening ear. Siegel (2004) affirms that psychiatrists also have an age bias when it comes to diagnosing problems for which older persons seek professional help. Siegel argues that psychiatrists need to take a new view of old age, appreciating the tremendous learning and personal growth that older adults have achieved. Psychiatrists should also be aware that older adults may have many different losses that younger people do not face, and they are also confronted with the oppressive youth-focused society, which ubiquitously presents negative views of older persons.

We Teach Our Children to be Ageist

In American society, as is the case in societies that are industrial, technological, and changing at a rapid pace, the emphasis is for workers to be mobile (to be able to go to where the new jobs crop up). Since the industrial revolution, Western societies have moved to a much smaller family unit, and one that most typically only includes the immediate (nuclear) family members (Branco & Williamson, 1982). As a result of this change in family structure, children have had much less contact with their grandparents (and other older persons). Some suggest that it is precisely this separation of older and younger generations that can lead to the development of age stereotypes in the minds of young children (Hagestad & Uhlenberg, 2005). Today, much of what children know about older persons, aside from sporadic actual contact with elderly relatives, comes from their school books (or television programs). Research has shown, however, that many classic fairy tales, as well as current school books, are biased against older persons. One study found that only 16% of 665 books for K-3 children (5–8-year-olds) contained an older character (Ansello, 1978). Older persons in these books were often depicted as problem creators, retired, and dependent. Thus, from a very young age children are taught ageist beliefs about older persons, and these persist and give rise to age prejudice and stereotypes. On a positive note, programs that are designed to bring children into contact with elders can greatly reduce the influence of stereotypes on the way that young children regard older people, and this change stays with the children as they get older (Murphy, Myers, & Drennan, 1982).

Conclusion

Research on ageism has a short history, relative to the general field of prejudice research. However, the available data allow us to draw several conclusions with a degree of confidence. First, age prejudice exists, and it is multifaceted. People have multiple, often contradictory, attitudes toward older individuals. Second, ageism is tied in part to that culture's views of (or fears about) death. Ageism is also tied to the emphasis that a culture places on change, mobility, and speed in the workforce. The greater the emphasis on these things, the more likely society is to perceive the older worker as not competitive, but rather he/she may be regarded as a burden on the resources of society.

Third, ageism is institutionalized in the U.S. The focus on youth, mobility, change, coupled with the intense fear of death in American culture, leads to derogation of older people, and anything associated with aging. Jokes about getting older, with the implicit message that it is bad or sad to get older, are regarded as benign humor. Americans believe that implicit message, however. Americans spend billions of dollars on products and surgeries designed to hide signs that they are growing older. Fourth, ageism is so pervasive that it is found even among those whose job it is to help older persons. This of course has tremendous implications for the physical and mental health of the older patient, as age stereotypes can bias the treatment recommendations that the therapist or physician has for the older patient.

Finally, ageist behavior is only perceived as offensive by those older persons who are high functioning (physically and mentally). Older people who have physical and/or mental deficiencies tend to believe that ageist behavior actually communicates a helping relationship between the younger person and the older individual, and might find that communication (though it is ageist) comforting.

The goal of this chapter is to identify areas of research on age prejudice that have yielded robust findings that would stand scrutiny in court proceedings, and to identify the nascent areas of research in which there is more empirical attention needed. We can have confidence in the following findings. Like other prejudices, ageism is learned, and often at an early age. Children are exposed to subtle ageist messages in the school books, in the media, and in society, and these attitudes become well entrenched and form the bases for the development of lifelong prejudice against older people. This prejudice against elders is activated rather automatically, often without the awareness of the perceiver. Younger adults have ambivalent feelings toward older adults. They regard elders with a mix of pity and affection. Ageism is one of the most socially condoned, institutionalized prejudices in the United States. People react to aging with fear. This fear often leads the individual to perceive anything associated with aging or death with fear. Because elders are closer to death, they are seen as reminders to young persons of their own mortality. To deny that reality, young people will often blame older people for aging, and they will deride, avoid, and feel hostility (and prejudice) toward older adults. We treat older adults like children in the way we remove their freedom (e.g., put them in nursing homes, and slowly remove their decision-making as they get older), and in the way we talk condescendingly to them.

There is much that we do not yet understand about ageism, however. What are the specific messages that children learn about ageism, through what medium, and how do those particular messages change over time to become fully elaborated prejudices and stereotypes about older adults? Knowing this, we might be better able to understand who is more likely to show prejudice toward elders. Once we understand that, we will be in a better position to find ways to prevent children from learning those messages, or (if already learned) to change their stereotypes about elders. More research needs to be directed to understanding the specific nature of implicit ageism, and how it can manifest itself in everyday life. This is an ongoing debate in the implicit stereotyping literature, centering around the question of personal responsibility for behavior that is affected by cognitive processes of which one is not aware (Banaji & Greenwald, 1994). If, for example, an older person were to file an age discrimination case against an employer, could the employer suggest that they were unaware that what they did constituted any age prejudice, that they harbor no prejudices against older adults, and that if their behavior were construed as ageist, then perhaps the employer's implicit ageist attitudes were responsible for the actions? As such, with no clear conscious intent to discriminate, and no ability to consciously influence implicit cognitive processes, would the employer be held accountable for their ageist actions?

We need more data on how ageism influences older persons. Specifically, we need to better understand why it has been found that the young-old differ from the old-old (Neugarten, 1974) in their perceptions of whether the behavior of younger people toward themselves constitutes ageism, and how they feel about that behavior (indignant or resigned) (Nelson, 2004). Much more research is needed on how employers, policy-makers, and laws can be informed about the influence of retirement on the older worker. Why is retirement regarded with dread by many older workers? In large part, it has to do with how there is a subtle stigma in American society about retired persons. They are seen as burdens, no longer contributing, but only taking from society (McCann & Giles, 2002). The retired person experiences a major loss of self-identity, which can often be traumatic. What specific things can employers do to help mitigate the negative connotations of retirement? In what ways might laws be changed to alter the way in which society regards retirement and retired persons?

While research on ageism is comparatively young, relative to our understanding of racism and sexism, there is much that we know.

Research since 1969 has revealed many counterintuitive and robust findings about age prejudice that can stand the scrutiny of court analyses, and the test of scientific replication. Yet ageism researchers are just getting started. It is especially timely that empirical attention be devoted to this issue, as American society will, in a few short years, begin to experience a massive change in its demographic characteristics. Specifically, the baby-boomers will begin to retire, resulting in what has been referred to as "the graying of America" (Nelson, 2002). This major influx of a very large segment of the population into retirement, and changing to senior citizens, will place unprecedented changes and consequences on society. As social scientists, to the degree that we understand how ageism arises, is maintained, and can be reduced, we can provide a solid scientific footing for the legal profession and policy-makers to fairly and objectively affect court proceedings relevant to older persons.

REFERENCES

Ansello, E. F. (1978). Age-ism: The subtle stereotype. *Childhood Education*, *54*(3), 118–122.

Atchley, R. (1982). The aging self. *Psychotherapy: Theory, Research, and Practice*, *19*(4), 388–396.

Banaji, M., & Greenwald, A. G. (1994). Implicit stereotypes and prejudice. In M. P. Zanna & J. M. Olson (Eds.), *The psychology of prejudice: The Ontario symposium* (Vol. 7, pp. 55–76). Hillsdale, NJ: Erlbaum.

Bell, J. (1992). In search of a discourse on aging: The elderly on television. *The Gerontologist*, *32*, 305–311.

Branco, K. J., & Williamson, J. B. (1982). Stereotyping and the life cycle: Views of aging and the aged. In A. G. Miller (Ed.), *In the eye of the beholder: Contemporary issues in stereotyping* (pp. 364–410). New York: Praeger.

Brewer, M. B. (1988). A dual-process model of impression formation. In T. K. Srull & R. S. Wyer (Eds.), *Advances in social cognition* (Vol. 1, pp. 1–36). Hillsdale, NJ: Erlbaum.

Butler, R. (1969). Age-ism: Another form of bigotry. *The Gerontologist*, *9*, 243–246.

Butler, R., Lewis, M., & Sunderland, T. (1991). *Aging and mental health: Positive psychosocial and biomedical approaches*. New York: Macmillan.

Bytheway, B. (1995). *Ageism*. Philadelphia, PA: Open University Press.

Caporael, L. (1981). The paralanguage of caregiving: Baby talk to the institutionalized aged. *Journal of Personality and Social Psychology*, *40*, 876–884.

Caporael, L., & Culbertson, G. (1986). Verbal response modes of baby talk and other speech at institutions for the aged. *Language and Communication, 6,* 99–112.

Caporael, L., Lukaszewski, M., & Culbertson, G. (1983). Secondary baby talk: Judgments by institutionalized elderly and their caregivers. *Journal of Personality and Social Psychology, 44,* 746–754.

Cottrell, W., & Atchley, R. (1969). *Women in retirement: A preliminary report.* Oxford, OH: Scripps Foundation.

Crockett, W. H., & Hummert, M. L. (1987). Perceptions of aging and the elderly. In K. Schaie & C. Eisdorfer (Eds.), *Annual review of gerontology and geriatrics* (Vol. 7, pp. 217–241). New York: Springer-Verlag.

Cuddy, A. J. C., & Fiske, S. T. (2002). Doddering but dear: Process, content, and function in stereotyping of older persons. In T. D. Nelson (Ed.), *Ageism: Stereotyping and prejudice against older persons* (pp. 3–26). Cambridge, MA: MIT Press.

Cuddy, A. J. C., Norton, M. I., & Fiske, S. T. (2005). This old stereotype: The pervasiveness and persistence of the elderly stereotype. *Journal of Social Issues, 61*(2), 267–286.

Falk, U., & Falk, G. (1997). *Ageism, the aged and aging in America.* Springfield, IL: Charles Thomas.

Fiske, S. T., & Neuberg, S. L. (1990). A continuum of impression formation, from category-based to individuating processes: Influences of information and motivation on attention and interpretation. In M. P. Zanna (Ed.), *Advances in experimental social psychology* (Vol. 23, pp. 1–74). New York: Academic Press.

Fiske, S. T., Cuddy, A. J. C., Glick, P. S., & Xu, J. (2002). A model of (often mixed) stereotype content: Competence and warmth respectively follow from perceived status and competition. *Journal of Personality and Social Psychology, 82,* 878–902.

Fiske, S. T., Xu, J., Cuddy, A. C., & Glick, P. (1999). (Dis)respecting versus (dis)liking: Status and interdependence predict ambivalent stereotypes of competence and warmth. *Journal of Social Issues, 55*(3), 473–489.

Garfinkel, R. (1975). The reluctant therapist: 1975. *The Gerontologist, 15,* 136–137.

Giles, H., Fox, S., Harwood, J., & Williams, A. (1994). Talking age and aging talk: Communicating through the life span. In M. Hummert, J. Weimann, & J. Nussbaum (Eds.), *Interpersonal communication in older adulthood: Interdisciplinary theory and research* (pp. 130–161).

Greenberg, J., Pyszczynski, T., & Solomon, S. (1986). The causes and consequences of a need for self-esteem: A terror management theory. In R. F. Baumeister (Ed.), *Public self and private self* (pp. 188–.212)

Greenberg, J., Schimel, J., & Martens, A. (2002). Ageism: Denying the face of the future. In T. D. Nelson (Ed.), *Ageism: Stereotyping and prejudice against older persons* (pp. 27–48). Cambridge, MA: MIT Press.

Greenwald, A. G., & Banaji, M. R. (1995). Implicit social cognition: Attitudes, self-esteem, and stereotypes. *Psychological Review, 102,* 4–27.

Greenwald, A. G., McGhee, D. E., & Schwartz, J. L. K. (1998). Measuring individual differences in implicit cognition: The Implicit Association Test. Journal of Personality and Social Psychology, 74, 1464–1480.

Hagestad, G., & Uhlenberg, P. (2005). The social separation of young and old: A root of ageism. *Journal of Social Issues, 61*(2), 343–360.

Hamilton, D. L., & Sherman, J. W. (1994). Stereotypes. In R. S. Wyer & T. K. Srull (Eds.), *Handbook of social cognition* (Vol. 2, 2nd ed., pp. 1–68). Hillsdale, NJ: Erlbaum.

Kastenbaum, R. (1964). The reluctant therapist. In R. Kastenbaum (Ed.), *New thoughts on old age* (pp. 237–249). New York: Springer.

Kite, M. E., & Wagner, L. S. (2002). Attitudes toward older adults. In T. D. Nelson (Ed.), *Ageism: Stereotyping and prejudice against older persons* (pp. 129–161). Cambridge, MA: MIT Press.

Koyano, W. (1989). Japanese attitudes toward the elderly: A review of research findings. *Journal of Cross-Cultural Gerontology, 4,* 335–345.

Lehr, U. (1983). In J. Birren, J. Munnichs, H. Thomae, & M. Marois (Eds.), *Aging: A challenge to science and society* (Vol. 3, pp. 101–112). New York: Oxford University Press.

Levy, B., & Langer, E. (1994). Aging free from negative stereotypes: Successful memory in China and among the American deaf. *Journal of Personality and Social Psychology, 66*(6), 989–997.

Lutsky, N. S. (1980). Attitudes toward old age and elderly persons. In C. Eisdorfer (Ed.), *Annual review of gerontology and geriatrics* (Vol. 1, pp. 287–336). New York: Springer.

Madey, S. F., & Gomez, R. (2003). Reduced optimism for perceived age-related medical conditions. *Basic and Applied Social Psychology, 25*(3), 213–219.

Martens, A., Goldenberg, J. L., & Greenberg, J. (2005). A terror management perspective on ageism. *Journal of Social Issues, 61*(2), 223–239.

Martens, A., Greenberg, J., Schimel, J., & Landau, M. J. (2004). Ageism and death: Effects of mortality salience and perceived similarity to elders on reactions to elderly people. *Personality and Social Psychology Bulletin, 30*(12), 1524–1536.

McCann, R., & Giles, H. (2002). Ageism in the workplace: A communication perspective. In T.D. Nelson (Ed.), *Ageism: Stereotyping and prejudice against older persons* (pp. 163–199). Cambridge, MA: MIT Press.

Monteith, M. J., Zuwerink, J. R., & Devine, P. G. (1994). Prejudice and prejudice reduction: Classic challenges, contemporary approaches. In P. G. Devine, D. L. Hamilton, & T. M. Ostrom (Eds.), *Social cognition: Impact on social psychology* (pp. 323–346). New York: Academic Press.

Montepare, J. M., & Zebrowitz, L. A. (1998) Person perception comes of age: The salience and significance of age in social judgments In M. Zanna

(Ed.), *Advances in experimental social psychology* (Vol. 30, pp. 77–125). New York: Academic Press.

Murphy, M., Myers, J., & Drennan, P. (1982). Attitudes of children toward older persons: What they are, what they can be. *The School Counselor, 29*(4), 281–288.

National Consumer's League (2004). New survey reveals consumers confused about, but overwhelmingly use, anti aging products and procedures. www. nclnet.org/pressroom/antiaging.htm.

Nelson, T. D. (Ed.) (2002). *Ageism: Stereotyping and prejudice against older persons.* Cambridge, MA: MIT Press.

Nelson, T. D. (2004, August). *Experiencing and expressing ageism.* Paper presented at the Annual Meeting of the American Psychological Association, Honolulu.

Nelson, T. D. (2005). Ageism: Prejudice against our feared future self. *Journal of Social Issues, 61*(2), 207–221.

Nelson, T. D. (2006). *The psychology of prejudice* (2nd ed.). New York: Allyn & Bacon.

Neugarten, B. (1974). Age groups in American society and the rise of the young old. *The Annals of the American Academy of Political and Social Science,* (September), 187–198.

Ng, S. H. (2002). Will families support their elders? Answers from across cultures. In T. D. Nelson (Ed.), *Ageism: Stereotyping and prejudice against older persons* (pp. 295–309). Cambridge, MA: MIT Press.

Nosek, B. A., Banaji, M. R., & Greenwald, A. G. (2002). Harvesting implicit group attitudes and beliefs from a demonstration web site. *Group Dynamics: Theory, Research, and Practice, 6,* 101–115.

Palmore, E. (1982). Attitudes toward the aged: What we know and need to know. *Research on Aging, 4,* 333–348.

Perdue, C. W., & Gurtman, M. B. (1990). Evidence for the automaticity of ageism. *Journal of Experimental Social Psychology, 26,* 199–216.

Pyszczynski, T., Greenberg, J., Solomon, S., Arndt, J., & Schimel, J. (2004). Why do people need self esteem? A theoretical and empirical review. *Psychological Bulletin, 130*(3), 435–468.

Reyes-Ortiz, C. (1997). Physicians must confront ageism. *Academic Medicine, 72*(10), 831.

Siegel, R. J. (2004). Ageism in psychiatric diagnosis. In P. J. Caplan & L. Cosgrove (Eds.), *Bias in psychiatric diagnosis* (pp. 89–97). Lanham, MD: Jason Aronson, Inc.

Snyder, M. (1987). *Public appearances, private realities: The psychology of self-monitoring.* New York: Freeman.

Solomon, S., Greenberg, J., & Pyszczynski, T. (1991). A terror management theory of social behavior: The psychological functions of self-esteem and world-views. In M. P. Zanna (Ed.), *Advances in experimental social psychology* (Vol. 24, pp. 91–159). New York: Academic Press.

Thornton, J. E. (2002). Myths of aging or ageist stereotypes. *Educational Gerontology, 28,* 301–312.

Troll, L. & Schlossberg, N. (1971). How age-biased are college counselors? *Industrial Gerontology, 10,* 14–20.

Tuckman, J., & Lorge, I. (1953). Attitudes toward old people. *Journal of Social Psychology, 37,* 249–260.

Williams, A., Ota, H., Giles, H., Pierson, H., Gallois, C., Ng, S., Lim, T., et al. (1997). Young people's beliefs about intergenerational communication: An initial cross-cultural comparison. *Communication Research, 24*(4), 370–393.

4

Gender Prejudice: On the Risks of Occupying Incongruent Roles

Alice H. Eagly and Anne M. Koenig

Analyses of prejudice have progressed over the years as people endeavor to make sense of prejudice in their daily lives and as social scientists advance in understanding prejudice in terms of social psychological principles. There is general agreement that prejudice is undesirable because it results in unfair treatment of individuals. But what exactly is prejudice? The common knowledge that emerges in daily life provides a starting point for social scientific analyses of prejudice, but, as we show in this chapter, everyday understandings are far too vague to explain or even to identify the phenomena of prejudice. Therefore, we provide an abstract definition of prejudice that refines the definitions that emerge from daily life as well as the definitions that social scientists proposed in earlier years. We apply this definition to achieve a better understanding of gender prejudice.

Our approach, known as the role congruity theory of prejudice (Eagly, 2004; Eagly & Diekman, 2005; Eagly & Karau, 2002), emphasizes the contextual quality of prejudice whereby members of particular groups are targets of prejudice in some situations but not in others. This theory has particular relevance to gender prejudice because it delineates the circumstances in which each sex is likely to be victimized by prejudice.

Definitions of Prejudice

In *The Nature of Prejudice,* a classic book that was influential in shaping early social psychological theories of prejudice, Gordon Allport (1954) defined prejudice as "antipathy based upon a faulty and inflexible generalization" (p. 9) and as "thinking ill of others without sufficient warrant" (p. 7). In Allport's definition, misinformation paired with hostility underlies prejudice. Allport therefore positioned inaccurate negative stereotypes at the core of prejudice. No doubt because he analyzed mainly the extreme prejudices that characterized midtwentieth-century American racism and European anti-Semitism, Allport elaborated prejudice only as a negative bias.

These classic ideas about antipathy and inaccuracy may seem at first glance to be sufficient to elucidate prejudice. "Negative inaccuracy" is indeed how many people think about prejudice in their daily lives: It derives from negative stereotypes and consists of discrimination against members of a group that is so characterized, with discrimination understood in terms of denial of access to jobs, housing, education, financial services, and other benefits.

Dictionary definitions, which succinctly express lay views of prejudice, also generally adhere to this approach by including both antipathy and irrationality (or inaccuracy) as components of prejudice. For example, one such definition is "an irrational attitude of hostility directed against an individual, a group, a race, or their supposed characteristics" (*Merriam-Webster Online Dictionary*, 2006). As we explain in this chapter, social psychological research and theory demonstrate that such ideas are far too simple to encompass many of the phenomena of prejudice. In contemporary contexts in the United States, few groups – and certainly not men or women – are subjected to generalized antipathy, but few observers would argue that prejudice has disappeared from the societal landscape. This situation has challenged social psychologists to refine their definition of prejudice.

Recognizing the complexity of the question about the accuracy of stereotypes, social psychologists have removed inaccuracy from most definitions of prejudice and stereotypes. There is increasing realization that prejudice does not necessarily stem from false or biased beliefs about groups (e.g., Lee, Jussim, & McCauley, 1995). A critical way that psychologists have moved beyond lay ideas about the inaccuracy of stereotypes is to distinguish between the characteristics of groups and of the members of these groups. Beliefs about groups may be entirely accurate based on group averages (e.g., Dutch people are tall; Americans are materialistic), but often inaccurate when applied to individuals within groups (e.g., Joost is a Dutchman so he must be tall; Jane is an American so she must be materialistic). Much of the inaccuracy of stereotypes stems from the application of group stereotypes to individuals, regardless of the accuracy of these stereotypes (see Eagly & Diekman, 2005).

A second critical insight from contemporary social psychological theory is that prejudice does not necessarily stem from negative attitudes, stereotypes, or emotions elicited by social groups. Some groups that are targets of prejudice and discrimination are not associated with negativity, but with neutrality or even with positivity. Prejudice against women provides a clear example of this phenomenon. Women elicit a predominantly positive evaluation because they are stereotypically nice, warm, and friendly, at least more so than men (Eagly & Mladinic, 1994; Langford & MacKinnon, 2000). The favorable beliefs and positive emotions that people commonly experience in relation to women in general can create the impression that people are unprejudiced toward women. In fact, those who discriminate against women in the workplace or elsewhere can also believe that women are wonderful and experience positive emotions toward women as a group. Therefore, to move beyond common understandings of prejudice, social scientific definitions of prejudice must be reconciled with the predominately positive evaluation of women and with the positive aspects of the stereotypes of some other social groups that can be targets of prejudice (e.g., Asian Americans; Lin, Kwan, Cheung, & Fiske, 2005).

In summary, two important insights from contemporary social psychology challenge everyday understanding of prejudice: (a) Prejudice against members of a group can reflect accurate as well as inaccurate beliefs about the group as a whole; and (b) prejudice toward group members is not necessarily accompanied by negative evaluations of the group as a whole. Instead, as we show in this chapter, prejudice toward particular groups occurs in some contexts and not in others, and this contextualism characterizes gender prejudice.

Role Congruity Theory of Prejudice

Role congruity theory of prejudice (Eagly, 2004; Eagly & Diekman, 2005; Eagly & Karau, 2002) states that prejudice arises from an incongruity between a group stereotype and the requirements of social roles. Prejudice occurs when members of a group enter or attempt to enter roles that are stereotypically mismatched to the attributes ascribed to their group. In this theory, prejudice is defined as a negative attitudinal shift that is elicited at the interface between stereotypical beliefs held by individuals and a social structure composed of social roles (Eagly, 2004). When social perceivers hold a stereotype about a social group that is inconsistent with the attributes required for success in a role, prejudice is activated in the context of this role to the extent that perceivers do not fully take into account whether the group member's individual traits and attributes fit with the role. Prejudice consists of a less favorable attitude-in-context toward an individual who is stereotypically mismatched with the requirements of a role, compared with attitudes toward individuals who are stereotypically well matched. Given no actual differences in the role-relevant attributes of the matched and mismatched individuals, this attitudinal decline is prejudicial. The greater the mismatch between the group stereotype and the role requirements, the greater prejudice is likely to be.

From the perspective of role congruity theory, it is important to assess prejudice by a comparative process because it consists of a lower evaluation of members of a stereotyped group as occupants of a particular role, compared with the evaluation of members of groups for whom the role is congruent. Even though an individual may be evaluated favorably in relation to a given role, that evaluation may be prejudicial. Whether a lower evaluation actually is prejudicial should be determined by comparing the role-relevant qualifications of individuals who are stereotypically matched and mismatched to the role. This is the approach often taken in the studies of wages and promotions conducted by economists and sociologists. They determine whether, controlling for job-relevant variables such as education and job experience, men and women have the same wages or rates of promotions. The usual conclusion from such studies is that women fare worse than men, even controlling for such variables (e.g., Baxter & Wright, 2000; Maume, 2004; U.S. Government Accountability Office, 2003).

As an example of role incongruity prejudice, let us consider a woman who occupies or is a candidate for a high status role such as Chief Financial Officer of a large corporation. She would most likely not elicit a negative attitude, given the prestige of this role, but rather a less positive attitude than an equivalent male executive. This attitude would be revealed by downward shifts in the expressions of attitudes in the particular context – that is, in beliefs held about the woman (e.g., she is not competitive enough), emotions felt in relation to her (e.g., anxiety that she cannot negotiate well enough), and behaviors directed toward her (e.g., unwillingness to give her very important assignments). Even if her qualifications were identical to those of her male counterparts, the activation of the female stereotype would produce this lowered evaluation. This outcome can occur, despite the favorable evaluation of the individual executive and despite the largely positive stereotypes associated with both women in general and corporate executives in general. The prejudicial phenomenon in this example stems from the juxtaposition of the nice, caring, and sensitive qualities associated with the stereotype of women, with the more aggressive, active, and resourceful qualities that corporate executives are expected to manifest. In such contexts, women are regarded as not having the "right stuff" for the role.

As this example makes clear, having a positive attitude or stereotype in relation to a group or feeling positive emotions does not guarantee lack of prejudice. Stereotypical attributes generally considered to be positive can be a liability for individuals in some roles (as gentleness might be a liability for a prosecuting attorney), and stereotypical attributes generally considered to be negative can become assets in some roles (as aggressiveness might be an asset for a prosecuting attorney). What matters for prejudicial responses is how the stereotype compares to the desired social role. When a group member attempts to fill a social role that requires attributes not associated with his or her group, prejudice is a likely outcome, regardless of the valence of those attributes in general.

Such biases are unfair because they derive from the characteristics culturally ascribed to one's group and not from evaluation of one's individual qualifications. However, it is not correct to label such biases as necessarily irrational. Instead, the biases arise from social perceivers treating group membership (in gender, race, or religious groups, for example) as a cue enabling them to predict future behavior. As we already stated, such predictions can be valid at the group level but invalid at the individual level. Perhaps this is the phenomenon that is inherent in the lay notion that stereotypes are prejudgments, represented in the dictionary definition of prejudice as "preconceived judgment or opinion" (*Merriam-Webster Online Dictionary*, 2006). However, as we shall see, not all prejudicial reactions involve a prejudgment.

Role congruity theory explains why prejudice is profoundly contextual: Members of particular groups do not elicit prejudice and discrimination in every context, and members of every group could be the recipients of prejudice given particular contexts. Prejudice toward women is not apparent in all contexts, and prejudice toward men is apparent in certain contexts. Because traits associated with women are seen as useful and necessary for female-dominated occupations but not for male-dominated occupations (e.g., Cejka & Eagly, 1999; Glick, 1991), the cultural consensus appears to be, for example, that women make better nurses and primary caretakers of young children than men, but men make better lawyers and stock brokers than women. Thus, men can be objects of prejudice in relation to roles that are incongruent with the cultural stereotype of men. Here again, social psychological research reaches beyond common knowledge to show that prejudice can occur even toward members of more privileged groups.

Role congruity theory is related to Heilman's (1983) lack-of-fit model of bias in work settings. According to this approach, to the extent that a workplace role is inconsistent with the attributes ascribed to an individual, based on group stereotypes or other information, she or he would suffer from a perceived lack of fit with the role, producing decreased performance expectations, increased expectations of failure, and decreased expectations of success. These effects could lower self-evaluation and evaluation by others. This theory thus addresses prejudice as well as related phenomena in the workplace. Although role congruity theory does not deal only with the workplace, the workplace is the most popular context for the study of prejudice.

Two types of prejudice

According to role congruity theory, prejudice toward potential role occupants and current role occupants often have different bases. These two types of prejudice derive from differing kinds of norms – *descriptive norms*, referring to what groups are like, or *injunctive norms*, referring to what they ideally should be like (Cialdini & Trost, 1998; Eagly, 2004; Eagly & Diekman, 2005). Descriptive norms are expectations derived from observations of what members of groups do, and these norms guide group members to the typical and (most likely) effective behaviors for their group. In contrast, injunctive or prescriptive norms are expectations about what members of groups should do, and these norms guide group members to socially desirable and admirable behaviors for their group.

In relation to women and men, much of the descriptive content of norms (i.e., gender stereotypes) pertains to either communion (e.g., sensitive, nurturing, cooperative) or agency (e.g., aggressive, competitive, dominant; Newport, 2001; Williams & Best, 1990). Women are perceived by others as especially communal and men as especially agentic (descriptive norms). Also, in defining injunctive (or prescriptive) norms, people think that women should be communal and men should be agentic (see, for example, Glick & Fiske, 1996). Because social scientists classically included this prescriptive aspect of expectations as an aspect of social roles, many social scientists refer to the cultural consensus about men and women as forming *gender roles*, not merely gender stereotypes.

Prejudice toward potential role occupants (e.g., hiring and promotion decisions) is based mainly on descriptive norms: Group members are assumed to possess the stereotypical characteristics of their group, which can prevent them from being considered well qualified for a given role. In contrast, prejudice toward current role occupants is based mainly on prescriptive norms: To the extent that fulfilling an incongruent role involves violations of prescriptive beliefs about one's group, role occupants receive negative reactions for their violation at the same time as they receive positive reactions based on their adequate fulfillment of the role.

Burgess and Borgida (1999) highlighted this distinction by identifying two types of workplace discrimination against women, one stemming from the descriptive beliefs about women and the other from the prescriptive beliefs. According to this analysis, descriptive stereotypes lead to discrimination that is labeled *disparate impact*, in which "institutional practices result in hiring and promotion decisions that are biased against a class of people" (p. 666), whereas prescriptive stereotypes lead to discrimination that is labeled *disparate treatment*, in which "women who violate prescriptive stereotypes of femininity are punished, either through hostile environment harassment or through the devaluation of their performance" (p. 666). This analysis is thus fully consistent with the importance that role congruity theory accords to descriptive and injunctive norms and extends the implications of the concepts to a legal context.

In natural settings, prejudice based on violations of prescriptive norms is often combined with prejudice based on descriptive norms. The Wal-Mart class action sex discrimination lawsuit, the largest employment discrimination case ever adjudicated in the United States, contains many such examples in the declarations from former employees. For example, one female managerial employee testified as follows (names have been omitted):

> Male Photo Division Management behaved in ways that demeaned and belittled women and minorities. In fall 1996, there was a Photo District Manager meeting in Valencia, California. Wal-Mart had just hired a second female Photo District Manager for the western region, Ms. A. During dinner, Mr. X introduced all of the District Managers to Ms. A using nicknames for the minorities and women. I was introduced as B, "the little Mexican princess." I was very offended by Mr. X's comment and left the dinner early. Throughout the meeting, men made sexual statements and jokes that I thought were very offensive. For example, a flyer with an offensive joke about women being stupid was left on my belongings. In February 1997, during an evaluation, I complained to One-hour Photo Divisional Manager Mr. Y about harassment based on gender at the previous Photo District Manager meeting. He replied that he would take care of it. I knew from trainings on Wal-Mart's sex harassment policy given by Wal-Mart Legal Department employee Ms. C that

company policy mandates that when someone complains of sexual harassment, an investigation must begin within twenty-four hours. Therefore, I expected to be interviewed as a part of an investigation. I was never called. A couple of weeks later, in March 1997, I saw Mr. Y at a meeting. I asked him if he had been conducting an investigation of my sexual harassment complaint. He replied that it was being taken care of. I was never aware of any action taken in response to my complaint. Six weeks after complaining about sexual harassment, I was terminated.

Betty Dukes et al. v. Wal-Mart Stores, Inc. (2003)

This woman was apparently victimized by descriptive stereotypes suggesting that women are incompetent sex-objects as well as by prescriptive stereotypes that proscribe assertive responses to discriminatory behavior.

Our distinction between two types of prejudice and discrimination draws attention to another way in which psychological research goes beyond common knowledge. The everyday belief that prejudice is a prejudgment fits with the application to individuals of descriptive stereotypes that derive from their sex, race, religion, or other group memberships. However, a negative attitudinal shift in a given context can also emerge in relation to an individual group member who already occupies a given role. For example, an aggressive, resourceful female business executive might be devalued relative to her male counterparts because prescriptively women are not supposed to behave in this way. Such prejudice is based on information gleaned about the target (e.g., her aggressiveness) and thus is not a prejudgment about likely future behavior but instead a reaction to current behavior.

Prejudice Toward Women

Are people prejudiced against women? Many people would probably hesitate to give an unqualified positive response to this question yet would agree that women are victims of prejudice and discrimination under some circumstances – for example, in relation to many leadership roles (Eagly & Karau, 2002). Moreover, given that women report being the targets of sexist incidents (Swim, Hyers, Cohen, & Ferguson, 2001) and of sexual harassment in the workplace (e.g., Fitzgerald, 1993) more frequently than men, it is not surprising that in public opinion polls, only about half of Americans endorse the view that women enjoy job opportunities equal to those of men (Jones, 2005, August 2).

It might seem that social category information would be irrelevant in most employment contexts, but gender roles spill over into all domains (Gutek & Morasch, 1982; Ridgeway, 1997), affecting perceivers' impressions of others even when the target's sex seems irrelevant to judgments of competence. This spillover occurs because sex is the strongest basis of social categorization (e.g., Fiske, Haslam, & Fiske, 1991) and stereotypes about men and women are easily and automatically activated (e.g., Banaji & Hardin, 1996; Blair & Banaji, 1996). Therefore, even when more specific roles (e.g., occupational, familial) provide more informative bases for reactions to individuals, gender stereotypes continue to have some influence.

Women as potential role occupants

People often give less favorable evaluations to women's potential for leadership roles and other male-dominated positions because they think that women will not be able to successfully fulfill such roles (Eagly & Karau, 2002). According to role congruity theory, such prejudice toward women results from the conflict between the communal qualities associated with women and the predominantly agentic qualities associated with male-dominated roles (in relation to managerial roles, see Powell, Butterfield, & Parent, 2002; Schein, 2001).

Experiments that vary the sex of a job applicant provide useful tests of the role congruity understanding of gender prejudice. Studies that have manipulated the sex of the target person while keeping other information identical are especially informative. This general method of examining prejudice is based on the *Goldberg paradigm*, which is named in honor of Phillip Goldberg's early experiment on biased evaluations of written essays (Goldberg, 1968). The participants each read an essay that was identical in content except for the author's name, which was either male or female. Thus, the ratings of the essay apparently authored by a woman could be compared to those of the essay apparently authored by a man, and any difference between the ratings was due to the sex of the writer of the essay. To disguise the purpose of the study, the participants who received these articles for evaluation did not realize that other students received the identical essay ascribed to a writer of the other sex. This initial experiment demonstrated an overall bias against women but not when the essay was in a feminine field.

This method was extended by researchers to the presentation of identical résumés or job applications with male or female names attached to them. Experiments of this type showed that men were preferred over women for jobs rated as masculine sex-typed (see meta-analysis by Davidson & Burke, 2000). The available research thus substantiates the conclusion that women are discriminated against when they vie for positions that are incongruent with the female gender role. Presumably this effect is due primarily to the descriptive stereotypes that people hold about women, which suggest that individual women would not be effective in masculine sex-typed roles.

Women as current role occupants

Gender prejudice does not stop once women are hired. If individuals adequately fulfill their new incongruent role, they may violate prescriptive gender norms, leading to negative reactions. For example, women who are effective as leaders often exhibit agentic behaviors in the context of this role and therefore may be seen as too agentic and not sufficiently communal. In other words, these women may fail to manifest prescribed feminine behaviors (by not being nice and kind) and may manifest proscribed masculine behaviors (by being aggressive and directive; see Prentice & Carranza, 2002). Thus, these violations of gender norms can lower evaluations of women in leadership positions (Eagly & Karau, 2002).

Prejudice toward role occupants based on prescriptive norms is substantiated by research investigating evaluations of men and women who occupy the same role. Many of these studies are experiments in the Goldberg paradigm that elicit evaluations from participants who have received equivalent information about the behavior or accomplishments of a man or a woman. For example, a meta-analysis of studies in which participants were given either behavioral information about a target (e.g., résumés) or a product created by the target showed that the difference in evaluations between male and female targets was negligible overall. However, women were evaluated less favorably than men when the stimulus materials were in a role-incongruent masculine or even in a gender-neutral domain, compared to a role-congruent feminine domain (Swim, Borgida, Maruyama, & Myers, 1989). The same type of effect occurred for Goldberg paradigm experiments in which participants evaluated the same leadership or managerial behaviors ascribed to women or men: Overall, women were slightly more negatively evaluated than men. However, this devaluation was more pronounced if the target used a masculine, autocratic style of leadership or occupied a male-dominated leadership role or led in an athletic context (Eagly, Makhijani, & Klonsky, 1992).

Prescriptive stereotypes may also contribute to women's own decisions to leave jobs. In a nationally representative sample, controlling for a variety of worker characteristics such as job tenure, education, and family status, male-dominated occupations were associated with increased odds of promotion for men but an increased probability of job exit for women (Maume, 1999). In addition, among the women who returned to work after leaving the labor force, most of those initially in female-dominated occupations remained in such positions, whereas half of those in male-dominated positions switched to female-dominated positions. Women's slower rates of promotion as well as their job exit and career changes likely reflect the increased stress and anxiety experienced by women in masculine occupations (Evans & Steptoe, 2002), which in turn reflects the prejudicial dynamics of such work environments for women.

In summary, violations of prescriptive stereotypes can also lead to role incongruity between individuals' gender role and their actions of fulfilling an incongruent role. The lowered evaluations of individuals who violate prescriptive norms can subsequently be manifested in lower performance evaluations, fewer promotions, and smaller salary increases (see Heilman, Wallen, Fuchs, & Tamkins, 2004).

What About Prejudice Toward Men?

Because there are far fewer men who attempt to enter female-dominated roles than women who attempt to enter male-dominated roles, prejudice toward men is not as culturally salient as prejudice toward women. However, when prejudice toward men does occur, it follows the same logic. Men are the targets of prejudice when they try to occupy or currently occupy roles that are incongruent with the group stereotype of men. In terms of men as potential role occupants, they are discriminated against when applying for jobs assumed to require feminine characteristics (Davidson & Burke, 2000), and the effect is only slightly smaller than the discriminatory effect associated with female applicants for masculine sex-typed jobs. Also, in divorce cases, judges appear to be reluctant to award child custody to fathers (Clarke, 1995; Stamps, 2002). In this situation, men suffer from role incongruity because, as men, they are thought to be less warm and nurturing than women and therefore less qualified for the role of child caretaker.

Not much research has addressed prejudice toward men as current role occupants. For example, men may meet with ambivalent reactions when they demonstrate caring, nurturing qualities in their on-the-job behavior as child care providers or nurses. In fact, men are recipients of sexual harassment when they violate their prescriptive gender role, just as women are (e.g., Waldo, Berdahl, & Fitzgerald, 1998). However, some researchers have argued that stereotypes of women have a stronger prescriptive component than stereotypes of men (see Rudman & Glick, 1999), making the range of men's acceptable behaviors wider than women's. Conversely, there is other research, especially involving children, that shows that the sanctions for males who violate their prescriptive gender norms are stronger than those for females (e.g., Martin, 1990). Clearly, prejudice toward men and boys warrants more attention in research.

Is Research on Gender Prejudice Generalizable?

When psychological research is brought into court cases, it is reasonable to ask whether it can be generalized to individual cases. Can the research that we have reviewed on gender prejudice provide guidance about the likelihood that a particular woman or man is the victim of prejudice and discrimination? Generalization from general scientific principles to new situations always involves some degree of risk. The risk may be larger or smaller, depending on the particular research base.

One function of scientific theory and research is to give people more systematic ways of thinking about phenomena, including gender prejudice. Theories in the physical and biological sciences give people ways of conceptualizing their world that were not available before scientists formulated the theories. For example, Darwin's theory of evolution gave people new ways of thinking about their relations to other species and the processes by which humans and other species came into being. Psychological research also gives people new ways of understanding phenomena. In particular, the principles offered by role congruity theory provide systematic ways of understanding prejudice. Its principles suggest that both men and women in role-incongruent settings are vulnerable to prejudice.

Research can go further than giving people ways of thinking about phenomena. It can suggest that particular new events or occurrences may be instances of the phenomena demonstrated in particular studies. Research thus allows observers to evaluate whether an individual person is in a situation likely to elicit gender prejudice. This type of generalization is more trustworthy to the extent that a large number of studies have demonstrated an effect. For example, as we have discussed, there exists a considerable body of research on evaluations of women and men in relation to male-dominated and female-dominated jobs. Most of the role incongruity findings that we have described have been replicated many times, across researchers and paradigms.

One reason that some generalizations are more secure than others based on psychological research is that researchers have used excellent methods of integrating the studies that have tested the same hypothesis. These methods, known as *meta-analysis*, implement statistically justified techniques for synthesizing research studies. Studies examining prejudice in congruent and incongruent roles have been systematically integrated with these methods. This modern method of integrating research constitutes a shift away from the informal, qualitative, or "narrative" reviews of studies that were common at earlier points in psychology and other fields (see Cooper & Hedges, 1994). In the past, researchers would read the available studies and provide verbal summaries of findings, drawing overall conclusions primarily from their impressions of findings and perhaps from simple counts of studies producing various outcomes.

Meta-analysts quantitatively combine all of the available studies that have tested a certain hypothesis, including any unpublished work and doctoral dissertations that can be obtained. This combination of findings is an average of the findings of the individual studies, with each of the findings expressed as an *effect size*. Each effect size for an individual study expresses the difference between two means, which is standardized by dividing it by the (pooled) standard deviation (i.e., variability around the mean). For example, to examine gender prejudice, a meta-analyst might compare the means of participants' evaluations of male and female job candidates in a particular Goldberg paradigm study in which the information about equivalent male and female candidates was presented to different groups of research participants. Single studies of this type are of course informative but do not necessarily provide reliable findings because a study may be biased or flawed in particular ways (e.g., from atypical participant samples or invalid measures or even from mistakes in data entry and analysis). Even identical studies are bound to have results that differ somewhat from one another simply by chance alone. Therefore, meta-analysts combine the results of large numbers of studies to provide much better evidence of the presence and magnitude of an effect. The average effect size is generally a reliable estimate, given that it balances the idiosyncrasies of single studies. Therefore, in this chapter, we give greater credence to meta-analyses of the research literature on gender prejudice than to single studies. And when research evidence is applied in legal contexts, appropriate meta-analyses should be given more weight than single studies.

Meta-analyses also examine the variability in the size of an effect across individual studies. This variability is also central to meta-analysis, which not only assesses the stability of findings in general but also allows for the discovery of conditions that moderate the effect of interest. For example, as we noted, meta-analyses have shown that prejudice toward women is greater when the task or position is masculine sex-typed, compared to when it is feminine sex-typed (e.g., Davidson & Burke, 2000).

Meta-analysis cannot remove limitations of the existing research base. For example, if such a review includes only studies performed in the laboratory or with student participants, then the average effect size can be generalized to other settings and demographic groups only with some risk. Therefore, it is important to investigate phenomena in a range of settings, including natural field settings. Research carried out in the field can reveal the generalizability of phenomena to natural settings and indicate whether the effect obtained in field settings is smaller or larger than the same effect obtained in laboratory studies. Indeed, there are some correlational survey studies with representative samples that are relevant to gender prejudice (e.g., Maume, 1999) as well as field experiments in which, for example, male versus female research assistants responded by telephone to job advertisements (Levinson, 1982) or applied for jobs in person (Neumark, Bank, & Van Nort, 1996). When research literatures are built on a range of methods, each offering advantages and limitations, they provide a stronger basis for generalization.

Conclusion

In summary, gender prejudice is illuminated by regarding prejudice as an unfavorable attitudinal shift in context. Role congruity theory states that such prejudice derives from the incongruity between group stereotypes and role characteristics. Thus, context is paramount – people can be prejudiced toward any social group when the group's stereotype conflicts with the characteristics needed for the roles they are trying to occupy.

Prejudice is not necessarily manifested by negative evaluations. Positive evaluations that are merely less positive than evaluations received by other individuals who possess the same qualifications also constitute prejudice. For example, when applying for a job, all candidates may receive positive evaluations, but the one with the most positive evaluation generally wins the job.

This understanding of prejudice reaches beyond common knowledge by (a) clarifying the sense in which prejudice can involve inaccuracy, (b) excluding the requirement that prejudice must be based on negative attitudes, (c) highlighting that members of majority groups as well as members of minority groups can be targets of prejudice, and (d) indicating that prejudice can be based on negative reactions to a violation of prescriptive stereotypes as well as to prejudgments based on descriptive stereotypes.

Psychological research has supported this definition of prejudice, especially for women in the context of masculine roles. Less research has focused on the impact of prejudice toward men in feminine roles, or toward other social groups, such as race and religious groups, in incongruent roles. However, the distinction between descriptive and prescriptive stereotypes (or norms) has general applicability for understanding prejudice.

The role incongruity principle gives people a way of reasoning about the conditions that are most likely to produce prejudice. Nevertheless, this theory cannot prove that prejudice was present in relation to a specific individual. To judge whether discrimination has occurred for a particular person in a particular situation, a wealth of specific facts must be known, to rule out that differential treatment was based on legitimate factors such as poor job performance. However, the role congruity approach does specify conditions in which prejudice is likely to occur. Coupled with information about the specifics of the situations of individuals, this approach sheds considerable light on prejudice and discrimination in natural settings.

The role incongruity view of prejudice has a decidedly rational flavor. After all, groups of people may not be well qualified for roles that have very different demands from those roles that were traditionally occupied by their group. However, unfairness derives from social perceivers' inappropriate weighting of group membership and thus not fully crediting the individual qualifications that individual group members possess for the new roles. This unfairness arises from assimilating individuals to stereotypes, a common psychological process. Nonetheless, irrationality can come to the fore as this basically rational process of perceivers predicting role performances from individuals' group memberships becomes co-opted by motivations. Persons who are frustrated or experiencing other negative states may especially seize on arguments that characterize members of out-groups as inadequate and unqualified (Spencer, Fein, Wolfe, Fong, & Dunn, 1998). Similarly, motivations to defend the privileges of one's own group may fuel especially stringent attention to a possible lack of qualifications in newcomers to the role (e.g., Sidanius & Pratto, 1999). However, stereotypes are not invented merely to defend people from their own inadequacies or to protect their own group's privileges. Instead, the processes of role incongruity provide the basic material that then enables motivated reasoning in defense of oneself or one's group.

REFERENCES

Allport, G. W. (1954). *The nature of prejudice.* Reading, MA: Addison-Wesley.

Banaji, M. R., & Hardin, C. D. (1996). Automatic stereotyping. *Psychological Science, 7,* 136–141.

Baxter, J., & Wright, E. O. (2000). The glass ceiling hypothesis: A comparative study of the United States, Sweden, and Australia. *Gender & Society, 14,* 275–294.

Betty Dukes et al. v. Wal-Mart Stores, Inc. U.S. District Court, Northern District of California, Case No. C-01-2252 MJJ. Retrieved on January 17, 2005 from www.walmartclass.com/staticdata/walmartclass/declarations (2003).

Blair, I. V., & Banaji, M. R. (1996). Automatic and controlled processes in stereotype priming. *Journal of Personality and Social Psychology, 70,* 1142–1163.

Burgess, D., & Borgida, E. (1999). Who women are, who women should be: Descriptive and prescriptive gender stereotyping in sex discrimination. *Psychology, Public Policy, and Law, 5,* 665–692.

Cejka, M. A., & Eagly, A. H. (1999). Gender-stereotypic images of occupations correspond to the sex segregation of employment. *Personality and Social Psychology Bulletin, 25,* 413–423.

Cialdini, R. B., & Trost, M. R. (1998). Social influence: Social norms, conformity, and compliance. In D. T. Gilbert, S. T. Fiske, & G. Lindzey (Eds.), *The handbook of social psychology* (4th ed., Vol. 2, pp. 151–192). Boston: McGraw-Hill.

Clarke, S. C. (1995). Advance report of final divorce statistics, 1989 and 1990. *Monthly Vital Statistics Report,* Vol. 45, No. 3, supp. Hyattsville, MD: National Center for Health Statistics.

Cooper, H., & Hedges, L. V. (Eds.). (1994). *The handbook of research synthesis.* New York: Russell Sage Foundation.

Davidson, H. K., & Burke, M. J. (2000). Sex discrimination in simulated employment contexts: A meta-analytic investigation. *Journal of Vocational Behavior, 56,* 225–248.

Eagly, A. H. (2004). Prejudice: Toward a more inclusive definition. In A. H. Eagly, R. M. Baron, & V. L. Hamilton (Eds.), *The social psychology of group identity and social conflict: Theory, application, and practice* (pp. 45–64). Washington, DC: APA Books.

Eagly, A. H., & Diekman, A. B. (2005). What is the problem? Prejudice as an attitude-in-context. In J. F. Dovidio, P. Glick, & L. Rudman (Eds.), *Reflecting on the nature of prejudice: Fifty years after Allport* (pp. 19–35). Malden, MA: Blackwell.

Eagly, A. H., & Karau, S. J. (2002). Role congruity theory of prejudice toward female leaders. *Psychological Review, 109*, 573–598.

Eagly, A. H., Makhijani, M. G., & Klonsky, B. G. (1992). Gender and the evaluation of leaders: A meta-analysis. *Psychological Bulletin, 111*, 3–22.

Eagly, A. H., & Mladinic, A. (1994). Are people prejudiced against women? Some answers from research on attitudes, gender stereotypes, and judgments of competence. In W. Stroebe & M. Hewstone (Eds.), *European review of social psychology* (Vol. 5, pp. 1–35). New York: Wiley.

Evans, O., & Steptoe, A. (2002). The contribution of gender-role orientation, work factors and home stressors to psychological well-being and sickness absence in male- and female-dominated occupational groups. *Social Science and Medicine, 54*, 481–492.

Fiske, A. P., Haslam, N., & Fiske, S. T. (1991). Confusing one person with another: What errors reveal about the elementary forms of social relations. *Journal of Personality and Social Psychology, 60*, 656–674.

Fitzgerald, L. F. (1993). Sexual harassment: Violence against women in the workplace. *American Psychologist, 48*, 1070–6.

Glick, P. (1991). Trait-based and sex-based discrimination in occupational prestige, occupational salary, and hiring. *Sex Roles, 25*, 351–378.

Glick, P., & Fiske, S. T. (1996). The Ambivalent Sexism Inventory: Differentiating hostile and benevolent sexism. *Journal of Personality and Social Psychology, 70*, 491–512.

Goldberg, P. (1968). Are women prejudiced against women? *Transaction, 5*, 316–322.

Gutek, B. A., & Morasch, B. (1982). Sex-ratios, sex-role spillover, and sexual harassment of women at work. *Journal of Social Issues, 38*, 55–74.

Heilman, M. E. (1983). Sex bias in work settings: The lack of fit model. *Research in Organizational Behavior, 5*, 386–395.

Heilman, M. E., Wallen, A. S., Fuchs, D., & Tamkins, M. M. (2004). Penalties for success: Reactions to women who succeed at male gender-typed tasks. *Journal of Applied Psychology, 89*, 416–427.

Jones, J. M. (2005, August 2). *Gender differences in views of job opportunity: Fifty-three percent of Americans believe opportunities are equal.* Retrieved August 5, 2005 from Gallup Brain, www.institution.gallup.com.turing. library.northwestern.edu/content/?ci=17614

Langford, T., & MacKinnon, N. J. (2000). The affective bases for the gendering of traits: Comparing the United States and Canada. *Social Psychology Quarterly, 63*, 34–48.

Lee, Y., Jussim, L., & McCauley, C. R. (Eds.). (1995). *Stereotype accuracy: Toward appreciating group differences.* Washington, DC: American Psychological Association.

Levinson, R. M. (1982). Sex discrimination and employment practices: An experiment with unconventional job inquiries. In R. Kahn-Hut, A. N. Daniels, & R. Colvard (Eds.), *Women and work: Problems and perspectives* (pp. 54–65). New York: Oxford University Press.

Lin, M. H., Kwan, V. S. Y., Cheung, A., & Fiske, S. T. (2005). Stereotype content model explains prejudice for an envied outgroup: Scale of Anti-Asian American Stereotypes. *Personality and Social Psychology Bulletin, 31,* 34–47.

Martin, C. L. (1990). Attitudes and expectations about children with nontraditional and traditional gender roles. *Sex Roles, 22,* 151–165.

Maume, D. J., Jr. (1999). Occupational segregation and the career mobility of White men and women. *Social Forces, 77,* 1433–1459.

Maume, D. J., Jr. (2004). Is the glass ceiling a unique form of inequality? Evidence from a random-effects model of managerial attainment. *Work and Occupations, 31,* 250–274.

Merriam-Webster Online Dictionary (2006). Retrieved January 19, 2006 from www.m-w.com/dictionary/prejudice

Neumark, D., Bank, R. J., & Van Nort, K. D. (1996). Sex discrimination in restaurant hiring: An audit study. *Quarterly Journal of Economics, 111,* 915–941.

Newport, F. (2001, February 21). *Americans see women as emotional and affectionate, men as more aggressive: Gender specific stereotypes persist in recent Gallup poll.* Retrieved January 25, 2001 from Gallup Brain, www.institution.gallup.com.turing.library.northwestern.edu/content/default.aspx?ci=1978.

Powell, G. N., Butterfield, D. A., & Parent, J. D. (2002). Gender and managerial stereotypes: Have the times changed? *Journal of Management, 28,* 177–193.

Prentice D. A., & Carranza, E. (2002). What women should be, shouldn't be, are allowed to be, and don't have to be: The contents of prescriptive gender stereotypes. *Psychology of Women Quarterly, 26,* 269–281.

Ridgeway, C. L. (1997). Interaction and the conservation of gender inequality: Considering employment. *American Sociological Review, 62,* 218–235.

Rudman, L. A., & Glick, P. (1999). Feminized management and backlash toward agentic women: The hidden costs to women of a kinder, gentler image of middle managers. *Journal of Personality and Social Psychology, 77,* 1004–1010.

Schein, V. E. (2001). A global look at psychological barriers to women's progress in management. *Journal of Social Issues, 57,* 675–688.

Sidanius, J., & Pratto, F. (1999). *Social dominance: An intergroup theory of social hierarchy and oppression.* New York: Cambridge University Press.

Spencer, S. J., Fein, S., Wolfe, C. T., Fong, C., & Dunn, M. A. (1998). Automatic activation of stereotypes: The role of self-image threat. *Personality and Social Psychology Bulletin, 24,* 1139–1152.

Stamps, L. E. (2002). Maternal preference in child custody decisions. *Journal of Divorce & Remarriage, 37,* 1–11.

Swim, J., Borgida, E., Maruyama, G., & Myers, D. G. (1989). Joan McKay versus John McKay: Do gender stereotypes bias evaluations? *Psychological Bulletin, 105,* 409–429.

Swim, J. K., Hyers, L. L., Cohen, L. L., & Ferguson, M. J. (2001). Everyday sexism: Evidence for its incidence, nature, and psychological impact from three daily diary studies. *Journal of Social Issues, 57,* 31–53.

U.S. Government Accountability Office. (2003). *Women's earnings: Work patterns partially explain difference between men's and women's earnings* (GAO-04-35). Washington, DC: Author. Retrieved July 30, 2004 from www.gao.gov/new.items/d0435.pdf

Waldo, C. R., Berdahl, J. L., & Fitzgerald, L. F. (1998). Are men sexually harassed? If so, by whom? *Law and Human Behavior, 22,* 59–79.

Williams, J. E., & Best, D. L. (1990). *Measuring sex stereotypes: A multination study* (rev. ed.). Newbury Park, CA: Sage.

5

From the Laboratory to the Bench: Gender Stereotyping Research in the Courtroom

Laurie A. Rudman, Peter Glick, and Julie E. Phelan

The study of stereotypes (beliefs about social groups), prejudice (biased feelings toward social groups), and discrimination (differential treatment of social groups) is a major subfield of social psychology (Fiske, 1998). The basic processes that govern these phenomena have often initially been established in laboratory studies with college students as participants, under conditions that afford rigorous tests of causal mechanisms. This scientific knowledge base has firmly established basic principles concerning how gender stereotypes and power differences relate to sex discrimination. Moreover, considerable research in field settings, including organizations such as the Armed Forces and large corporations, has confirmed that these basic principles operate similarly among working adults and within work organizations (e.g., Boyce & Herd, 2003; Eagly, Makhijani, & Klonsky, 1992; Ely, 1994; Heilman, Block, & Martell, 1995; Heim, 1990; Schein, 2001; Sonnert & Holton, 1995).

In this chapter, we first describe how gender stereotypes foster discrimination toward women in the workplace. The remainder of the chapter focuses on two areas of complexity within the gender stereotyping literature that can lead to confusion when research findings are presented in the courtroom. Specifically, we consider: (a) whether individuating information thwarts stereotypical judgments (and sex discrimination) and (b) how subjectively positive female stereotypes can actively harm women in performance settings. We selected these topics because, in each case, empirical evidence contradicts common knowledge. First, although it might seem intuitive to expect stereotypes to diminish in the face of personalized information (e.g., after you learn that a woman is a competent accountant you should no longer stereotype her as unskilled at math), the research literature presents a more complex picture that argues against this simplified view. Second, common knowledge suggests that favorable beliefs about women, including that they are more modest, supportive, and cooperative than men, should benefit them; however, empirical evidence suggests that these favorable beliefs can harm women by undermining their credibility and prestige.

Gender Stereotypes and Sex Discrimination

Gender stereotypes generally cast women as more *communal* (empathetic, nurturing, understanding) than men and men as more *agentic* (independent, ambitious, good leaders) than women (Eagly, 1987). In short, women are viewed as warmer but less competent, and men as more competent but less warm. Overall, these stereotypes lead evaluators to judge men as more suited to high status, leadership roles (which typically emphasize competence) and women to lower-status support roles (for which warmth is a qualification). Women and men are therefore "matched" to different types of jobs, which are themselves stereotyped as requiring agentic or communal traits (Glick, 1991; Heilman, 1983). Although such matching discriminates against men who apply for "feminine" occupations (e.g., nurse, day care worker, receptionist), the overall effect is to segregate women into lower-paying and lower-status roles (Heilman, this volume; Reskin & Ross, 1992; Reskin & Padavic, 2002).

Because they reflect conventional gender roles and men's power advantage, gender stereotypes are widely shared and often *prescriptive* (specifying how men and women *should* act) as well as *descriptive* (a set of expectancies about how men and women are *likely* to act) (Burgess & Borgida, 1999; Fiske & Stevens, 1993; Heilman, 2001; Prentice & Carranza, 2002). Descriptive gender stereotyping can lead to discrimination when individuals are assimilated into the stereotype (e.g., a female job candidate is assumed to be less competent than a similarly qualified male candidate), which can occur automatically and without a perceiver's awareness (Fiske, 1998). That is, gender stereotypes are learned so early in life that they become *implicit*, meaning that people stereotype others according to gender quickly, automatically, and without being conscious that they do so. Even individuals who explicitly endorse egalitarian views can be prone to implicit stereotyping, leading to unintentional discrimination. A considerable research literature shows that automatic gender stereotypes are not only pervasive, but significantly affect how people judge and treat men versus women (e.g., Banaji & Greenwald, 1995; Rudman & Glick, 2001; Rudman & Kilianski, 2000).

Prescriptive stereotypical beliefs also lead to sex discrimination. Although there has been a significant trend toward more egalitarian gender attitudes as women have entered the paid workforce in increasing numbers, gender prescriptions still foster sex discrimination (Spence & Buckner, 2000). In comparison to descriptive stereotypes, prescriptive stereotyping creates more intentional, motivated, and hostile discriminatory behavior. Although both men and women face rejection (and even sabotage) for violating gender stereotypes (Rudman & Fairchild, 2004), women are much more likely to suffer prescriptively based discrimination at work. Gender prescriptions for men typically match prescriptions for work roles – being agentic is required in most jobs (especially those with the most prestige and pay, e.g., management; Glick, 1991). In contrast, prescriptive stereotypes that women ought not to be too ambitious or dominant conflict with the demands of high powered work roles. This places women in a bind, in so far as demonstrating that they are qualified for the job can lead to social rejection by coworkers and superiors (Rudman, 1998).

Does Individuating Information Eliminate Stereotypes and Discrimination?

Can descriptive stereotyping be short-circuited by providing information that an individual does not fit the stereotype of his or her gender? Impressions can range from being wholly category-based (i.e., stereotypical) to being completely personalized (i.e., individuated and not biased by category membership). Some theorists propose that people initially form a category-based impression and subsequently attend to individuating information if they have the opportunity and are motivated to do so (Brewer, 1988; Fiske & Neuberg, 1990). Others propose that stereotypes and individuating information simultaneously influence impressions (Kunda & Thagard, 1996). In either case, as research has repeatedly shown, stereotypes dominate impressions when no individuating information is available or when it is ambiguous. Therefore, clear, unambiguous information about targets' counterstereotypical attributes is essential to undermining stereotypes (Fiske, 1998; Hamilton & Sherman, 1994; Kunda & Thagard, 1996).

However, some defense attorneys and expert psychologists have interpreted past research (e.g., Locksley, Borgida, Brekke, & Hepburn, 1980) as indicating that clear, individuating information easily "dissolves" stereotypes (e.g., Barrett & Morris, 1993; *Huffman v. Pepsi-Cola Bottling Co.*, 1994; *Jensen v. Eveleth Taconite Mining Co.*, 1993; Jussim, Eccles, & Madon, 1996; Kunda & Thagard, 1996). Given that individuating information is invariably present in personnel decisions (e.g., hiring and promotions are not determined knowing only a candidate's gender), it is tempting to conclude that stereotyping has negligible effects in the workplace. A considerable body of research shows, however, that this is a false conclusion: Gender discrimination has been repeatedly demonstrated in hiring decisions for male-dominated jobs, with male applicants favored over female applicants when individuating information suggests similar qualifications (for comprehensive reviews, see Fiske, Bersoff, Borgida, Deaux, & Heilman, 1991; Fiske, 1998; Deaux & LaFrance, 1998; Eagly & Karau, 2002). As a result, women continue to be underrepresented in managerial and high-status professions (e.g., Bielby & Baron, 1986; Giele, 1988; Reskin & Ross, 1992). Moreover, even when women break through the glass ceiling, they continue to suffer economic discrimination (i.e., to receive less money for the same position; Babcock & Laschever, 2003; Reskin & Padavic, 2002; Roos & Gatta, 1999). If individuating information trumps stereotypes, such discriminatory effects would be rare and negligible. They are not.

The role that individuating information plays in stereotypical thinking is arguably the most complex aspect of the data base on gender stereotyping (Borgida, Rudman, & Manteufel, 1995). The notion that individuating information effectively counteracts gender stereotypes and (in turn) sex discrimination is a gross oversimplification of this research for several reasons, which we elaborate on below. First, perceivers preferentially solicit stereotype-confirming individuating information and interpret ambiguous information in stereotype-consistent ways. Second, "shifting standards" that affect subjective evaluations of men and women can mask stereotyping effects, which become evident in personnel decisions, such as hiring, promotion, and the assignment of valued tasks. Third, stereotype-disconfirming targets are often evaluated negatively for having violated gender prescriptions, rendering moot the benefits of individuation. We consider each of these complexities in turn to show how they subvert the oversimplified view of earlier research, and therefore, common knowledge, regarding the putatively weak influence of stereotypes on perceivers' decisions and behavior (see also Bodenhausen, Macrae & Sherman, 1999).[1]

Stereotypes bias how individuating information is gathered and interpreted

The likelihood that perceivers will gather or pay close attention to stereotype-disconfirming information is affected by people's general preference to confirm (rather than disconfirm) their stereotypes (e.g., Cameron & Trope, 2004; Gawronski, Ehrenberg, Banse, Zukova, & Klauer, 2003; Trope & Thompson, 1997; for reviews, see Miller & Turnbull, 1986; Snyder, 1984). Moreover, perceivers use different evidentiary standards to evaluate individuating information, requiring more compelling information to disconfirm than to confirm a stereotypic expectation (Biernat, 2003; Biernat & Ma, 2005). Finally, perceivers with particularly strong stereotypic associations tend to have poor recall for individuating information; they also falsely recall information about the target in a stereotype-consistent manner (Gawronski et al., 2003; Miller & Turnbull, 1986; Snyder, 1984).

In addition to biased information gathering, perceivers interpret individuating information through stereotypic lenses. As a result, if the information is open to interpretation it is likely to be viewed as confirming a stereotype. For example, a housewife who "hit someone," was judged to be less aggressive than a construction worker about whom the same individuating information was provided. Gender stereotyping was eliminated only when a clear and detailed description of the behavior (e.g., "punched a neighbor in the arm") was given (Kunda & Sherman-Williams, 1993; see also Krueger & Rothbart, 1988). When individuating information is open to interpretation, stereotypes guide how the information is construed. In the example above, participants were more likely to assume that "hit someone" indicated mild aggression by the housewife (e.g., she spanked her child) and more extreme aggression by the construction worker (e.g., he was in a bar fight).

Individuating information can also be dismissed by perceivers depending on stereotypical interpretations of the causes of a target's

---

[1]   Although it is beyond the scope of this review, Bodenhausen et al. (1999) also point to the many methodological flaws in much of the research suggesting that individuating information overrides stereotypes. These include demand characteristics, social desirability bias, and disparities in information salience that likely draw more attention to personal than categorical information.

behavior. For example, women's successes on stereotypically masculine tasks are often construed as being due to luck or extreme effort, whereas men's successes are attributed to skill (for a meta-analysis, see Swim & Sanna, 1996). Moreover, when women and men work in teams, women's contributions are devalued because they are presumed to be less competent, less influential, and less likely to have played a leadership role (Heilman & Haynes, 2005).

In short, individuating information is not likely to undermine stereotypic assumptions unless it is completely unambiguous and specific. For example, female candidates for a managerial position were evaluated as less suitable than male counterparts even when they were described as "successful;" to undermine sex discrimination, the women had to be described as successful *managers* (Heilman et al., 1995). Based on a comprehensive literature review, Fiske and Taylor (1991) concluded that stereotyping is only likely to be counteracted "when the potentially diluting behavioral information is clearly, unambiguously judgment relevant, *to the point of redundancy with the judgment*" (p. 136, emphasis added).

Shifting standards

Early research on individuating information appeared to show that it is effective at counteracting stereotyping, as measured by subjective rating scales. Subsequent research, however, revealed that such rating scales obscure important stereotyping effects. Consider a woman and a man whom perceivers each rate with a "4" on a 5-point scale in which 1 = "not at all aggressive" and 5 = "extremely aggressive." Do similar ratings indicate that the "very aggressive" man is actually perceived as similar to the "very aggressive" woman? Research on shifting standards (e.g., Biernat, 2003; Biernat & Fuegen, 2001) suggests that perceivers compare men and women to different standards on subjective rating scales – e.g., she may be viewed as "very aggressive for a woman" (but not "for a man") in the same way that 50-degree weather may be viewed as "very cold" for Miami (but not for Minneapolis). On more objective or behavioral measures (e.g., how likely would he or she be to punch a stranger?) stereotype effects that are obscured by subjective rating-scale measures become evident.

For example, shifting standards research demonstrates that although a female and a male job applicant may both be rated as "extremely well qualified" on a subjective rating scale, on objective ratings (e.g., How much money should she be paid?; Is she likely to complete a specific task successfully?) the woman is likely to be rated more poorly than the man. When it comes to such decisions as who gets a job or who receives limited resources, stereotyping effects that are masked by shifting standards on subjective rating scales become apparent. Such "zero-sum" decisions (and not the subjective rating scales initially favored by researchers) reflect the important "real-world" outcomes that favor men over women (Biernat, 2003).

Not only may men and women be judged according to different standards, but perceivers may shift job criteria to give men an advantage over women for male-dominated jobs. For example, when the candidates for a police chief were described as a "streetwise man" and an "educated woman," evaluators rated being streetwise as more important than having a formal education. However, when the choice was between an "educated man" and a "streetwise woman," education received more weight (Uhlmann & Cohen, 2005). Thus, even though the candidates were individuated (e.g., a streetwise male and a street-wise female candidate were perceived as similarly competent), people shifted the job criteria to favor a male candidate's strengths. Real-life examples of such gender-biased evaluative criteria include Sears and Roebuck's "vigor test," which favored applicants with deep voices who liked to hunt and fish (*Equal Employment Opportunity Commission v. Sears, Roebuck & Co., 1986*). Criteria such as this result in women being less likely to be hired than men owing to a perceived "lack of fit" with the job (Burgess & Borgida, 1999; Heilman, 1983).

Negative consequences of disconfirming prescriptive stereotypes

Even if an individual woman successfully manages to contradict being stereotyped as "feminine" by providing individuating information, she may find that she has stepped from the frying pan into the fire. Prescriptive stereotypes carry a powerful burden of *should nots* for women, including many of the agentic traits and behaviors (e.g., self-promotion, ambition, and competitiveness) that are valued for high status work roles. Ann Hopkins, a successful accountant who was denied partnership at her firm for being "too masculine," exemplifies the dilemma that women face. The Supreme Court ruled in her favor, arguing that women are placed in an "intolerable catch-22: out of a job if they behave aggressively and out of a job if they don't."[2]

Unfortunately, owing to descriptive stereotyping, a female candidate for a masculine-typed occupation is likely to be judged as less

---

[2]   *Price-Waterhouse v. Hopkins* (1989, p. 1791).

suitable than a man unless she provides strong, counterstereotypical information (Glick, Zion, & Nelson, 1988). At the same time, she is likely to face social and economic reprisals (termed *backlash effects*; Rudman, 1998) if she violates gender stereotypic assumptions. For example, agentic female job applicants are perceived as highly qualified for managerial jobs, but they are also viewed as unlikable and abrasive, compared with agentic men, which results in hiring discrimination (Heilman, Wallen, Fuchs, & Tamkins, 2004; Rudman, 1998; Rudman & Glick, 1999, 2001). Similarly, female leaders are judged more harshly than men when they behave in an autocratic and directive manner (though not when they lead with a participatory style; Eagly et al., 1992) and women who successfully compete in male-dominated domains risk being sabotaged by their peers (Rudman & Fairchild, 2004; see also Heim, 1990). Women who work in male-dominated occupations are also likely to be subjected to sexual harassment (Fiske & Stevens, 1993; *Robinson v. Jacksonville Shipyards, Inc.*, 1991). In some occupations, the mere presence of women violates gender pre-scriptions, resulting in nasty reprisals. Thus, in many cases unambiguous, individuating information can backfire, resulting in negative reactions based on the violation of prescriptive stereotypes (Gill, 2004; Rudman & Glick, 2001).

In sum, gender stereotypes are remarkably resistant to individuating information, unless the information is virtually redundant with the judgment task. This occurs for several reasons. Individuating information is often gathered in a biased manner and, if at all ambiguous, is interpreted in stereotype-consistent ways (reinforcing rather than disconfirming the stereotype). Owing to shifting standards, stereo-types (once individuating information has been provided) may appear to vanish if subjective rating scales are used to assess them, but are evident in zero-sum decisions (e.g., whether to hire a female candidate or a male competitor). Moreover, even when individuating information leads perceivers to view a woman as atypical, she may be treated with hostility for violating gender prescriptions (Rudman, 1998). In short, individuating information, though important, is not a panacea for stereotype-based discrimination.

Subjectively Positive Female Stereotypes Elicit Patronizing Discrimination

According to common knowledge, discrimination typically arises from intergroup hostility. In gender relations, however, attitudes toward women combine hostility toward some women with paternalistic benevolence toward those women who conform to feminine ideals (Glick & Fiske, 1996). Because the communal stereotype of women reflects these feminine ideals (e.g., to be warm and supportive of others), women are evaluated more favorably than men (Eagly & Mladinic, 1989; Eagly, Mladinic, & Otto, 1994). Laypersons are likely to misconstrue such ostensibly favorable, but stereotypical, attitudes toward women as evidence of "reverse discrimination." For example, when Rudman and Goodwin (2004) reported that women automatically preferred women to men, they were barraged with hostile email from men who believed it signified how men are treated unfairly (oddly, no one seemed to mind that male participants also often preferred women to men in this research). However, paternalistic pro-female orientations are dependent on women occupying low-status roles; in contrast, female authority figures are evaluated more negatively than male counterparts (Eagly & Karau, 2002; Rudman & Kilianski, 2000). That is, women are only perceived to be "wonderful" (e.g., more nurturing, modest, and morally pure than men; Glick & Fiske, 1996) if they remain weak and dependent.

The perception that women are warm but incompetent can lead to patronizing discrimination, defined by Glick and Fiske (in press) as " behavior that is ostensibly benevolent, but demeans and excludes by reinforcing assumptions that the target is incompetent and low status" (see also Glick & Fiske, 1996; Jackman, 1994). For example, men may offer more praise for a female (as compared to a male) subordinate's accomplishments as a substitute for meaningful rewards (e.g., promotion or pay raises), which are more likely to be allocated to men (Vescio, Gervais, Snyder, & Hoover, 2005). Moreover, the expectation that women will not perform as well as men can lead to soft forms of bigotry (e.g., overhelping, taking over, or limiting women's responsibilities). Shifting standards for excellence can result in high competence ratings for women who perform well in masculine domains (Deaux & Taylor, 1973), but they do not translate into tangible rewards – reflecting the notion that "she is excellent . . . for a woman" (Biernat & Fuegen, 2001; Rudman, 1998; Rudman & Glick, 1999).

The invisibility of paternalism

Paternalistic prejudice is particularly insidious because recipients and perpetrators alike may not recognize patronizing behavior as a form of discrimination (Jackman, 1994). Indeed, women sometimes score higher than men on measures of support for paternalism, but only in nations where the endorsement of hostile sexism toward women who pursue equal status and power is highest. Across two studies involving a total of 26 nations, women were more benevolently sexist than men in the 5 nations in which men most strongly endorsed hostile sexism (Glick et al., 2004, 2000). At least some women may happily receive the patronizing help and attention of a male supervisor, either because they fail to realize how this reinforces traditional gender stereotypes and cements them into lower status, dependent roles (see Kilianski & Rudman, 1998), or because they believe that it is better to be patronized than to face hostility and overt derogation.

Moreover, even when a woman does resist paternalism, efforts to seek legal recourse may be stymied by a failure of the courts to recognize paternalism as discrimination. For example, a chemistry professor was denied tenure despite a favorable faculty vote, external funding, and glowing letters of recommendation because an ad hoc committee considered her scholarship to be weak. These evaluators assumed a patronizing tone, referring to her only by her first name and described her as "perfectly nice," "caring," and "nurturing." These stereotypically feminine qualities were used to highlight the professor's perceived intellectual weakness (assimilating her into the stereotype of women as "nice, but not competent"). The court issued a summary judgment in which the majority rejected the plaintiff's claim of sex discrimination, ruling that "Any reasonable person of either sex would like to be considered 'nice'" and pointing out that, unlike Ann Hopkins, the plaintiff "faced no . . . carping" about her perceived femininity.[3]

A lone judge protested that the plaintiff deserved her day in court. Citing the patronizing tone of the ad hoc committee, the dissenter wrote:

> This case presents the mirror image of Price Waterhouse. The decision to deny tenure was based – ironically – on Weinstock's perceived success at projecting a stereotypically "feminine" image at work. She was described as gentle and caring, "nice," a "pushover," and nurturing. Unfortunately . . . a stereotypically "feminine" person is not viewed in a male dominated field as a driven, scientifically-minded, competitive academic researcher. The inappropriate focus on Weinstock's "feminine" qualities in the tenure process led [her evaluators] to discount her "masculine" success as a researcher and professor. While Hopkins

---

[3] _Weinstock v. Columbia University_ (2000, p. 8).

was punished for failing to perform a "feminine" role, Weinstock was punished for performing it too well . . . Hopkins was punished because her "masculinity" appeared inconsistent with gendered stereotypes of how women should look and behave; Weinstock was punished because her "femininity" appeared inconsistent with "masculine" success as a researcher. Yet if she had chosen to project a more "masculine" image, she could very well have suffered the same fate as Hopkins.[4]

In sum, although the dissenting judge recognized the dilemma faced by women in traditionally masculine occupations, the majority missed the influence of positive female stereotyping (and its undercurrent of paternalism) because it appears to benefit "any reasonable person." The result is a system-level barrier to gender equity stemming from judges blindly relying on their common knowledge, as opposed to the scientific literature.

Paternalism represents inappropriate sex-role spillover

Paternalistic prejudice may be driven by the simple fact that oppression, when cloaked in a velvet glove, is more hospitable to victims than when it is enforced through an iron fist (Jackman, 1994). That is, soft forms of bigotry lead to less resistance and more acceptance of the status quo. However, in the case of gender, paternalism is also tied to the fact that men and women are uniquely intimate and interdependent in heterosexual romantic relationships and domestic life (Glick & Fiske, 1996; in press).

The norms that govern heterosexual relations tend to be replicated in the workplace; this has been labeled "sex-role spillover" (Gutek, 1985). For example, the fact that, traditionally, women have gained social and economic status through marriage to men (i.e., their sex appeal) has repercussions for women in performance settings. If there are few women occupying leadership roles in an organization, those who succeed are viewed as having done so illegitimately (i.e., by "sleeping their way to the top;" Ely, 1994). Attractive female managerial applicants are therefore disadvantaged, relative to male counterparts (Heilman & Stopek, 1985), especially if they emphasize their sex appeal (Glick, Larsen, Johnson, & Branstiter, 2005).

In addition, women's sex appeal can result in biased evaluations by male supervisors. Men primed to think of women as sexual objects (as compared to non-primed men) evaluated female job applicants as less

---

[4] *Weinstock* (2000, p. 17).

competent, though also friendlier and more hirable for an entry-level position (Rudman & Borgida, 1995). Not surprisingly, romantic expectations can cloud the judgment of male evaluators, who may judge poor performance as equivalent to good performance on a task (Goodwin, Fiske, Rosen, & Rosenthal, 2002). This type of favoritism is harmful to everyone in the organization, including the female recipients. Even though some women may benefit materially, appearance-based hiring is a patronizing form of discrimination that reinforces the belief that women typically gain power through their sex appeal, not their intelligence. Moreover, attractive women's advantage in the workplace is evident only for low-status, not high-status, occupations (Glick et al., 2005). Thus, power based on sex appeal has limited effectiveness for women, underscoring the dubious benefits of paternalistic prejudice.

Paternalistic assumptions about women's physical limitations and "proper place" as housewives and mothers can also foster patronizing discrimination. For example, pregnant women often receive unsought help and are addressed by diminutive endearments, such as "honey" (Walton et al., 1988). At the same time, many people look askance at pregnant career women (and working mothers; Cuddy, Fiske, & Glick, 2004) because they perceive a conflict between fulfilling home and workplace responsibilities (Crosby, Williams, & Biernat, 2004). As a result, pregnant female job candidates can suffer both patronizing and hostile discrimination. For example, women who wore a pregnancy prosthesis while posing as a customer were patronized (e.g., smiled at and called "honey"), but when they applied for a job they received more hostility (e.g., scowling and rudeness), compared with the same women who did not wear the prosthesis (Hebl, King, Glick, Singletary, & Kazama, in press). Paternalism toward women rewards them with affection for conforming to traditional low-power feminine roles, but can yield to hostility when women stray from those roles in an effort to obtain or perform well in nontraditional occupations.

Conclusion

This chapter represents a brief overview of the relationship between gender stereotyping and sex discrimination. We chose to highlight two particularly complex and potentially confusing areas of the gender stereotyping literature because they are prone to misrepresentation in the courtroom. First, we have attempted to clarify why the ability of individuating information to mitigate stereotypical judgments is often overestimated. Specifically, targets are seldom "purely" personalized (i.e., judged without reference to stereotypes), in part because gender categories influence how perceivers elicit, interpret, and recall individuating information. Further, the typical methodology of assessing stereotypes through subjective rating scales (due to shifting standards) initially obscured the effects of gender stereotypes on the kinds of decisions that actually matter in the workplace – which candidate gets hired, promoted, or assigned valued resources and opportunities. Moreover, even when individuating information "works" (i.e., changes how a person is perceived), atypical targets are not necessarily rewarded with stereotype-free evaluations; instead, they are often punished for violating prescriptive gender stereotypes.

Second, we have pointed out the ways in which subjectively positive female stereotypes represent a barrier to gender equity. Women are traditionally evaluated more favorably than men, but only because they are viewed as wonderful but weak. Women's putative niceness puts them at risk of patronizing discrimination, which relegates them to low-status roles and occupations and excludes them from leadership roles that are linked to masculine, aggressive qualities. Once the connection between perceptions of women's warmth and incompetence is revealed, it is not difficult to see how positive female stereotypes can undermine women in the workplace. Unfortunately, whether it is because women suspect they have to choose between being patronized or treated in a hostile manner, or because, like men, they take subjectively "profemale" beliefs at face value, paternalism readily masquerades as benevolence toward "the fairer sex" and is not easily resisted. Intergroup relations researchers have only recently expanded their definition of prejudice to include the soft bigotry of paternalism (Dovidio, Glick, & Rudman, 2005; Glick et al., 2000). Optimistically, we expect the legal profession (and laypersons) to follow suit, but, realistically, change may be slow. Convincing laypeople that "being nice" can be a form of harmful discrimination is likely to take a large body of evidence on the effects of patronizing discrimination; psychologists have only recently begun this task. The evidence collected thus far, however, makes a persuasive case that patronizing discrimination is a largely invisible barrier to gender equity that must be unmasked and dismantled.

REFERENCES

Babcock, L. & Laschever, S. (2003). *Women don't ask*. Princeton, NJ: Princeton University Press.

Banaji, M. R., & Greenwald, A. G. (1995). Implicit gender stereotyping in judgments of fame. *Journal of Personality and Social Psychology, 68,* 181–198.

Barrett, G. V., & Morris, S. B. (1993). Sex stereotyping in Price Waterhouse v. Hopkins *American Psychologist, 48,* 54–55.

Bielby, W. T., & Baron, J. N. (1986). Men and women at work: Sex segregation and statistical discrimination. *American Journal of Sociology, 91,* 759–799.

Biernat, M. (2003). Toward a broader view of social stereotyping. *American Psychologist, 58,* 1019–1027.

Biernat, M., & Fuegen, K. (2001). Shifting standards and the evaluation of competence: Complexity in gender-based judgment and decision making. *Journal of Social Issues, 57,* 707–724.

Biernat, M., & Ma, J. E. (2005). Stereotypes and the confirmability of trait concepts. *Personality and Social Psychology Bulletin, 31,* 483–495.

Bodenhausen, G. V., Macrae, C. N., & Sherman, J. W. (1999). On the dialectics of discrimination. Dual processes in social stereotyping. In S. Chaiken & Y. Trope (Eds.), *Dual-process theories in social psychology* (pp. 271–290). New York: Guilford Press.

Borgida, E., Rudman, L. A., & Manteufel, L. L. (1995). On the courtroom use and misuse of gender stereotyping research. *Journal of Social Issues, 51,* 181–192.

Boyce, L. A., & Herd, A. M. (2003). The relationship between gender role stereotypes and requisite military leadership characteristics. *Sex Roles, 49,* 365–378.

Brewer, M. B. (1988). A dual process model of impression formation. In T. K. Skrull & R. S. Wyer, Jr. (Eds.), *Advances in social cognition* (Vol. 1, pp. 1–36). Hillsdale, NJ: Erlbaum.

Burgess, D., & Borgida, E. (1999). Who women are, who women should be: Descriptive and prescriptive gender stereotyping in sex discrimination. *Psychology, Public Policy, and Law, 5,* 665–692.

Cameron, J. A., & Trope, Y. (2004). Stereotyped-biased search and processing of information about group members. *Social Cognition, 22,* 650–672.

Crosby, F., J., Williams, J., & Biernat, M. (2004). The maternal wall. *Journal of Social Issues, 60,* 675–682.

Cuddy, A. J. C., Fiske, S. T., & Glick, P. (2004). When professionals become mothers, warmth doesn't cut the ice. *Journal of Social Issues, 60,* 701–718.

Deaux, K., & LaFrance, M. (1998). Gender. In D. T. Gilbert, S. T. Fiske, & G. Lindzey (Eds.), *The handbook of social psychology* (4th ed., pp. 788–827). New York: McGraw-Hill.

Deaux, K., & Taylor, J. (1973). Evaluation of male and female ability: Bias works two ways. *Psychological Reports, 32,* 261–262.

Dovidio, J. F., Glick, P., & Rudman, L. A. (Eds.) (2005). *On the nature of prejudice: Fifty years after Allport.* Malden, MA: Blackwell.

Eagly, A. H. (1987). *Sex differences in social behavior: A social role interpretation*. Hillsdale, NJ: Erlbaum.

Eagly, A. H., & Karau, S. J. (2002). Role congruity theory of prejudice toward female leaders. *Psychological Review, 109*, 573–598.

Eagly, A. H., Makhijani, M. G., & Klonsky, B. G. (1992). Gender and the evaluation of leaders: A meta-analysis. *Psychological Bulletin, 111*, 3–22.

Eagly, A. H., & Mladinic, A. (1989). Gender stereotypes and attitudes toward women and men. *Personality and Social Psychology Bulletin, 15*, 543–558.

Eagly, A. H., Mladinic, A., & Otto, S. (1994). Cognitive and affective bases of attitudes toward social groups and social policies. *Journal of Experimental Social Psychology, 30*, 113–137.

Ely, R. J. (1994). The effects of organizational demographics and social identity on relationships among professional women. *Administrative Science Quarterly, 39*, 203–238.

Equal Employment Opportunity Commission v. Sears, Roebuck & Co. 628 F. Supp. 1264 (N.D. Ill. 1986) *aff'd*, 839 F.2d 302 (7th Cir. 1988).

Fiske, S. T. (1998). Stereotyping, prejudice and discrimination. In D. T. Gilbert, S. T. Fiske, & G. Lindzey (Eds.), *The handbook of social psychology* (4th ed., pp. 357–414). New York: McGraw-Hill.

Fiske, S. T., Bersoff, D. N., Borgida, E., Deaux, K., & Heilman, M. E. (1991). Social science research on trial: Use of sex stereotyping research in Price Waterhouse v. Hopkins. *American Psychology, 46*, 1049–1060.

Fiske, S. T., & Neuberg, S. L. (1990). A continuum of impression formation, from category-based to individuating processes: Influences of information and motivation on attention and interpretation. In M. Zanna (Ed.), *Advances in experimental social psychology* (Vol. 23, pp. 1–74). New York: Academic Press.

Fiske, S. T., & Stevens, L. E. (1993). What's so special about sex? Gender stereotyping and discrimination. In S. Oskamp, & M. Costanzo (Eds.), *Gender issues in contemporary society* (pp. 173–196). Thousand Oaks, CA: Sage Publications, Inc.

Fiske, S. T., & Taylor, S. E. (1991). *Social cognition* (2nd ed.). New York: McGraw-Hill.

Gawronski, B., Ehrenberg, K., Banse, R., Zukova, J., & Klauer, K. C. (2003). It's in the mind of the beholder: The impact of stereotypic associations on category-based and individuating impression formation. *Journal of Experimental Social Psychology, 39*, 16–30.

Giele, J. Z. (1988). Gender and sex roles. In N. J. Smelser (Ed.), *Handbook of sociology* (pp. 291–323). Newbury Park, CA: Sage.

Gill, M. J. (2004). When information does not deter stereotyping: Prescriptive stereotyping can foster bias under conditions that deter descriptive stereotyping. *Journal of Experimental Social Psychology, 40*, 619–632.

Glick, P. (1991). Trait-based and sex-based discrimination in occupational prestige, occupational salary, and hiring. *Sex Roles, 25*, 351–378.

Glick, P., & Fiske, S. T. (1996). The Ambivalent Sexism Inventory: Differentiating hostile and benevolent sexism. *Journal of Personality and Social Psychology, 70,* 491–512.

Glick, P., & Fiske, S. T. (in press). Sex discrimination: The psychological approach. To appear in: F. J. Crosby, M. S. Stockdale, & S. A. Ropp (Eds.), *Sex discrimination in the workplace.* Malden, MA: Blackwell Publishing.

Glick, P., Fiske, S. T., Mladinic, A., Saiz, J. L., Abrams, D., Masser, B., et al. (2000). Beyond prejudice as simple antipathy: Hostile and benevolent sexism across cultures. *Journal of Personality and Social Psychology, 79,* 763–775.

Glick, P., Lameiras, M., Fiske, S. T., Eckes, T., Masser, B., Volpato, C., et al. (2004). Bad but bold: Ambivalent attitudes toward men predict gender inequality in 16 nations. *Journal of Personality and Social Psychology, 86,* 713–728.

Glick, P., Larsen, S., Johnson, C., & Branstiter, H. (2005). Evaluations of sexy women in low and high status jobs. *Psychology of Women Quarterly, 29,* 389–395.

Glick, P., Zion, C., & Nelson. C. (1988). What mediates sex discrimination in hiring decisions? *Journal of Personality and Social Psychology, 55,* 178–186.

Goodwin, S. A., Fiske, S. T., Rosen, L. D., & Rosenthal, A. M. (2002). The eye of the beholder: Romantic goals and impression biases. *Journal of Experimental Social Psychology, 38,* 232–241.

Gutek, B. A. (1985). *Sex and the workplace.* San Francisco: Jossey-Bass.

Hamilton, D. L., & Sherman, J. W. (1994). Stereotypes. In R. S. Wyer, Jr., & T. K. Srull (Eds.), *Handbook of social cognition* (2nd ed., pp. 1–68). Hillsdale, NJ: Erlbaum.

Hebl, M. R., King, E., Glick, P., Singletary, S. L., & Kazama, S. M. (in press). *Hostile and benevolent reactions toward pregnant women: Complementary interpersonal punishments and rewards that maintain traditional roles. Journal of Applied Psychology.*

Heilman, M. E. (1983). Sex bias in work settings: The lack of fit model. *Research in Organizational Behavior, 5,* 269–298.

Heilman, M. E. (2001). Description and prescription: How gender stereotypes prevent women's ascent up the organizational ladder. *Journal of Social Issues, 57,* 657–674.

Heilman, M. E., Block, C. J., & Martell, R. F. (1995). Sex stereotypes: Do they influence perceptions of managers? *Journal of Social Behavior & Personality, 10,* 1995.

Heilman, M. E., & Haynes, M. C. (2005). No credit where credit is due: Attributional rationalization of women's success in male–female teams. *Journal of Applied Psychology, 90,* 905–916.

Heilman, M. E., & Stopek, M. H. (1985). Being attractive: advantage or disadvantage? Performance-based evaluations and recommended personnel actions as a function of appearance, sex, and job type. *Organizational Behavior and Human Decision Processes, 35*, 202–215.

Heilman, M. E., Wallen, A. S., Fuchs, D., & Tamkins, M. M., (2004). Penalties for success: Reactions to women who succeed at male gender-typed tasks. *Journal of Applied Psychology, 89*, 416–427.

Heim, P. (1990). Keeping the power dead even. *Journal of American Medical Women's Association, 45*, 232–243.

Huffman v. Pepsi-Cola Bottling Co. of Minneapolis-St. Paul, et al., Hennepin County Trial Court, File # MC 92-10995. Decided June 20, 1994.

Jackman, M. R. (1994). *The velvet glove: Paternalism and conflict in gender, class, and race relations.* Berkeley, CA: University of California Press.

Jensen v. Eveleth Taconite Mining Co. 824 F. Supp. 847 (D. Minn 1993).

Jussim, L., Eccles, J., & Madon, S. (1996). Social perception, social stereotypes, and teacher expectations: Accuracy and the quest for the powerful self-fulfilling prophecy effect. In M. P. Zanna (Ed.), *Advances in experimental social psychology* (Vol. 28, pp. 281–388). San Diego, CA: Academic Press.

Kilianski, S. E., & Rudman, L. A. (1998). Wanting it both ways: Do women approve of benevolent sexism? *Sex Roles, 39*, 333–352.

Krueger, J., & Rothbart, M. (1988). Use of categorical and individuating information in making inferences about personality. *Journal of Personality and Social Psychology, 55*, 187–195.

Kunda, Z., & Sherman-Williams, B. (1993). Stereotypes and the construal of individuating information. *Personality and Social Psychology Bulletin, 19*, 90–99.

Kunda, Z., & Thagard, P. (1996). Forming impressions from stereotypes, traits, and behaviors: A parallel-constraint-satisfaction theory. *Psychological Review, 103*, 284–308.

Locksley, A., Borgida, E., Brekke, N., & Hepburn, C. (1980). Sex stereotypes and social judgment. *Journal of Personality and Social Psychology, 39*, 821–831.

Miller, D. T., & Turnbull, W. (1986). Expectancies and interpersonal processes. *Annual Review of Psychology, 37*, 233–256.

Prentice, D. A., & Carranza, E. (2002). What women and men should be, shouldn't be, are allowed to be, and don't have to be: The contents of prescriptive gender stereotypes. *Psychology of Women Quarterly, 26*, 269–281.

Price-Waterhouse v. Hopkins, 109 S. Ct. 1775 (1989).

Reskin, B. F., & Padavic, I. (2002). *Women and men at work* (2nd ed.). Thousand Oaks, CA: Pine Forge Press.

Reskin, B. F., & Ross, C. E. (1992). Jobs, authority, and earnings among managers: The continuing significance of sex. *Work and Occupations, 19*, 342–365.

Roos, P. A., & Gatta, M. L. (1999). The gender gap in earnings: Trends, explanations, and prospects. In Powell, G. N. (Ed), *Handbook of gender and work* (pp. 95–123). Thousand Oaks, CA, Sage.

Robinson v. Jacksonville Shipyards, Inc., 760 F. Supp 1486 (M. D. Fla 1991).

Rudman, L. A. (1998). Self-promotion as a risk factor for women: The costs and benefits of counterstereotypical impression management. *Journal of Personality and Social Psychology, 74,* 629–645.

Rudman, L. A., & Borgida, E. (1995). The afterglow of construct accessibility: The behavioral consequences of priming men to view women as sexual objects. *Journal of Experimental Social Psychology, 31,* 493–517.

Rudman, L. A., & Fairchild, K. (2004). Reactions to counterstereotypic behavior: The role of backlash in cultural stereotype maintenance. *Journal of Personality and Social Psychology, 87,* 157–176.

Rudman, L. A., & Glick, P. (1999). Feminized management and backlash toward agentic women: The hidden costs to women of a kinder, gentler image of middle-managers. *Journal of Personality and Social Psychology, 77,* 1004–1010.

Rudman, L. A., & Glick, P. (2001). Prescriptive gender stereotypes and backlash toward agentic women. *Journal of Social Issues, 57,* 743–762.

Rudman, L. A., & Goodwin, S. A. (2004). Gender differences in automatic ingroup bias: Why do women like women more than men like men? *Journal of Personality and Social Psychology, 87,* 494–509.

Rudman, L. A., & Kilianski, S. E. (2000). Implicit and explicit attitudes toward female authority. *Personality and Social Psychology Bulletin, 26,* 1315–1328.

Schein, V. E. (2001). A global look at psychological barriers to women's progress in management. *Journal of Social Issues, 57,* 675–688.

Snyder, M. (1984). When belief creates reality. In L. Berkowitz (Ed.), *Advances in experimental social psychology* (Vol. 18, pp. 248–305). San Diego, CA: Academic Press.

Sonnert, G., & Holton, G. (1995). *Who succeeds in science? The gender dimension.* New Brunswick, NJ: Rutgers University Press.

Spence, J. T., & Buckner, C. E. (2000). Instrumental and expressive traits, trait stereotypes, and sexist attitudes. *Psychology of Women Quarterly, 24,* 44–62.

Swim, J. K., & Sanna, L. J. (1996). He's skilled, she's lucky: A meta-analysis of observers' attributions for women's and men's successes and failures. *Personality and Social Psychology Bulletin, 22,* 507–519.

Trope, Y., & Thompson, E. P. (1997). Looking for truth in all the wrong places? Asymmetric search of individuating information about stereotyped group members. *Journal of Personality and Social Psychology, 73,* 229–241.

Uhlmann, E. L., & Cohen, G. L. (2005). Constructed criteria: Redefining merit to justify discrimination. *Psychological Science, 16,* 474–480.

Vescio, T. K., Gervais, S. J., Snyder, M., & Hoover, A. (2005). Power and the creation of patronizing environments: The stereotype-based behaviors of the powerful and their effects on female performance in masculine domains. *Journal of Personality and Social Psychology, 88,* 658–672.

Walton, M. D., Sachs, D., Ellington, R., Hazlewood, A., Griffin, S., & Bass, D. (1988). Physical stigma and the pregnancy role: Receiving help from strangers. *Sex Roles, 18,* 323– 311.

Weinstock v. Columbia University, 224 F.3d 33 2nd Cir. (2000).

6

(Un)common Knowledge: The Legal Viability of Sexual Harassment Research

Louise F. Fitzgerald and
Linda L. Collinsworth

Research on sexual harassment, though only slightly more than 20 years old, is already notable for its richness and coherence. A search of the literature[1] reveals over a thousand journal articles and a wealth of integrative chapters that give testimony to the increasing theoretical maturity of the field. One of the most striking characteristics of this body of work is its consistency; in an area considered by its nature controversial, the empirical literature here is notable for its lack of controversy. Theoretical formulations are incremental and complementary rather than competitive (compare, e.g., Pryor's Person X Environment Interaction Model [Pryor, Giedd, & Williams, 1995], and the Comprehensive Model developed by Fitzgerald and the Illinois group [Fitzgerald, Hulin, & Drasgow, 1995; Fitzgerald, Hulin, Drasgow, Gelfand, & Magley, 1997]). Similarly, Gutek's sex-role spillover concept (1985) holds a key place not only in these two formulations, but also within Fiske and Glick's (1995) ambivalent sexism framework. We suggest that even findings possibly considered counterintuitive (e.g., that most victims never report, that reporting leads to negative consequences) enjoy a consistency largely unknown in other areas of behavioral and social science and counterexamples, where they exist, are rare.

Not surprisingly, much of this research has found its way to court, where controversy and argument are the order of the day and clashing "theories" abound. How does harassment research fare in

---

[1] The literature review covers 1984 to the present.

this environment? What are its most valuable contributions, and what are its vulnerabilities? Are these vulnerabilities scientific or legal? In this chapter, we address these questions, focusing our discussion on three areas of work, each well developed scientifically but enjoying differing degrees of acceptance by experts and/or the courts: (1) the victim response literature; (2) the empirical connection between sexual harassment and posttraumatic stress disorder (PTSD); and (3) the voluminous literature on organizational climate.

The first is the most straightforward; despite public, organizational, and even legal expectation that "real" victims report their experiences and seek organizational relief, victims continue to resist doing so. This discrepancy between normative expectations and actual behavior, bolstered by the consistency of research on the topic, has led even judges traditionally suspicious of the social scientific enterprise in general and testifying experts in particular to rule that testimony on this topic may be helpful to the jury (*Ferrante v. Sciaretta et al.*, 2003; *Griffin v. City of Opa-locka*, 2000). We begin with a brief summary of the research in this area, and then review ways in which such data can be helpful to triers of fact.

Victim[2] Response to Sexual Harassment: Theory and Research

From a psychological perspective, reporting harassment is one of a number of coping methods that victims employ (see, e.g., Fitzgerald, Swan & Fischer, 1995; Gutek & Koss, 1993). Although organizations cannot be held liable for conduct of which they have no knowledge[3] understanding when and how victims will report (or not) requires a broader understanding of victim response more generally. There is consensus in the research literature that victims employ multiple strategies to manage their situation and several frameworks have been proposed to organize these strategies conceptually (Fitzgerald, Swan, et al., 1995; Gruber, 1992; Gutek & Koss, 1993; Knapp, Faley, Ekeberg, & Dubois, 1997; Magley, 2002).

---

[2]   Terminology here is less than satisfactory. We follow the customary practice of employing the word "victim" with no implication that any particular individual has been legally wronged; similarly, we refer to victims as "she" and offenders as "he" while acknowledging that such is not always the case.
[3]   Legal distinctions between liability for supervisor versus coworker harassment and actual versus constructive knowledge need not concern us here.

Most of these systems are multidimensional in nature;[4] for example, Gutek and Koss (1993) proposed a 2 × 2 classification system sorting harassing behaviors into indirect and direct responses, made either individually or with the assistance of others. Indirect responses reflect nonassertive behaviors and include such things as ignoring the behavior, avoiding the harasser, or joking about the experience. Direct responses include assertive strategies such as confronting the harasser (Gutek & Koss, 1993). Knapp et al.'s (1997) theoretical framework is similar, incorporating one dimension that reflects an internal–external distinction (e.g., denial vs. reporting) and a second that focuses on the presence or absence of support utilized in response processes. This dimensional intersection culminates in four cells: "(1) avoidance/denial; (2) social coping; (3) confrontation/negotiation; and (4) advocacy seeking" (Knapp et al., 1997, p. 690).

Fitzgerald, Swan, et al.'s (1995) research on how victims cope with sexual harassment, probably the most widely known theoretical framework, posits two independent dimensions: Specifically grounded in Lazarus and Folkman's (1984) classic paradigm of stress and coping, it proposes that victim responses can be classified as either *internally* (endurance or extinction; denial, detachment, reattribution, and illusory control) or *externally* focused (avoidance, appeasement, assertion, seeking institutional relief, and seeking social support). Internal strategies are characterized by attempts to manage the thoughts and emotions associated with the experience (e.g., "I just tried to forget about it;" "I told myself it didn't matter") whereas externally focused strategies are problem solving in nature (e.g., "I told him to leave me alone"; "I stayed away from him as much as possible"; "I reported him").

Magley (2002) reconceptualized these categories of internal and external responses into a four-category, two-dimensional space, one dimension of which reflects the internal–external distinction (e.g., denial/detachment vs. reporting the harasser) and the other dividing the space between responses conceived as engagement (e.g., reporting the harasser) and disengagement (e.g., avoiding the harasser, denying the experience), but it is unclear that the multidimensional approaches provide any increase in explanatory power.

Against the background of these theoretical frameworks, a wealth of empirical studies have appeared, the results of which can be summarized as follows:

---

[4] See Gruber, 1992, for an early exception.

1. *Avoidance is ubiquitous.* Virtually every study conducted has documented that most victims go to great lengths to avoid a harasser, avoid being alone with him, and even avoid the workplace altogether when possible (Bastian, Lancaster, & Reyst, 1996; Cochran, Frazier, and Olson, 1997; Culbertson, Rosenfeld, Booth-Kewley, & Magnusson, 1992; Fitzgerald, et al., 1988; Gutek, 1985; McKinney, Olson, & Satterfield, 1988; Pryor, 1995; Schneider, 1991; U.S. Merit Systems Protection Board, 1981; 1988; 1995). Victim testimony often reads like classic ethnography, as plaintiffs – often without being directly asked – describe such efforts in exquisite detail.

2. *Assertiveness is common.* Victims rarely remain passive in the face of objectionable behavior; in addition to avoiding the harasser, the majority go to some length to make clear his behavior is unwelcome (Bastian et al., 1996; Cochran et al., 1997; Gruber & Bjorn, 1982; Pryor, 1995; Richman, Rospenda, Flaherty, & Freels, 2001; Schneider, Swan, & Fitzgerald, 1997).

3. *Appeasement is not uncommon.* A sizeable minority of victims attempt to manage their situation by placating the harasser(s) in some manner (e.g., laughing at inappropriate jokes and remarks; cloaking their refusals in socially acceptable euphemisms) (Gruber & Smith, 1995; Gutek & Koss, 1993; Magley, 2002).

4. *Seeking social support is unpredictable.* Many victims discuss the harassment with at least one other person, but a large number never tell anyone. The classic sources of social support (e.g., family, spouse) are, in this case, sometimes the least likely to be told, and many victims are more likely to confide in a friend or acquaintance at work than to seek support from husbands, partners, or families.[5]

5. *Reporting is relatively rare.* Like all forms of sexual victimization and abuse, sexual harassment is woefully underreported, as victims attempt to avoid the embarrassment and discomfort of making a formal complaint. Such discomfort combines with pervasive fear of organizational or coworker consequences to ensure that the

---

[5]   Testimony across multiple cases indicates that plaintiffs often hint of their difficulties to their personal physicians, most usually in general terms. Medical records reveal entries such as "Under a lot of stress at work", "Difficulties with her supervisor" and the like; in our experience, it is unusual to find "sexual harassment at work" clearly identified in medical records, even in fairly egregious cases.

majority of this problem – even (or sometimes particularly) when it is very serious[6] – goes unreported.

Victim Response: Legal Relevance and Issues

Victim behavior is relevant to a number of the liability and damage issues arising in the course of sexual harassment litigation. For example, although Equal Employment Opportunity Commission's (1990) *Policy Guidance* suggests that failure to report harassment does not necessarily indicate that the situation was welcome,[7] and at least one court has underscored the point,[8] defense counsel continue to raise this hypothesis and some courts have considered it favorably (*Weinsheimer v. Rockwell International Corp.*, 1990; *Perkins v. General Motors Corp.*, 1989).

More generally, because victim behavior is commonly misunderstood and often counterintuitive, "(e)gregious conduct may be legally condoned because the plaintiff first reacted by trying to ignore it or to 'fit in' by participating in trashy sex talk, rather than by confronting her tormentors and risking making her situation in the workplace even more unpleasant or tenuous" (Coombs, 1999, p. 140). It is precisely this situation that renders the social science of victim response relevant to legal decision-making, as it is clear that real victims are considerably more likely to "try to ignore it" (endurance) or "fit in" (appeasement) than to confront or (especially) report.

Of course, if reporting is required by law as an element of liability, empirical findings to the contrary are beside the point; but that is not

---

[6]   There is a moderate correlation between harassment severity and reporting (Bergman, Langhout, Palmieri, Cortina, & Fitzgerald, 2002; Brooks & Perot, 1991; and others); however, some of the most egregious situations – those in which the victims are psychologically and physically violated over long periods of time by a high-level and powerful perpetrator – are hidden for years (see *Lizee v. Washington State Hospital et al.*, 2001, for a classic example).

[7]   When confronted with conflicting evidence as to welcomeness, the Commission looks "at the record as a whole and at the totality of circumstances . . ." (29 C.F.R. § 1604.11[b]), evaluating each situation on a case-by-case basis. When there is some indication of welcomeness or when the credibility of the parties is at issue, the charging party's claim will be considerably strengthened if she made a contemporaneous complaint or protest (EEOC, 1990).

[8]   *Stricker et al., v. Cessford Construction Company et al.* (2001). "There is simply no requirement that the plaintiffs have reported the conduct to company officials to establish that the conduct was 'unwelcome,' . . ."

(or, at least, not always) the case. The nature of victim response has assumed an even higher profile since the Supreme Court's creation of an affirmative defense for employers in cases in which the plaintiff is deemed to have "unreasonably" failed to take advantage of organizational complaint procedures (*Faragher v. City of Boca Raton*, 1998; *Ellerth v. Burlington Industries*, 1998). Sometimes interpreted as requiring the victim officially to report her experiences,[9] this defense exists in tension with the consistent empirical finding that reporting is the least likely of all responses. What is reasonable as a matter of law can differ dramatically from what real people believe is in their best interest.

The *Faragher/Ellerth* decisions have also given rise to another line of reasoning, however, situated somewhat in contrast to that cited above and recognizing to a greater extent the context-dependent variability in behavior. In *Cerros v. Steel Technologies, Inc.* (2005), the Seventh Circuit disagreed that "a plaintiff's failure to follow the reporting mechanisms outlined in an employer's harassment policy is a sufficient basis in itself for finding no employer liability." Writing for the Court, Judge Diane Wood noted: "[T]he [Ellerth/Faragher] Court made clear that compliance with an employer's designated complaint procedure is not the sole means by which an employee can fulfill her 'coordinated duty to avoid or mitigate harm' [citation omitted]. Rather, under the functional approach established in *Ellerth/Faragher*, an employer must prove that 'the plaintiff employee unreasonably failed to take advantage of any preventive or corrective opportunities provided by the employer *or to avoid harm otherwise*'" (citation omitted; emphasis Judge Wood's).

Although *Cerros* reads the dictum to *avoid harm otherwise* principally to broaden the concept of reporting beyond the employer's "official" notification channels,[10] it seems reasonable that it could be expanded to include other methods of "avoiding harm"

---

[9]   See, for example, *Caridad v. Metro-North Commuter Railroad* (1999); *Breeding v. Cendant Corporation* (2003); *Leopold v. Baccarat, Inc.* (2001) in the Second Circuit as well as *Woods v. Delta Beverage Group, Inc.* (2001) in the Fifth.

[10]   "At bottom, the employer's knowledge of the misconduct is what is critical, not how the employer came to have that knowledge (citation omitted). The relevant inquiry is therefore whether the employee adequately alerted her employer to the harassment, thereby satisfying her obligation to avoid the harm, not whether she followed the letter of the reporting procedures set out in the employer's harassment policy" (*Cerros v. Steel Technologies, Inc.*, 2005).

(e.g., avoiding the harasser, appeasement), particularly in light of research demonstrating that assertive responses such as confronting the harasser or filing a complaint are not only frequently ineffective, but often actually make things worse. For example, Hesson-McInnis and Fitzgerald (1997) found that although the majority of respondents said that assertiveness "made things better," in actuality they had worse outcomes than other victims. Bergman et al. (2002) found that assertive responding was associated with more negative psychological and job-related outcomes even after severity of harassment was controlled. They also noted that reporting harassment had little practical effect and what impact did exist was negative. Stockdale (1998) reported that individuals who used confrontational strategies to cope with frequent harassment tended to experience worse outcomes than other victims. Furthermore, use of such responses tended to amplify associations between harassment pervasiveness and consequences; in other words, the effects of frequent harassment were more damaging when the target confronted the problem directly. Finally, Richman et al. (2001) found that reporting (or confronting) the harasser did not predict harassment cessation, but did predict subsequent problematic drinking behavior (Richman et al., 2001).

Given such results, it is difficult to conclude that "failing to report" definitionally violates plaintiff's burden to "avoid harm otherwise." We recognize, of course, that organizational liability requires organizational knowledge; as *Cerros* suggests, however, there are many ways in which organizations acquire knowledge; when this is the case, social science testimony on typical victim response can provide juries with appropriately comprehensive understanding on which to base their decisions. Numerous courts appear to agree with this analysis and the behavioral science research on victim response has become a familiar fixture in sexual harassment litigation (see, e.g., *Denhof et al. v. City of Grand Rapids*, 2005; *United States of America v. John R. Koch*, 2003).

Sexual Harassment and PTSD

From victim response, we turn our attention to victim outcomes, reviewing the data demonstrating that sexual harassment can give rise to PTSD, even in the absence of the single traumatic stressor traditionally envisaged by the Diagnostic and Statistical Manual (DSM-IV-TR;

American Psychiatric Association, 2000).[11] Here we acknowledge more controversy, but argue that this inheres not in the research linking harassment to trauma symptoms, but in the conflict between theory (which holds that victims by definition cannot develop PTSD absent a traditional Criterion A event) and data (which show that they do). Here we find a somewhat peculiar situation: Courts, long accustomed to mental health testimony in a variety of contexts, are less skeptical about such testimony than some members of the behavioral research community (e.g., Grove & Barden, 1999), including, at times, ourselves.

There appears little doubt that sexual harassment can be associated with significant psychological damage, as research here has been nothing if not consistent. From the earliest studies to the most recent, findings of negative psychological health and work consequences permeate the literature, and are documented across numerous settings and populations. Once dismissed as a trivial complaint, sexual harassment is now firmly linked to a broad range of psychological and health-related problems. Summarizing the findings to that time, Gutek and Koss (1993) reported that emotional responses to harassment included anger, fear, depression, anxiety, irritability, lowered self-esteem, feelings of humiliation, alienation, helplessness, and vulnerability.

Symptoms associated specifically with PTSD have been empirically linked to experiences of sexual harassment for at least the past decade. For example, Schneider et al. (1997) found in a sample of female employees that symptoms of posttraumatic stress (e.g., sleep disturbance, physiological arousal) were the best differentiators of women who had been sexually harassed. Three recent studies have documented a connection between sexual harassment and PTSD symptoms among female military personnel; harassment significantly predicted PTSD even when the variance attributable to being in combat had been accounted for (Fontana, Litz, & Rosenheck, 2000; Kang, Dalager, Mahan, & Ishii, 2005; Wolfe et al., 1998).

Although important, such studies document the presence of PTSD *symptoms* in response to harassment; they do not establish a formal link between harassment and the diagnosis itself. Such links, however,

---

[11] "A. The person has been exposed to a traumatic event in which both of the following were present: (1) the person experienced, witnessed, or was confronted with an event or events that involved actual or threatened death or serious injury, or a threat to the physical integrity of self or others; (2) the person's response involved intense fear, helplessness, or horror" (DSM-IV-TR, p. 467).

have now begun to appear. Dansky and Kilpatrick (1997) reported the first systematic examination of sexual harassment, depression, and PTSD at the diagnostic level. A national sample of 3,006 women was interviewed via telephone about experiences of unwanted sexual attention and sexual coercion, and formally assessed on DSM-III symptom criteria for PTSD and depression. The results indicated that sexual harassment significantly predicted both diagnoses, even after accounting for the effects of rape and other types of assaults.

In 1999 Fitzgerald and her colleagues (Fitzgerald, Buchanan, Collinsworth, Magley, & Ramos, 1999) examined psychological damage among a sample of sexual harassment plaintiffs; each participant underwent a comprehensive diagnostic evaluation lasting at least eight hours and in some cases two full days. Diagnosis was based on the Clinician-Administered Post-Traumatic Stress Disorder Scale (CAPS, a structured diagnostic interview; Blake et al., 1995), long considered the gold standard for PTSD diagnosis, or on the PTSD module of the SCID-I. They reported that 33 out of a total of 48 (68%) met DSM-IV criteria for PTSD. Continuing this study over the next five years, these researchers have documented similar findings in a sample now numbering over 120 plaintiffs.

Palmieri and Fitzgerald (2005) studied 1,241 members of a nationwide class action alleging sexual harassment and gender discrimination while employed by a major financial services firm. Using standard scoring rules for the Posttraumatic Checklist, a self-report instrument assessing the presence and intensity of PTSD symptomatology (PTSD Checklist – Civilian Version; Weathers, Litz, Herman, Huska, & Keane, 1993), to assess symptoms, they found that 33% met full diagnostic criteria for PTSD related to their experiences at the defendant organization; when more conservative scoring rules were employed, the figure was 17%. Noting that sexual harassment experiences vary in nature and severity, the researchers deleted participants who alleged sexual assault as part of their claims and reanalyzed the data, finding that diagnostic percentages dropped by only 3%. Diagnostic status was significantly correlated with severity of harassment (as measured by frequency); symptom severity was also related to length of employment at the company, an estimate of stressor exposure not subject to the possible demand effects of self-report among legal claimants. This research provides additional support for the argument that low magnitude, frequent stressors can give rise to PTSD, even in the absence of a traditional Criterion A event.

These empirical findings exist in the tension with controversy among the scientific community as to whether clinicians overdiagnose PTSD

(Pitman, Sparr, Saunders, & McFarlane, 1996); whether low magnitude events can cause it (March, 1993); whether Criterion A is necessary (Solomon & Canino, 1990); and even whether PTSD exists at all as a diagnosable entity (Faust & Ziskin, 1988; Grove & Barden, 1999). What are courts to make of such controversy? Should experts be precluded from testifying on the topic, as urged by a few vocal commentators? Our answer, reminiscent of Gordon Paul's classic dictum concerning whether psychotherapy works, can be framed as follows: Which expert? Using what methodology? Based on what data?

To begin, we note that the issue of whether PTSD (or any other psychological disorder) exists as an entity independent of its symptoms and measurement is an epistemological issue that need not concern us here; the nature of reality and its relationship to our symbol system (i.e., language) is a discussion that has engaged scientists and philosophers for centuries. As a practical matter, we note that the majority of professionals accept the *existence* of PTSD to at least the same degree that they do other psychological disorders.

Although the conceptual wisdom of Criterion A continues to be debated in the scientific literature, we believe this may be a red herring for the courts. Even if (1) the necessity of such a "gate" criterion is conceded and (2) it is agreed that a particular set of allegations does not meet it, it seems largely irrelevant to legal resolution of the matter. Psychological disorder is not an element of proof in the establishment of liability (*Harris v. Forklift Systems, Inc.*, 1993).

We are somewhat more inclined to sympathize with the view that clinicians may misdiagnose PTSD (and other psychological disorders more generally) and chagrined that we must agree that this is far too often the case. We argue, however, that this state of affairs is not an inherent feature of the process itself but rather of the methodology of the particular evaluation. Structured interviews and other diagnostic tools for reliable assessment are widely available, detailed procedures for damages assessment in litigation (including sexual harassment litigation) appear in the literature (see, e.g., Fitzgerald & Collinsworth, 2002; Simon, 2003), textbooks on forensic assessment abound, and the Academy of Forensic Psychology regularly offers indepth professional education on this topic. Not to put too fine a point on it, the fact that there are sloppy diagnosticians does not imply that the process of diagnosis is inherently unreliable.

It is both curious and unfortunate that courts (and commentators) often treat mental health "professionals" as generic and fungible when this is most assuredly not the case. First, there seems to be a tendency to conflate the work of treating professionals with the testimony of consulting diagnosticians, despite the fact that their purpose, their procedures, and (generally) their experience are very different. The fact that possession of an MD or PhD allows a witness to offer opinions as an expert does not ipso facto make him or her a specialist in a particular area. This is not to denigrate the perspective and skill of the seasoned treating practitioner, but rather to emphasize the importance of specific methodology and indepth knowledge of the instant issue. Unfortunately, our experience suggests that busy courts are sometimes understandably too willing to accept a professional degree as surrogate for the detailed (and often unfamiliar) methodological inquiry necessary to establish testimonial reliability.[12]

Summary

We conclude that the presence of "reasoned disagreement" concerning the nature of PTSD and its diagnostic requirements is typical of the process of consensus development in any field of science and, thus, no basis for precluding testimony on this topic. The fate of Criterion A may continue in doubt for some time, as the process of DSM-V development is only now beginning (see www.dsm5.org/ for the American Psychiatric Association's timeline for activities leading to the publication of the DSM-V). In our view, arguments concerning whether sexual harassment qualifies under the current formulation more often than not deflect attention from the more relevant questions of what, if any, psychological distress a plaintiff is suffering; whether such can be linked to her workplace experiences with a reasonable degree of certainty; and what is the reliability of the methodology employed by the expert?

"Lookin' for a home": The Connection Between Harassment and Organizational Climate

Our final section examines the research on organizational climate, reliably shown to be a powerful facilitator of sexual harassment in the

---

[12] In a recent example, particularly striking to us, one court allowed diagnostic testimony by a psychologist who had never met with either plaintiff (see *Kessell and Meador v. Cook County et al.*, 2000); in another, a defense expert, testifying in his deposition, based his claim to neutrality on the fact that he knew nothing about sexual harassment, had never read any of the professional literature, and thus could not be considered "biased." It would be difficult to find a rationale other than expediency for allowing such testimony.

workplace. Naylor, Pritchard, and Ilgen (1980) conceptualize organizational climate as "shared perceptions, among members of a relevant group, department, or organization, of contingencies between specific behaviors and their consequences, both private and public, positive and negative" (Naylor et al., 1980, as cited by Hulin, Fitzgerald, & Drasgow, 1996, p. 133). More specifically, organizational climate for sexual harassment can be defined as employee perceptions of the tolerance of sexual harassment in the workplace (Hulin et al., 1996), as well as the availability, accessibility, and effectiveness of organizational policies and procedures for addressing harassment. To assess climate for harassment, survey respondents are typically asked their perceptions about all or part of the climate for harassment in their workgroups and/or organizations. More sophisticated studies delete data from each focal individual in a step-wise fashion, or employ work-group level data minus each focal individual, to eliminate demand effects or self-consistency bias (see, for example, Glomb et al., 1997).

Several studies have shown that perceptions of organizational climate for sexual harassment relate to reports of and perceptions about sexual harassment. A number have used the Organizational Tolerance of Sexual Harassment Inventory (OTSHI; Hulin et al., 1996), a measure that taps the perceived degree of risk for victims who make complaints, the degree to which such complaints are likely to be taken seriously, and the perceived likelihood of meaningful sanctions against harasser(s). Fitzgerald et al. (1997) found that perceptions of organizational tolerance of sexual harassment in the workplace predicted higher levels of sexual harassment experiences. Cortina, Fitzgerald, and Drasgow (2002) and Glomb et al. (1997) also identified a relationship between OTSHI scores and sexual harassment experiences described by working women. Other studies support the general finding that an organizational climate in which sexual harassment is tolerated or condoned increases the likelihood of sexual harassment experiences (e.g., Bergman et al., 2002; Fitzgerald, Drasgow, & Magley, 1999; Hesson-McInnis & Fitzgerald, 1997; Mueller, DeCoster, & Estes, 2001).

A specific aspect of organizational climate that appears to be the major driving force in the relationship between climate and harassment is the willingness of leadership to sanction offenders in a meaningful way. Based on a large sample of military personnel, Williams, Fitzgerald, and Drasgow (1999) found that the perception that harassment policies are implemented, both formally and informally, explained variance in reports of harassment incidence. In particular, the study demonstrated that perceptions that the organization actually *did something about harassment* better predicted harassment than did perceptions of organizational resources for harassment targets or organizational training. This study illuminates the importance of organizational *action* against harassment perpetrators, relative to the mere presence of policies, procedures, and training.

A parallel line of research is that of Pryor and his colleagues who have repeatedly demonstrated the importance of management norms, coworker perceptions of climate, and the like. For example, Pryor, LaVite, and Stoller (1993) found that women in workgroups where the supervisor ignored or encouraged sexual harassment were more likely to report having been harassed. In a reanalysis of the 1988 Department of Defense study on gender and workplace issues, Pryor et al. (1993) found that the proportion of sexually harassed women was higher when they perceived that their commanding officers (COs) encouraged sexual harassment than when they were indifferent and also when COs were indifferent than when they discouraged sexual harassment. Pryor et al. (1993) also reported similar results for a large civilian organization.

In an interesting and unusually compelling study of climate, Pryor et al. (1995) found that men's beliefs that their supervisors were indifferent to sexual harassment predicted their female coworkers' sexual harassment experiences, confirming that "the [empirical] relationship between experiencing sexual harassment and judgments about the reactions of management do not simply reflect a hypersensitivity to sexual harassment on the part of women who were harassed" (p. 73).

Finally, given the relationship between harassment and workplace norms, it is not surprising that the impact of climate extends beyond those who directly experience sexual harassment at work. Glomb et al. (1997) introduced the construct of *ambient sexual harassment*, defined as the "frequency of sexually harassing behaviors perpetrated against others in a woman's workgroup" (Glomb et al., 1997, p. 314). Based on structural equations modeling, the authors found a significant path from organizational climate (as measured by the OTSHI) to ambient sexual harassment, in addition to a significant path from organizational climate to sexual harassment. Thus, organizational tolerance of sexual harassment relates to both direct and indirect experiences of sexual harassment.

Implications of Organizational Climate Research for Sexual Harassment Litigation

What are the implications and limitations of climate research for assisting the trier of fact in sexual harassment litigation? As with research on PTSD, limitations inhere not in the data themselves; studies are clear and consistent that organizations in which employees believe that the topic of harassment is not taken seriously, it is risky to complain, and there are unlikely to be meaningful sanctions for perpetrators have greater problems with harassment. Importantly, a tolerant climate is also associated with psychological damage to targets and other employees over and above that done by the harassment itself (Fitzgerald, Hulin et al., 1995; Bergman et al., 2002). Such findings have been reported by multiple investigators, employing differing methods, in different settings, for nearly 20 years, and appear to qualify as legally admissible on their scientific merits. Despite its reliability and importance, however, *climate* evidence has proven difficult to get before a jury, as judges must determine whether it may not be more prejudicial than probative. We examine these arguments, reviewing the potential and possible uses of climate research for assisting jurors to decide sexual harassment cases.

Liability

The principal objection to climate research is generally similar to that raised against *profiling* and *syndrome* evidence more broadly (i.e., that it is more prejudicial than probative). Defendants express concern that evidence that a particular organization demonstrates the characteristics of a tolerant climate (as operationally defined) may imply that, by definition, a hostile environment exists.

We suggest that such concern is misplaced for a number of reasons. First, it is certainly possible and sometimes thought preferable for experts to take the stand to explain the concept of climate for a jury without attempting to apply the concept to the facts of the particular case. To those who would object that such evidence is not grounded in the relevant facts and thus not relevant, we reply that such arguments misunderstand the broader purpose of expert testimony in general and social framework in particular, that is, to assist the trier of fact. Given the nature of litigation, which is often to sever facts from their context, such testimony provides an educational context in which to understand the interactions at issue.

Second, there seems to us a fundamental difference between profile evidence in general[13] and the specific construct of organizational

---

[13]   Profile or syndrome evidence typically consists of (1) correlations of atheoretical variables with the variable of interest and (2) the probabilities associated with that variable, given the presence of the others.

climate for harassment, which consists only of elements relevant to the case (e.g., the organization has ignored or minimized past complaints, offenders have received no or minimal sanctions, managers and supervisors have participated in harassment). This concept, grounded in the empirical, scientific literature, provides the jury with a framework to integrate sometimes disparate testimony and decide for themselves whether the fact pattern does or does not support an inference of organizational tolerance.

Damages determination

In the event that defendant organizations are found liable, plaintiffs typically seek some form of emotional distress damages to compensate them for psychological pain and suffering. It is here that mental health testimony is introduced, generally by both parties.[14] Rule 26 of the Federal Rules of Civil Procedure requires that any expert report "shall contain a complete statement of all opinions to be expressed *and the basis and reasons therefore*" (Federal Rules of Civil Procedure 26[a][2][B], emphasis added).

We read this rule to require that the expert explain the link between her or his diagnosis (if any) and the facts and conditions alleged in the case. Assuming that these occurred largely as alleged, is such a pattern capable of causing any condition from which the plaintiff may suffer? Was there a preexisting condition, or concurrent stressors that might account for any such condition? And what is the analytic path by which the expert got from the facts to the diagnosis, that is, what is the reasoning by which the expert arrived at the diagnosis? This last requires a sound and indepth knowledge of sexual harassment research and the factors that are known to lead to damage in such cases. Among these is organizational climate (Fitzgerald, Hulin et al., 1995).

Fitzgerald, Swan & Magley (1997) identified the factors that give rise to harm from sexual harassment, a formulation that has come to be referred to as the Model of Harm. Drawing on modern cognitive frameworks for understanding stressful life events, these authors outline three sets of factors that influence severity: *stimulus factors*[15]

---

[14] But see Fitzgerald (2003) for the proposal that social framework evidence be substituted for the traditional mental health examination where possible.

[15] Stimulus factors encompass the well-known dimensions of stressor severity: frequency, intensity, and duration. Frequency and duration are self-explanatory; intensity refers to the magnitude of the stressor and includes multiple perpetrators, powerful perpetrators, behavior that is physical, frightening, direct, sexual, and/or hostile, and limited opportunity for escape.

(i.e., the behavior itself), *individual factors*,[16] that is the vulnerability of the individual target; and *contextual factors* (i.e., the context in which the harassment takes place). It is this last that concerns us here.

The relevant finding in this area is not that harassment is more common and more severe in settings tolerant of such behavior, although that is empirically the case (Fitzgerald, Hulin et al., 1995; Fitzgerald et al., 1997). Rather, for purposes of damages determination, it is important to understand that *victims have worse outcomes in such settings* – tolerance being defined as the perception that the issue is not taken seriously, that there is high risk for complaining, and little chance that perpetrators will be sanctioned (Fitzgerald et al., 1997; Hulin et al., 1996). Other aspects of tolerance include the lack of policies or procedures for dealing with sexual harassment, normative behavior that appears to tolerate harassment, and simply being in an environment where other women are being harassed (such a situation is known to social scientists as ambient harassment, or "bystander stress"). Glomb and her colleagues (Glomb et al., 1997) demonstrated that ambient harassment and a tolerant climate produced psychological distress equivalent to that of being directly harassed.

Summary

The social science research on organizational climate is plentiful, reliable, and consistent, and should be able to withstand a traditional *Daubert*-based challenge. Its legal vulnerability arises from challenges based on relevance, that is, the question of whether it may be more prejudicial than probative in any particular case. As with any scientific evidence, this may be so in any particular case; however, we see no reason to believe that it will always be the case. Climate theory and research will almost always be useful to the jury.

Implications

We close our chapter by reconsidering the questions we posed when we began. How does harassment research fare in the legal environment? What is its "added value," that is, its insights above and beyond common knowledge and sense that advance our understanding? What are its vulnerabilities? Are these scientific or legal?

---

[16]   Vulnerability factors include previous victimization and mental health status, personal resources, and cognitive variables such as attitudes, attributions, and sense of control.

In our view, this research is faring very well, making important contributions to harassment jurisprudence at every level; testimony on the psychology of victim response is routinely admitted in trial courts across the country. Appellate briefs in high profile cases routinely incorporate it into their arguments,[17] and some parties have even commissioned social fact studies of particular organizations to assist in determinations of class certification[18] or assist in settlement negotiations.[19] Although any particular study must stand or fall on its merits, the legal arguments that are made about it,[20] and the predilections of the particular judge, the social science of sexual harassment appears increasingly well established in legal circles (Beiner, 2005). Though we are less sanguine about the quality of generic mental health testimony in such cases, we reiterate that what flaws exist inhere in the knowledge base of the particular practitioner, not the field itself, and repeat our call for the development of professional guidelines for practice in this area.

Although the research base that exists is sound, there are – as always – unanswered questions. In particular, the details of the process by which reporting leads to increased psychological harm are unknown. The impact of sexual harassment training programs is beginning to be examined but for now they remain, like beauty, their own excuse for being (Antecol & Cobb-Clark, 2003; Bell, Quick, & Cycyota, 2002; Fitzgerald & Shullman, 1993; Wilkerson, 1999). Research on retaliation is beginning to appear, but the fact that retaliatory practices, while toxic, are more often social rather than organizational renders the legal usefulness and viability of this research unclear.[21] Clearly, a number of

---

[17]   See, for example, the amicus brief of the American Psychological Association in *Harris v. Forklift Systems, Inc.*, (1993), as well as that of the National Employment Lawyers Association in *Ellerth v. Burlington Industries, et al.* (1998).

[18]   *Elkins, et al., v. American Showa, Inc.* (2002).

[19]   *Martens et al. v. Smith Barney, Inc.* (2001) and *Cremin et al. v. Merrill-Lynch* (1997).

[20]   See, e.g., *EEOC v. The Dial Corporation* (2003); in which the trial judge barred a particular social-fact study offered by the plaintiffs but allowed social framework testimony on the relevant topics.

[21]   While we were editing this chapter, the Supreme Court handed down its decision in *Burlington Northern and Santa Fe Railway Co. v. White* (2006), broadening the definition of retaliatory acts. The Court stated, "This Court agrees with the Seventh and District of Columbia Circuits that the proper formulation [for a retaliation claim] requires a retaliation plaintiff to show that the challenged action "well might have 'dissuaded a reasonable worker from making or supporting a charge of discrimination.'" It remains to be seen what impact this will have on the admissibility of retaliation research.

important questions remain, and we expect them to keep us busy for some time to come.

ACKNOWLEDGMENTS

The authors would like to acknowledge the contributions of Nicole F. Lindemeyer, Esq., whose legal research, practical experience, and conceptual acumen made this paper considerably better than it would have been otherwise. We are also grateful for the patience and support of our editors, Gene Borgida and Susan Fiske, who advanced us extra chips when we had used ours up.

REFERENCES

American Psychiatric Association (2000). (DSM-IV-TR) Diagnostic and statistical manual of mental disorders, 4th ed., text revision. Washington, DC: American Psychiatric Press, Inc.

Antecol, H., & Cobb-Clark, D. (2003). Does sexual harassment training change attitudes? A view from the federal level. *Social Science Quarterly, 84*(4), 826–842.

Bastian, L. D., Lancaster, A. R., & Reyst, H. E. (1996). *Department of Defense 1995 sexual harassment survey* (Rep. No. 96–014.). Arlington, VA: Defense Manpower Data Center. (DTIC/NTIS No. AD-A323 942).

Beiner, T.M. (2005). *Gender myths v. working realities: Using social science to reformulate sexual harassment law.* New York: New York University Press.

Bell, M. P., Quick, J. C., & Cycyota, C. S. (2002). Assessment and prevention of sexual harassment of employees: An applied guide to creating healthy organizations. *International Journal of Selection and Assessment, 10*(1–2), 160–167

Bergman, M. E., Langhout, R. D., Palmieri, P. A., Cortina, L. M., & Fitzgerald, L. F. (2002). The (un)reasonableness of reporting: Antecedents and consequences of reporting sexual harassment. *Journal of Applied Psychology, 87*, 230–242.

Blake, D. D., Weathers, F. W., Nagy, L. M., Kaloupek, D. G., Gusman, F. D., Charney, D. S., & Keane, T. M. (1995). The development of a clinician-administered PTSD scale. *Journal of Traumatic Stress, 8*, 75–90.

Breeding vs. Cendant Corporation, WL 1907971 (SDNY) (2003).

Brooks, L., & Perot, A.R. (1991). Reporting sexual harassment: Exploring a predictive model. *Psychology of Women Quarterly, 15*(1), 31–47.

Burlington Industries, Inc. v. Ellerth, 524 U.S. 742 (1998).

Burlington Northern and Santa Fe Railway Co. v. White, No. 05-259 (2006).

Caridad v. Metro-North Commuter Railroad. 191 F.3d 283 (2nd Cir. 1999).

Cerros v. Steel Technologies, Inc., 398 F.3d 944, 950–51 (7th Cir. 2005).

Cochran, C. C., Frazier, P.A., & Olson, A. M. (1997). Predictors of responses to unwanted sexual attention. *Psychology of Women Quarterly*, *21*(2), 207–226.

Coombs, M. (1999). Title VII and homosexual harassment after Oncale: Was it a victory? *Duke Journal of Gender, Law, and Policy*, 6, 13.

Cortina, L. M., Fitzgerald, L. F., & Drasgow, F. (2002). Contextualizing Latina experiences of sexual harassment: Preliminary tests of a structural model. *Basic and Applied Social Psychology*, 24, 295–311.

Cremin et al. v. Merrill-Lynch, 957 F. Supp. 1460 (N. D. Ill. 1997).

Culbertson, A. L., Rosenfeld, P., Booth-Kewley, S., & Magnusson, P. (1992). *Assessment of sexual harassment in the Navy: Results of the 1989 Navy-wide survey, TR-92-11.* San Diego, CA: Naval Personnel Research and Development Center.

Dansky, B. S., & Kilpatrick, D. S. (1997). The effects of sexual harassment. In W. O'Donohue (Ed.), pp. 152–174. *Sexual harassment: Theory, research, and treatment.* Boston: Allyn & Bacon, Inc.

Denhof et al. v. City of Grand Rapids & City of Grand Rapids Police Department et al. State of Michigan in the Circuit Court for the County of Kent. 01-00789-NZ (2005).

Equal Employment Opportunity Commission (1990). Policy Guidance on Current Issues of Sexual Harassment. N-915-050. www.eeoc.gov/policy/docs/currentissues.html.

EEOC v. The Dial Corporation, N.D. Illinois No. 99 C 3356 (2003).

Elkins et al., v. American Showa, Inc. Case No. C-1-99-988, Southern District of Ohio, Western Division (2002).

Faragher v. City of Boca Raton, 524 U.S. 775 (1998).

Faust, D., & Ziskin, J. (1988). *Coping with psychiatric and psychological testimony* (4th ed.) Marina del Rey, CA: Law and Psychology Press.

Federal Rules of Civil Procedure (2006). Washington, DC: U.S. Government Printing Office.

Ferrante v. Sciaretta et al., 365 N.J. Super. 601 (2003).

Fiske, S. T., & Glick, P. (1995). Ambivalence and stereotypes cause sexual harassment: A theory with implications for organizational change. *Journal of Social Issues*, *51*(1), 97–115.

Fitzgerald, L. F. (2003). Sexual harassment and social justice: Reflections on the distance yet to go. *American Psychologist*, 58, 915–924.

Fitzgerald, L. F., Buchanan, N., Collinsworth, L. L., Magley, V. M., & Ramos, A. (1999). Junk logic: The abuse defense in sexual harassment litigation. *Psychology, Public Policy, and Law*, 5, 730–759.

Fitzgerald, L. F., & Collinsworth, L. L. (2002). The forensic psychological evaluation in sexual harassment litigation. In Isabela Schultz (Ed.). *Handbook of psychological injuries: Evaluation, treatment, and compensable damages.* Chicago, IL: American Bar Association.

122   *Louise F. Fitzgerald and Linda L. Collinsworth*

Fitzgerald, L. F., Drasgow, F., & Magley, V. J. (1999). Sexual harassment in the Armed Forces: A test of an integrated model. *Military Psychology, 11,* 329–343.

Fitzgerald, L. F., Hulin, C., & Drasgow, F. (1995). The antecedents and consequences of sexual harassment in organizations: An integrated process model. In S. Sauter & G. Keita (Eds.). *Job stress 2000: Emergent issues.* Washington, DC: American Psychological Association.

Fitzgerald, L. F., Hulin, C. L., Drasgow, F., Gelfand, M., & Magley, V. (1997). The antecedents and consequences of sexual harassment in organizations: A test of an integrated model. *Journal of Applied Psychology, 82,* 578–589.

Fitzgerald, L. F., & Shullman, S. L. (1993). Sexual harassment: A research analysis and agenda for the '90s. *Journal of Vocational Behavior, 42,* 5–27.

Fitzgerald, L. F., Shullman, S. L., Bailey, N., Richards, M., Swecker, J., Gold, Y., Ormerod, A., & Weizman, L. (1988). The dimensions and extent of sexual harassment in higher education and the workplace. *Journal of Vocational Behavior, 32,* 152–175.

Fitzgerald, L. F., Swan, S., & Fisher, K. (1995). Why didn't she just report him? The psychological and legal context of women's responses to sexual harassment. *Journal of Social Issues, 51,* 117–183.

Fitzgerald, L. F., Swan, S., & Magley, V. (1997). But was it really sexual harassment: Psychological, behavioral, and legal definitions of sexual harassment. In W. O'Donohue (Ed.). *Sexual harassment: Research, theory, and treatment* (pp. 5–28). New York: Allyn & Bacon.

Fontana, A., Litz, B., & Rosenheck, R. (2000). Impact of combat and sexual harassment on the severity of posttraumatic stress disorder among men and women peacekeepers in Somalia. *Journal of Nervous and Mental Disease, 188*(3), 163–169.

Glomb, T. M., Richman, W. L., Hulin, C. L., Drasgow, F., Schneider, K. T., & Fitzgerald, L. F. (1997). Ambient sexual harassment: An integrated model of antecedents and consequents. *Organizational Behavior and Human Decision Processes, 71,* 309–328.

Griffin v. City of Opa-locka, U.S. Dist. Ct., S.D. Fla., No. 98-1550 (2000).

Grove, W. M., & Barden, R. C. (1999). Protecting the integrity of the legal system: The admissibility of testimony from mental health experts under Daubert/Kumho analyses. *Psychology, Public Policy, and the Law, 5,* 224–242.

Gruber, J. E. (1992). Methodological problems and policy implications in sexual harassment research. *Population Research and Policy Review, 9,* 235–254.

Gruber, J. E., & Bjorn, L. (1982). Blue-collar blues: The sexual harassment of women autoworkers. *Work & Occupations, 9*(3), 271–298.

Gruber, J. E., & Smith, M. D. (1995). Women's responses to sexual harassment: A multivariate analysis. *Basic and Applied Social Psychology, 17*(4), 543–562.

Gutek, B. (1985). *Sex and the workplace.* San Francisco: Jossey-Bass.

Gutek, B., & Koss, M. P. (1993). Changed women and changed organizations: Consequences of and coping with sexual harassment. *Journal of Vocational Behavior, 42,* 28–48.

Harris v. Forklift Systems, Inc., 510 U.S. 17 (1993).

Hesson-McInnis, M., & Fitzgerald, L. F. (1997). Sexual harassment: A preliminary test of an integrative model. *Journal of Applied Social Psychology, 27*(10), 877–901.

Hulin, C., Fitzgerald, L. F., & Drasgow, F. (1996). Organizational influences on sexual harassment. In B. Gutek and M. Stockdale (Eds.), *Women and work,* Vol. 6. Newberry Park, CA: Sage.

Kang, H., Dalager, N., Mahan, C., & Ishii, E. (2005). The role of sexual assault on the risk of PTSD among Gulf War veterans. *Annals of Epidemiology, 15,* 191–195.

Kessel & Meador v. Cook County et al., Northern District of Illinois. 00 CV 03980 (2000).

Knapp, D. E., Faley, R. H., Ekeberg, S. E., & Dubois, C. L. Z. (1997). Determinants of target responses to sexual harassment: A conceptual framework. *Academy of Management Review, 22*(3), 687–729.

Lazarus, R. S., & Folkman, S. (1984). *Stress, appraisal, and coping.* New York: Springer.

Leopold v. Baccarat, Inc. 239 F.3d 243 (2d Cir. 2001).

Lizee v. Washington State Hospital, et al. Superior Court of State of Washington. No. CO1-2-09414-4.

Magley, V. J. (2002). Coping with sexual harassment: Reconceptualizing women's resistance. *Journal of Personality and Social Psychology, 83*(4), 930–946.

March, J. S. (1993). What constitutes a stressor? The "Criterion A" issue. In J. R. T. Davidson & E. B. Foa (Eds.), *Posttraumatic stress disorder: DSM-IV and beyond* (pp. 37–56). Washington, DC: American Psychiatric Press, Inc.

Martens, et al. v. Smith Barney, Inc., U.S. District Court for the Southern District of New York (2001).

McKinney, K., Olson, C. V., & Satterfield, A. (1988). Graduate students' experiences with and responses to sexual harassment: A research note. *Journal of Interpersonal Violence, 3,* 319–325.

Mueller, C. W., De Coster, S., & Estes, S. B. (2001). Sexual harassment in the workplace: Unanticipated consequences of modern social control in organizations. *Work & Occupations, 28,* 411–446.

Naylor, J. C., Pritchard, R. D., & Ilgen, D. R. (1980). *A theory of behavior in organizations.* New York: Academic Press.

Palmieri, P. A., & Fitzgerald, L. F. (2005).Confirmatory factor analysis of posttraumatic stress symptoms in sexually harassed women. Journal of Traumatic Stress. 2005, December; *18*(6), 657–66.

Perkins v. General Motors Corp., 709 F. Supp. 1487, 1499 (W.D. Mo. 1989).

Pitman, R. K., Sparr, L. F., Saunders, L. S., & McFarlane, A. C. (1996). Legal issues in posttraumatic stress disorder. In B. A. van der Kolk, A. C. McFarlane, & L. Weisaeth (Eds.), (1996). *Traumatic stress: The effects of overwhelming experience on mind, body, and society.* (pp. 378–397). New York: Guilford Press.

Pryor, John B. (1995). The psychosocial impact of sexual harassment on women in the U.S. Military. *Basic and Applied Social Psychology, 17*(4), 581–603.

Pryor, J. B., Giedd, J. L., & Williams, K. B. (1995). A social psychological model for predicting sexual harassment. *Journal of Social Issues, 51*(1), 69–84.

Pryor, J. B., LaVite, C. M., & Stoller, L. M. (1993). A social psychological analysis of sexual harassment: The person/situation interaction. *Journal of Vocational Behavior, 42*, 68–83.

Richman, J. A., Rospenda, K. M., Flaherty, J. A., & Freels, S. (2001). Workplace harassment, active coping, and alcohol-related outcomes. *Journal of Substance Abuse, 13*, 347–366.

Schneider, B. E. (1991). Put up or shut up: Workplace sexual assault. *Gender and Society, 5*, 533–548.

Schneider, K. T., Swan, S., & Fitzgerald, L. F. (1997). Job-related and psychological effects of sexual harassment in the workplace: Empirical evidence from two organizations. *Journal of Applied Psychology, 82*, 401–415.

Simon, R. (Ed.) (2003). *Posttraumatic stress disorder in litigation: Guidelines for forensic assessment.* 2nd ed. Washington, DC: American Psychiatric Publishers.

Solomon, S. D., & Canino, G. J. (1990). Appropriateness of DSM-III–R criteria for posttraumatic stress disorder. *Comprehensive Psychiatry, 31*(3), 227–237.

Stockdale, M. S.(1998). The direct and moderating influences of sexual-harassment pervasiveness, coping strategies, and gender on work-related outcomes. *Psychology of Women Quarterly, 22*, 521–535.

Stricker et al. vs. Cessford Construction Company et al. U.S. District Court, Northern District of Iowa Central Division. C00-3022-MWB (2001).

United States of America v. John R. Koch (2003).

U.S. Merit Systems Protection Board (1981). *Sexual harassment of federal workers: Is it a problem?* Washington, DC: U.S. Government Printing Office.

U.S. Merit Systems Protection Board (1988). *Sexual harassment of federal workers: An Update.* Washington, DC: U.S. Government Printing Office.

U.S. Merit Systems Protection Board (1995). *Sexual harassment of federal workers: An Update.* Washington, DC: U.S. Government Printing Office.

Weathers, F. W., Litz, B. T., Herman, D. S., Huska, J. A., & Keane, T. M. (1993, October). *The PTSD Checklist: Reliability, validity, and diagnostic utility.* Paper presented at the Annual Meeting of the International Society for Traumatic Stress Studies, San Antonio, TX.

Weinsheimer v. Rockwell International Corp., 754 F. Supp. 1559, 1564 (M.D.Fla.1990).

Wilkerson, J. M. (1999). The impact of job level and prior training on sexual harassment labeling and remedy choice. *Journal of Applied Social Psychology,* *29*(8), 1605–1623

Williams, J. H., Fitzgerald, L. F., & Drasgow, F. (1999). The effects of organizational practices on sexual harassment and individual outcomes in the military. *Military Psychology, 11,* 303–328.

Wolfe, J., Sharkansky, E. J., Read, J. P., Dawson, R., Martin, J. A., & Ouimette, P. C. (1998). Sexual harassment and assault as predictors of PTSD symptomatology among U.S. female Persian Gulf War military personnel. *Journal of Interpersonal Violence, 13,* 40–57.

Woods v. Delta Beverage Group, Inc., 274 F.3d 295, 300 n.3 (5th Cir. 2001).

Subjectivity in the Appraisal Process: A Facilitator of Gender Bias in Work Settings

Madeline E. Heilman and Michelle C. Haynes

Subjectivity in organizational decision-making practices is an issue that has taken center stage in numerous legal proceedings involving discrimination in the workplace. This is particularly true with respect to performance appraisal, the formal evaluative process that is used in organizations to make personnel decisions and is key to equal employment opportunity litigation involving salary equity, promotions and terminations (Arvey & Murphy, 1998; Bernardin & Tyler, 2001). The focus on subjectivity derives from the critical role it can play in giving rise to biased evaluations and their subsequent behavioral expression, discrimination. In fact, the argument that there is subjectivity in the appraisal process often is an evidentiary precursor of bias and discriminatory practices in organizations.

But how do we get from subjectivity to discrimination? The answer lies in the links between stereotypes, the expectations they engender, and the subsequent impact of those expectations on cognitive processing and evaluative judgments. It is in this last link that the role of subjectivity is critical; the greater the subjectivity, the more opportunity for stereotype-based expectations to influence evaluative judgments.

In this chapter we examine why, how and when subjectivity can give rise to biased evaluative judgments, with particular emphasis on performance appraisal. We will review research that examines the conditions that promote subjectivity, as well as the conditions that affect the strength and prevalence of stereotype-based performance expectations and the likelihood of their biasing effects. Although we concentrate on the impact of subjectivity on women in the workplace, much of what we discuss is likely to apply to situations involving members of other groups about whom there exist stereotypes that generate work-relevant expectations. Our aim in this chapter is to identify general principles that have emerged in the study of gender stereotyping from both social and organizational psychology and discuss the utility of these principles in assessing whether, in any given situation, gender discrimination has in fact occurred.

Subjectivity: A Much Needed Definition

There has been much disagreement about the definition of subjectivity. For example, some have argued than *any* evaluative judgment is by definition subjective, given that all evaluations are the product of human cognitive processing, and as such are judgments that have passed through a particular person's lens (Arvey & Murphy, 1998; van der Heijden & Nijhof, 2004). While this no doubt is true, our use of the term "subjectivity" in the context of performance appraisal is more fine-grained and specific. It denotes an evaluative orientation that requires inference because judgments are based primarily on outcomes and criteria that are open to interpretation. This can be contrasted to "objectivity", an evaluative orientation in which the need for inference is minimal because judgments are based primarily on concrete outcomes that are independently arrived at and measured against a prescribed reference point for comparison.

Subjectivity in performance appraisal is not simply an "either/or" matter. Rather, the extent to which inference about performance effectiveness is required to make an evaluative judgment about an individual is a function of contextual conditions, in particular the amount of ambiguity inherent in the evaluation process. Ambiguity necessitates inference, and therefore the more ambiguity there is, the greater the likelihood and degree of subjectivity. We will be discussing the different types of ambiguity that can promote subjectivity later in this chapter.

Importantly, subjectivity does not in itself produce bias; rather, it induces a judgment process that, because it is based on inference, is highly susceptible to bias. In these situations, expectations can become highly influential. We now turn to a discussion of the ways in which expectations can shape evaluative outcomes.

Expectations: How Subjectivity Impacts Performance Appraisal

To fully understand why subjectivity can be so problematic in performance appraisal processes, it is necessary to consider how evaluative judgments can be affected by expectations. Since the mid-1970s performance appraisal researchers have taken a cognitive, information processing approach (Bretz, Milkovich, & Read, 1992; Ilgen, Barnes-Farrell, & McKellin, 1993). As such, many researchers have characterized the performance appraisal process as the product of a series of cognitive tasks (e.g. Borman, 1978; Cooper, 1981; DeNisi, Cafferty, & Meglino, 1984; Feldman, 1981; Landy & Farr, 1980). For example, Feldman (1981) argued there are several essential mental operations that comprise the performance appraisal process. First, supervisors must *identify and attend to evaluation-relevant information*. Second, unless an evaluation immediately follows a work behavior, supervisors must *organize and store the information* so that it can be retrieved at a later date. Third, at the time of evaluation, supervisors must be able to *recall the information* such that they can subsequently use the information for the final task of creating some sort of summary evaluative judgment.

Evidence that expectations can influence these mental operations is critical to the claim that subjectivity can give rise to biased evaluative judgments. In considering the substantial literature on expectancies, it is clear that performance expectations do affect a variety of cognitive processes, including each of the mental operations that have been identified as part of performance appraisal. To these we add another: *making comparisons among employees* in the allocating of resources and rewards.

Identifying and attending to evaluation-relevant information

Expectations can influence the extent to which information is noticed and attended to. For example, Favero & Ilgen (1989) found that raters spent less time attending to work behaviors of individuals about whom there were stereotype-based expectations. This finding is critical, given that time spent observing an individual's behavior is positively related to accuracy in the rating of individuals' behavior (Favero & Ilgen, 1989; Heneman & Wexley, 1983). Moreover, there is a tendency for expectations to act as a perceptual filter, directing attention toward consistent information and away from inconsistent information (Johnson & Judd, 1983; Srull & Wyer, 1980, 1983). Thus, a supervisor may fail to notice an astute comment made by a subordinate about whom he has negative expectations, but be very attentive to a blunder that the subordinate makes even if, for that individual, blunders are very rare (Rothbart, Evans, & Fulero, 1979). This is not to say that expectancy inconsistent information is never attended to but, as we will discuss in the next section, if it is, it is often distorted or attributed in a manner that allows the original expectations to stay intact.

Once an individual has attended to information that is consistent with his/her expectation, additional information search tends to be halted (see Fiske, 1998, for a review). So, one blunder is likely to be sufficient to cast as incompetent the subordinate about whom there are negative expectations whereas far more information would be necessary to make that assessment of a subordinate about whom there are positive expectations. Similarly, there is research that suggests that one less-than-stellar evaluation is likely to be sufficient for a low competence assessment of an individual about whom there are negative expectations, but if expectations are positive more evidence is likely to be sought to validate the information (Ditto & Lopez, 1992).

Lastly, when negative expectations are held, more evidence tends to be needed to demonstrate convincingly that an individual possesses an unexpected attribute. Thus, individuals about whom there are negative performance expectations may have to work harder, be more productive and/or produce higher quality work to be regarded just as favorably as individuals about whom there are positive expectations. Their performance must be extraordinary to be noted as similarly competent. Evidence corroborates this point: A stricter inference standard is used for those about whom negative expectations exist (Biernat, 2003; Biernat & Kobrynowicz, 1997; Foschi, 1996, 2000).

Organizing and storing the information

One of the most robust findings in the expectancy literature is that expectations can exert a substantial impact on how information is interpreted, particularly when information is ambiguous (see Olson, Roese, & Zanna, 1996, for a review). In general, information is interpreted in line with expectations. As such, expectations can serve to direct the manner in which particular information is encoded. For example, the identical behavior performed by individuals about whom there are different expectations may be interpreted differently, e.g., the same deliberativeness may be seen as "judicious" when performed by men but as "tentative" by women, or the same work demeanor may be seen as indicative of a "go-getter" when exhibited by men, but as "abrasive" when exhibited by women (Heilman & Okimoto, in press; Heilman, Wallen, Fuchs, & Tamkins, 2004; Kunda, Sinclair, & Griffin, 1997). The meaning of the behavior can vary depending upon what is expected, and therefore it may get encoded and stored in memory differently.

Interpretation of a behavior and causal attribution for it are closely related. Causal inferences are made when unexpected behavior that challenges the validity of expectations occurs and cannot be ignored. Causal attributions can function to protect the original expectation by discounting the unexpected behaviors as uninformative about the actor. Accordingly, researchers have found that behavior that is consistent with gender-based expectancies is often attributed to stable dispositional attributes, whereas behavior that is inconsistent with gender-based expectancies is often attributed to external factors or temporary elements of the situation (Swim & Sanna, 1996). Thus information about the success of a woman in an unexpected work domain can be explained away as either a result of a lucky quirk of fate (Deaux & Emswiller, 1974) or as a result of the efforts of someone else who might have been a behind-the-scenes source of assistance (Heilman & Haynes, 2005). Either way, the expectation-inconsistent information is often written off as a fluke.

Recalling the information

Expectations have been shown to influence what people remember about a particular individual. Typically, memory is biased in the direction of expectation consistent attributes – what fits the expectation is remembered more completely and more accurately than what does not fit the expectation. This is particularly true when people are bombarded with the many competing cognitive tasks typical of work settings. Accordingly, expectations have been shown to supersede raters' memory for the events they have observed when they make behavioral ratings (Baltes & Parker, 2000; Cooper, 1981; DeNisi et al., 1984; Feldman & Lynch, 1988; Martell, Guzzo, & Willis, 1995). Thus, that blunder by the employee about whom there are negative expectations is apt to be readily recalled whereas the same blunder by an employee about whom there are positive expectations is more likely to be forgotten.

Moreover, evidence suggests that evaluators engage in a limited memory search until they find the information required to make an evaluation. Thus, it is the most accessible information – the information that is most readily remembered – that provides the basis for evaluations. This is true even if more diagnostic yet less accessible information is stored in memory (Feldman & Lynch, 1988). Because expectation consistent information is often more accessible, it is the information more likely to be recalled and used in evaluative judgments.

Making comparisons among employees

Expectations also can affect comparative judgments. This can happen even when two individuals are rated equally if there are different underlying expectations of them. According to Biernat (2003) this is because we tend to use a within-category mentality when rating individuals (e.g., she is competent *for a woman*) that masks beliefs about cross-category expectations (women are less competent than men). So, although two employees may have received the same high rating on a performance evaluation measure, the rating for the employee about whom there are more positive expectations is likely to be higher in absolute terms than the rating for the employee about whom there are less positive expectations. Consequently, when forced to rank the two employees in order of competence, the evaluator is likely to place the one about whom there are more positive expectations in the top position (Eidelman & Biernat, 2003). This tendency is apt to have serious, but often hidden, consequences not only for evaluative judgments, but also for decisions about the allocation of rewards. Thus, for example, women often make it to the "short list", but when final promotion decisions are made they are less likely than men to be the ones selected (Biernat & Fuegen, 2001).

In sum, expectations can profoundly impact cognitive processes that are critical in performance appraisal. They seem to have their own defense system, tenaciously protecting themselves against disconfirming evidence, and inclining the expectation holder to think and act in a manner that "proves them true". Thus, when subjectivity exists, and inference is required for making evaluative judgments, expectations are likely to exert a powerful influence on evaluative outcomes.

If, as we are asserting, gender stereotypes are an important source of performance expectations, then when conditions promote subjectivity, these stereotype-based expectations are likely to be highly influential. Therefore it is instructive to consider the nature of these expectations and how they originate.

From Gender Stereotypes to Expectations

A full examination of gender stereotyping can be found elsewhere in this volume, but, to review briefly, a stereotype is a set of attributes ascribed to a group and believed to characterize its individual members simply because they belong to that group. In the case of gender stereotypes, these are attributes ascribed to individual men and women simply by virtue of their sex. Men, but not women, are thought to possess agentic characteristics, such as being forceful, assertive, and achievement oriented, whereas women, but not men, are thought to possess communal characteristics, such as being understanding, caring and relationship-oriented (Bakan, 1966; Deaux & Lewis, 1984; Eagly & Karau, 2002; Eagly & Steffen, 1984; Heilman, 2001). These conceptions of women and men are pervasive; concurrence has been found regardless of the perceiver's sex, age, education level or emotional health. Moreover, there is evidence that gender stereotypes influence not only how women and men are characterized in social and domestic settings but also in employment settings (Dodge, Gilroy, & Fenzel 1995; Heilman, Block, & Martell, 1995; Heilman, Block, Martell, & Simon, 1989; Schein, 2001).

However, stereotypes about women do not in themselves produce negative performance expectations for women at work. Indeed, there is much evidence that women and the attributes assumed to characterize them are favorably regarded and highly valued (Eagly & Mladinic, 1989; Eagly, Mladinic, & Otto, 1991). Expectations about how successful or unsuccessful an individual will be when working at a particular job are determined by the fit between the perceived attributes of the individual and the attributes thought to be required to perform the job well (Heilman, 1983, 2001; see also Eagly & Karau, 2002). If the fit is a good one, then success is expected; if the fit is poor, then failure is expected. Thus, it is only when a job is thought to be masculine in nature, or "male sex-typed", that negative performance expectations of women arise.

Jobs that are the highest in authority, responsibility, and prestige in organizations typically also are the ones that are considered to be male in sex-type (Lyness, 2002). The perceived requirements for success in many male sex-typed jobs, such as decisiveness, toughness under pressure, and leadership skills, are congruent with the male stereotype, but incongruent with the female stereotype. As such, women are often perceived to be deficient in the attributes thought to be required for success at upper level and high power jobs (Heilman et al., 1989; Schein, 2001). It is this "lack of fit" between female stereotypic attributes and perceptions of male sex-typed job requirements that leads to the conclusion that women are ill equipped to handle male sex-typed work, and the expectation that they are unlikely to succeed in traditionally male roles (Heilman, 1983, 2001).

Factors regulating the link from gender stereotypes to negative expectations of women

If the incongruity between how women are typically viewed and the attributes believed to be required to succeed at important and powerful jobs is the source of negative expectations about how women will perform, then the larger the incongruity the more negative the expectations should be. The size of the incongruity can be affected by either the degree to which stereotypes about women are assumed to characterize a particular woman or the degree to which a particular job is male sex-typed. Variations in either of these components of the fit formulation should affect the extent to which there are negative expectations and also should affect the likelihood that negative performance evaluations will result.

Support for these ideas can be found in investigations of performance evaluations in which "fit" has varied. In these investigations, different levels of fit have led to different evaluative outcomes. Thus, it has been shown that women with personal attributes that amplify the saliency of their gender, such as physical attractiveness (Heilman & Stopeck, 1985a, 1985b) or motherhood status (Fuegen, Biernat, Haines, & Deaux, 2004; Heilman & Okimoto, 2006), elicit more negative performance expectations and evaluations than depictions of women who do not have these personal attributes. Similarly, organizational elements that highlight a woman's gender, such as token or minority status (Heilman & Blader, 2001; Sackett, DuBois, & Noe, 1991), or focus on affirmative action or diversity initiatives (Heilman, Block, & Stathatos, 1997; Heilman & Welle, 2006), have been shown to result in more negative performance expectations and evaluations for women than men for the same male sex-typed job. For example, Sackett et al. (1991), using archival data from a wide variety of jobs and organizations, found that performance ratings of women were negatively related to their proportional representation in the work group even after controlling for the effects of ability, education, and experience.

There also is evidence that the sex-type of jobs affects women's performance evaluations, with negativity resulting only when a job is thought to be "male" (Davison & Burke, 2000). The results of a large-scale field study of over 3,000 senior officers in the Israeli Defense Forces conducted by Pazy and Oron (2001) indicated that women's competence and performance was rated significantly lower than men's in organizational units in which women were underrepresented but not in those in which they were well represented. Corroborating these findings, a study of performance evaluations in a large multinational financial services company demonstrated that women were rated less favorably than men in line jobs (which tend to be highly male sex-typed), but not in staff jobs (Lyness & Heilman, in press).

In sum, there is support for the idea that expectations of incompetence can arise from the content of the female stereotype and the perceived lack of fit that results when the jobs in question are male in sex-type. Moreover, there is evidence that there are personal and organizational factors that can exacerbate or attenuate the magnitude of the perceived lack of fit and the negative performance expectations that ensue. Finally, there is evidence supporting the notion that these negative performance expectations can ultimately impact evaluation. We now consider the organizational factors that promote subjectivity, and therefore pave the way for these stereotype-based performance expectations to color evaluations.

When Subjectivity Flourishes and Expectations Can Take Hold

As we said earlier, ambiguity feeds subjectivity. The more ambiguity there is in a particular situation, the more inference is required for evaluation. And, the more inference is required, the less guidance there is about the "correct" evaluation, leaving the situation ripe for expectations to exert their influence. More than 25 years ago Nieva and Gutek (1980), after reviewing the extant literature, concluded that evaluative decisions that require inference are more susceptible to gender bias than those that do not. In the many years since, their thesis has been repeatedly supported. Although the terms used to characterize the ambiguous situations in which decisions require inference have been many, and the processes by which bias is thought to dominate in such situations have been debated, the basic premise has held up well to scientific scrutiny. Ambiguity is likely to be high when there is: an absence of relevant, specific information; poorly defined evaluative criteria; lack of clarity about what performance actually is; and confusion about the source of performance outcomes. It is these same conditions that promote subjectivity in performance appraisal processes, thus leaving the door open for stereotype-based expectations to bias evaluative judgments.

Ambiguity in the type and amount of information available to the evaluator

Research has shown that ambiguity in the information available to a rater is related to whether gender stereotyped expectations are used in making evaluative judgments (Davison & Burke, 2000; Tosi & Einbender, 1985). Information that is impoverished or uninformative has been found to facilitate the use of stereotype-based expectations. This is particularly true when evaluators have either very little relevant information or the information that they do have is unclear in its implications, either because it is vague or presents a mixed picture.

Research findings suggest that unless information is highly job-relevant and diagnostic of performance success it does little to limit the effect of expectations on evaluations (Heilman, 1984; Renwick & Tosi, 1978). Indeed, there is evidence that irrelevant information produces no better evaluations than the absence of any information at all (Heilman, 1984). In fact, evidence that irrelevant information can reinforce, rather than challenge, stereotype-driven expectations has been provided by other studies as well (Locksley, Borgida, Brekke, & Hepburn, 1980; Rasinski, Crocker, & Hastie, 1985). Moreover, even if the performance information is job relevant, it must be very specific and virtually impossible to distort if it is to quell the impact of negative stereotype-based expectations in evaluative judgments (Heilman, Martell, & Simon, 1988). For example, it was found that even though they were all rated in the highest performance category available, it was only when the category was labeled the "top 2% of employees", that women were rated as equally favorably as their male counterparts in male sex-typed jobs; when the category was labeled the "top 25% of employees", although it was the highest rating category available, women were rated significantly less competent than men (Heilman et al., 1997; Heilman & Haynes, 2005).

Thus, mitigating the influence of stereotype-based expectations appears to require not only that information be job relevant, but also unequivocal in its implications and therefore unassailable. Information, by itself, does not protect against bias in performance evaluations – it must be information that undercuts ambiguity and therefore the need for inference. The absence of this type of information promotes subjectivity, with bias in the evaluative process the potential result.

Ambiguity in evaluative criteria

It is a generally accepted idea in the psychology of social cognition that the more vague and poorly defined the judgment criteria, the more easily information can be distorted to fit an expected outcome (Fiske & Taylor, 1991). In the domain of performance appraisal, dimensions of the evaluative criteria can be vague in multiple ways that fuel subjectivity, making evaluations susceptible to bias. One issue is the nature of the performance outcome. Thus, it is more difficult to distort test scores, dollar earnings, or number of widgets produced in a given period of time, than to distort work output that is not measurable in standard and discrete units. A related issue is the nature of the evaluative focus. Distortion is more likely to creep into assessments of whether an individual is a "good team player", or a "charismatic leader," than into assessments of his or her actual work behaviors or work outcomes. There is, for example, evidence that supervisors rate performance of communication competence and interpersonal competence less reliably, on average, than rating of productivity or quality (Viswesvaran, Ones, & Schmidt, 1996). In fact, some appraisal researchers have concluded that an appraisal system that entails behavioral or results-based standards for jobs and a specific definition of performance criteria is less apt to induce rating bias than appraisal systems that entail less specific criteria (Heneman, 1986; Huber, 1989; Schrader & Steiner, 1996).

A lack of specification about how various evaluative criteria are to be combined also fuels subjectivity by requiring individual raters to derive their own systems for integrating information into an evaluative summary. Thus, the more unstructured the evaluative procedure, the more opportunity there is for negative performance expectations about women to weigh heavily in the overall evaluation (Baltes & Parker, 2000; Bauer & Baltes, 2002). Ganzach (1995), who conducted research challenging the idea of a linear relationship between individual ratings and an overall performance evaluation, found that more weight is given to negative attributes than to positive ones, and that the combination of ratings may be nonlinear in character. Additionally, McIntyre and James (1995) demonstrated in a policy capturing study that the combination and weighting of information about an individual can be target specific and that raters may be particularly sensitive to negative information. Structure in the evaluative process works against these tendencies. It forces the consideration of multiple sources of information about an individual and the attending to a particular set of criteria, any one of which might be ignored without the constraint of having to attend to it. It ensures that particular attributes are assessed for everyone and that they are given equal weight in the evaluation process no matter who the target of the evaluation might be. The ambiguity resulting from the absence of structure can encourage the differential emphasis on different performance elements for different people – a condition that is highly conducive to bias.

Ambiguity about the job performance domain

A related issue is the definition of job performance. Distinctions have been made between task performance and what has been termed "contextual" performance (Arvey & Murphy, 1998). Task performance concerns the proficiency with which workers perform core activities whereas contextual performance concerns extra activity, not part of formal job responsibilities, that contributes favorably to the social and psychological work environment. The idea of contextual performance is related to that of organizational citizenship behavior (Organ, 1988), prosocial behavior (Brief & Motowidlo, 1986), and organizational spontaneity (George & Brief, 1992).

Taxonomies of contextual work behaviors have been advanced, one based on supervisory ratings of over 18,000 employees in 42 different entry-level retail jobs (Hunt, 1996). Debates have occurred about whether behaviors deemed to be contextual are actually discretionary and outside of one's job description (Morrison, 1994; Organ, 1997; Tepper, Lockhart, & Hoobler, 2001; Van Dyne, Cummings, & Parks, 1995). But at least one set of studies has indicated that a behavior deemed to be contextual – altruistic citizenship behavior – is not equally optional for men and for women (Heilman & Chen, 2005).

The Heilman and Chen series of studies demonstrated that helping others in work settings is considered a "should" for women, and therefore is a tacit job requirement, whereas it is considered to be discretionary for men. Thus women who did not engage in altruism were penalized in their performance ratings whereas this did not happen for men. The results additionally made clear that beliefs about required work behaviors for women include not only helping others, such as resolving conflicts among coworkers and assisting new employees settle into their jobs, but also nonhelping behaviors such as being tidy and maintaining a positive attitude. The idea that there are gender-linked requirements for these types of behaviors is consistent with other research (Kidder, 2002; Kidder & Parks, 2001). The implication is that different types of performance may be considered part of overall job responsibilities when the individual being evaluated is a man or a woman, with the requirements for women being more demanding. The absence of clarity about the precise domains of performance that are the focus of an evaluation, which is said to be increasingly common given the general move toward more flexible definitions of work roles and the view of jobs as dynamic (Arvey & Murphy, 1998), thus promotes subjectivity, with gender-based expectations determining which standards are operative.

Ambiguity about the source of performance

Another form of ambiguity in the evaluation setting that can promote subjectivity and therefore induce bias in evaluation is the ambiguity that arises when it is not clear who has been responsible for a particular performance outcome. When there is this kind of source ambiguity, stereotype-based expectations are likely to help people fill in the blanks in their assignment of credit for positive outcomes. Research supporting this idea has indicated that when a woman works together with a man on a joint task, she is given less credit for a successful group outcome, is seen as making a smaller contribution to it, and is seen as less competent than her male teammate (Heilman & Haynes, 2005). Furthermore, additional studies indicated that this tendency to allow stereotype-based expectations color evaluations occurred unless the task was structured so that the contribution of both members of the team was undeniable or the woman was explicitly said to be very competent at the task at hand.

The importance of these findings goes beyond women working in dyads with men. In today's performance settings work is rarely accomplished in isolation, and it is often impossible to tease out who is responsible for what. Furthermore, there are all kinds of relationships, such as mentoring and coaching, which also create ambiguity about responsibility for work outcomes. These, also, can affect the way in which responsibility is attributed. Whenever source ambiguity exists, whatever its origin, it is likely to promote a subjective orientation in which expectations can exert a strong biasing influence.

A word about rating format

Reviews of research on performance appraisal systems have concluded that all types of rating scale formats are subject to cognitive distortion (Arvey & Murphy, 1998; Bernardin, Hennessey, & Peyrefitte, 1995; Ilgen et al., 1993). Thus, behaviorally anchored rating scales as well as summated or behavioral observation scales, have been found to affect rater observation and recall (e.g., DeNisi et al., 1984; Murphy & Constans, 1987; Nathan & Alexander, 1985). More recently, Kane, Bernardin, Villanova, and Peyrefitte (1995) demonstrated that both lenient and harsh evaluators tend to maintain their stance regardless of rating format. This suggests that no one type of rating format is more or less vulnerable to rating bias, a conclusion that is echoed in some major reviews of the performance evaluation literature (for example, Arvey & Murphy, 1998). It also implies that the degree of subjectivity induced by rating format does not affect the occurrence of bias.

Nonetheless, a meta-analysis by Bommer, Johnson, Rich, Podsa-koff, and Mackenzie (1995) that examined the relationship between more and less objective measures of employee performance suggested that the measures were not totally interchangeable. Moreover, recent research by Bauer and Baltes (2002) demonstrated the effectiveness of a structured free recall intervention, using specific observed behaviors rather than an overall judgment of an employee, in counteracting the impact of gender stereotypes on the accuracy of performance evaluations. These findings suggest that the nature of the rating instrument, and the degree to which it necessitates inference, does indeed affect the strength of stereotype-based expectations on the accuracy of ratings. Thus, although there are claims that the distinctions are unlikely to be as great as once thought, it seems imprudent to conclude that the type of rating format, particularly in the level of subjectivity it promotes, is totally irrelevant to rating bias.

Factors that Can Mitigate the Influence of Expectations Despite Subjectivity

Even if the organizational landscape is filled with ambiguity, and therefore likely to promote a subjective evaluative orientation, there are elements of the context that can cause people to be more cautious and deliberative in making inferences about others, relying less on expectations when making evaluative judgments. Thus, despite subjectivity, gender bias is not inevitable. Of relevance is a substantial body of research documenting motivation as an important factor in the application of stereotypes (Brewer, 1988; Fiske, 1989, 2004; Fiske & Neuberg, 1990). Specifically, the tendency to rely on stereotype-based expectations can give way to more controlled and reasoned thought processes when the evaluator is strongly motivated to make accurate judgments. This is likely to occur when: (1) the evaluator is in an interdependent relationship with the evaluated such that his or her outcomes rely on the accuracy of the evaluation; or (2) the evaluator knows that he or she is going to have to account to others for the decisions made. In either of these instances, the influence of stereotype-based expectations on evaluations may well be tempered.

Anticipated interdependence

Self-interest enters into the judgment of others when the evaluator and the target of the evaluation have interdependent outcomes. Interdependence, simply put, is when one person's outcome depends on another's performance. To do well for themselves, individuals with interdependent outcomes are motivated to judge the other accurately, recognizing his or her strengths and weaknesses (Fiske, 2000). This, in turn, encourages paying careful attention to whatever individuating information is available, however meager, rather than relying exclusively on stereotype-based expectations. In organizational contexts this is of relevance when a manager's future prospects are directly tied to the target of the performance evaluation, such as when the manager is making a choice about who to work with on a highly visible project or whom to best handle a task for which the manager is ultimately responsible. In these situations, the use of expectations as the primary basis of evaluation is far less likely than when the target's future behavior is of little consequence to the manager personally. And this would be the case even if the organizational conditions are otherwise ones that promote subjectivity.

Accountability

Accountability refers to being individually responsible and answerable for the decisions one makes. In organizations, managers may be asked to justify their evaluations and decisions based on these evaluations to a variety of organizational constituencies that may be important for them to impress favorably, including supervisors, subordinates, and even researchers (Murphy & Cleveland, 1991). Accountability, because it motivates people to appear competent (Simonson & Nye, 1992), can curb the use of expectations in evaluative judgments by encouraging more complex judgment strategies (Tetlock, 1983a): Individuals are apt to exert more effort in information search and process information more deeply. Mero and colleagues (1995, 2003) have found that accountability ultimately results in increased accuracy in making evaluative judgments. Moreover, they reported evidence that being held accountable makes individuals take action and exhibit behaviors (such as being more attentive when observing performance and taking more extensive notes when gathering information) that better prepares them to justify their ratings, which in turn produces more accurate evaluative judgments. These activities can reduce, and perhaps even eliminate, the influence of stereotype-based performance expectations on evaluations despite the existence of conditions that promote subjectivity.

However, making evaluators accountable does not automatically ensure less bias in evaluative judgments. Research suggests that when accountable decision-makers know their audiences' views, they tend to make decisions that are consistent with these views (Klimoski & Inks, 1990; Tetlock, 1985). They are motivated by the need for approval (Jones & Wortman, 1977) and the motivation to present themselves as favorably as possible to those to whom they are accountable (Tetlock, 1983b; Tetlock, Skitka, & Boettger, 1989). These findings suggest that although making evaluators accountable for their evaluations can lessen their dependency on gender-based expectations, biased outcomes may still occur if the organizational norms support them.

It should be noted that while motivational dynamics can act to discourage the bias that is fostered by subjectivity, the total absence of features in the environment that motivate people to make accurate judgments can actually encourage bias. When the evaluator has virtually no stake in the outcome of his/her decisions, there is little reason not to rely on expectation-based inferences in making evaluative judgments. It is easy and efficient to do so, especially when there are limited cognitive resources available (van Knippenberg & Dijksterhuis, 2000). This is likely to be the case when the evaluator is doing many different things simultaneously (Gilbert & Hixon, 1991) or there are severe time pressures (Pratto & Bargh, 1991), situations very commonly found in work settings.

Assessing the Likelihood that Subjectivity Has Resulted in a Biased Judgment

The ideas we have presented throughout this chapter can be helpful in determining whether subjectivity has in fact given rise to gender bias in evaluations. Although the particular way in which these ideas are realized in any one work setting may differ, the basic principles we have outlined can serve as a guide. Taken together they provide a crude checklist specifying potential contributors to stereotype-based bias in the performance appraisal process. A summary of these potential contributors follows.

Performance expectations are critical; subjectivity will give rise to gender bias only when there are stereotype-based negative performance expectations which can impact the inferences about performance effectiveness that are required to make evaluative judgments. These expectations are produced by the perceived lack of fit between stereotypically female attributes and the attributes required to perform male sex-typed jobs. Therefore, they are more likely in situations in which gender is salient, such as when the woman is the solo woman in the work setting or she has been designated as the beneficiary of an affirmative action or diversity initiative, or when her personal attributes highlight her sex because of her appearance or her marital or parental status. Similarly, negative performance expectations are more likely when the position for which a woman is being evaluated is considered to be highly male in sex-type, either because of the rarity of women among typical job holders or the stereotypically male nature of what are commonly assumed to be the job requirements.

Even if there are negative performance expectations of women, their influence will differ in strength depending upon the degree to which conditions promote subjectivity and therefore inference is required to make evaluative judgments. This is determined by the extent to which ambiguity predominates in the evaluative process. Ambiguity comes in many forms, and we have identified a number of sources that seem particularly pernicious in terms of potentially leading to biased judgments: (1) the information available to the evaluator, particularly its lack of specificity and relevance to performance; (2) the nature of the evaluative criteria and the degree to which they are vague or poorly defined, or lack a structure for their weighting; (3) the absence of specification of the domains of performance that are the focus of the evaluation; and (4) the lack of clarity regarding the origin of the performance outcome.

There are organizational features, namely anticipated interdependence and accountability, that, despite subjectivity, can constrain stereotype-based performance expectations from having a biasing effect on evaluations of women. They have this effect because they increase the evaluator's motivation to be accurate in assessing performance, and thereby decrease the dependence on expectations as the basis for inferences about performance effectiveness. Paradoxically, contexts that are devoid of features that motivate evaluators to be accurate in their judgments can actually increase reliance on stereotype-based expectations. Specifically, if the evaluator has no self-interest in evaluating a woman accurately because the evaluator's outcomes are not linked with her in any meaningful way, or if the evaluator does not have to answer to anyone for his or her judgments, there is very little impetus to refrain from using performance expectations in forming evaluative inferences.

This list is not exhaustive. We have sought to identify variables that produce negative performance expectations about women, that promote subjectivity and therefore pave the way for the use of these expectations in the evaluation process, and that are likely to affect the reliance on expectation-based inferences when evaluative judgments are made. As we have said, it is not possible to specify all the ways in which these variables might manifest themselves in different organizational contexts; the variety of possible realizations is endless. That is why we urge that general principles rather than particular expressions of these principles be used to assess the incidence of subjectivity-facilitated bias.

State of the Literature: Debates and Dilemmas

In the course of this chapter we have presented research from social and organizational psychology that utilized various methodologies and that was conducted both in the laboratory and the field. The results of these research endeavors converge to paint a relatively unified picture: Subjectivity in performance appraisal processes can give rise to gender biased evaluations. While no one study provides unequivocal evidence, nor by itself tells the whole story, it is the cohesive package that lends strong support for this argument.

Some critics challenge the validity of laboratory experiments as a basis for providing evidence for organizational processes (e.g., Copus, 2005). We believe, however, that together with field evidence, findings from the laboratory not only strengthen our claims but are essential to them. Nonetheless, these criticisms are important to address. The crux of the argument against the value of laboratory research generally rests on three issues: (1) its lack of generalizability to organizational settings because of physical and demographic differences; (2) its irrelevance because of the artificiality of the research setting and its inability to incorporate the complexities of the organizational environment; and (3) its triviality because of its typically small effect sizes. We shall briefly address each of these concerns.

Built into the criticisms about generalizability of research findings is the assumption that research done in any one setting can be best extrapolated to another setting if the two settings are "similar". But this assumption can be misleading. The critical features that must be similar if research results are to be extrapolated from one setting to another are not necessarily those that are apparently similar, such as the age of the respondents or the appearance of the physical setting.

What is critical to generalizability is the similarity of the elements that are central to the theoretical principles that specify when and why gender bias occurs. If, for instance, evaluators feel accountable for their judgments in one organization, the role of subjectivity in giving rise to gender bias is likely to be very different from that in another organization in which evaluators do not feel accountable, no matter how similar the organizations are in other ways, but may not differ very much at all from a laboratory study in which accountability is present. Thus, the "phenotype" is far less important than the "genotype" in generalizing across research settings.

A second criticism of the usefulness of laboratory research in drawing conclusions about what happens in organizations is that it is irrelevant because of the artificiality and tight control of the setting. This criticism, first of all, ignores the incredibly important function of experimental research in systematically building a theory with organizing principles that help identify variables that are critical in regulating the occurrence of particular outcomes, in this case gender bias. A comprehensive theory enables prediction, and is essential to drawing conclusions about whether gender bias has in fact occurred. Thus, one can make the case that experimental laboratory research is, in fact, very practical. Another aspect of the criticism about the artificiality and tight control of the laboratory setting revolves around the absence of the typical complexities of real work settings. The concern underlying this complaint is that it is easier to find gender bias in the laboratory than in the field, and that laboratory results, because things have been simplified to their barest level, are exaggerated. Indeed, typically there is little information available about the person being evaluated, and also the prospects of future interaction with him or her are limited, both of which are factors thought to heighten the tendency to biased judgment. But there also are elements of the laboratory that make it much *less* likely to find gender bias. For one, the participants tend to be students and as such are likely to be both younger and more embracing of cultural mores of gender equality than people who are organization members. Also, participants are not as pressed for time or pulled in as many directions as are organizational decision-makers, making them less likely to be reliant on stereotype-based expectations in making inferences about performance effectiveness. This is not to suggest that it is more difficult to find gender bias in the laboratory than in organizational settings, but that the two settings are different, and that comparisons of this sort are not fruitful. For this reason we believe that it is the accumulation of evidence from multiple venues, with multiple methods, that provides compelling evidence that subjectivity in the performance appraisal process can promote biased evaluations.

The argument that the effect sizes found in the results of laboratory experiments are typically small and therefore trivial also seems misguided. It fails to recognize the importance of the fundamental principle of compounding, often applied to economic matters. Simply put, small differences can have a large impact over time. To illustrate how small effects can translate into large real-world consequences, Martell and colleagues (1996) conducted a computer simulation designed to simulate the promotion of employees within the pyramid structure of an organization, such that employees with higher performance scores became eligible for promotion to the next level. The simulation mimicked an 8-level organization, with 500 positions at the lowest level and 10 at the top level. Beginning with equal numbers of men and women at the lowest level of the organization, they found that despite an effect size so small that it only accounted for 1% of the initial difference between men and women's performance scores, only 35% of women were represented at the top level of the organization. The take home message is that small effects over time can be compounded, with very substantial repercussions.

Interpreting research results

It is very important to note that because there are many possible moderators of gender biased judgments, the results of research investigations that fail to attend to them may be of only limited usefulness in increasing our understanding of gender bias in performance appraisal or our awareness of when it is of most concern. Even more problematic, these investigations may appear to have produced results conflicting with those of other investigations when in fact they have not. For example, if job sex-type is not taken into account in field research, then finding no gender bias may only indicate that the particular jobs focused upon are not male sex-typed, such as when the targets are nonmanagerial employees (e.g., Pulakos, White, Oppler, & Borman, 1989). Moreover, the absence of distinctions between the job types studied (e.g., Hennessey & Bernardin, 2003) may obscure effects that are actually there – but only for the male jobs. We simply do not know. Thus, the failure to consider the effects of this and other repeatedly demonstrated moderator variables can be very misleading not only when doing research but also when drawing general implications about the occurrence of sex bias in performance evaluations (e.g., Barrett & Morris, 1993). Also misleading can be the interpretation of the absence of statistical main effects in laboratory studies as evidence that no gender bias occurred (e.g., Barrett & Morris, 1993), when the hypotheses clearly were aimed at exploring moderating variables, and therefore interaction effects, not overall main effects, were predicted.

Meta-analyses, which are important in so many ways, do not really help with these problems. Meta-analyses are informative only about moderator variables that are investigated in a substantial number of studies that are reviewed. They are limited by the research that is available; if a moderator variable has not been the focus of multiple studies, it cannot be examined. It is critical to keep this in mind when reviewing research results.

Thus, there are no simple steps to arriving at definitive answers about the issues raised in this chapter. What is critical is that there is a convergence of evidence, collected in many places from many different types of people, and using different research methods, that supports a general theoretical scheme. While social science theory is always being modified and elaborated, and therefore is never "settled", the overwhelming consistency of evidence and its support of a set of organizing principles certainly provides guidance "beyond common knowledge" in the determination of whether gender bias has occurred and whether it has been facilitated by conditions promoting subjectivity.

Conclusions

In this chapter we have examined subjectivity and its influence on performance evaluations. We have argued that in situations in which conditions promote subjectivity, stereotype-based performance expectations can have a biasing influence on evaluations of women if they provide a strong basis for inference about performance effectiveness. We also have argued that without subjectivity even the most negative performance expectations will not be reflected in evaluative judgments because it is only when inference is required that these expectations can have an impact on the evaluation process. Finally, we have asserted that even if there is both subjectivity and negative performance expectations of women, gender bias is unlikely if motivational concerns intervene to cause more deliberative processing in the forming of evaluative judgments. These ideas, and the results of the research upon which they are based, should be of use to researchers and practitioners alike in their quest to better understand bias in the performance appraisal process and to target situations that are particularly prone to biased judgments.

REFERENCES

Arvey, R. D., & Murphy, K. R. (1998). Performance evaluation in work settings. *Annual Review of Psychology*, *49*, 141–168.
Bakan, D. (1966). *The duality of human existence: An essay on psychology and religion*: Chicago: Rand McNally.
Baltes, B. B., & Parker, C. P. (2000). Reducing the effects of performance expectations on behavioral ratings. *Organizational Behavior and Human Decision Processes*, *82*(2), 237–267.
Barrett, G. V., & Morris, S. B. (1993). Sex stereotyping in Price Waterhouse v. Hopkins. *American Psychologist*, *48*(1), 54–55.
Bauer, C. C., & Baltes, B. B. (2002). Reducing the effects of gender stereotypes on performance evaluations. *Sex Roles*, *47*(9–10), 465–476.
Bernardin, H. J., Hennessey, H. W., Jr., & Peyrefitte, J. S. (1995). Age, racial, and gender bias as a function of criterion specificity: A test of expert testimony. *Human Resource Management Review*, 5, 63–77.
Bernardin, H. J., & Tyler, C. L. (2001). Legal and ethical issues in multisource feedback. In D. W. Bracken, C. W. Timmwreck & A. H. Church (Eds.), *The handbook of multisource feedback* (pp. 447–462). San Francisco: Jossey-Boss.
Biernat, M. (2003). Toward a broader view of social stereotyping. *American Psychologist*, *58*(12), 1019–1027.
Biernat, M., & Fuegen, K. (2001). Shifting standards and the evaluation of competence: Complexity in gender-based judgment and decision making. *Journal of Social Issues*, *57*(4), 707–724.
Biernat, M., & Kobrynowicz, D. (1997). Gender- and race-based standards of competence: Lower minimum standards but higher ability standards for devalued groups. *Journal of Personality and Social Psychology*, *72*(3), 544–557.
Bommer, W. H., Johnson, J., Rich, G. A., Podsakoff, P. M., & Mackenzie, S. B. (1995). On the interchangeability of objective and subjective measures of employee performance: A meta-analysis. *Personnel Psychology*, *48*(3), 587–605.
Borman, W. C. (1978). Exploring upper limits of reliability and validity in job performance ratings. *Journal of Applied Psychology*, *63*(2), 135–144.
Bretz, R. D., Milkovich, G. T., & Read, W. (1992). The current state of performance appraisal research and practice: Concerns, directions, and implications. *Journal of Management*, *18*(2), 321–352.
Brewer, M. B. (1988). A dual process model of impression formation. In T. K. Srull & R. S. Wyer (Eds.), *Advances in social cognition* (Vol. 1, pp. 1–36). Hillsdale, NJ: Erlbaum.

Brief, A. P., & Motowidlo, S. J. (1986). Prosocial organizational behaviors. *Academy of Management Review, 11*(4), 710–725.

Cooper, W. H. (1981). Conceptual similarity as a source of illusory halo in job performance ratings. *Journal of Applied Psychology, 66*(3), 302–307.

Copus, D. (2005). A lawyer's view: Avoiding junk science. In F. Landy (Ed.), *Employment discrimination litigation: Behavioral, quantitative, and legal perspectives* (pp. 450–462). San Francisco, CA: Jossey-Bass.

Davison, H. K., & Burke, M. J. (2000). Sex discrimination in simulated employment contexts: A meta-analytic investigation. *Journal of Vocational Behavior, 56,* 225–248.

Deaux, K., & Emswiller, T. (1974). Explanations of successful performance on sex-linked tasks: What is skill for the male is luck for the female. *Journal of Personality & Social Psychology, 29,* 80–85.

Deaux, K., & Lewis, L. L. (1984). Structure of gender stereotypes: Interrelationships among components and gender label. *Journal of Personality and Social Psychology, 46*(5), 991–1004.

DeNisi, A. S., Cafferty, T. P., & Meglino, B. M. (1984). A cognitive view of the performance appraisal process: A model and research propositions. *Organizational Behavior & Human Performance, 33*(3), 360–396.

Ditto, P. H., & Lopez, D. F. (1992). Motivated skepticism: Use of differential decision criteria for preferred and non-preferred conclusions. *Journal of Personality and Social Psychology, 63*(4), 568–584.

Dodge, K. A., Gilroy, F. D., & Fenzel, M. L. (1995). Requisite management characteristics revisited: Two decades later. *Journal of Social Behavior & Personality, 10*(6), 253–264.

Eagly, A. H., & Karau, S. J. (2002). Role congruity theory of prejudice toward female leaders. *Psychological Review, 109*(3), 573–598.

Eagly, A. H., & Mladinic, A. (1989). Gender stereotypes and attitudes toward women and men. *Personality & Social Psychology Bulletin, 15*(4), 543–558.

Eagly, A. H., Mladinic, A., & Otto, S. (1991). Are women evaluated more favorably than men? An analysis of attitudes, beliefs, and emotions. *Psychology of Women Quarterly, 15*(2), 203–216.

Eagly, A. H., & Steffen, V. J. (1984). Gender stereotypes stem from the distribution of women and men into social roles. *Journal of Personality & Social Psychology, 46*(4), 735–754.

Eidelman, S., & Biernat, M. (2003). Derogating black sheep: Individual or group protection? *Journal of Experimental Social Psychology, 39*(6), 602–609.

Favero, J. L., & Ilgen, D. R. (1989). The effects of ratee prototypicality on rater observation and accuracy. *Journal of Applied Social Psychology, 19*(11), 932–946.

Feldman, J. M. (1981). Beyond attribution theory: Cognitive processes in performance appraisal. *Journal of Applied Psychology, 66*(2), 127–148.

Feldman, J. M., & Lynch, J. G. (1988). Self-generated validity and other effects of measurement on belief, attitude, intention, and behavior. *Journal of Applied Psychology, 73*(3), 421–435.

Fiske, S. T. (1989). Examining the role of intent: Toward understanding its role in stereotyping and prejudice. In J. S. Uleman & J. A. Bargh (Eds.), *Unintended thought* (pp. 253–283). New York: Guilford Press.

Fiske, S. T. (1998). Stereotyping, prejudice, and discrimination. In D. T. Gilbert, S. T. Fiske & G. Lindzey (Eds.), *The handbook of social psychology* (Vol. 2, 4th ed., pp. 357–411). New York: McGraw-Hill.

Fiske, S. T. (2000). Interdependence and the reduction of prejudice. In S. Oskamp (Ed.), *Reducing prejudice and discrimination. "The Claremont Symposium on Applied Social Psychology"* (pp. 115–135). Mahwah, NJ: Lawrence Erlbaum Associates.

Fiske, S. T. (2004). Intent and ordinary bias: Unintended thought and social motivation create casual prejudice. *Social Justice Research, 17*(2), 117–127.

Fiske, S. T., & Neuberg, S. L. (1990). A continuum of impression formation, from category-based to individuating processes: Influences of information and motivation on attention and interpretation. In M. P. Zanna (Ed.), *Advances in experimental social psychology* (Vol. 23, pp. 1–74). San Diego, CA: Academic Press.

Fiske, S. T., & Taylor, S. E. (1991). *Social cognition* (2nd ed.). McGraw Hill series in social psychology. New York: Mcgraw Hill, 717.

Foschi, M. (1996). Double standards in the evaluation of men and women. *Social Psychology Quarterly, 59*(3), 237–254.

Foschi, M. (2000). Double standards for competence: Theory and research. *Annual Review of Sociology, 26*, 21–42.

Fuegen, K., Biernat, M., Haines, E., & Deaux, K. (2004). Mothers and fathers in the workplace: how gender and parental status influence judgments of job-related competence. *Journal of Social Issues, 60*(4), 737–754.

Ganzach, Y. (1995). Negativity (and positivity) in performance evaluation: Three field studies. *Journal of Applied Psychology, 80*(4), 491–499.

George, J. M., & Brief, A. P. (1992). Feeling good – doing good: A conceptual analysis of the mood at work–organizational spontaneity relationship. *Psychological Bulletin, 112*(2), 310–329.

Gilbert, D. T., & Hixon, J. G. (1991). The trouble of thinking: Activation and application of stereotypic beliefs. *Journal of Personality and Social Psychology, 60*(4), 509–517.

Heilman, M. E. (1983). Sex bias in work settings: The Lack of Fit model. *Research in Organizational Behavior, 5*, 269–298.

Heilman, M. E. (1984). Information as a deterrent against sex discrimination: The effects of applicant sex and information type on preliminary employment decisions. *Organizational Behavior and Human Decision Processes, 33*(2), 174–186.

Heilman, M. E. (2001). Description and prescription: How gender stereotypes prevent women's ascent up the organizational ladder. *Journal of Social Issues, 57*(4), 657–674.

Heilman, M. E., & Blader, S. L. (2001). Assuming preferential selection when the admissions policy is unknown: The effects of gender rarity. *Journal of Applied Psychology, 86*(2), 188–193.

Heilman, M. E., Block, C. J., & Martell, R. F. (1995). Sex stereotypes: Do they influence perceptions of managers? *Journal of Social Behavior and Personality, 10*(6), 237–252.

Heilman, M. E., Block, C. J., Martell, R. F., & Simon, M. C. (1989). Has anything changed? Current characterizations of men, women, and managers. *Journal of Applied Psychology, 74*(6), 935–942.

Heilman, M. E., Block, C. J., & Stathatos, P. (1997). The affirmative action stigma of incompetence: Effects of performance information ambiguity. *Academy of Management Journal, 40*(3), 603–625.

Heilman, M. E., & Chen, J. J. (2005). Same Behavior, Different Consequences: Reactions to Men's and Women's Altruistic Citizenship Behavior. *Journal of Applied Psychology, 90*(3), 431–441.

Heilman, M. E., & Haynes, M. C. (2005). No credit where credit is due: Attributional rationalization of women's success in male–female teams. *Journal of Applied Psychology, 90*(5), 905–916.

Heilman, M. E., Martell, R. F., & Simon, M. C. (1988). The vagaries of sex bias: Conditions regulating the undervaluation, equivaluation, and overvaluation of female job applicants. *Organizational Behavior and Human Decision Processes, 41*(1), 98–110.

Heilman, M. E., & Okimoto, T. G. (in press). Averting penalities for women's success: Rectifying the perceived communality deficiency. *Journal of Applied Psychology.*

Heilman, M. E., & Okimoto, T. G. (2006). *Motherhood: Adverse consequences for career advancement. Unpublished manuscript.*

Heilman, M. E., & Stopeck, M. H. (1985a). Attractiveness and corporate success: Different causal attributions for males and females. *Journal of Applied Psychology, 70*(2), 379–388.

Heilman, M. E., & Stopeck, M. H. (1985b). Being attractive, advantage or disadvantage? Performance-based evaluations and recommended personnel actions as a function of appearance, sex, and job type. *Organizational Behavior and Human Decision Processes, 35*(2), 202–215.

Heilman, M. E., Wallen, A. S., Fuchs, D., & Tamkins, M. M. (2004). Penalties for success: Reactions to women who succeed at male gender-typed tasks. *Journal of Applied Psychology, 89*(3), 416–427.

Heilman, M. E., & Welle, B. (2006). Disadvantaged by diversity? The effects of diversity goals on competence perceptions. *Journal of Applied Social Psychology, 36*(5), 1291–1319.

Heneman, R. L. (1986). The relationship between supervisory ratings and results-oriented measures of performance: A meta-analysis. *Personnel Psychology, 39*(4), 811–826.

Heneman, R. L., & Wexley, K. N. (1983). The effects of time delay in rating and amount of information observed on performance rating accuracy. *Academy of Management Journal, 26*(4), 677–686.

Hennessey, H. W., Jr., & Bernardin, H. J. (2003). The relationship between performance appraisal criterion specificity and statistical evidence of discrimination. *Human Resource Management*, 42(2), 143–158.

Huber, O. (1989). Information-processing operators in decision making. In H. Montgomery & O. Svenson (Eds.), *Process and structure in human decision making*. (pp. 3–21): Oxford, UK: John Wiley & Sons.

Hunt, S. T. (1996). Generic work behavior: An investigation into the dimensions of entry-level, hourly job performance. *Personnel Psychology*, 49(1), 51–83.

Ilgen, D. R., Barnes-Farrell, J. L., & McKellin, D. B. (1993). Performance appraisal process research in the 1980s: What has it contributed to appraisals in use? *Organizational Behavior and Human Decision Processes*, 54(3), 321–368.

Johnson, J. T., & Judd, C. M. (1983). Overlooking the incongruent: Categorization biases in the identification of political statements. *Journal of Personality and Social Psychology*, 45(5), 978–996.

Jones, E. E. & Wortman, C. (1977). *Ingratiation: An attributional approach.* Morristown, NJ: General Learning Press.

Kane, J. S., Bernardin, H. J., Villanova, P., & Peyrefitte, J (1995). Stability of rater leniency: Three studies. *Academy of Management Journal*, 38(4), 1036–1051.

Kidder, D. L. (2002). The influence of gender on the performance of organizational citizenship behaviors. *Journal of Management*, 28(5), 629–648.

Kidder, D. L., & Parks, J. M. (2001). The good soldier: Who is s(he)? *Journal of Organizational Behavior*, 22(8), 939–959.

Klimoski, R., & Inks, L. (1990). Accountability forces in performance appraisal. *Organizational Behavior and Human Decision Processes*, 45(2), 194–208.

Kunda, Z., Sinclair, L., & Griffin, D. (1997). Equal ratings but separate meanings: Stereotypes and the construal of traits. *Journal of Personality & Social Psychology*, 72(4), 720–734.

Landy, F. J., & Farr, J. L. (1980). Performance rating. *Psychological Bulletin*, 87(1), 72–107.

Locksley, A., Borgida, E., Brekke, N., & Hepburn, C. (1980). Sex stereotypes and social judgment. *Journal of Personality and Social Psychology*, 39(5), 821–831.

Lyness, K. S. (2002). Finding the key to the executive suite: Challenges for women and people of color. In R. Silzer (Ed.), *The 21st century executive: Innovative practices for building leadership at the top* (pp. 229–273). San Francisco: Jossey-Boss.

Lyness, K. S., & Heilman, M. E. (in press). When fit is fundamental: Performance evaluation and promotions of upper-level female and male managers. *Journal of Applied Psychology*.

Martell, R. F., Guzzo, R. A., & Willis, C. E. (1995). A methodological and substantive note on the performance-cue effect in ratings of work-group behavior. *Journal of Applied Psychology*, 80(1), 191–195.

Martell, R. F., Lane, D. M., Emrich, C. (1996, February). Male–female differences: A computer simulation. *American Psychologist*, 51(2), 157–158.

McIntyre, M. D., & James, L. R. (1995). The inconsistency with which raters weight and combine information across targets. *Human Performance*, 8(2), 95–111.

Mero, N. P., & Motowidlo, S. J. (1995). Effects of rater accountability on the accuracy and the favorability of performance ratings. *Journal of Applied Psychology*, 80(4), 517–524.

Mero, N. P., Motowidlo, S. J., & Anna, A. L. (2003). Effects of accountability on rating behavior and rater accuracy. *Journal of Applied Social Psychology*, 33(12), 2493–2514.

Morrison, E. W. (1994). Role definitions and organizational citizenship behavior: The importance of the employee's perspective. *Academy of Management Journal*, 37(6), 1543–1567.

Murphy, K. R., & Cleveland, J. N. (1991). *Performance appraisal: An organizational perspective*. Human resource management series. Needham Heights, MA, US: Allyn & Bacon, 349.

Murphy, K. R., & Constans, J. I. (1987). Behavioral anchors as a source of bias in rating. *Journal of Applied Psychology*, 72(4), 573–577.

Nathan, B. R., & Alexander, R. A. (1985). The role of inferential accuracy in performance rating. *Academy of Management Review*, 10(1), 109–115.

Nieva, V. G., & Gutek, B. A. (1980). Sex effects on evaluation. *Academy of Management Review*, 5, 267–276.

Olson, J. M., Roese, N. J., & Zanna, M. P. (1996). Expectancies. In E. T. Higgins & A. W. Kruglanski (Eds.), *Social psychology: Handbook of basic principles* (pp. 211–238). New York: Guilford Press.

Organ, D. W. (1988). *Organizational citizenship behavior: The good soldier syndrome*. Issues in organization and management series. Lexington, MA: Lexington Books/D. C. Heath and Co., 132.

Organ, D. W. (1997). Organizational citizenship behavior: It's construct clean-up time. *Human Performance*, 10(2), 85–97.

Pazy, A., & Oron, I. (2001). Sex proportion and performance evaluation among high-ranking military officers. *Journal of Organizational Behavior*, 22(6), 689–702.

Pratto, F., & Bargh, J. A. (1991). Stereotyping based on apparently individuating information: Trait and global components of sex stereotypes under attention overload. *Journal of Experimental Social Psychology*, 27(1), 26–47.

Pulakos, E. D., White, L. A., Oppler, S. H., & Borman, W. C. (1989). Examination of race and sex effects on performance ratings. *Journal of Applied Psychology*, 74(5), 770–780.

Rasinski, K. A., Crocker, J., & Hastie, R. (1985). Another look at sex stereotypes and social judgments: An analysis of the social perceiver's use of subjective probabilities. *Journal of Personality and Social Psychology*, 49(2), 317–326.

Renwick, P. A., & Tosi, H. (1978). The effects of sex, marital status, and educational background on selection decisions. *Academy of Management Journal, 21*(1), 93–103.

Rothbart, M., Evans, M., & Fulero, S. (1979). Recall for confirming events: Memory processes and the maintenance of social stereotypes. *Journal of Experimental Social Psychology, 15*(4), 343–355.

Sackett, P. R., DuBois, C. L., & Noe, A. W. (1991). Tokenism in performance evaluation: The effects of work group representation on male–female and White–Black differences in performance ratings. *Journal of Applied Psychology, 76*(2), 263–267.

Schein, V. E. (2001). A global look at psychological barriers to women's progress in management. *Journal of Social Issues, 57*, 675–688.

Schrader, B. W., & Steiner, D. D. (1996). Common comparison standards: An approach to improving agreement between self and supervisory performance ratings. *Journal of Applied Psychology, 81*(6), 813–820.

Simonson, I., & Nye, P. (1992). The effect of accountability on susceptibility to decision errors. *Organizational Behavior and Human Decision Processes, 51*(3), 416–446.

Srull, T. K., & Wyer, R. S. (1980). Category accessibility and social perception: Some implications for the study of person memory and interpersonal judgments. *Journal of Personality and Social Psychology, 38*(6), 841–856.

Srull, T. K., & Wyer, R. S. (1983). The role of control processes and structural constraints in models of memory and social judgment. *Journal of Experimental Social Psychology, 19*(6), 497–521.

Swim, J. K., & Sanna, L. J. (1996). He's skilled, she's lucky: A meta-analysis of observers' attributions for women's and men's successes and failures. *Personality and Social Psychology Bulletin, 22*(5), 507–519.

Tepper, B. J., Lockhart, D., & Hoobler, J. (2001). Justice, citizenship, and role definition effects. *Journal of Applied Psychology, 86*(4), 789–796.

Tetlock, P. E. (1983a). Accountability and complexity of thought. *Journal of Personality and Social Psychology, 45*(1), 74–83.

Tetlock, P. E. (1983b). Accountability and the perseverance of first impressions. *Social Psychology Quarterly, 46*(4), 285–292.

Tetlock, P. E. (1985). Accountability: The neglected social context of judgment and choice. *Research in Organizational Behavior, 7*, 297–332.

Tetlock, P. E., Skitka, L., & Boettger, R. (1989). Social and cognitive strategies for coping with accountability: Conformity, complexity, and bolstering. *Journal of Personality and Social Psychology, 57*(4), 632–640.

Tosi, H. L., & Einbender, S. W. (1985). The effects of the type and amount of information in sex discrimination research: A meta-analysis. *Academy of Management Journal, 28*(3), 712–723.

van der Heijden, B. I. J. M., & Nijhof, A. H. J. (2004). The value of subjectivity: Problems and prospects for 360-degree appraisal systems. *International Journal of Human Resource Management, 15*(3), 493–511.

Van Dyne, L., Cummings, L. L., & Parks, J. M. (1995). Extra-role behaviors: In pursuit of construct and definitional clarity (A bridge over muddied waters). In B. M. Staw & L. L. Cummings (Eds.), *Research in organizational behavior* (Vol. 17, pp. 215–285). Greenwich, CT: JAI Press.

van Knippenberg, A., & Dijksterhuis, A. (2000). Social categorizations and sterotyping: A functional perspective. In W. Stroebe & M. Hewstone (Eds.), *European review of social psychology* (Vol. 11, pp. 105–144). Chichester, UK: Wiley.

Viswesvaran, C., Ones, D. S., & Schmidt, F. L. (1996). Comparative analysis of the reliability of job performance ratings. *Journal of Applied Psychology*, *81*(5), 557–574.

Part II

Psychological Science on Legal System Processes

8

Eyewitness Identification: Issues in Common Knowledge and Generalization

Gary L. Wells and Lisa E. Hasel

Kirk Bloodsworth had never before been in trouble with the law. However, based on the eyewitness identification testimony of five eyewitnesses Bloodsworth was charged, convicted, and sentenced to Maryland's gas chamber for the 1984 rape and murder of a 9-year-old girl. Lucky for him, forensic DNA testing managed to prove him innocent after nine years of harsh prison life (Junkin, 2004). Since the advent of forensic DNA testing in the 1990s, more than 200 people who were convicted by juries and were serving hard time (some on death row) have been proven innocent with DNA testing (see the up-to-date list of exonerations on the Innocence Project website www.innocenceproject.org/know/Browse-Profiles.php). Approximately 75% of these cases of the conviction of the innocent involve mistaken eyewitness identification evidence.

Long before forensic DNA testing was developed, psychological scientists were publishing articles warning that eyewitness identification evidence appears to be at once both highly persuasive to jurors yet highly subject to error. The interest of psychological scientists in eyewitness memory was clearly evidenced in the early part of the twentieth-century in the writings of Munsterberg (1908). But, it was not until the 1970s that psychological scientists began to launch systematic experiments involving lineups.[1] The study of memory has tended to be primarily a domain for cognitive psychologists. However, social psychologists have made the largest share of contributions to the

[1] James Doyle, a Boston defense lawyer, has written a brilliant and interesting scholarly book on the history of the interface between psychological science and the legal system as it relates to eyewitness evidence, from Munsterberg to today (Doyle, 2005).

eyewitness identification literature, perhaps because social psychologists have understood from the outset that eyewitness identification is not just a memory issue; there are social factors at play. The result has been a healthy literature that has had some impact on the legal system (Wells et al., 2000). Since late 2001 reforms have been made to how police conduct lineups in a number of jurisdictions (such as the states of New Jersey, North Carolina, and Wisconsin, and the cities and counties of Boston and Minneapolis) that cover approximately 30 million citizens. These reforms are based on the findings from psychology research experiments, and psychological scientists have been directly involved in effecting these reforms. Nevertheless, these reformed jurisdictions cover only about 10% of the population of the United States (Wells, 2006) and it remains very difficult, if possible at all, to have expert testimony on eyewitness identification issues admitted in many jurisdictions in the United States.

It is not the purpose of this article to advocate for or against the admission of expert testimony on eyewitness identification issues, nor is it our purpose to review the vast literature on eyewitness identification research (see reviews by Cutler & Penrod, 1995; Wells & Loftus, 2003; Wells & Olson, 2003). Instead, we confine this chapter to the overall questions raised in this volume, namely are there research findings on eyewitness identification that have levels of reliability and generalizability to withstand the scrutiny of the legal system and do these findings go beyond mere common knowledge? We first address the question of reliability and generalization. Then we describe some research that has been done on the question of whether findings in the area go beyond common knowledge. In a final section, we place a new twist on the question of whether the findings are merely a matter of common knowledge by pointing to evidence that the legal system itself (e.g., prosecutors, judges, and police) apparently does not understand or appreciate certain aspects of eyewitness identification.

Can Eyewitness Research Findings Withstand the Legal System's Scrutiny?

Before attempting to answer that question, it is important to note that expert testimony on eyewitness identification issues has been admitted in some court at some point in almost every jurisdiction in the United States. In this sense, it has passed the scrutiny of some courts some of the time. However, it is nearly impossible to know how often it is admitted because written opinions are largely confined to cases in which the expert testimony was excluded. When expert testimony on eyewitness identification issues is excluded, the exclusions are based largely on one of two arguments. One argument is that the findings are not reliable enough or generalizable enough to assist the trier of fact. The other argument is that the findings are just a matter of common knowledge and that jurors already know these things. The latter argument is addressed in the next section (Are the Findings Just a Matter of Common Knowledge?). The former argument is really two issues, namely reliability and generalizability.

The legal system uses the term reliability to mean what scientists usually construe as validity. Validity, of course, depends on reliability, but validity is not the same as reliability. A finding can be reliable (e.g., consistently observed) without being valid (e.g., attributed to the actual cause). Reliability is easier to demonstrate than validity and to some extent is demonstrated in every article describing a particular finding because the results are analyzed for statistical significance. But, a higher level of reliability is demonstrated through meta-analytic procedures in which the results of many different studies are combined. It is not the purpose of this chapter to review the eyewitness identification literature, but we single out four examples of findings that we believe meet the test of reliability as evidenced from meta-analyses. First, there is reliable empirical evidence showing that cross-race identifications are more difficult for eyewitnesses than are within-race identifications. A meta-analysis by Meissner and Brigham (2001) indicates that this effect is true not only for White people attempting to identify Black people, but also Black people attempting to identify White people. Furthermore, the effect is not just true for racial categories but also for ethnic categories (e.g., Hispanics). Second, there is highly reliable empirical evidence to indicate that the failure to warn eyewitnesses prior to viewing a lineup that the actual perpetrator might not be present serves to increase the chances of a mistaken identification when the perpetrator is not in the lineup, with relatively little effect on accurate identifications when the perpetrator is in the lineup. A meta-analysis by Steblay (1997) indicates strong effects for this warning. Third, there is highly reliable evidence to indicate that the presence of a weapon while witnessing a crime diminishes the ability of the eyewitness to later accurately identify the face of the perpetrator (see meta-analysis by Steblay, 1992). Finally, there is highly reliable empirical evidence indicating that postidentification confirming feedback to eyewitnesses distorts their recollections of their own certainty (Douglass & Steblay, 2006).

Because these four reliable findings are based on true experiments (rather than correlations, for example), a basic level of causal validity is inherent in these results. That is, we can clearly say that the differences in accurate identification rates observed in these studies are attributable to the manipulated variables. We cannot be so sure, however, about the process through which the variables exert their influence. For example, although the data tend to rule out prejudice per se as a cause of the cross-race identification effect, there remains some uncertainty as to the precise mechanisms responsible for the effect. Similarly, although we know that postidentification confirming feedback to eyewitnesses distorts their retrospective reports of certainty, there are competing theoretical accounts of the processes underlying this effect.

At some level, validity of explanation (i.e., a good understanding of the theoretical processes underlying the finding) is not necessarily an impediment for making use of a finding in terms of applying it to real-world cases. However, validity of explanation can be important at times for purposes of generalization because no collection of experiments can possibly represent the exact set of circumstances that occur in an actual case. Consider, for example, the postidentification feedback effect. The dominant explanation for the postidentification feedback effect is that eyewitnesses use the feedback to infer that their identification was correct and then make an inference that they were certain based on their elevated senses that their decision was correct. But, the experiments have operationalized postidentification feedback in only two ways, either by telling the eyewitness that she or he identified the suspect, rather than a filler, in the lineup or by telling the eyewitness that another eyewitness identified the same person that they did. What about a case in which the eyewitness learns that the defendant's fingerprints were found at the scene or that the defendant has a prior record? If there is validity to the interpretation of the postidentification feedback effect, then the absence of studies manipulating fingerprint feedback or prior-record feedback matters little because both would be expected to have the same effect as that demonstrated in the other postidentification feedback effect studies. Hence, generalization depends somewhat on having a valid understanding of the psychological process underlying the phenomenon.

One argument against generalizing from laboratory studies of eyewitnesses to actual cases is that the experimental eyewitnesses know that their identification decisions do not have severe consequences for the accused whereas real eyewitnesses would be far more cautious.

Fortunately, data on real lineups can help shed light on this issue. In an experiment, the perpetrator is actually an accomplice of the experimenter, so we can be certain as to whether any identification is of the actual perpetrator versus an innocent person. In actual cases, the identity of the perpetrator cannot be known with absolute certainty. However, there is a special situation in the study of actual lineups in which we can in fact know whether the eyewitness identified the wrong person, namely when the eyewitness identifies a filler (foil or distractor) from the lineup. In properly constructed lineups, there is only one suspect (who might or might not be the actual perpetrator) and the remaining lineup members are merely fillers. In studies of actual lineups, eyewitnesses to real crimes tend to identify fillers approximately 20% of the time (Behrman & Davey, 2001; Wright & McDaid, 1996). These rates are quite similar to what are found in laboratory studies of eyewitness identification, suggesting that the laboratory studies are capturing generalizable phenomena.

Another way to make a strong case for generalization is to conduct experiments with actual eyewitnesses to real crimes. A very strong example of this was recently conducted on the postidentification feedback effect. The postidentification feedback effect is arguably one of the most important and reliable laboratory phenomena on eyewitness identification evidence discovered in the past several years. In the original laboratory study, eyewitnesses who made mistaken identifications were randomly assigned to receive confirming feedback ("Good, you identified the suspect"), disconfirming feedback ("Actually, the suspect was a different person in this lineup"), or no feedback (Wells & Bradfield, 1998). Later, all eyewitnesses were asked to recall how certain they were at the time of their identification as well as to report on how much attention they paid during the witnessed event, how good their view was of the culprit while witnessing, and other testimony-relevant questions. Compared to the no-feedback control condition, confirming feedback led witnesses to recall having been certain all along, having paid more attention, and having had a better view. Disconfirming feedback had the opposite effect. These retrospective distortions of certainty, attention, and view as a function of feedback are highly robust effects that have been replicated widely in laboratory studies (see meta-analysis by Douglass & Steblay, 2006). Again, the argument could be made that real eyewitnesses to actual crimes would not prove so malleable on measures of this sort, perhaps owing to the serious consequences that exist in actual cases versus the more trivial consequences that are associated with a laboratory experiment. However, a recent experiment using 134 eyewitnesses to actual crimes revealed that the postidentification feedback effect *is* robust. With the cooperation of the Sussex (United Kingdom) Police Department, Wright and Skagerberg (2007) had eyewitnesses answer various questions (e.g., "How good a view did you have of the culprit during the crime?" and "How much attention did you pay to the culprit during the crime?") either immediately after making their identifications or after learning whether the person they had identified was a suspect versus an innocent filler. Just as has been found in laboratory studies, these eyewitnesses to actual crimes changed their recollections on these questions as a function of what they had learned about their identification.

Generalization from controlled laboratory studies to the real world also is benefited by documenting individual real-world cases of the conviction of innocent people. In particular, findings in the eyewitness identification area have benefited greatly from the advent of forensic DNA testing, which has resulted in the release of over 200 people who were convicted of serious crimes for which DNA later proved them innocent. Importantly, over 75% of these DNA exoneration cases are instances of mistaken eyewitness identification (Scheck, Neufeld, & Dwyer, 2000; Wells et al, 2000). These cases help extend the laboratory findings in several ways. First, they illustrate that mistaken identification is not just a laboratory phenomenon. Second, these cases show that confident eyewitnesses tend to trump other evidence that is exculpatory (such as alibis) and are consistent with the laboratory findings indicating that eyewitness identification evidence holds more weight than it should. The observation that eyewitness identification testimony is readily accepted by jurors fits nicely with the broader social psychological literature on how mental systems believe. Gilbert (1991), for instance, has reviewed a wide variety of evidence indicating that comprehension and acceptance occur simultaneously, which makes acceptance of a statement (e.g., "That is the person I saw commit the crime") a starting point in human judgment. Adjustments from a starting point are commonly insufficient (Epley & Gilovich, 2001; Tversky & Kahneman, 1973). Third, these DNA exoneration cases show a disproportionate representation of cross-race identifications as well as high rates of poorly constructed lineups, failures to warn eyewitnesses appropriately prior to the lineup that the culprit might not be in the lineup, and giving eyewitnesses confirming feedback (even though their identifications were mistaken). In other words, these DNA exoneration cases show patterns that are consistent with the findings of laboratory studies and in this sense tend to assist in generalizing from the laboratory to actual cases.

Are the Findings Just a Matter of Common Knowledge?

There are different ways in which researchers have attempted to find out if the scientific findings by eyewitness researchers are merely a reflection of common knowledge. Three methodologies that have been utilized are: (1) surveying people's knowledge through questionnaires; (2) assessing people's ability to predict the outcome of eyewitness identification experiments; and (3) examining people's verdicts and opinions about written or videotaped trials (Devenport, Penrod, & Cutler, 1997, Wells, 1984, Wells & Olson, 2003). In survey studies, participants typically read statements about factors that may or may not influence eyewitness identifications or testimony and give ratings on how much they agree or disagree with them. In prediction studies, participants are typically presented with the methods section of a previously conducted eyewitness identification experiment and are asked to predict the outcome of the study. These predictions are then compared with the outcome of the original study in order to assess whether or not people have an understanding of how different situations affect eyewitness behavior. In trial studies, participants are usually given a description of a crime and an investigation, either through a written scenario or through a videotaped mock trial, and asked to make judgments about the information presented. Participants are typically asked whether or not they would find the defendant/suspect guilty and are asked to make other judgments regarding the evidence or the defendant. Across all three of these methodologies, it appears as though some, but not a majority, of the findings of eyewitness researchers could just be a matter of common knowledge.

In a direct comparison of potential juror and expert knowledge in a survey study, it was found that participants disagreed with experts on 13 of 21 statements but agreed with experts on 8 of 21 statements about factors that affect identification accuracy (Kassin & Barndollar, 1992). For example, only 50% of the nonexperts who were surveyed, as opposed to 87% of the experts, agreed with the statement that "an eyewitness's confidence is not a good predictor of his or her identification accuracy." This indicates a discrepancy between common knowledge and what experts have to say regarding how indicative an eyewitness's confidence statement is of his or her actual accuracy. Additionally, only 39% of the nonexperts who were surveyed agreed with the statement that "the more the members of a lineup resemble the suspect, the higher the likelihood that identification of the suspect is accurate," which is a finding that is highly endorsed by eyewitness experts. This, once again, demonstrates a disconnect between common knowledge and what experts know about factors that influence eyewitness identification accuracy. Contrary to the prior examples, 90% of the persons who were surveyed agreed with the statement that "an eyewitness's testimony about an event can be affected by how the questions put to that witness are worded," which is highly consistent with the scientific literature. Therefore, it appears as though people have common knowledge of how the wording of questions can influence a witness's responses to those questions. However, does this mean that they can apply this understanding to different situations? For example, would a potential juror realize the different type of answer that "Did you notice *the* briefcase?" as opposed to "Did you notice *a* briefcase?" can elicit from an eyewitness? Even though potential jurors may be able hypothetically to reason that certain events might influence an eyewitness's description of a crime, when presented with a particular instance of the event, they might not realize that the hypothetical situation applies to the specific instance.

Similarly, 82% of the nonexperts who were surveyed agreed with the statement that "very high levels of stress impair the accuracy of eyewitness testimony," which is largely in agreement with scientific findings (Kassin & Barndollar, 1992). However, potential jurors consistently believe witnesses who are highly confident in their identifications more than they do witnesses who are not confident in their identifications (e.g., Bradfield & Wells, 2000, Brewer & Burke, 2002, Fox & Walters, 1986; Wells, Lindsay & Ferguson, 1979; Wells & Murray, 1984). Therefore, given an actual case in which it is known that a witness experienced high stress during the crime but expresses high certainty in his or her identification, will the eyewitness's certainty influence the jurors so much that they do not believe that the high stress made a difference? It is likely that in this situation the high confidence of the eyewitness would trump the jurors' hypothetical belief that a high level of stress will impair eyewitness testimony. Additionally, although research has shown that high levels of stress impairs memory for events (Morgan et al., 2004), many people also believe that if a person is in a highly stressful situation, then their senses will be heightened and will cause them to remember things even better than they would if they were not under stress. When attorneys for the different parties or other jurors present a jury with two opposing sides that offer competing intuitions about the role of stress in memory, how will they ultimately decide which theory to accept and apply to the situation? This will depend on how convincing the arguments are when they are originally offered and how they "fit" with the rest of the evidence for the crime.

In the same comparison study of experts' and nonexperts' understanding of the factors that influence eyewitness testimony, a statistically significant difference was found between the percentage of experts (95%) and nonexperts (68%) who agreed with the statement that "police instructions can affect an eyewitness's willingness to make an identification and/or the likelihood that he or she will identify a particular person" (Kassin & Barndollar, 1992). According to the analyses conducted in the study, this indicates that this statement is beyond common knowledge, even though over 50% of the potential jurors who read this statement agreed with the experts. What percentage of nonexperts would need to agree with a statement for it to be considered common knowledge? We cannot expect people to be in agreement with each statement 100% of the time before we decide that the statement is common knowledge. After all, even the experts in the field do not agree 100% of the time.

In 1992 eyewitness researchers were split (57% agreed and 43% disagreed) regarding the statement that "the presence of a weapon impairs an eyewitness's ability to accurately identify the perpetrator's face" (Kassin & Barndollar, 1992). However, less than a decade later, a survey conducted in the same way as the first found that 87% of the eyewitness researchers who were surveyed agreed with this statement (Kassin, Tubb, Hosch, & Memon, 2001). Kassin and his colleagues hypothesized that a meta-analysis of the weapon-focus effect (Steblay, 1992) and new studies of the effect (e.g., Pickel, 1999), which were published after the first survey of experts and before the second survey of the experts, account for the greater agreement about this effect among experts in the second survey. Of course, there is no reason that nonexperts during this same time period would have increased their knowledge about this effect. In 1992 agreement with the weapon-focus statement was 60% among nonexperts, which was not significantly different than the 57% of experts who agreed with the statement; however, had the survey of nonexperts been conducted in 2001, there probably would have been a significant difference between the nonexpert and expert belief in this statement. This is because the scientific literature continues to evolve, but knowledge about the scientific literature may not spread to nonexperts without some sort of educational effort by the experts in the field.

Attempts have been made and continue to be made to assess which aspects of the eyewitness research findings are common knowledge and which are not, but this is extremely difficult to do. Some of this difficulty is inherent in defining a criterion for common knowledge. However, we believe that much of the difficulty stems from a distinction between people's having knowledge per se and their application of that knowledge in the context of an actual case. As discussed earlier, it may be difficult for jurors to apply their hypothetical knowledge about a phenomenon to a particular instance of that phenomenon. This type of problem is not unique to the eyewitness area. Consider, for example, what a person might say if asked "How should one decide to buy a car? Is it better to rely on *Consumer Reports*, which is based on hundreds of people's experience with the car or to rely on only one other person's experience?" Clearly, people would endorse the former. But, if his/her neighbor were to buy the car and have nothing but trouble, the neighbor's experience would be likely to persuade the person to ignore *Consumer Reports*. Hence, having what appears to be good common knowledge and applying that common knowledge to a given instance can be two very different things. Jurors may also be presented with opposing sides that offer competing intuitions about a phenomenon and may reach different conclusions, depending on the rest of the evidence or how strongly each of the sides are argued. Lastly, jurors may fail to recognize an instance of the problem because it is somehow masked or presented in a way that is different from their understanding of the phenomenon.

Does the System Itself Have Common Knowledge About Eyewitness Identification?

In the previous section, we discussed various reasons to suspect that some findings in the eyewitness area might not be a part of jurors' common knowledge or at least jurors' abilities to apply that knowledge to individual cases. In the eyewitness area, however, we raise an even more disturbing possibility. Specifically, we argue that there is evidence that the broader justice system, including judges, prosecutors, and police, apparently do not have common knowledge of important variables and psychological processes that affect the accuracy of eyewitness identification. To the extent that this is true, it would be somewhat bizarre to argue that jurors know things that judges, prosecutors, and police apparently do not know.

In making this argument, we do not rely on surveys or simulated trials, but rather on the practices of police, prosecutors, and judges as a way to uncover their apparent assumptions, understanding, and knowledge of factors that influence eyewitness identification accuracy.

Consider, for instance, the numerous ways in which the conductance of lineups by law enforcement agencies creates confounds that would never be permitted to occur in a social psychological experiment. Wells and Luus (1990) described a strong analogy between police conducting a lineup and social psychologists conducting an experiment: The *officer* conducting the lineup is like an *experimenter*, the eyewitnesses are the subjects, *instructions* to the witness can be likened to an experimenter's *protocol*, the *suspect* is the *stimulus*, the selection of lineup fillers and *positioning* of the suspect are part of the *design*. Continuing this analogy, police have a *hypothesis* (e.g., that #3 is the culprit), they have created a design and *procedure* to test their hypothesis, collect *data* from the subject/witness, *interpret* the result, and so on. In general, all of the same types of things that can go wrong in conducting a social psychology experiment can go wrong in conducting a lineup. For instance, officers conducting lineups are not blind to condition (i.e., which lineup member is the suspect and which are fillers), pre-lineup instructions to witnesses are commonly suggestive, fillers are often chosen in ways that make it obvious which person is the suspect, the position of the suspect is rarely counterbalanced or rotated in any way in multiple-witness cases, relevant data are often not recorded (e.g., whether the witness picked a filler versus selected no one), witnesses are commonly debriefed before being asked relevant questions (e.g., told whether they picked a filler versus the suspect before being asked about their certainty), and disconfirming data tend to be ignored or explained away (e.g., not picking the suspect is interpreted as the result of a witness having a poor memory).

Hence, social psychologists have been particularly strong advocates of implementing various principles of experimental design into actual police lineups. But, if this contribution from social psychology were already a part of the common sense of the legal system, then why are these problems occurring? Wells and Luus (1990) argued that these problems are not at all obvious to the legal system. They seem obvious to social psychologists because the logic of good experimentation is ingrained in social psychologists' thinking and training. In fact, graduate education in psychology has been shown to lead to profoundly different and better thinking on problems of this sort than in any other discipline (see Lehman, Lempert, & Nisbett, 1988). Interestingly, even the simple idea of control groups tends to not be a part of people's everyday reasoning. This should not be particularly surprising since the first formal treatment of the need for control groups did not occur until the problem was articulated by Mill (1851), and Boring

(1954) notes that the use of control groups is a twentieth-century phenomenon.

The contrast between the eyewitness identification practices of the legal system and the principle of a good social psychology experiment seems to be strong evidence that what psychology has to offer is not obvious to the legal system. In the following two sections, we give a more detailed treatment of two common practices that further illustrate our argument that the legal system apparently does not intuitively understand what psychology has to offer because, if the system understood these things, then why do these practices exist? These two examples are: (a) an assumption that eyewitnesses can retrospectively report the influence of a variable as evidenced by the practice of asking them to do so, and (b) an assumption that the knowledge, expectations, and desires of a tester do not influence the person being tested as evidenced by the failure to require double-blind identification procedures.

The assumption of accurate retrospective reporting on influence variables

Among the reasons for excluding expert testimony on eyewitness identification at trial is the argument that one can simply ask the witness whether some variable influenced them. For example, a defense attorney might argue at a suppression trial that the identification of the defendant from a lineup was tainted by the fact that the eyewitness watched a news broadcast that depicted the defendant's face before viewing the lineup. Commonly, prosecutors will argue that the defense is free to cross-examine the eyewitness and ask the eyewitness if that newscast influenced them. This argument is commonly accepted by judges who note that the defense can ask if the eyewitness made the lineup identification based on his or her memory of the perpetrator from the crime scene or was instead based on simply identifying the person seen on the newscast. Of course, social psychologists have long known that people do not have the kind of introspective access that would permit reliance on their response to such questions. People often report that a variable did not influence them when it actually did, as well as reporting that a variable influenced them when it actually did not (Nisbett &Wilson, 1977).

Another example occurs when there is postidentification tainting of the certainty of the eyewitness. The certainty of the eyewitness is a profoundly strong determinant of whether or not the prosecutor will charge the defendant, whether or not the judge will permit the witness to testify, and whether or not jurors will vote to convict the defendant. To some extent, moderate use of certainty can be justified under special conditions in which the certainty statement is obtained at the time of identification by a neutral tester (see Wells, Olson, & Charman, 2002). However, once the eyewitness learns the "status" of the identified person, the certainty of the eyewitness is dramatically influenced. There is now compelling scientific evidence that confirming feedback to eyewitnesses who have made mistaken identifications (e.g., "Good, you identified the actual suspect") makes eyewitnesses believe that they were certain in the accuracy of their identification all along (see Bradfield, Wells, & Olson, 2002; Hafstad, Memon, & Logie, 2004; Semmler, Brewer, & Wells, 2004; Wells & Bradfield, 1998; Wells & Bradfield, 1999; Wells, Olson, & Charman, 2003).

The practice of not securing a statement as to the certainty of the eyewitness at the time of identification, before other variables can influence the eyewitness's certainty, seems to rest on the assumption that eyewitnesses can make accurate retrospective reports about the uncertainty that they felt before other variables influenced their certainty. At a pretrial hearing, for instance, an argument by defense counsel that there was a failure to secure a certainty statement from the eyewitness at the time of identification does not succeed in getting a judge to prevent the eyewitness from stating his or her certainty at trial. Even if the defense can show that the police or prosecutor briefed the eyewitness (e.g., "Good job, Miss Jones, you identified the guy who we believe did this"), the failure to secure a certainty statement from the eyewitness prior to the briefing is not a persuasive argument. Instead, the judge accepts the prosecution's claim that the defense can simply ask the eyewitness to recall how certain the eyewitness was at the time of the identification. In fact, however, these retrospective reports of certainty are not only distorted, but those eyewitnesses who say that the feedback did not influence how certain they recall being are in fact no less influenced than are those who say that the feedback did influence them (Wells & Bradfield, 1998).

Lack of introspective access (Nisbett & Wilson, 1977) and hindsight biases (Choi & Nisbett, 2000) are not the only psychological processes affecting eyewitness identification testimony that the legal system seems to not understand. However, these serve as examples of practices by legal system actors that illustrate an apparent gap between the science and common knowledge. If judges and prosecutors seem not to understand or appreciate these factors, in what sense can it be said that jurors understand?

The assumption that testers do not influence the person tested

It has been more than two decades since Harris and Rosenthal (1985) published a massive meta-analysis of experimenter expectancy effects summarizing the profound influence of testers' knowledge on those being tested. Also, it has been argued by eyewitness researchers since the late 1980s that the person who conducts a lineup should not know which lineup member is the suspect and which lineup members are merely fillers (Wells, 1988). Psychological scientists and those in other sciences are well aware of the need for double-blind testing. In any face-to-face testing of humans (as well as testing of animals), the needs, knowledge, and expectations of the person conducting the test can influence the individual being tested. Neither intentionality nor aware-ness on the part of either the tester or the person being tested is required for this influence to take place.

The concept of double-blind testing is so fundamental in science that it is difficult for some scientists to believe that photographic lineup procedures, which place the liberty and life of suspects at risk, are rou-tinely administered by the case detective rather than a neutral party. Most identifications of criminal suspects are conducted by the case detective with photo-lineups for which there is no presence of defense counsel and no audio or video recordings. The case detective is the same person who "developed the suspect" in the first place (i.e., decided that this person is the likely perpetrator). Hence, the lineup administrator is highly aware of which lineup photo is the suspect and which are merely filler photos. The administration of the lineup test is highly interactive and rich in both verbal and nonverbal communication. In this context, research shows that the lineup administrator's assumption regarding which lineup member is the suspect influences not only the choices made by eyewitnesses but also the certainty that they express in their identifications (see Garrioch & Brimacombe, 2001; Haw & Fisher, 2004; Phillips, McAuliff, Kovera, & Cutler, 1999).

Despite the obvious flaw of permitting the case detective (or anyone else who knows the "correct" answer) to administer a lineup, only a few jurisdictions now require double-blind lineup procedures, and these jurisdictions only implemented the double-blind requirement since 2001 based on significant pressure and education by eyewitness researchers.[2] Apparently, the need for double-blind lineups was not at

---

[2]   These jurisdictions are New Jersey (all), North Carolina (most), Wisconsin (most), Boston, Minneapolis, and some scattered local jurisdictions in Virginia, Iowa, and California.

all intuitive to these jurisdictions. If the psychological processes influencing eyewitness identification were truly a matter of common knowledge to the inside actors in the legal system (judges, prosecutors, police), would not a rational system have required double-blind lineups? And, if the inside actors in the legal system fail this common knowledge test, why would we expect jurors to have such common knowledge and apply it?

Conclusions

We have described some findings in eyewitness identification that we believe are reliable enough to withstand the challenges of the legal system. We acknowledge that generalization from these findings to actual cases is a judgment call. However, these judgment calls on generalization are facilitated by studying actual cases, conducting field experiments, and by having an underlying conceptual framework for understanding the processes. Some of these findings do not appear to be common knowledge to the average person and, hence, might be beneficial to share with jurors. In the eyewitness identification area, however, it might be more informative to ask what the system itself knows about the variables and processes that affect eyewitness identification. Attributing common knowledge to jurors when that common knowledge appears to not exist in the justice system's primary assumptions and practices seems to be an indictment of the very foundation on which the system often refuses to admit experts.

REFERENCES

Behrman, B. W., & Davey, S. L. (2001). Eyewitness identification in actual criminal cases: An archival analysis. *Law and Human Behavior, 25,* 475–491.

Boring, E. G. (1954). The nature and history of experimental control. *American Journal of Psychology, 67,* 573–589.

Bradfield, A. L., & Wells, G. L. (2000). The perceived validity of eyewitness identification testimony: A test of the five Biggers criteria. *Law and Human Behavior, 24,* 581–594.

Bradfield, A. L., Wells, G. L., & Olson, E. A. (2002). The damaging effect of confirming feedback on the relation between eyewitness certainty and identification accuracy. *Journal of Applied Psychology, 87,* 112–120.

Brewer, N., & Burke, A. (2002). Effects of testimonial inconsistencies and eyewitness confidence on mock juror judgments. *Law and Human Behavior, 26,* 353–364.

174   *Gary L. Wells and Lisa E. Hasel*

Choi, I., & Nisbett, R. E. (2000). Cultural psychology of surprise: Holistic theories and recognition of contradiction. *Journal of Personality and Social Psychology, 79*, 890–905.

Cutler, B. L., & Penrod, S. D. (1995). *Mistaken identification: The eyewitness, psychology, and the law.* New York: Cambridge University Press.

Devenport, J. L., Penrod, S. D., & Cutler, B. L. (1997). Eyewitness identification evidence: evaluating commonsense evaluations, *Psychology, Public Policy, and Law, 3*, 338–361.

Douglass, A. B. & Steblay, N. (2006) *Memory distortion in eyewitnesses: A meta-analysis of the post-identification feedback effect. Applied Cognitive Psychology, 20*, 991–1007.

Doyle, J. M. (2005). *True witness.* New York: Palgrave Macmillan.

Epley, N., & Gilovich, T. (2001). Putting the adjustment back in the anchoring and adjustment heuristic: Differential processing of self-generated and experimenter-provided anchor. *Psychological Science, 12*, 391–396.

Fox, S. G., & Walters, H. A. (1986). The impact of general versus specific expert testimony and eyewitness confidence upon mock juror judgment. *Law and Human Behavior, 10*, 215–228.

Garrioch, L. & Brimacombe, C. A. E. (2001). Lineup administrators' expectations: Their impact on eyewitness confidence. *Law and Human Behavior, 25*, 299–315.

Gilbert, D. T. (1991). How mental systems believe. *American Psychologist, 46*, 107–119.

Hafstad, G. S., Memon, A., & Logie, R. (2004). Post-identification feedback, confidence and recollections of witnessing conditions in child witnesses. *Applied Cognitive Psychology, 18*, 901–912.

Harris, M. J., & Rosenthal, R. (1985). Mediation of interpersonal expectancy effects: 31 meta-analyses. *Psychological Bulletin, 97*, 363–386.

Haw, R. M., & Fisher, R. P. (2004). Effects of administrator-witness contact on eyewitness identification accuracy. *Journal of Applied Psychology, 89*, 1106–1112.

Junkin, T. (2004) *Bloodsworth: The true story of the first death row inmate exonerated by DNA.* Chapel Hill, NC: Algonquin.

Kassin, S. M., & Barndollar, K. A. (1992). The psychology of eyewitness testimony: A comparison of experts and prospective jurors. *Journal of Applied Social Psychology, 22*, 1241–1249.

Kassin, S. M., Tubb, V. A., Hosch, H. M., & Memon, A. (2001). On the "general acceptance" of eyewitness testimony research. *American Psychologist, 56*, 405–416.

Lehman, D. R., Lempert, R. O., & Nisbett, R. E. (1988). The effects of graduate training on reasoning: Formal discipline and thinking about everyday-life events. *American Psychologist, 43*, 431–442.

Meissner, C. A., & Brigham, J. C. (2001). Twenty years of investigating the own-race bias in memory for faces: A meta-analytic review. *Psychology, Public Policy, and Law, 7*, 3–35.

Mill, J. S. (1851). *A system of logic, ratiocinative and inductive: being a connected view of principles of evidence and methods of scientific investigation.* London: J. W. Parker.

Morgan, C. A., Hazlett, G., Doran, A., Garrett, S., Hoyt, G., Thomas, P., Baranoski, M., & Southwick, S. M. (2004) Accuracy of eyewitness memory for persons encountered during exposure to highly intense stress. *International Journal of Psychiatry and the Law, 27,* 265–279.

Munsterberg, H. (1908). *On the witness stand.* New York: Doubleday.

Nisbett, R. E., & Wilson, T. D. (1977). Telling more than we can know: Verbal reports on mental processes. *Psychological Review, 84,* 231–259.

Phillips, M. R., McAuliff, B. D., Kovera, M. B., & Cutler, B. L. (1999). Double-blind photoarray administration as a safeguard against investigator bias. *Journal of Applied Psychology, 84,* 940–951.

Pickel, K. L. (1999). The influence of context on the "weapon focus" effect. *Law and Human Behavior, 23,* 299–311.

Scheck, B., Neufeld, P., & Dwyer, J. (2000). *Actual innocence.* New York: Random House.

Semmler, C., Brewer, N., & Wells, G. L. (2004). Effects of postidentification feedback on eyewitness identification and nonidentification. *Journal of Applied Psychology, 89,* 334–346.

Steblay, N. M. (1992). A meta-analytic review of the weapon focus effect. *Law and Human Behavior, 16,* 413–424.

Steblay, N. M. (1997). Social influence in eyewitness recall: A meta-analytic review of lineup instruction effects. *Law and Human Behavior, 21,* 283–298.

Tversky, A., & Kahneman, D. (1973). Avaliability: A heuristic for judging frequency and probability. *Cognitive Psychology, 5,* 207–232.

Wells, G. L. (1984). How adequate is human intuition for judging eyewitness testimony? In G. L. Wells & E. F. Loftus (Eds.), *Eyewitness testimony: Psychological perspectives* (pp. 256–272). New York: Cambridge University Press.

Wells, G. L. (1988). *Eyewitness identification: A system handbook.* Toronto: Carswell Legal Publications.

Wells, G. L. (2006). Eyewitness identification: Systemic reforms. *Wisconsin Law Review, 2006,* 615–643.

Wells, G. L., & Bradfield, A.L. (1998). "Good, you identified the suspect:" Feedback to eyewitnesses distorts their reports of the witnessing experience. *Journal of Applied Psychology, 83,* 360–376.

Wells, G. L., & Bradfield, A. L. (1999). Distortions in eyewitnesses' recollections: Can the postidentification feedback effect be moderated? *Psychological Science, 10,* 138–144.

Wells, G. L., Lindsay, R. C. L., & Ferguson, T. J. (1979). Accuracy, confidence, and juror perceptions in eyewitness identification. *Journal of Applied Psychology, 64,* 440–448.

Wells, G. L., & Loftus, E. F. (2003). Eyewitness memory for people and events. In A. Goldstein (Ed.). *Comprehensive handbook of psychology*, Vol. 11, Forensic psychology. New York: John Wiley and Sons.

Wells, G. L., & Luus, E. (1990). Police lineups as experiments: Social methodology as a framework for properly-conducted lineups. *Personality and Social Psychology Bulletin, 16*, 106–117.

Wells, G. L., Malpass, R. S., Lindsay, R. C. L., Fisher, R. P., Turtle, J. W., & Fulero, S. (2000). From the lab to the police station: A successful application of eyewitness research. *American Psychologist, 55*, 581–598.

Wells, G. L., & Murray, D. (1984). Eyewitness confidence. In G. L. Wells & E. F. Loftus (Eds.), *Eyewitness testimony: Psychological perspectives*. New York: Cambridge University Press.

Wells, G. L., & Olson, E. (2003). Eyewitness identification. *Annual Review of Psychology, 54*, 277–295.

Wells, G. L., Olson, E., & Charman, S. (2002). Eyewitness identification confidence. *Current Directions in Psychological Science, 11*, 151–154.

Wells, G. L., Olson, E., & Charman, S. (2003). Distorted retrospective eyewitness reports as functions of feedback and delay. *Journal of Experimental Psychology: Applied, 9*, 42–52.

Wright, D. B., & McDaid, A. T. (1996). Comparing system and estimator variables using data from real lineups. *Applied Cognitive Psychology, 10*, 75–84.

Wright, D. B., & Skagerberg, E. M. (2007). Post-identification feedback affects real eyewitnesses. *Psychological Science, 18*, 172–178.

9

Repressed and Recovered Memory

Elizabeth F. Loftus, Maryanne Garry, and Harlene Hayne

In the twentieth century, the notion of repression wormed its way deep into western culture. How? Many scholars point to Freud. Yet Freud was maddeningly vague about repression: As Crews (1995) has long noted, Freud could not decide if what becomes repressed were real events or merely fantasies, or if the repression mechanism operates consciously or unconsciously. The essence of repression is a protective process that shuttles truly disturbing memories, thoughts, or behaviors out of awareness, where they lurk, ready to reappear when the anxiety associated with them is removed through the course of therapy. Fittingly, Freud was also responsible for developing a method to uncover repressed memories – or, as Crews says, Freud "pioneered the modern memory sleuths' technique of thematically matching a patient's symptom with a sexually symmetrical 'memory'."

Although Freud eventually renounced his fuzzy theory, modern therapists repatriated it, adding their own refinements. By the late 1980s many mental health professionals were sure that what was repressed were real memories for real events, and so what was unrepressed were accurate memories of these real events (see, for example, Briere & Conte, 1993; Herman, 1992; Terr, 1988, 1995). The generally accepted view they espoused is that victims of abusive experiences push their traumatic memories for these experiences out of consciousness for some period of time after which the memories resurface in their original, pristine format.

None of us questions the reality of physical and sexual abuse. Far too many children are abused at the hands of people whom they love and trust, and for many, this abuse leaves lasting psychological scars that may remain throughout their lifetime. But the central issue here is whether it is possible for victims of abuse temporarily to banish traumatic memories from consciousness only to have them return, in almost perfect condition, years and sometimes decades later. In our view, scientific research on memory sheds considerable light on the notion of repressed and recovered memories. Here, we review research on the process of forgetting. On the basis of these data, we argue that there is no empirical evidence for repression and that claims of repression (in cases where the event really happened) are merely instances of plain old everyday forgetting. We will also review research on false memories. On the basis of these data we conclude that it is possible (and, in fact, relatively easy) for people to develop memories for events that they have never experienced.

Repression versus Normal Forgetting

The notion of repression taps into at least two widely held but unsupported beliefs about the nature of memory. First, there is a pervasive belief that memory works like a video camera, recording all of our experiences and laying them down in some mental equivalent of a DVD library. In such a view, remembering means locating where the particular DVD is and simply playing it back. Yet there is no credible scientific evidence to support such a belief, and – as we shall see – there is plenty of evidence against it. Yet this view remains widespread (see, for example, Garry, Loftus, Brown, & DuBreuil, 1997; McNally, 2004).

The belief that memory is a veridical record of our past experience fits with the view expressed by some of the most prominent proponents of recovered memory therapy. For example, Terr (1990) wrote: "The memory of trauma is shot with higher intensity light than is ordinary memory. And the film doesn't seem to disintegrate with the usual half-life of ordinary film. Only the best lenses are used, lenses that will pick up every last detail, every line, every wrinkle, and every fleck" (p. 170).

A similar belief was expressed by authors of *The Courage to Heal*. This self-help book is sometimes described as the "bible" of the recovered memory movement (for an excellent review, see Tavris, 1993). First published in 1988 by Bass and Davis, many people who have long been aware of their sexual abuse have found consolation in its pages, but the trouble began with the book's impact on those readers who initially had no memories of abuse. Among the book's implicit assumptions is that the brain stores information permanently, and forgetting is merely an inability to find that stored information. Take, for example, this warning in an early chapter: "If you are unable to remember any specific instances like the ones mentioned above but still have a feeling that something abusive happened to you, it probably did" (p. 21). As alarming as these unsubstantiated claims might seem, readers may be tempted to think that the impact of the book – now nearly 20 years old – has waned. Yet it has not. In the last two months of 2005 alone, *The Courage to Heal* was ranked as highly as 896 among Amazon's book sales (see tictap.com).

Forgetting is one of the oldest topics in the field of psychological science, dating back at least to Ebbinghaus (1885) who first showed the rapid forgetting of newly learned nonsense syllables. More than a century later it is tempting to say sure, Ebbinghaus did research that was interesting for its time, but his work tells us nothing about real life, because in real life our experiences are important, meaningful, and emotional. In fact, the pattern Ebbinghaus discovered actually does tell us about real life. For example, memories for important personal experiences, such as car accidents and hospitalizations, also follow the same rapid and steep forgetting function that Ebbinghaus originally documented for nonsense syllabus. For example, in a nationwide U.S. health survey investigators interviewed 590 people who had been involved in an injury-producing car accident within the previous 12 months. The investigators compared the information that each person reported during the interview with information on the official report from the time of the accident. They found that approximately 14% of the people did not even report being in such an accident. Moreover, as the time between the accident and the interview increased, the number of people who reported having been in a car accident also decreased. By the time 9–12 months had elapsed, more than a quarter of the people failed to report the accident (for a complete description, see Cash & Moss, 1972).

People also often forget even repeated, risky behaviors. For example, Garry, Sharman, Feldman, Marlatt and Loftus (2002) found that college students reported approximately one-third fewer sexual part-ners than they had really had, but reported having far more sex than they had really had. The role of social desirability in their responses was minimized in this study because subjects reported their experi-ences to a computer, and research shows that people report a greater number of sensitive sexual behaviors when interviewed using a com-puter (Turner et al., 1998).

Should we describe these occasions of forgetting of car accidents and sexual encounters as examples of repression? If so, we are left with trying to explain why the need to repress car accidents would increase over time, or why people remembering sex would repress some sexual partners while at the same time remembering that they had more sexual activity than they really had. In short, repression does not provide a parsimonious explanation for the kind of forgetting we all experience, even for significant events in our lives.

There are simple explanations for everyday forgetting. One hypothesis is that unrehearsed information tends to decay more than rehearsed information. Another hypothesis is that some experiences are encoded inadequately to begin with, or some other experience interferes with the memory consolidation process. Despite these perfectly good (and well-documented) explanations for ordinary forgetting, there is still a widespread belief that forgetting means something sinister. Take, for just one example, a national memory survey in the US with over 1,500 respondents. People of all ages and educational backgrounds often said that when people have "spotty" memories, it is usually a sign that something traumatic has happened to them (Garry et al., 1997).

The fact is, we often go through cycles of remembering: We go without thinking about something for a while, then we remember it again, then go without thinking about it, then remember it yet again. The sense of discovering something new when it is really not new may contribute to a belief that one has suddenly uncovered a repressed memory. There is both theoretical and empirical evidence for such a process. Schooler and colleagues (1997) have suggested that at least some instances of memory recovery are the result of people remembering traumatic experiences in qualitatively different ways over the course of their lives. For example, a woman who thinks of her sexual abuse as very disturbing may not recall that a decade earlier she thought of it as only moderately upsetting – thus, she will not remember that she has previously remembered being abused. Schooler and colleagues call this illusion of forgetting the "forgot-it-all-along effect."

More real-life empirical evidence for the forgot-it-all-along effect comes from Read and Lindsay (2000; see also Lindsay & Read, 2006, for an excellent review of related issues). In research that has been used as evidence for repressed and recovered memory, people are said to have experienced amnesia for traumatic events if they say yes to this question: Was there ever a period of time when you remembered less about the event than you do now? (see, for example, Elliot & Briere, 1995). Yet when Read and Lindsay asked people to try to remember more about a long-ago experience such as their high school graduation, they also gave answers that fit with the definition of amnesia. For those who might criticize this study on the grounds that high school graduation is not remotely like childhood sexual abuse, we say – yes, but that is exactly the point. Freud did not propose a mechanism that would repress both terrifying abuse and an everyday coming-of-age ritual.

The second widely held, but unsupported, belief about memory is that despite the presumed clarity of memories for sexual abuse, these memories are highly susceptible to repression, particularly if the abuse is prolonged and extremely traumatic (see Terr, 1991). Yet recent research, in which victims of childhood sexual abuse have been followed prospectively over time, shows that these abusive events are not forgotten. In fact, victims can often provide very accurate accounts of their abuse, even when they are interviewed over long delays (Alexander et al., 2005; Goodman et al., 2003).

It is extremely difficult to study the mechanism of repression in the controlled conditions of the laboratory. The net result of this difficulty is that much of the popular speculation regarding repressed and recovered memory has emerged in the course of clinical practice rather than as a result of empirical research. That is, the "reality" of repressed and recovered memory has been based primarily on clinical intuition rather than on data. For obvious reasons, empirical research on this issue has been practically and ethically difficult to conduct. In order to find genuine evidence that these phenomena exist we would have to meet two criteria. First, we would have to obtain verifiable evidence that the target event took place; second, we would have to obtain verifiable evidence that the memory of the event had been inaccessible for some period of time and then that it was subsequently recovered by a process beyond ordinary forgetting and remembering.

Some researchers have attempted to meet these criteria. For example, Linda Williams (1994) studied 129 women whose parents, suspecting sexual abuse, took them to an emergency room for examination when they were children. Some 17 years later, the women were interviewed about their past, including questions about sexual victimization. Forty-nine – or 38% – of the women did not tell the interviewers of the target incident that had led to their hospital visit. Williams describes her findings as "quite dramatic" (p. 4). Are they? Ofshe and Watters (1994), who rigorously examined the Williams study, say "no." Of the 49 women who did not tell the interviewers about the target incident, 33 described other abuse incidents. Are we to understand that although 49 women had experienced – as Williams told a science journalist – some kind of "amnesia" (Bower, 1993, p. 18), 33 of the women had amnesia for the wrong episode? Again, we emphasize the need for readers to distinguish between ordinary forgetting and something more special: Once we reclassify these 33 women as those who told the interviewer about at least one abuse incident, we are left with 16 women (12%) who did not tell about any abuse, a percentage similar to those who forget car accidents, hospitalisations, or who had "amnesia" for high school graduation.

In 1997 psychiatrist David Corwin and a colleague published a case history that was viewed by many as proof of a recovered memory (Corwin & Olafson, 1997). Corwin interviewed Jane Doe in 1984, when she was five years old, recording his final interview shortly after her sixth birthday. Jane's divorced parents were in the middle of a bitter custody dispute. Jane's father and stepmother accused the mother of sexually and physically abusing Jane, and Corwin was brought in to evaluate these allegations. Corwin met with young Jane three times, videotaping each session. At their final session, Jane told Corwin specific details of abuse at the hands of her mother: She "rubs her finger up my vagina" in the bathtub, and did so "more than twenty times . . . probably ninety-nine times." Jane also told Corwin that her mother had burned her feet (Corwin concludes Jane was burned on a kitchen stove coil). Jane's mother lost both custody and visitation rights.

Eleven years later, when Corwin spoke to Jane during his routine contacts to gain her ongoing consent for him to show the tapes of her earlier interviews, the grownup Jane asked to see them. Although she remembered what she had told Corwin many years earlier, Jane said she was not sure whether what she said was really true. Corwin met with her, and videotaped their session. When he asked Jane if she remembered anything about possible sexual abuse, she said: "No. I mean, I remember that was part of the accusation, but I don't remember anything – wait a minute, yeah, I do." Almost immediately, Jane described an abusive episode in the bathtub, one that – as Neisser (1997) pointed out in his commentary – was different from what she had reported 11 years earlier. Nonetheless, the case of Jane Doe came to be seen as compelling evidence of a repressed and recovered memory.

But Loftus and Guyer (2002a, b) were more sceptical. When they dug into the facts of the case, they discovered that there was never any objective corroborating evidence of Jane's alleged abuse, nor was there any evidence that she had repressed the allegations. There was, however, a nasty custody battle that Jane's stepmother said they won because of the "sexual angle." And the burned feet? Well, not only did Jane's mother not have a stove with coils, but Jane had a hereditary fungal condition that could have caused what looked like a healing burn wound. Furthermore, there was also no evidence that Jane had ever forgotten the allegations of abuse. In fact, both her foster mother and her stepmother reported that Jane talked about these events frequently. At the end of this ordeal what we are left with is a videotape of a young woman's emotional reaction to herself as a child reporting an experience with detail, sincerity, and emotion. Yet none of these factors are related to the accuracy of the original allegations and provide no empirical support for the phenomenon of repressed and recovered memory.

Other researchers have turned their attention to gathering evidence for a neural mechanism for repression. For example, Anderson et al. (2004) asked their subjects to take part in a three-phase experiment. In the first phase, subjects learned 40 word pairs (e.g., ordeal, roach). In the second phase, subjects were cued with one word in the pair (ordeal) and instructed to recall its partner (roach), cued but instructed to suppress the partner, or not cued at all. There were 16 "recall" trials and 16 "suppress" trials. On each of these 32 trials, Anderson and colleagues used fMRI to measure subjects' brain activity. Finally, in the third phase of the experiment, subjects were again instructed to remember words from the first phase, but this time they were cued with an old cue (ordeal) or a new cue that was semantically related to the partner (insect).

Anderson et al. (2004) reported three findings. First, when subjects had tried to recall partner words in phase two, they were better at recalling them in phase three. Second, if they had been instructed to suppress partner words in phase two, they were sometimes – but not always – worse at recalling them in phase three. Third, subjects showed different patterns of brain activity, as measured by fMRI, when they tried to recall words than when they tried to suppress them. For example, when subjects tried to remember words, they showed more activity in the hippocampus; when they tried to suppress words, they showed more activity in other regions. Anderson et al. (2004) concluded that their data fit with Freud's notion of repression, because they show evidence of a "mechanism that pushes unwanted memories out of awareness."

If we look more closely at their data, however, we see that not much of anything was being pushed anywhere. That is, after *not* trying to suppress the partner words, subjects recalled about 87% of them; after trying 16 times to suppress the partner words, subjects recalled about 80% of them. These results raise an important question: If 16 attempts to bury a single word were successful only 7% of the time, how much harder might it be to bury a string of horrible experiences that might have occurred repeatedly throughout childhood?

As for the fMRI results, they too are uninformative. For example, remembering was associated with activity in the hippocampus; this finding is not news. Attempts at suppression were associated with activity in other regions, a finding that might simply reflect subjects' attempts to think about something else, funnelling their cognitive resources to other parts of the brain. In order to adequately interpret the fMRI results, Anderson et al. (2004) needed to provide data on two additional patterns of brain activity, one they could produce and one they probably could not. First, they needed to compare brain activity associated with *successful* attempts to suppress the words with brain activity that is associated with *unsuccessful* attempts to suppress. In their paper, they reported brain activity that reflects the attempt to suppress, regardless of the outcome. Second, they needed to provide a measure of baseline brain activity – that is, brain activity for the uncued words. But they could not, because subjects never had to practice doing anything with those words. The fact that these data are missing means that we cannot compare subjects' brain activity when they attempt to suppress a word with their activity when they are doing nothing to a word. Finally, it is worth noting that Bulevich, Roediger, Balota and Butler (in press) tried several times to replicate Anderson et al.'s findings and could not. That is not to say the suppression effect does not exist. Instead, it means that the effect of suppression is not only small, it is fragile – and hardly the kind of mechanism that Judith Herman (1992) had in mind when she wrote that "the ordinary response to atrocities is to banish them from consciousness" (p. 1).

False Memories

Another way of understanding claims of repressed and recovered memory is to investigate whether there are certain techniques that help people "recover" memories for experiences that never really happened. In other words, if people can produce what looks like a recovered memory and it feels like recovered memory, but is really only a false memory, then such a result would call into question the validity of other memories reported under similar circumstances.

For a long time we have known that it is possible to alter the details of subjects' memories for events they have witnessed (for a review see Belli & Loftus, 1996), but in 1995, Loftus and Pickrell (see also Loftus, 1993) asked whether it was also possible for subjects to create a coherent and detailed memory for something they never did. Their design was simple: They recruited people in pairs; both members of each pair belonged to the same family. One family member became a confederate, whose job it was to tell the experimenters about some real events that the other family member – who became the subject – had experienced during childhood. The subject received a booklet containing short written descriptions of several childhood events: three true ones that the confederate had supplied, and one false one, about getting lost in a shopping mall. The confederate helped the experimenters create a description of the false event, supplying them with idiosyncratic details about which shopping mall, who was at the mall, and so on. Despite these idiosyncratic details, the main features of the false event were always the same: The subject became lost, and was eventually found by an elderly lady who helped to reunite the family.

Over three sessions, the subjects reported what they could remember about each event. By the end of the study, approximately one quarter of the subjects had created a partial or full false memory of being lost in the mall as a child. Even when they had been told the real purpose of the study, some subjects found it hard to believe the memory was false.

These lost-in-the-mall studies were the first demonstrations that entirely false memories could be implanted in people's autobiographies. Other scientists adopted the paradigm, and showed that false memories could be implanted for events as diverse as causing mayhem at a family wedding (Hyman, Husband, & Billings, 1995), being attacked by an animal (Porter, Yuille, & Lehman, 1999), and being rescued from drowning by a lifeguard (Heaps & Nash, 2001).

Now, more than 10 years after the publication of the first lost-in-the-mall study, it is easy to underestimate the importance of this line of research in helping to change beliefs about the validity of suddenly remembered *repressed* memories. Yet as recently as the early 1990s, there was very little scientific evidence that there could be a systematic means to implant false events in memory. In fact, it was common for nonscientists to claim that even the cumulative weight of memory studies – dating back 100 years – told us nothing about memory for real experiences, let alone traumatic ones. For example, "trauma sets up new rules for memory," wrote Terr (1990, p. 52).

Even some scientists thought the implanted false events were too ordinary, too plausible, to shed much light on recovered memories for the kinds of significant experiences that led people to court. Take Pezdek, Finger, and Hodge (1997) for example. They hypothesized that it would be very difficult to implant a false memory for an implausible event, and set about trying to get subjects to remember receiving a rectal enema in childhood. No one did. Thus, concluded Pezdek et al., false memories can be implanted for plausible experiences, but not for implausible ones, which they must have assumed included sexual abuse.

One problem with such a conclusion is that, of course in real life, people actually do falsely remember implausible experiences, such as being abducted by aliens, or tortured by a satanic cult. Thus, Mazzoni, Loftus, and Kirsch (2001) suggested that instead of asking if people can develop plausible false memories, it would be better to ask how they come to do so. Mazzoni et al. (2001) found that when they exposed people to information about an implausible experience – witnessing demonic possession – it became more plausible. Eventually, 18% of subjects were confident that it had probably happened to them.

Considered as a whole, a large body of research now shows that remarkably simple techniques (i.e., talking about a past event or reading about someone else's experience) can implant false memories. Increasingly, we have at our disposal an arsenal of even more sophisticated techniques that might also foster false memories of prior experiences. For example, it was not so long ago that only movie producers and criminal conspirators had the tools to doctor photographs. These days, nearly everyone has a desktop computer, digital camera, and image editing software, and removing an old boyfriend from a photo is almost as easy as removing red-eye. Does changing the photographic documentation of an event change memory itself? More to the point, can creating a photograph of a false event create memory for it?

Wade, Garry, Read, and Lindsay (2002) designed an experiment to answer these questions. Wade et al. (2002) adapted the lost-in-the-mall method originally described by Loftus and Pickrell (1995), but replaced the narratives with photographs: The false event was a doctored photo showing the subject and family members on a hot air balloon ride, an event that family members confirmed was false. To create the doctored photograph, Wade et al. cobbled together real photographs of the subject, other family members, and a dummy photograph of a hot air balloon. After three interviews in which subjects tried to remember the experience, 50% came to remember at least some details about the ride. These reports were often richly detailed, and when subjects were debriefed, they tended to express astonishment that the balloon ride never happened.

In a follow-up study, Garry and Wade (2005) compared the relative effects of narratives and photographs on the development of false memories. They showed half of the subjects a doctored photograph of the balloon ride, and provided the other half with a written narrative describing the ride. Garry and Wade made sure that subjects received the same amount of information about each event by asking judges to extract all the information they could from the balloon photograph, and then using that information to create the narrative. By the end of the study, one medium proved to be the clear winner in its ability to cultivate false memories – but it was the narratives. Eighty percent of the subjects who read a false narrative came to remember at least some details about their false hot air balloon ride, compared with 50% of those who saw the photo. In addition, when Garry and Wade (2005) asked their subject which medium worked better to "jog" their memories, narrative subjects said photos worked better, while photo subjects said narratives worked better. This interesting crossover effect may reflect a process similar to what Winkielman, Schwarz, & Belli (1998) found when they asked people to remember either a few or many childhood experiences. That is, when people find it difficult to remember something, they often make the wrong attributions about the source of that difficulty.

As interesting as these doctored photo studies may be, the fact is that most people do not encounter massively doctored photos of false events; instead, they routinely review undoctored (or cosmetically enhanced) photos of real events. Can exposure to real photographs hurt our memories? To answer this question, Lindsay, Hagen, Read, Wade, and Garry (2004) examined the power of a real photograph to elicit a false memory. They adapted the lost-in-the-mall method, and asked subjects to remember three primary school experiences from different years. Two of the experiences really happened, but the third one did not. In this false event, the subject got in trouble for putting Slime (the goopy green children's toy) into the teacher's desk drawer. All subjects read a summary of each event, but half of them also received a memory aid – a real class photo from the year that each event happened. Lindsay et al. found that just under half of the summary-only subjects reported something about the Slime episode, but more than 70% of the summary-plus-photo subjects did. In short, even our real photographs can play havoc with memory.

While some research has used pseudodocumentation– narratives or photographs ostensibly provided by family members – to suggest a false event, other research has examined the role of more subtle techniques in changing people's autobiography. For example, imagining what might have happened during childhood was a staple strategy in many abuse recovery books and it was also one of the tools in recovered-memory therapists' toolboxes. A key feature of these imagination techniques is visualizing how one might have been abused without worrying about the accuracy of that scenario (e.g., Bass & Davis, 1988). Garry, Manning, Loftus, and Sherman (1996) wondered whether this exercise could play havoc with memory.

To address this issue, Garry et al. (1996) asked their subjects to review a list of childhood events and to report their confidence that each of those events had happened. Later, subjects briefly imagined some of the events from the list but not others. Finally, Garry et al. asked their subjects to redo their answers to the questions, falsely claiming that the original tests had been misplaced. Compared with childhood events that they did not imagine, subjects became more confident that the events they imagined really did happen. Garry et al. referred to this confidence-boosting increase as *imagination inflation*. Their results suggest that imagining a childhood event, even for only a few minutes, is an extremely powerful technique in altering our confidence that these events actually took place.

Other research has since produced imagination inflation using a variety of materials and situations (Heaps & Nash, 1999; Paddock et al., 1999). For example, we have learned that imagination inflation is not limited to long ago experiences; inflation can also happen to recent experiences and to bizarre experiences. Moreover, the more times subjects imagine an experience, and the more sensory details they add into their imaginings, the more inflation we can expect (Goff & Roediger, 1998; Thomas, Bulevich, & Loftus, 2003; Thomas & Loftus, 2002). In fact, more recent studies have shown that imagination is not necessary to produce imagination inflation-type effects. Instead, similar increases in confidence can be induced by asking subjects to paraphrase sentences (Sharman, Garry, & Beuke, 2004), or by asking them to solve anagrams (Bernstein, Godfrey, Davison, & Loftus, 2004; Bernstein, Whittlesea, & Loftus, 2002), rather than imagining the target event. It may be, then, that any process that exposes people to a "what if" scenario can produce inflation.

The fact that there are many routes to imagination inflation is especially worrying considering the research showing that false beliefs can morph into memory. For example, Mazzoni and Memon (2003) convinced subjects in the UK that when they were children, a nurse took a skin sample from their little finger to carry out some kind of national health test – but the test was entirely false. Imagining the experience led subjects to become more confident that it had really happened to them and some of those subjects developed false memories that were rich with sensory detail. These findings show that imagination by itself does not merely inflate confidence that a false event was real; in some cases, it can produce memories for that false event.

How Strong Is the Evidence?

As we have reported here, evidence to support the phenomenon of repression is circumstantial at best, with claims for its validity more a matter of clinical faith than scientific reality. In short, the lack of empirical evidence for the phenomenon should leave any jury in a chronic state of "reasonable doubt" when faced with a claim of repressed and recovered memory of abuse. Yet recent research suggests juries might arrive at reasonable doubt only with the assistance of an expert witness. In a survey of people with various roles in the criminal justice system, Benton, Ross, Bradshaw, Thomas, and Bradshaw (2006) found that 73% of jurors, 50% of judges, and 65% of police officers believed in the concept of repression (Kassin, Tubb, Hosch, & Memon, 2001). Thus, despite considerable progress in unraveling the myths of repressed and recovered memory, current scientific findings have yet to work their way down to the coal face of the courtroom, a state of affairs that argues for the presence of an expert witness to assist triers-of-fact in understanding the empirical literature.

What about agreement within the psychological community? Benton et al.'s (2006) survey data gives us part of the answer: Only 22% of psychological scientists believe that there is evidence to support the notion of repression. Within the wider community of researchers from various disciplines, however, there is more dissent. For example, although there is mounting evidence that it is possible for otherwise reasonable, well-adjusted people to develop memories for events that never really happened, some early critics downplayed the strength of the evidence by arguing that "it seems to be impossible to 'implant' vivid flashbacks of imaginary events into human beings" (van der Kolk, McFarlane, & Weisaeth, 1996, p. 567). Other critics argued that it was inappropriate to draw conclusions about clinically relevant memories on the basis of laboratory research for personally irrelevant events (Freyd & Gleaves, 1996; cf., Roediger & McDermott, 1995). But the corpus of data collected to date clearly refutes these early arguments. The research we have reviewed in this chapter shows that some adults do develop vivid false memories for personally relevant experiences. Furthermore, some of the most effective false-memory induction techniques (such as conversation, imagination, and dream interpretation) are the same techniques that feature over and over again in cases of repressed and recovered memory.

Unfortunately for the legal system, there is no reliable way to listen to a memory report and judge whether it is true or false. The simple fact is, false memories often – although not always – feel to people like their real memories do. Although Loftus and Pickrell (1995) found that their subjects used fewer words when describing being lost in the mall than when describing their memories of real experiences and that they rated their memory of the false event as less clear than their memory for real events, Lindsay et al. (2004) found no difference in the quality of people's true and false memories. Lindsay et al. asked their subjects to rate the three events they talked about in terms of their sense of reliving when describing the event, the degree to which they felt as if they were remembering it, and their confidence that the event really happened. Those subjects who developed a false memory of putting Slime in the teacher's desk rated their true and false memories the same way on these three scales. In fact, even people's physiological responses to their false memories resemble the physiological responses typically seen in response to real trauma. For example, when McNally et al. (2004) asked people who claimed to have been abducted by aliens to remember their abduction experience, the pattern of physiological responses they exhibited was similar to that exhibited by people diagnosed with Post-Traumatic Stress Disorder (PTSD) who were asked to recall real traumatic experiences.

Conclusion

In conclusion, repressed memory appears to be a notion that lacks credible empirical support. When allegedly repressed memories are reported, especially after suggestive psychotherapy, we need to worry that false-memory induction could be at the root. Future research in this area will help to identify those individuals who may be most susceptible to developing false memories as well as the range of therapeutic techniques that might be the most dangerous. In the meantime, the legal system ought to treat with skepticism expert testimony from mental health professionals who claim that repression exists.

REFERENCES

Alexander, K. W., Quas, J. A., Goodman, G. S., Ghetti, S., Edelstein, R. S., Redlich, A. D., Cordon, I. M., & Jones, D. P. H. (2005). Traumatic impact predicts long-term memory for documented child sexual abuse. *Psychological Science, 16,* 33–40.

Anderson, M. C., Ochsner, K. N., Kuhl, B., Cooper, J., Robertson, E., Gabrilei, S. W., Glover, G. H., & Gabrieli, J. D. E. (2004). Neural systems underlying the suppression of unwanted memories. *Science, 303,* 232–235.

Bass, E., & Davis, L. (1988). *The courage to heal.* New York: Harper & Row.

Belli, R. F., & Loftus, E. F. (1996). The pliability of autobiographical memory: Misinformation and the false memory problem. In D. C. Rubin (Ed.), Remembering our past: Studies in autobiographical memory (pp. 157–179). New York: Cambridge University Press.

Benton, T. R., Ross, D. F., Bradshaw, E., Thomas, W. N., & Bradshaw, G. S. (2006). Eyewitness memory is still not common sense: Comparing jurors, judges and law enforcement to eyewitness experts. *Applied Cognitive Psychology, 20,* 115–129.

Bernstein, D. M., Godfrey, R. D., Davison, A., & Loftus, E. F. (2004). Conditions affecting the revelation effect for autobiographical memory. *Memory & Cognition, 32,* 455–462.

Bernstein, D. M., Whittlesea, B. W. A., & Loftus, E. F. (2002). Increasing confidence in remote autobiographical memory and general knowledge: Extensions of the revelation effect. *Memory & Cognition, 30,* 432–438.

Bower, B. (1993). Sudden recall. *Science News, 144,* 184–186.

Briere, J., & Conte, J. (1993). Self-reported amnesia in adults molested as children. *Journal of Traumatic Stress, 6,* 21–31.

Bulevich, J. B., Roediger, H. L., Balota, D. A., & Butler, A. C. (in press). Failures to find suppression of episodic memories in the think/no-think paradigm. *Memory & Cognition.*

Cash, W. S., & Moss, A. J. (1972, April). Optimum recall period for reporting persons injured in motor vehicle accidents. (U.S. Public Health Service, DHEW-HSM Publication No. 72–1050). Washington, DC: U.S. Government Printing Office.

Corwin, D. L., & Olafson, E. (1997). Videotaped discovery of a reportedly unrecallable memory of child sexual abuse: Comparison with a childhood interview videotaped 11 years before. *Child Maltreatment, 2,* 91–112.

Crews, F. C. (1995). *The memory wars: Freud's legacy in dispute.* New York: The New York Review of Books.

Ebbinghaus, H. (1885) *Uber das Gedachtris.* Leipzig: Dunker. (Trans. H. Ruyer & C. E. Bussenius, Memory. New York: Teachers College Press, 1913).

Elliot, D. M., & Briere, J. (1995). Posttraumatic stress associated with delayed recall of sexual abuse: A general population study. *Journal of Traumatic Stress, 8,* 629–647.

Freyd, J. J., & Gleaves, D. H. (1996). "Remembering" words not presented in lists: Relevance to the current recovered/false memory controversy.

Journal of Experimental Psychology: Learning, Memory, and Cognition, 22, 811–813.

Garry, M., Loftus, E. F., Brown, S. W., & DuBreuil, S. C. (1997). Womb with a view: Beliefs about memory, repression and memory-recovery. In P. Conrad (Ed.), *Intersections in Basic and Applied Memory Research* (pp. 233–255). Hillsdale, NJ: Lawrence Erlbaum Associates.

Garry, M., Manning, C. G., Loftus, E. F., & Sherman, S. (1996). Imagination inflation: Imagining a childhood event inflates confidence that it occurred. *Psychonomic Bulletin & Review, 3,* 208–214.

Garry, M., Sharman, S. J., Feldman, J. Marlatt, G. A., & Loftus, E. F. (2002). Examining memory for heterosexual college students' sexual experiences using an electronic mail diary. *Health Psychology, 21,* 629–634.

Garry, M., & Wade, K. A. (2005). Actually, a picture is worth less than 45 words: Narratives produce more false memories than photographs do. *Psychonomic Bulletin & Review, 12,* 359–366.

Goff, L. M., & Roediger, H. L. III. (1998). Imagination inflation for action events: repeated imaginings lead to illusory recollections. *Memory & Cognition, 26,* 20–33.

Goodman, G. S., Ghetti, S., Quas, J. A., Edelstein, R. S., Alexander, K. W., Redlich, A. D., Cordon, I. M., & Jones, D. P. H. (2003). A prospective study of memory for child sexual abuse: New findings relevant to the repressed-memory controversy. *Psychological Science, 14,* 113–117.

Heaps, C. M., & Nash, M. (1999). Individual differences in imagination inflation. *Psychonomic Bulletin & Review, 6,* 313–318.

Heaps, C. M., & Nash, M. (2001). Comparing recollective experience in true and false autobiographical memories. *Journal of Experimental Psychology: Learning, Memory, and Cognition, 27,* 920–930.

Herman, J. L. (1992). *Trauma and recovery.* New York: Basic Books.

Hyman, I. E., Husband, T. H., & Billings, F. J. (1995). False memories of childhood experiences. *Applied Cognitive Psychology, 9,* 181–197.

Kassin, S. M., Tubb, V. A., Hosch, H. M., & Memon, A. (2001). On the "general acceptance" of eyewitness testimony research. *American Psychologist, 56,* 405–416.

Lindsay, D. S., Hagen, L., Read, J. D., Wade, K. A., & Garry, M. (2004). True photographs and false memories. *Psychological Science, 15,* 149–154.

Lindsay, D. S., & Read, J. D. (2006). Adults' memories of long-past events. In L. G. Nilsson & N. Ohta (Eds.), *Memory and society: Psychological perspectives* (pp. 51–72). New York: Psychology Press.

Loftus, E. F. (1993) The reality of repressed memories. *American Psychologist, 48,* 518–537.

Loftus, E. F., & Guyer, M. (2002a). Who abused Jane Doe?: The hazards of the single case history, Part I, *Skeptical Inquirer,* Vol. 26, No. 3 (May/June), 24–32.

Loftus, E. F., & Guyer, M. J. (2002b). Who abused Jane Doe? Part II. *Skeptical Inquirer,* Vol. 26, No. 4 (July/August), 37–40, 44.

Loftus, E. F., & Pickrell, J. E. (1995). The formation of false memories. *Psychiatric Annals, 25,* 720–725.

Mazzoni, G. A. L., Loftus, E. F., & Kirsch, I. (2001). Changing beliefs about implausible autobiographical events: A little plausibility goes a long way. *Journal of Experimental Psychology: Applied, 7,* 51–59.

Mazzoni, G., & Memon, A. (2003). Imagination can create false autobiographical memories. *Psychological Science, 14,* 186–188.

McNally, R. J. (2004). The science and folklore of traumatic amnesia. *Clinical Psychology: Science and Practice, 11,* 29–33.

McNally, R. J., Lasko, N. B., Clancy, S. A., Macklin, M. L., Pitman, R. K., & Orr, S. P. (2004). Psychophysiologic responding during script-driven imagery in people reporting abduction by space aliens. *Psychological Science, 15,* 493–497.

Neisser, U. (1997). Jane Doe's memories: Changing the past to serve the present. *Child Maltreatment, 2,* 123–125.

Ofshe, R., & Watters, E. (1994). *Making monsters: False memories, psychotherapy, and sexual hysteria.* Los Angeles: University of California Press.

Paddock, J. R., Noel, M., Terranova, S., Eber, H. W., Manning, C., & Loftus, E. F. (1999). Imagination inflation and the perils of guided visualization. *Journal of Psychology, 133,* 581–595.

Pezdek, K., Finger, K., & Hodge, D. (1997). Planting false childhood memories: The role of event plausibility. *Psychological Science, 8,* 437–441.

Porter, S., Yuille, J. C., & Lehman, D. R. (1999). The nature of real, implanted and fabricated memories for emotional childhood events: Implications for the false memory debate. *Law & Human Behavior, 23,* 517–538.

Read, J. D., & Lindsay, D. S. (2000). "Amnesia" for summer camps and high school graduation: Memory work increases reports of prior periods of remembering less. *Journal of Traumatic Stress, 13,* 129–147.

Roediger, H. L. III., & McDermott, K. B. (1995). Creating false memories: Remembering words not presented in lists. *Journal of Expeirmental Psychology: Learning, Memory, and Cognition, 21,* 803–814.

Schooler, J. W., Ambadar, Z., & Bendiksen, M. (1997). A cognitive corroborative case study approach for investigating discovered memories of sexual abuse. In J. D. Read & D. S. Lindsay (Eds.), *Recollections of trauma: Scientific evidence and clinical practice* (pp. 379–387). New York: Plenum Press.

Sharman, S. J., Garry, M., & Beuke, C. J. (2004). Imagination or exposure causes imagination inflation. *American Journal of Psychology, 117,* 157–168.

Tavris, C. (1993). Beware the incest-survivor machine. *The New York Times Book Review.* January 3, p. 1.

Terr, L. (1988). What happens to early memories of trauma? A study of 20 children under age five at the time of documented traumatic events.

Journal of the American Academy of Child and Adolescent Psychiatry, 27, 96–104.

Terr, L. C. (1990). *Too scared to cry.* New York: Harper & Row.

Terr, L. (1991). Childhood traumas: An outline and overview. *American Journal of Psychiatry, 148,* 10–20.

Terr, L. (1995). *Unchained memories: True stories of traumatic memories, lost, and found.* New York: Basic Books.

Thomas, A. K., Bulevich, J. B., & Loftus, E. F. (2003). Exploring the role of repetition and sensory elaboration in the imagination inflation effect. *Memory & Cognition, 31,* 630–640.

Thomas, A. K., & Loftus, E. F. (2002). Creating bizarre false memories through imagination. *Memory & Cognition, 30,* 423–431.

Turner, C. F., Ku, L., Rogers, S. M., Lindberg, L. D., Pleck, J. H., & Sonenstein, F. L. (1998, May 8). Adolescent sexual behavior, drug use, and violence: Increased reporting with computer survey technology. *Science, 280,* 867–873.

van der Kolk, B. A., McFarlane, A. C., & Weisaeth, L. (1996). *Traumatic stress: The effects of overwhelming experience on mind, body, and society.* New York: The Guilford Press.

Wade, K. A., Garry, M., Read, J. D., & Lindsay, D. S. (2002). A picture is worth a thousand lies. *Psychonomic Bulletin & Review, 9,* 597–603.

Williams, L. M. (1994). Recall of childhood trauma: A prospective study of women's memories of child sexual abuse. *Journal of Consulting and Clinical Psychology, 62,* 1167–1176.

Winkielman, P., Schwarz, N., & Belli, R. F. (1998). The role of ease of retrieval and attribution in memory judgments: Judging your memory as worse despite recalling more events. *Psychological Science, 9,* 124–126.

10

Expert Testimony on the Psychology of Confessions: A Pyramidal Framework of the Relevant Science

Saul M. Kassin

Increasingly, psychologists are being called to serve as consultants and expert witnesses in criminal cases involving coerced – and possibly false – confessions.[1] In some instances, the main purpose is to assess a defendant's competence or vulnerability, an inquiry that brings into focus individual characteristics such as age, intelligence, mental health, criminal justice experience, and personality traits such as interrogative compliance and suggestibility. In other instances, the main purpose is to evaluate the social influence conditions under which the accused waived his or her *Miranda* rights and then confessed. This latter inquiry brings into play a number of foundational principles of psychology and, more specifically, social psychology.

The trials and tribulations of John Kogut, Dennis Halstead, and John Restivo are a case in point. In 1986, largely on the basis of his confession, Kogut and the two other young men that he had implicated were tried for the rape and murder of a 16-year-old girl. Two trials were held in Nassau County, New York, at which these defendants were convicted and sentenced to prison. They remained incarcerated for 17 years until DNA tests on the semen originally recovered from the victim's body conclusively excluded all three men, rendering the confession an inaccurate description of the crime. Through the

---

[1] There is no way to determine the precise number of times that experts have testified on confessions because a record for appeal is created only in cases in which experts have been excluded or limited in their testimony (for a review, see Fulero, 2004). Through an informal, unpublished survey of 12 known experts in the area, which I conducted in 2005, I found that there were 335 reported instances of testimony in federal and military courts and in 36 different states (some were at suppression hearings; some at postconviction relief hearings; most in jury and bench trials).

intervention of the Innocence Project, the convictions were vacated in 2003. Shortly afterward, however, the district attorney – unwilling to concede that the original confession was false, and despite the absence of additional evidence – decided to retry Kogut, the confessor.

If successful, the district attorney would have established a danger-ous precedent, being the first to reconvict someone of a crime for which they had been exonerated by DNA evidence. In anticipation of this trial, Kogut's legal defense team, led by Centurion Ministries, proffered expert testimony on the psychology of confessions. The intended and circumscribed purpose of this testimony was not to offer an *ultimate opinion* as to whether the original confession had been true or false but to educate the judge or jury about general principles of relevance to making this assessment. The district attorney's office objected, arguing that the subject matter did not pass New York's criterion of "general acceptance" within the scientific community. The court thus granted a *Frye* hearing "to determine whether the meth-odology of social psychology was generally accepted and whether the voluntariness of the defendant's confession was a proper subject of expert testimony." Occurring through the spring and summer of 2005, this hotly contested hearing contained testimony from 4 experts, took 12 days to complete, and generated 1,734 pages of transcript. It also attracted a great deal of news coverage (including a story by ABC *Primetime*) and was accompanied by a surprising press release in which the Nassau County district attorney advocated for the first time the videotaping of interrogations.

On September 15, 2005, Judge Victor Ort released an 11-page opinion in which he ruled that ". . . psychological studies on the vol-untariness of confessions generally and the phenomenon of eliciting false confessions will be admissible at trial" (*People of the State of New York v. Kogut*, 2005, p. 10). The judge specifically concluded that the methodology and analysis are generally accepted within the field, and that jurors, who presume that innocent persons would not confess to crimes they did not commit, would benefit from the resulting testi-mony. Addressing the prosecutor's expert, the judge stated: "The fact that social psychology is not yet able to plot the curve showing the relationship between the decision to confess and the variables involved does not rebut the significance of Dr. Kassin's findings" (p. 9).[2]

---

[2]   Subsequent to this ruling, the defendant waived his right to a jury in favor of a bench trial. The expert testimony was admitted, as ruled, and the defendant was acquit-ted. At that point, the charges against Halstead and Restivo, the other men initially convicted and imprisoned because of Kogut's false confession, were dismissed.

Different standards are used to determine the admissibility of expert testimony. In New York and several other states, the classic and conservative *Frye* test (1923) states that to be admissible expert testimony must conform to generally accepted principles within a discipline (*Frye v. United States*, 1923). The Federal Rules of Evidence (FRE), codified in 1975, shifted the emphasis, stating that expert testimony is admissible if the expert is qualified, if the testimony is reliable, and if the testimony assists the trier of fact. In *Daubert v. Merrell Dow Pharmaceuticals, Inc.* (1993), the U.S. Supreme Court urged trial judges to serve as even more active gatekeepers of scientific evidence by ascertaining for themselves whether an expert proffers information that is scientific – as measured by such criteria as being testable, falsifiable, peer reviewed, reliable, valid, and generally accepted (for a discussion of *Daubert* and its implications, see Faigman & Monahan, 2005).

Using the *Frye* hearing in the Kogut case as an illustration, this chapter is written with three objectives in mind. The first is to propose a three-tiered *pyramidal framework* for conceptualizing a body of relevant psychology. The second is to more fully develop this framework by illustrating its use in the psychology of interviewing, interrogation, the elicitation of confessions, and their consequences. The third objective is to address a relevant legal question concerning expert testimony that is extrinsic to this framework – a question concerning the extent to which expert testimony is needed or whether lay jurors are sufficiently informed as a matter of common sense.

The Pyramid: General Framework

It is both accurate and important to represent the corpus of expert knowledge on confessions in the form of a three-tiered pyramid – with individual cases at the vertex; relevant core principles of psychology at the base; and content-specific forensic research in the middle. Indeed, this three-tiered pyramidal framework brings to the forefront a means of depicting any body of knowledge and is implicit in all subdisciplines of forensic psychology. Whether the subject matter is eyewitness testimony, race or gender discrimination, rape trauma syndrome, or confessions, experts have routinely sought to link real-world instances of a phenomenon to basic principles of psychology and, when available, to research specifically aimed at hypothesis-testing in a particular context.

At the vertex, unconnected to science, are actual accounts of post-conviction DNA exonerations, litigated acts of discrimination, instances of rape and other forms of crime victimization, and the like. As reported in books, newspapers, magazines, and television documentaries, these stories may shock the public conscience and reveal that these events occur, with some unknown frequency; that they share certain common features; and that they seem more common in some types of people and in some settings than in others. Knowing that concrete and vivid anecdotes are persuasive, psychological experts testifying in court will often use these accounts to illustrate key points.

Depending on the subject matter, individual case data can be derived from first- and secondhand case materials such as police reports, medical and forensic tests, trial testimony, employment records, and victim interviews from a single case. This is the part of the pyramid that is visible to the public, but without scientific explanation as to causes or correlates. Case studies have served an invaluable purpose in the history of psychology. Through the study of split brain patients, child prodigies, amnesiacs, great leaders, lucid dreamers, chess masters, and others who are exceptional in some way, the in-depth study of single cases has provided a basis for generating theories to be tested by more systematic means.

At the base of the pyramid is the warehouse of core psychological principles, research findings, and propositions. The product of theory testing, this warehouse contains the basic research of psychological science – from the nineteenth-century laws of psychophysics to twenty-first century advances in the neuroimaging of perception and memory, the social-cognitive roots of stereotyping and prejudice, and the consequences of posttraumatic stress and other disorders. Designed for theory testing, the core is rich in context-free research collected in laboratory settings and built to maximize internal validity. It is common, in the early (some would say, "premature") growth stages of an applied science, for writers and expert witnesses to rely exclusively on core principles, leaping from the laboratory to the setting to be predicted. This was evident in the modern but early days of the eyewitness area, where experts testified about arousal, weapon focus, and the other-race bias on the basis of general theories of attention and memory, and basic laboratory experiments, even before these propositions had been tested in a forensic context.

The middle, linkage, part of the pyramid is always the last to develop within an applied science. Assuming the importance of the problem revealed by the cases at the vertex, and in recognition of the external validity limits inherent in the core principles and basic research, researchers interested in a forensic subdiscipline conduct content-specific research that is inspired by actual cases and resembles in mundane ways the settings and behaviors in question. For example, in the eyewitness area, which is at a relatively advanced stage of maturity, this transition from a reliance on core principles to content-specific research was seen, over the past quarter century, in the numerous studies by Wells and Lindsay and their colleagues, Malpass, Brigham, and others, and was marked by a shift from the study of estimator variables to system variables (Wells, 1978; for an historical overview, see Doyle, 2005). Currently, when experts testify about lineup composition, instructions, and presentation format, they do so by relying on realistic, content-specific forensic studies. At this point in the development of a domain, one might argue that this middle level of the pyramid renders the base less relevant.

The Pyramid: Psychology of Confessions

A three-tiered pyramidal framework can be used to depict any body of knowledge of relevance to forensic psychology. In the remainder of this chapter, the burgeoning study of police interviewing, interrogations, and confessions will be used to illustrate this framework (see figure 10.1; for more comprehensive reviews of this literature, see Gudjonsson, 1992, 2003; Kassin, 1997, 2005; Kassin & Gudjonsson, 2004; Wrightsman & Kassin, 1993).

At the vertex: The archives of proven false confessions

Beginning with the Salem witch trials of the seventeenth century, the landscape of American legal history is littered with erroneous convictions of innocent men and women who were prosecuted, wrongfully convicted, and sentenced to prison or death because of confessions to crimes they did not commit. There are four ways in which confessions are proved false: (1) It turns out that the confessed crime did not occur; (2) the real perpetrator is apprehended; (3) postconfession evidence reveals that the confessor's story was physically impossible; and (4) DNA or other exculpatory evidence is discovered.

Although numerous confessions have been proven false without dispute, a precise prevalence rate of the problem is not known, and is likely not knowable. What is clear, however, is that 12% of prisoners who were interrogated, 3–4% of college students, and 1–2% of older university students self-report having given false confessions to police (Gudjonsson, 2003); and that 20–25% of all DNA exonerations had

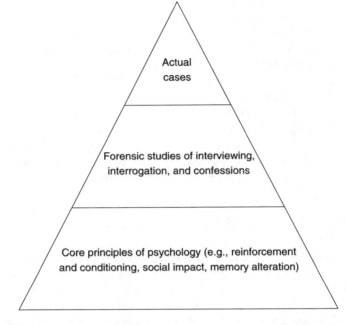

Figure 10.1   Pyramidal model of expert testimony on confessions

contained confessions in evidence (Scheck, Neufeld, & Dwyer, 2000; www.innocenceproject.org/). Importantly, these discovered cases represent only the tip of a much larger iceberg, as they do not take into account the many false confessions that are quietly rejected by police or prosecutors before trial, false confessions to minor crimes that result in guilty pleas, and false confessions in juvenile proceedings that are confidential (Drizin & Leo, 2004).

At the top of this pyramid are the horror stories of false confessions taken from juveniles and other vulnerable suspect populations and in the presence of prolonged detention and isolation, deprivation of needs, physical discomfort, implicit or explicit promises and threats, and various high-influence tactics of police interrogation. Over the years, case studies of this nature have proved useful in the development of this research area. By comparing and contrasting several known cases throughout history, for example, and by drawing on theories of social influence, Kassin and Wrightsman (1985) introduced a taxonomy that distinguished among three types of false confessions. *Voluntary* false confessions are self-incriminating statements offered without external pressure. Coerced-*compliant* false confessions are those in which a suspect confesses in order to escape an aversive interrogation, avoid an explicit or implied threat, or gain a promised or implied reward. This confession is a mere act of public compliance by a suspect who knows that he or she is truly innocent. Third, coerced-*internalized* false confessions are those in which an innocent but vulnerable person – in response to certain highly suggestive procedures – comes to believe that he or she committed the crime, sometimes forming a false memory in the process. This classification scheme has provided a useful framework for the study of false confessions and has been widely used and refined by others.

In short, the study of actual cases has proved informative, revealing that false confessions occur with some unknown frequency, in different ways, and for different reasons; that they share certain common features; and that they seem to be associated with the presence of some conditions, indicating potential risk factors, more than others. Of course, no analysis of these cases can afford conclusions concerning the causal nexus of factors associated with the elicitation of confessions.

At the base: Relevant core principles of psychology

In the scientific study of confessions, it is important for experts to communicate to the courts that our relevant knowledge is firmly grounded not only in content-specific research but in universally accepted core principles of psychology. This is an important point because opponents will try to force experts in this area to construe the field in the narrowest of terms – terms that exclude the 100-plus years of knowledge that forms the base of the pyramid.

Depending on the fact pattern of a particular case involving a disputed confession, there are numerous basic phenomena that may prove relevant – for example, pertaining to the effects of isolation, stress, alcohol, childhood and adolescence, false evidence, and the processing of pragmatic implications (as when leniency in exchange for confession is implied by minimization tactics). For example, the scientific research literature on sleep deprivation is relevant in a number of cases. In *Kogut*, the defendant had been interrogated for 15 hours when he signed the confession and for more than 18 hours when he appeared in a videotaped statement. Interrogated through the night, he had also not slept for close to 30 hours. Except for one study showing that interrogative suggestibility scores increase with prolonged sleep deprivation (Blagrove, 1996), no research has examined the effects of sleep deprivation on the behavior of suspects in the interrogation room. Nevertheless, there is a wealth of relevant empirical knowledge that is reliable and generally accepted. Across a range of cognitive, affective, and behavioral measures, including information processing and decision-making performance, studies of college students, medical interns, motorists, fighter pilots, and others have shown that sleep deprivation "strongly impairs human functioning" (Pilcher & Huffcut, 1996; see also Harrison & Horne, 2000).

In very general terms, it is reasonable to identify three broad, well-established sets of principles that are ripe for expert testimony on confessions – all of which are beyond dispute in the scientific community (this is by no means an exhaustive list). The first core principle, dating back to Thorndike's (1911) law of effect, is that people are highly responsive to reinforcement and subject to the laws of conditioning, and that behavior is influenced more by perceptions of short-term than long-term consequences, which are strategically manipulated by trained police investigators. Of distal relevance to a psychological analysis of interrogation are the thousands of operant animal studies of reinforcement schedules, punishment, and appetitive, avoidance, and escape learning, as well as behavioral modification applications in clinics, schools, and workplaces. Looking through a behavioral lens, one is struck by the ways in which interrogators shape suspects to confess to particular narrative accounts of crimes like they were rats in a Skinner box (Skinner, 1938; Herrnstein, 1970).

Similarly relevant to an analysis of choice behavior in the interrogation room are studies of human decision-making in the behavioral economics paradigm. A voluminous body of research has shown that people make choices believed to maximize their wellbeing given the constraints they face, making the best of the situation they are in – what Herrnstein has called the *matching law* (Herrnstein, Rachlin & Laibson, 1997). With respect to a suspect's response to interrogation, studies on the discounting of rewards and costs show that people tend to be myopic and impulsive in their orientation, preferring outcomes that are immediate rather than delayed, the latter depreciating over time in their subjective value (Rachlin, 2000). This tendency is particularly evident in juvenile populations and among smokers and other substance users (e.g., Bickel, Odum, & Madden, 1999; Kollins, 2003).

Rooted in the observation that people are inherently social beings, a second set of core principles is that individuals are highly vulnerable to influence from change agents who seek their compliance. Of direct relevance to an analysis of interrogation are the extensive literatures on attitudes and persuasion (Petty & Cacioppo, 1986), informational and normative influences (e.g., Asch, 1956), the use of sequential request strategies, as in the foot-in-the-door effect (Cialdini, 2001), and the gradual escalation of commands, issued by figures of authority, to effectively obtain self- and other-defeating acts of obedience (Milgram, 1974). Conceptually, Latane's (1981) social impact theory provides a coherent predictive model that can account for the influence of police interrogators – who bring *power, proximity,* and *number* to bear on their exchange with suspects (for a range of social psychological perspectives on interrogation, see Bem, 1966; Zimbardo, 1967; Davis & O'Donohue, 2003).

A third set of core principles consists of the "seven sins of memory" that Schacter (2001) has identified from cognitive and neuroscience research – a list that includes memory transience, misattribution effects, suggestibility, and bias. When Kassin and Wrightsman (1985) first identified coerced-internalized false confessions, they were puzzled. At the time, existing models of memory could not account for the phenomenon whereby innocent suspects would come to internalize responsibility for crimes they did not commit. These cases occur when a suspect is dispositionally or situationally rendered vulnerable to manipulation and the interrogator then misrepresents the evidence, a common ploy. In light of a now extensive research literature on misinformation effects and the creation of illusory memories (e.g., Loftus, 1997, 2005), and a source monitoring perspective to explain how people, once confused, can be induced to distort their recollections, experts can now better grasp the process by which people internalize guilt for a crime they did not commit and the conditions under which this may occur (see Henkel & Coffman, 2004).

In the middle: Content-specific forensic research

In recent years, increasing numbers of researchers have begun to conduct content-specific forensic research on the processes of interviewing and interrogation and the elicitation of confessions.

As one would expect, multiple methods are used to investigate this chain of events in the criminal justice system. Leo and Ofshe (1998) used an aggregated case study method to compare and contrast 60 proven or probable false confession cases. More recently, Drizin and Leo (2004) analyzed 125 proven false confession cases in the United States, occurring between 1971 and 2002, the largest sample ever studied. Leo (1996a), in the United States, and Moston, Stephenson, and Williamson (1992), in Great Britain, used naturalistic observations to study processes and outcomes in live and videotaped police interrogations. Gudjonsson (1992, 2003) and his colleagues have also used self-report methods to examine correlations between various personal suspect characteristics – such as interrogative compliance and suggestibility – and the tendency to confess or resist confession. My colleagues and I have developed experimental paradigms to test specific causal hypotheses about interrogation tactics that increase the risk of false confessions (e.g., Kassin & Kiechel, 1996; Russano, Meissner, Narchet, & Kassin, 2005) – and, more recently, to assess how accurately investigators make preinterrogation judgments of truth and deception (Meissner & Kassin, 2002; Kassin, Meissner & Norwick, 2005).

What follows is a brief overview of a research literature that is characterized by eclectic methods that have produced convergent results. Specifically, this overview examines four steps in the chain of events:

1. the accuracy with which police investigators make judgments of truth and deception from suspect interviews;
2. the *Miranda* warning and waiver, a process by which police apprise suspects of their rights to silence and counsel and elicit a waiver of these rights;
3. the interrogation, a process of social influence in which police employ various techniques to elicit confessions, sometimes by people who are innocent; and
4. the consequences of confession evidence as later evaluated by police, prosecutors, judges, and juries.

Interview-based truth and deception judgments. In countless numbers of false confessions, the police chose to interrogate an innocent person because they had made an incorrect judgment, based on an initial interview, that he or she was lying and hence culpable. Thomas Sawyer had blushed and looked away; Peter Reilly, Gary Gauger, and Michael Crowe exhibited too little emotion; Jeffrey Deskovic seemed overly distraught; Timothy Bickel broke down and cried. Many law enforcement professionals are trained to use these common-sense types of cues. For example, Inbau, Reid, Buckley, and Jayne (2001), authors of the well-known and widely used manual *Criminal Interrogations and Confessions* (4th edition), advise investigators to use various verbal cues (e.g., qualified or rehearsed responses), nonverbal cues (e.g., gaze aversion, frozen posture, slouching), and "behavioral attitudes" (e.g., unconcerned, anxious, guarded) to identify deception. Using these cues, they claim that investigators can be trained to judge truth and deception at an 85% level of accuracy.

Despite popular conceptions, deception detection research has failed to support the claim that groups can attain such high average levels of performance. Most experiments have shown that people on average perform at no better than chance level – regardless of professional experience or training (for reviews of this literature, see Bond & DePaulo, 2006; Granhag & Strömwall, 2004; Vrij, 2000). One might argue that performance in the laboratory is poor because of the low-stakes nature of the task, which weakens deception cues (DePaulo et al., 2003). However, forensic studies using high-stake lies have produced mixed results, with one study suggesting that police can sometimes make these judgments at modestly high levels of accuracy (Mann, Vrij, & Bull, 2004). One might also argue that professionals would be more accurate if they were to personally conduct the interviews rather than merely observe the sessions. However, research fails to support this notion as well (Buller, Strzyzewski, & Hunsaker, 1991; Hartwig, Granhag, Strömwall, & Vrij, 2004).

A number of studies have examined whether special training increases judgment accuracy in a specifically forensic context. Kassin and Fong (1999) trained some college students but not others in the Reid technique of lie detection and then presented videotaped denials of mock suspects who were truly guilty or innocent of a mock crime. As in studies in nonforensic settings, observers performed at no better than chance level – and those who underwent training were *less* accurate than naïve controls (though they were more confident and exhibited a response bias toward seeing deception). In a follow-up study, Meissner and Kassin (2002) administered the same task to experienced investigators from the United States and Canada, many of whom had received special training, and found that investigators – compared to college students – exhibited lower (chance-level) accuracy, significantly higher confidence, and a response bias toward deception. Similar results have been obtained with law enforcement samples in England (Vrij & Mann, 2001), Israel (Elaad, 2003), Spain (Garrido, Masip, & Herrero, 2004), and Sweden (Hartwig et al., 2004).

Miranda warnings and waivers. For suspects who are judged deceptive, the questioning becomes highly confrontational. There is, however, one procedural safeguard to protect the accused from this transition. In *Miranda v. Arizona* (1966), the U.S. Supreme Court ruled that police must inform all suspects placed in custody of their Constitutional rights to silence and to counsel – and suspects must voluntarily, knowingly, and intelligently waive these rights (for a review of the legal status of *Miranda*, see White, 2003).

Research suggests two reasons why *Miranda* may not afford the protection it was supposed to provide. The first is that many juvenile suspects (Grisso, 1981; Oberlander & Goldstein, 2001) and adults who are cognitively limited (Fulero & Everington, 1995) do not fully comprehend or know how to apply these rights. Second, naturalistic observations reveal that a vast majority of suspects voluntarily waive their rights and submit to questioning (Leo, 1996b; Moston, Stephenson, & Williamson, 1993).

This latter tendency may be most characteristic of innocents who stand falsely accused. Replicating a result previously observed in Great Britain, Leo (1996b) found that individuals with no prior record are more likely to waive their rights than are those who have criminal justice "experience." In light of recidivism rates in criminal behavior, this difference suggests that innocent people in particular are at risk to waive their rights. To test this hypothesis in a controlled setting, Kassin and Norwick (2004) had participants commit or not commit a mock theft of $100, after which they were apprehended for investigation. Motivated to avoid further commitments of time without compensation, they were confronted by a male "detective" who sought a waiver of their *Miranda* rights. As predicted, participants who were innocent were substantially more likely to sign a waiver than those who were guilty (81% to 36%). Asked to explain their decisions, most innocents said afterward that they waived their rights precisely because they were innocent (e.g., "I did nothing wrong," "I didn't have anything to hide").

Social influences in the interrogation room. By definition, interrogation is an accusatory process of influence purposefully designed by a person in authority to elicit a confession from a suspect who is presumed guilty. For innocent people initially misjudged, one would hope that investigators would remain open-minded and reevaluate their beliefs. However, a great deal of research suggests that once people form an impression, they unwittingly seek, interpret, and create behavioral data in self-verifying ways. This last phenomenon – variously referred to by the terms self-fulfilling prophecy, interpersonal expectancy effect, and behavioral confirmation bias – was demonstrated by Rosenthal and Jacobson (1968) in their classic field study of teacher expectancy effects, with similar results later obtained not only in the laboratory (e.g., Snyder & Swann, 1978) but in military, business, and other organizational settings (McNatt, 2000).

Importing the laboratory paradigm to the study of police interrogations, Kassin, Goldstein and Savitsky (2003) led student interrogators to believe that they would be questioning someone who was likely guilty or innocent of a mock crime. Then they randomly paired these interrogators with suspects who were actually guilty or innocent. Overall, those who were led to expect guilt asked more guilt-presumptive questions, used more techniques, exerted more pressure to get a confession, and made innocent suspects sound more anxious and defensive to observers. They (as well as neutral observers who later listened to the interviews on tape) were later more likely to see these suspects in incriminating terms. The presumption of guilt, which underlies interrogation, thus unleashed a process of behavioral confirmation, shaping the interrogator's behavior, the suspect's behavior, and ultimately the judgments of neutral observers.

In general terms, it is clear that police interrogation is a guilt-presumptive process that can set into motion a range of cognitive and behavioral confirmation biases. But it is also important to assess the specific techniques that are employed that may lead people to confess to crimes they did not commit. As derived from popular training manuals (Inbau et al., 2001), and as seen in practice (e.g., Leo, 1996a; Kassin et al., in press), modern police interrogations are conducted in a sequence of steps, essentially reducible to three processes: (1) *isolation*, often in a special interrogation room, which increases anxiety and the incentive to escape; (2) *confrontation*, in which the suspect is accused of the crime, presented with evidence, real or manufactured, and blocked from denial; and (3) *minimization*, in which the crime is morally excused by a sympathetic interrogator, leading suspects to see confession as a possible means of gaining leniency (see Kassin, 1997, 2005).

As noted earlier, a long history of psychological science indicates without dispute that people are responsive to reinforcement and conditioning, influenced more by perceptions of immediate than delayed consequences, and vulnerable to influence from social impact agents who use sequential request strategies and authority to elicit self-defeating acts of compliance. With regard to studies specifically aimed at testing the tactics of interrogation, two lines of research in particular have implicated tactics that put innocent people at risk to confess.

The first tactic pertains to the presentation of false evidence. Once suspects are isolated, interrogators confront them with bold assertions of guilt, a process that may even involve misrepresentations of the evidence (e.g., pretending to have the suspect's fingerprints, a blood or hair sample, and eyewitness identification, or a failed polygraph). In the United States, this false evidence ploy is permissible (*Frazier v. Cupp*, 1969). It is perhaps not surprising that although this tactic is not frequently used (Leo, 1996a; Leo et al., 2006), it can be seen in virtually all proven false confession cases. Crime suspects report that their perception of the strength of the evidence was their primary reason for confession or denial (Moston et al., 1992). Moreover, laboratory experiments have shown that false evidence can lead innocent people to confess to acts they did not commit. In the first such study, college students engaged in a typing and reaction time task were accused of causing the experimenter's computer to crash by pressing a key they were instructed to avoid, and were asked to sign a confession (Kassin & Kiechel, 1996). All participants were innocent and all initially denied the charge. In some sessions, a confederate told the experimenter that she witnessed the participant hit the forbidden key; in others she said she did not witness what happened. This false evidence significantly increased the number of students who signed a written confession, from 48% to 94% (this manipulation also increased the number of participants who internalized responsibility for this outcome they did not produce). Follow-up studies have replicated this effect, even when the confession was said to bear a financial consequence (Horselenberg, Merckelbach, & Josephs, 2003; Horselenberg et al., 2006), and particularly among juveniles who are more compliant and more suggestible than adults (Redlich & Goodman, 2003).

A second tactic that has received research attention concerns the use of minimization. Once interrogators have thrust a suspect into feeling trapped by evidence, they begin to suggest that the crime was spontaneous, accidental, provoked, drug-induced, or otherwise justified by circumstances. Over the years, most courts have rejected as involuntary confessions taken by promises of leniency, acknowledging the risk to innocent people. But what about promises that are implied, even if not spoken? In one study, readers of an interrogation transcript in which the interrogator made minimizing remarks inferred by pragmatic implication that leniency in sentencing would follow from confession, even without an explicit promise (Kassin & McNall, 1991).

In a second study, a laboratory paradigm was used to assess the behavioral effects of minimization on the elicitation of true and false confessions (Russano et al., 2005). Participants were paired with a confederate for a problem-solving study and half were induced by that confederate to cheat by collaborating on a problem that was supposed to be solved alone. The experimenter "discovered" the similarity in the solutions, accused the participant of cheating, and tried to extract a signed confession by promising leniency, making minimizing remarks, using both tactics, or using no tactics. Overall, the confession rate was higher among guilty than innocent participants when leniency was promised than when it was not, and when minimization was used than when it was not. On calculations of diagnosticity (as measured by the ratio of true to false confessions), the results showed that diagnosticity was highest in the no-tactics cell (where 46% of guilty suspects confessed vs. only 6% of innocents) and that minimization – just like an explicit offer of leniency – reduced diagnosticity by tripling the rate of false confessions (81% vs. 18%). In short, minimization serves as the implicit functional equivalent to a promise of leniency, putting innocents at risk to make false confessions.

Consequences of confession evidence in court. A fourth line of inquiry concerns the credibility and impact of confessions – first on police and prosecutors, but ultimately on judges and juries. In cases involving a disputed confession, a preliminary hearing is held for a judge to determine its voluntariness and admissibility. In American courts, confessions deemed voluntary are then admitted to the jury (with or without special instruction). The question is, with what effect?

Research on the impact of confessions throughout the criminal justice system is not encouraging. Mock jury studies have shown that confessions have more impact than eyewitness and character testimony, other potent forms of human evidence (Kassin & Neumann, 1997). Moreover, people trust confessions and do not fully discount them even when it is logically and legally appropriate to do so. For example, Kassin and Sukel (1997) presented mock jurors with one of three versions of a murder trial: one that contained a low-pressure confession, a second that contained a high-pressure confession, and a third that lacked a confession. Faced with the high-pressure confession, participants appeared to respond in the legally prescribed manner, as assessed by two measures: Relative to those in the low-pressure condition, they judged the statement to be involuntary and said it did not influence their decisions. Yet on the all-important measure of verdicts, these confessions, which should have been discounted, significantly boosted the conviction rate.

Archival analyses of criminal justice statistics provide real-world corroboration of this disturbing pattern. When proven false-confessors have pled not guilty and proceeded to trial, the jury conviction rates have ranged from 73% (Leo & Ofshe, 1998) to 81% (Drizin & Leo, 2004). These figures led Drizin and Leo (2004) to describe confession evidence as "inherently prejudicial and highly damaging to a defendant, even if it is the product of coercive interrogation, even if it is supported by no other evidence, and even if it is ultimately proven false beyond any reasonable doubt" (p. 959).

Outside the Pyramid: Factoring In "Common Knowledge"

Both the *Frye* test of general acceptance and the more recent *Daubert* criteria for assessing the validity of scientific, technical or other specialized knowledge, can be sufficiently addressed within the three-tiered pyramidal framework. To address the more extrinsic question of whether an expert's testimony will assist the trier of fact – apart from how generally accepted and valid it may be – requires additional inquiry into the realm of common-sense psychology.

In recent years American courts have struggled with this question in a number of cases. In *People of the State of New York v. Kogut* (2005), Judge Ort noted that jurors may benefit from expert testimony even if they know in general terms that police interrogation is psychologically oriented. Drawing a parallel to the eyewitness area, the judge stated: "As with psychological studies of eyewitness identification, it cannot be said that the typical juror is familiar with psychological research concerning the voluntariness of confessions or the tendency of certain techniques to contribute to a false confession" (p. 9).

Another recent case is also instructive on this point. In *United States v. Belyea* (2005), the defendant confessed to the theft of a firearm after being terrified into thinking that the weapon was used in a murder, that his fingerprints were on it, and that he could avoid jail by co-operating (the confession contradicted subsequently discovered key details of the crime). The defendant moved to introduce expert trial testimony on false confessions, but the district court rejected this motion because "Jurors [already] know people lie." Belyea was convicted, but the U.S. Court of Appeals for the Fourth Circuit overturned the verdict, noting that the law requires a nuanced analysis of whether expert testimony would be useful in a particular case. Specifically, the Court argued that whereas jurors know that people lie, they may not know that certain people under certain conditions will confess, against their own self-interest, to crimes they did not commit. In this Court's judgment, "The phenomenon of false confessions is counter-intuitive and is not necessarily explained by the general proposition that 'jurors know people lie'" (p. 10).

It is beyond the scope of this chapter to discuss lay theories of reinforcement and motivation, human decision-making, truth and lie detection, and other issues of potential relevance to expert testimony in this area. In general, however, it seems clear that there are few, if any, phenomena of human behavior that are less intuitive than that of false confessions. Indeed, all confession-based wrongful convictions are a product of two problems: the first being that innocent people can be led to confess, the second being that police detectives, prosecutors, judges, and juries routinely believe these false confessions.

There are three bases for pessimism on the question of whether jurors are sufficiently equipped to evaluate confession evidence without assistance. First, generalized common sense leads us to trust confessions, a behavior that breaches self-interest in a profound way (most people believe they would never confess to a crime they did not commit and they cannot image the circumstances under which anyone would do so). Over the years, social psychologists have found in a wide range of contexts that people fall prey to the "fundamental attribution error" – that is, they tend to make dispositional attributions for a person's actions, taking behavior at face value, while neglecting the role of situational factors (Ross, 1977; Jones, 1990; Gilbert & Malone, 1995). This tendency to underestimate social impact was seen in dramatic form when Milgram (1974) found that people vastly underpredicted the percentage of subjects who would exhibit total obedience in his experiment. Illustrating this point in a forensic context are studies showing that mock juries are corrupted by confessions regardless of whether they judge them to be voluntary or coerced (e.g., Kassin & Sukel, 1997). Hence, it comes as no surprise that in actual cases, false-confessors who proceed to trial are usually convicted (Leo & Ofshe, 1998; Drizin & Leo, 2004).

A second basis for pessimism is that people are typically not adept at deception detection. Even professional lie catchers are accurate in only 45–60% of judgments, with a mean of 54% (Vrij, 2000). We saw earlier that neither trained college students nor experienced police investigators can accurately separate true from false denials. But what about the assumption that "I'd know a false confession if I saw one?" In a two-part study, Kassin et al. (2005) videotaped male prison inmates giving two narrative confessions: one to the crime for which they were in prison, a second to a crime that they did not commit. Then we created a stimulus videotape containing 10 different inmates, each giving a single true or false confession to one of five crimes. The result was that neither college students nor police investigators performed significantly better than chance, though police were significantly more confident in their judgments and exhibited significantly more false alarms in their errors.

A third basis for pessimism is that police-induced confessions, unlike other types of verbal statements, are corrupted by the very process of interrogation that elicits them – designed for persuasion, even if false. In most documented false confessions, the statements ultimately presented in court are compelling, often containing vivid and accurate details about the crime. Sometimes these details had become known to the innocent suspect through leading questions, photographs, visits to the crime scene, and other secondhand sources of information. To further obfuscate matters, many false confessions contain statements of motivation, apologies and expressions of remorse, and even physical reenactments. In some cases, innocent suspects correct minor errors that appear in the statements, corrections that interrogators are trained to insert and get corrected for tactical purposes. Hence, to the naïve juror, false confessions often appear to be voluntary, textured with detail, and the product of personal experience – not staged, rehearsed, and enacted, as they are, like a Hollywood drama (Kassin, 2002).

This point is clearly illustrated in the case of John Kogut, who was exonerated by DNA after 17 years in prison, retried on his original confession, and acquitted. The confession Kogut had signed contained a striking degree of colorful detail, not only on central aspects of the murder, but on peripheral details as well – such as a description of the victim's "gold colored chain with what looked like a double heart on it with a piece broken off of it."[3] The statement Kogut signed also contained errors that he presumably corrected and initialed. Yet at trial, his interrogator admitted that he inserted the errors, made the corrections, and directed Kogut to initial these corrections.

Using Psychology to Promote Justice

Voluntarily or under pressure, it is inevitable that people will sometimes confess to crimes they did not commit, thus placing the burden on the courts to serve as a safety net. Yet judges and juries cannot be expected to intuit as a matter of common knowledge the relevant research literatures on reinforcement and conditioning, human decision-making, reconstructive memory, social influence, and other core

---

[3] The confession was handwritten by one of the interrogators and signed by Kogut. Importantly, this statement contained no information that was not already known to police and led police to no evidence they did not already have.

principles that define the 100-plus years of psychological science. Predictable by studies of the fundamental attribution error, it is particularly clear that people accept confessions uncritically, even when coerced. Toward this end, expert testimony provides a necessary mechanism for assisting juries to more accurately assess this evidence – and how and from whom it was produced.

Another important mechanism is to ensure that trial judges, juries, and appellate courts can observe the process by which confessions are produced. In Great Britain, the Police and Criminal Evidence Act of 1986 mandated that all custodial sessions be taped in their entirety. In the United States, five states (Minnesota, Alaska, Illinois, Maine, and Wisconsin) and the District of Columbia presently have mandatory videotaping requirements, though the practice is found elsewhere on a voluntary basis.[4]

There are many advantages to a videotaping policy (e.g., the presence of a camera should deter interrogators from using coercive tactics; disable frivolous defense claims of coercion; and provide a full and accurate record of the transaction, a common source of dispute in courts). For the purpose of the current discussion, the following hypothesis presents itself: A mandatory videotaping policy will increase the fact finding accuracy of judges and juries. In ruling on voluntariness, judges will observe firsthand the suspect's physical and mental state, the conditions of interrogation, and the tactics that were used; and juries, in rendering a verdict, will observe not only how the statements were taken but from whom the crime details, if accurate, originated.

As a matter of policy, it is important not only that entire sessions be recorded but that the camera adopt a neutral "equal-focus" perspective that shows both the accused and his or her interrogators. In a series of studies on illusory causation effects, Lassiter and his colleagues found that people are more attuned to the situational factors that draw confessions when the interrogator is on camera than when the sole focus is on the suspect (for a review, see Lassiter & Geers, 2004). Under these former circumstances, juries make more informed judgments of voluntariness and guilt when they see not only the final confession but the conditions that prompted it and the source of the details that it contained (Lassiter, Geers, Handley, Weiland, & Munhall, 2002).

---

[4]   In *Commonwealth of Massachusetts v. DiGiambattista* (2004), the Supreme Judicial Court of Massachusetts stopped short of a mandatory videotaping requirement but ruled that any confession resulting from an unrecorded interrogation will entitle the defendant to a jury instruction that urges caution in the use of that confession.

REFERENCES

Asch, S. E. (1956). Studies of independence and conformity: A minority of one against a unanimous majority. *Psychological Monographs, 70,* 416.

Bem, D. J. (1966). Inducing belief in false confessions. *Journal of Personality and Social Psychology, 3,* 707–710.

Bickel, W. K., Odum, A. L., & Madden, G. L. (1999). Impulsivity and cigarette smoking: Delay discounting in current, never, and ex-smokers. *Psychopharmacology, 146,* 447–454.

Blagrove, M. (1996). Effects of length of sleep deprivation on interrogative suggestibility. *Journal of Experimental Psychology: Applied, 2,* 48–59.

Bond, C. F., Jr., & DePaulo, B. M. (2006). Accuracy of deception judgments. *Personality and Social Psychology Review, 10,* 214–234.

Buller, D. B., Strzyzewski, K. D., & Hunsaker, F. G. (1991). Interpersonal deception: II. The inferiority of conversational participants as deception detectors. *Communication Monographs, 58,* 25–40.

Cialdini, R. B. (2001). *Influence: Science and practice* (4th ed.). Needham Heights, MA: Allyn & Bacon.

Commonwealth of Massachusetts v. DiGiambattista, 442 Mass. 423 (2004).

Daubert v. Merrell Dow Pharmaceuticals, Inc., 509 U.S. 579 (1993).

Davis, D., & O'Donohue, W. (2003). The road to perdition: "Extreme influence" tactics in the interrogation room. In W. O'Donohue, P. Laws, & C. Hollin (Eds.), *Handbook of forensic psychology* (pp. 897–996). New York: Basic Books.

DePaulo, B. M., Lindsay, J. J., Malone, B. E., Muhlenbruck, L., Charlton, K., & Cooper, H. (2003). Cues to deception. *Psychological Bulletin, 129,* 74–112.

Doyle, J. M. (2005). *True witness: Cops, courts, science, and the battle against misidentification.* New York: Palgrave Macmillan.

Drizin, S. A., & Leo, R. A. (2004). The problem of false confessions in the post-DNA world. *North Carolina Law Review, 82,* 891–1007.

Elaad, R. (2003). Effects of feedback on the overestimated capacity to detect lies and the underestimated ability to tell lies. *Applied Cognitive Psychology, 17,* 349–363.

Faigman, D. L., & Monahan, J. (2005). Psychological evidence at the dawn of the law's scientific age. *Annual Review of Psychology, 56,* 631–659.

Frazier v. Cupp, 394 U.S. 731 (1969).

Frye v. United States, 293 F. 1013 (D.C. Circuit, 1923).

Fulero, S. M. (2004). Expert psychological testimony on the psychology of interrogations and confessions. In G. D. Lassiter (Ed.), *Interrogations, confessions, and entrapment* (pp. 247–263). New York: Kluwer Academic.

Fulero, S. M., & Everington, C. (1995). Assessing competency to waive *Miranda* rights in defendants with mental retardation. *Law and Human Behavior, 19,* 533–543.

Garrido, E., Masip, J., & Herrero, C. (2004). Police officers credibility judgments: Accuracy and estimated ability. *International Journal of Psychology, 39*, 254–275.

Gilbert, D. T., & Malone, P. S. (1995). The correspondence bias. *Psychological Bulletin, 117*, 21–38.

Granhag, P. A., & Strömwall, L. (Eds.) (2004). *Deception detection in forensic contexts.* Cambridge, England: Cambridge University Press.

Grisso, T. (1981). *Juveniles' waiver of rights: Legal and psychological competence.* New York: Plenum.

Gudjonsson, G. H. (1992). *The psychology of interrogations, confessions, and testimony.* London: Wiley.

Gudjonsson, G. H. (2003). *The psychology of interrogations and confessions: A handbook.* Chichester, England: John Wiley & Sons.

Harrison, Y., & Horne, J. A. (2000). The impact of sleep deprivation on decision making: A review. *Journal of Experimental Psychology: Applied, 6*, 236–249.

Hartwig, M., Granhag, P. A., Strömwall, L. A., & Vrij, A. (2004). Police officers' lie detection accuracy: Interrogating freely vs. observing video. *Police Quarterly, 7*, 429–456.

Henkel, L. A., & Coffman, K. J. (2004). Memory distortions in coerced false confessions: A source monitoring framework analysis. *Applied Cognitive Psychology, 18*, 567–588.

Herrnstein, R. J. (1970). On the law of effect. *Journal of the Experimental Analysis of Behavior, 7*, 243–266.

Herrnstein, R. J., Rachlin, H., & Laibson, D. I. (Eds.) (1997). *The matching law: Papers in psychology and economics.* New York: Russell Sage Foundation.

Horselenberg, R., Merckelbach, H., & Josephs, S. (2003). Individual differences and false confessions: A conceptual replication of Kassin & Kiechel (1996). *Psychology, Crime and Law, 9*, 1–18.

Horselenberg, R., Merckelbach, H., Smeets, T., Franssens, D., Ygram Peters, G-J., & Zeles, G. (2006). False confessions in the lab: Do plausibility and consequences matter? *Psychology, Crime and Law, 12*, 61–75.

Inbau, F. E., Reid, J. E., Buckley, J. P., & Jayne, B. C. (2001). *Criminal interrogation and confessions* (4th ed.). Gaithersberg, MD: Aspen. www.innocenceproject.org/

Jones, E. E. (1990). *Interpersonal perception.* New York: Freeman.

Kassin, S. M. (1997). The psychology of confession evidence. *American Psychologist, 52*, 221–233.

Kassin, S. M. (2002, November 1). False confessions and the jogger case. *New York Times*, p. A31.

Kassin, S. M. (2005). On the psychology of confessions: Does *innocence* put *innocents* at risk? *American Psychologist, 60*, 215–228.

Kassin, S. M., & Fong, C. T. (1999). "I'm innocent!" Effects of training on judgments of truth and deception in the interrogation room. *Law and Human Behavior, 23*, 499–516.

Kassin, S. M., Goldstein, C. J., & Savitsky, K. (2003). Behavioral confirmation in the interrogation room: On the dangers of presuming guilt. *Law and Human Behavior, 27,* 187–203.

Kassin, S. M., & Gudjonsson, G. H. (2004). The psychology of confession evidence: A review of the literature and issues. *Psychological Science in the Public Interest, 5,* 35–69.

Kassin, S. M., & Kiechel, K. L. (1996). The social psychology of false confessions: Compliance, internalization, and confabulation. *Psychological Science, 7,* 125–128.

Kassin, S. M., Leo, R. A., Meissner, C. A., Richman, K. D., Colwell, L. H., Leach, A. M., & La Fon, D. (in press). Police interviewing and interrogation: A self-report survey of police practices and beliefs. *Law and Human Behavior, 31.*

Kassin, S. M., & McNall, K. (1991). Police interrogations and confessions: Communicating promises and threats by pragmatic implication. *Law and Human Behavior, 15,* 233–251.

Kassin, S. M., Meissner, C. A., & Norwick, R. J. (2005). "I'd know a false confession if I saw one": A comparative study of college students and police investigators. *Law and Human Behavior, 29,* 211–227.

Kassin, S. M., & Neumann, K. (1997). On the power of confession evidence: An experimental test of the "fundamental difference" hypothesis. *Law and Human Behavior, 21,* 469–484.

Kassin, S. M., & Norwick, R. J. (2004). Why suspects waive their *Miranda* rights: The power of innocence. *Law and Human Behavior, 28,* 211–221.

Kassin, S. M., & Sukel, H. (1997). Coerced confessions and the jury: An experimental test of the "harmless error" rule. *Law and Human Behavior, 21,* 27–46.

Kassin, S. M., & Wrightsman, L. S. (1985). Confession evidence. In S. Kassin & L. Wrightsman (Eds.), *The psychology of evidence and trial procedure* (pp. 67–94). Beverly Hills, CA: Sage.

Kollins, S. H. (2003). Delay discounting is associated with substance use in college students. *Addictive Behaviors, 28,* 1167–1173.

Lassiter, G. D., & Geers, A. L. (2004). Evaluation of confession evidence: Effects of presentation format. In G. D. Lassiter (Ed.), *Interrogations, confessions, and entrapment.* New York: Kluwer Press.

Lassiter, G. D., Geers, A. L., Handley, I. M., Weiland, P. E., & Munhall, P. J. (2002). Videotaped confessions and interrogations: A change in camera perspective alters verdicts in simulated trials. *Journal of Applied Psychology, 87,* 867–874.

Latane, B. (1981). The psychology of social impact. *American Psychologist, 36,* 343–356.

Leo, R. A. (1996a). Inside the interrogation room. *The Journal of Criminal Law and Criminology, 86,* 266–303.

Leo, R. A. (1996b). Miranda's revenge: Police interrogation as a confidence game. *Law and Society Review, 30,* 259–288.

Leo, R. A., Kassin, S. M., Richman, K. D., Colwell, L. H., Leach, A., La Fon, D., & Meissner, C. (2006). *Police interviewing and interrogation: A national self-report survey of police practices and beliefs.* Paper presented at the American Psychology-Law Society, St. Petersburg, FL.

Leo, R. A., & Ofshe, R. J. (1998). The consequences of false confessions: Deprivations of liberty and miscarriages of justice in the age of psychological interrogation. *Journal of Criminal Law and Criminology, 88*, 429–496.

Loftus, E. F. (1997). Creating false memories. *Scientific American, 277*, 70–75.

Loftus, E. F. (2005). Planting misinformation in the human mind: A 30-year investigation of the malleability of memory. *Learning & Memory, 12*, 361–366.

Mann, S., Vrij, A., & Bull, R. (2004). Detecting true lies: Police officers' ability to detect suspects' lies. *Journal of Applied Psychology, 89*, 137–149.

McNatt, D. B. (2000). Ancient Pygmalion joins contemporary management: A meta-analysis of the result. *Journal of Applied Psychology, 85*, 314–322.

Meissner, C. A., & Kassin, S. M. (2002). "He's guilty!": Investigator bias in judgments of truth and deception. *Law and Human Behavior, 26*, 469–480.

Milgram, S. (1974). *Obedience to authority: An experimental view.* New York: Harper & Row.

Miranda v. Arizona, 384 U.S. 336 (1966).

Moston, S., Stephenson, G. M., & Williamson, T. M. (1992). The effects of case characteristics on suspect behaviour during questioning. *British Journal of Criminology, 32*, 23–40.

Moston, S., Stephenson, G. M., & Williamson, T. M. (1993). The incidence, antecedents and consequences of the use of the right to silence during police questioning. *Criminal Behavior and Mental Health, 3*, 30–47.

Oberlander, L. B., & Goldstein, N. E. (2001). A review and update on the practice of evaluating *Miranda* comprehension. *Behavioral Sciences and the Law, 19*, 453–471.

People of the State of New York v. Kogut (2005). Supreme Court of Nassau County, Unpublished opinion, Indictment No. 61029/85, September 15, 2005.

Petty, R. E., & Cacioppo, J. T. (1986). *Communication and persuasion: Central and peripheral routes to attitude change.* New York: Springer-Verlag.

Pilcher, J. J., & Huffcut, A. (1996). Effects of sleep deprivation on performance: A meta-analysis. *Sleep, 19*, 318–326.

Rachlin, H. (2000). *The science of self-control.* Cambridge, MA: Harvard University Press.

Redlich, A. D., & Goodman, G. S. (2003). Taking responsibility for an act not committed: Influence of age and suggestibility. *Law and Human Behavior, 27*, 141–156.

Rosenthal, R., & Jacobson, L. (1968). *Pygmalion in the classroom: Teacher expectation and pupils' intellectual development.* New York: Holt, Rinehart, & Winston.

Ross, L. (1977). The intuitive psychologist and his shortcomings: Distortions in the attribution process. *Advances in Experimental Social Psychology, 10,* 174–221.

Russano, M. B., Meissner, C. A., Narchet, F. M., & Kassin, S. M. (2005). Investigating true and false confessions within a novel experimental paradigm. *Psychological Science, 16,* 481–486.

Schacter, D. L. (2001). *The seven sins of memory: How the mind forgets and remembers.* Boston: Houghton Mifflin.

Scheck, B., Neufeld, P., & Dwyer, J. (2000). *Actual innocence.* Garden City, NY: Doubleday.

Skinner, B. F. (1938). *The behavior of organisms.* NY: Appleton-Century-Crofts.

Snyder, M., & Swann, W. B., Jr. (1978). Hypothesis-testing processes in social interaction. *Journal of Personality and Social Psychology, 36,* 1202–1212.

Thorndike, E. L. (1911). *Animal intelligence: Experimental studies.* New York: MacMillan.

United States v. Belyea. U.S. Court of Appeals for the Fourth Circuit, Unpublished opinion, No. 04-4415 (2005, December 28).

Vrij, A. (2000). *Detecting lies and deceit: The psychology of lying and the implications for professional practice.* London: Wiley.

Vrij, A., & Mann, S. (2001). Who killed my relative?: Police officers' ability to detect real-life high-stake lies. *Psychology, Crime and Law, 7,* 119–132.

Wells, G. L. (1978). Applied eyewitness-testimony research: System variables and estimator variables. *Journal of Personality and Social Psychology, 30,* 1546–1557.

White, W. S. (2003). *Miranda's waning protections: Police interrogation practices after Dickerson.* Ann Arbor: University of Michigan Press.

Wrightsman, L. S., & Kassin, S. M. (1993). *Confessions in the courtroom.* Newbury Park, CA: Sage Publications.

Zimbardo, P. G. (1967, June). The psychology of police confessions. *Psychology Today, 1,* 17–20, 25–27.

11

Polygraph Testing

William G. Iacono

In an episode of one of the most popular TV shows in the United States, a woman took a polygraph test to prove that she was not involved in her husband's death. The test included questions about any romantic feelings she might hold toward a male companion. Although she denied having any, the twitch of the polygraph pens suggested she was lying. Instead of charging that the polygraph was in error, the woman concluded that she might indeed be in love, and used the test results to justify pursuing a relationship with her friend. Much of public perception about polygraph testing is probably derived from such mysterious and magical portrayals. However, polygraphs are not capable of mind-probing revelations. Moreover, although polygraphs may appear to be inscrutably complex, they are nevertheless based on fairly simple procedures and psychological assumptions that are easy to comprehend.

Tens of thousands of polygraph tests are administered in this country every year, mostly by government agencies, and many of these tests are administered to resolve crimes. Although the accuracy of polygraph examinations has been vigorously challenged (most recently in a report form the National Academy of Sciences, National Research Council, 2003), their utility, or the degree to which they can be used as a tool to help solve crimes, has not. Polygraph examiners take advantage of the shroud of mystery surrounding their techniques and public ignorance about their validity to use the polygraph as a tool to extract admissions and confessions from unsophisticated subjects. This information-eliciting aspect of polygraph testing has led government agencies concerned with security and law enforcement to defend and support their expanded use despite the criticism that they lack scientific foundation and cannot possibly be as accurate as polygraphers claim. Much of the controversy surrounding the evidentiary value of polygraph tests thus can be traced to the way in which utility and accuracy become conflated in the practice of polygraphy. That is, despite the strongly disputed scientific standing of polygraphy, the viability of polygraphy derives from the examiners' belief that "it works" because many suspects confess under the pressure of an examination. This state of affairs in turn confuses courts and the public alike as it is difficult to grasp how a procedure can sustain long-term and widespread use, be generally acknowledged as effective, and yet not be accurate.[1]

In this chapter, I will develop more thoroughly the basis for these conclusions, in the process explaining why a test that elicits admissions of guilt need not be accurate. I will begin by demystifying the polygraph, making explicit the assumptions on which these tests are based. Exposing the basis of the technique reduces it to a set of psychological principles that most educated persons can grasp and evaluate. I will then discuss how expert testimony is developed around selected key scientific reports to illustrate how knowledgeable scientists disagree on the interpretations that can be drawn from the literature used to evaluate polygraph accuracy. I will conclude by considering how the scientific literature and pertinent expert testimony regarding polygraph evidence is likely to improve the decision-making of fact finders beyond what they can determine from understanding the psychological assumptions that provide the foundation for polygraph tests.

How Does a Polygraph Test Work?

William Marston (Marston, 1917), a psychologist who was also trained as a lawyer, introduced a primitive "lie detector" that monitored the changes in blood pressure arising when a suspect denied wrongdoing. Marston's invention became famous when he tested and found nondeceptive accused murderer James Frye. This case eventually came before the U.S. Supreme Court which ruled against Frye (*Frye v. United States*, 1923), in the process deciding what constituted valid scientific evidence. The *Frye* criteria are still used to evaluate scientific

[1]   Recently, the New Mexico Supreme Court revealed the difficulty it had coming to grips with these apparent inconsistencies when it ruled in favor of polygraph admissibility citing "principles of fairness." The court noted that despite government opposition to admissibility based in part on the conclusions of the National Academy of Sciences (National Research Council, 2003), government use of and reliance on polygraphs is widespread (NM Supreme Court, 2004).

evidence in many state courts and remain relevant to current federal court standards under *Daubert* (*Daubert v. Merrell Dow Pharmaceuticals, Inc.*, 1993).

Polygraph testing has evolved substantially since Marston tested Frye. In addition to recording blood pressure, the modern field polygraph is capable of recording respiration and palmar sweating. Although some examiners still record these physiological signals as ink tracings on long strips of chart paper, advances in computer technology allow this information to be digitally recorded. It can then be displayed by a computer that simulates how the signals would appear on chart paper.

The notion that one can determine whether a person is lying simply by monitoring their physiological reactions when they deny wrongdoing has been thoroughly discredited: There is no unique physiological signature associated with lying. The physiological response only tells us that a person was disturbed by a question. It cannot tell us why the person was disturbed. Because of this, polygraph tests include several different types of questions that are designed to elicit emotional reactions. The truthfulness of a subject is decided by comparing the responses to these different questions.

There are many types of polygraph tests, but the only one that is routinely used in forensic settings is the control question technique (CQT). Introduced by John Reid in 1947 (Reid, 1947), the CQT is itself a collection of procedures that vary according to the structure and placement of different kinds of questions as well as the rules used to interpret the physiological data. However, all CQTs have in common the inclusion of relevant and control questions, and these are the questions used to determine whether a test is passed or failed (Raskin, 1986; Raskin & Honts, 2002). To illustrate how a CQT is intended to work, it is instructive to consider a common application.

Polygraph tests are frequently given in situations where compelling evidence is lacking. Hence, they are often administered in sex crimes where there is little physical evidence and the question at hand may involve the use of force or whether contact between the victim and alleged perpetrator occurred. Suppose, for instance, that a day care provider has concluded that your 3-year-old child, Kara, is displaying language and behavior that sexually molested children sometimes display. An investigation by child protection services, a physician, and the police is inconclusive, but the only plausible suspect is you, the child's primary caretaker. You have agreed to take a polygraph test with the understanding that the investigation will cease only if you pass a CQT. During your test, you will be asked a series of *relevant* questions, each of which directly addresses your possible involvement in the alleged crime. Sample questions include "Did you place your mouth on Kara's genitals?" or "Have you fondled Kara's private parts?" You will also be asked a series of *control* questions. These questions involve some misdeed that presumably everyone has been guilty of in their lives. For your test, they will include "Have you ever lied to someone who trusted you?" or "Have you ever engaged in sexual behavior you are ashamed of?" You are expected to answer all questions "no."

Your responses to the control questions are presumed to bother you, ideally because you are lying when you answer them or are at least uncertain about your denial. These questions thus hypothetically establish the degree to which you react physiologically when you lie. The magnitude of these responses is then compared to the magnitude of your response to the relevant questions. If you are telling the truth when you answer the relevant questions, the response to them is expected to be smaller than the response to the control questions because it is only the latter questions that disturb you. If you lie to the relevant questions, your response to them should exceed your response to the control questions because these lies are of greater concern to you.

Before the physiological data are collected, the polygraph examiner reviews all the test questions after first emphasizing that complete honesty is required to pass the test. In addition, the expectation that all questions can be answered truthfully with a "no" response is made explicit. Under these circumstances, many examinees will divulge information related to control questions. For instance, for the sample control questions presented above, the subject may admit lying to a parent or having once had a homosexual encounter. If this occurs, the examiner is trained to ask for an explanation and attempts to convince the subject that any further admissions will lead the examiner to conclude that the subject is dishonest and thus guilty. Once the subject stops revealing information, the control questions are modified such that they begin with a phrase that excepts the revelation from being covered by the question, e.g., "*Other than what you told me about,* have you ever lied to someone who trusted you?"

At the conclusion of the pretest interview that is used to formulate and review questions, the sensors are attached and the questions are read while the subject's physiological reactions are recorded on a chart or computer that can output the equivalent of a chart. A typical test might consist of about 10 questions spaced at 20 second intervals followed by a brief break that allows the subject to move about. Three pairs of relevant and control questions are included along with other questions that are not used to determine whether the subject is lying.

This process is repeated several times (each one yielding a "chart"), with the question order varied slightly for each chart. Many examiners will also include a special procedure, inserted before or after the first chart, that is called a *stim* or *acquaintance* test (so named because it stimulates the subject to respond or acquaints the examinee with the procedure). Its real purpose, however, is to convince subjects that they will be caught if they lie. The many variants of the stim test all include a procedure whereby the subject attempts to "conceal" information from the examiner by denying possession of the information while physiological reactions are monitored. For instance, the subject may choose a card from a marked deck that is numbered 6. The examiner will query "Is your number 3? ... Is your number 7? ... Is your number 6? ..." etc., and eventually reveal to the subject the correct answer. Whatever version of the stim test is used, the results are arranged so the examiner is able to portray the result as indicating the subject was easily detectable.

Evaluation of the CQT

It should be apparent from the preceding section that the CQT is more a procedure than a test. As such, it is not standardized; there is no way to assure that two examiners independently evaluating the same suspect would use the same relevant and control questions. Nor would they necessarily be expected to be equally successful in convincing the examinee that all the questions are supposed to be answered honestly, that failing any question could lead to a deceptive verdict, or that it is not in the subject's interest to divulge dishonest or embarrassing incidents associated with the control questions. Not only would no two tests be the same, there is no way to tell whether one test or one examiner is better than another. In addition, not all examiners use a stim test, it is not known to what degree subjects find stim test demonstrations convincing, and it is not known how important a stim test is to obtaining an accurate verdict.

As noted by Lykken over 30 years ago (Lykken, 1974), the control question does not provide an adequate control for the psychological impact of the accusation contained in the relevant question.[2] In the

---

[2]   Accepting that the control question does not provide a true control for the psychological processes tapped by the relevant question, after 50 years of reference to these questions as controls, the American Polygraph Association recently renamed them comparison questions, preserving the CQT acronym in the process.

hypothetical child sexual abuse case described above, how often would it be reasonable to expect the innocent to be relatively calm when asked about engaging in sexual perversions with their offspring but relatively disturbed when asked about lying to an acquaintance? How likely is it that the innocent person is in fact aroused by or lying to the control question, e.g., because they can't think of a specific lie or the lie they think of is inconsequential? How likely is it that the innocent person comes to believe the falsehood that lying to a control question could lead to their failing the test? The answers to these questions are, of course, unknown. However, for the CQT to work as well as proponents charge, innocent subjects cannot be too bothered by the accusation embedded in the relevant question, they need to find their response to possibly innocuous control questions disturbing, and they must not come to think that control questions are probably unimportant given the alleged crime.

The assumptions of the CQT can also be challenged when considering guilty suspects. Clearly, the CQT could be expected to work best with guilty individuals who do not understand the purpose of the control and relevant questions. If they did, they could consciously adopt strategies to influence test outcome. For instance, they would realize that it is to their advantage to respond strongly to the control questions. Hence, they should make no important admissions to the examiner when reviewing the control questions. In addition, they should think of highly emotionally disturbing incidents associated with the control questions (e.g., lying to their spouse about an extramarital affair, masturbating in public, etc.). Finally, they can use countermeasures to augment their responses to control questions. Research has shown that simple maneuvers like pressing one's toes on the floor or performing mental arithmetic exercises when asked control questions enables guilty subjects in laboratory studies to appear truthful on the CQT (Honts, Hodes, & Raskin, 1985; Honts, Raskin, & Kircher, 1994). These results were obtainable with unsophisticated subjects who received no more than a half hour of explanation teaching them how to recognize control and relevant questions, and instructions about how to self-stimulate in response to control questions. Moreover, these same studies indicated that examiners cannot detect the use of these maneuvers.

It is apparent from the description of the CQT that the test has the best chance of conforming to examiner expectations if the examinee is naïve, knows nothing about the procedure, and is unable to discern the intent of the different types of questions. The degree to which examinees are likely to be naïve is unknown, but it is now relatively straightforward for anyone undergoing a polygraph test to access information explaining the technique and how to manipulate the outcome. This can be accomplished by accessing popular books (Lykken, 1998), scientific articles on countermeasures (Honts et al., 1985; Honts et al., 1994), and websites that expose the basis of the CQT and provide information regarding how to use countermeasures effectively (e.g., antipolygraph.org; polygraph.com).

The information I have presented thus far, although not common knowledge, can be readily obtained by anyone who wishes to learn about polygraph testing. The basis of CQT polygraph testing can also be easily explained to triers of fact. Armed with such knowledge, it seems likely that the educated lay person would be skeptical about claims that polygraphs in general are highly accurate. In addition, it would be difficult to decide what to make of a specific individual's test outcome given the many unknowns that could affect the result.

Why Polygraph Examiners Believe the CQT Is Nearly Infallible

Notwithstanding the many criticisms that have been leveled against the CQT, polygraph examiners and the scientists who support this profession insist that speculation regarding CQT deficiencies is irrelevant. In their hands, the CQT works exceptionally well,[3] and that is all that matters. This sincerely held belief has its roots in the selective feedback individual examiners receive in the course of their testing careers. The nature of polygraph testing is such that examiners often learn when they are correct, but almost never learn when they are incorrect. Examiners will swear under oath that they have given thousands of polygraph tests and have either never once been shown to be incorrect or are aware of only a couple of instances where they made an error. How is this possible?

Police-administered polygraph tests are typically given in situations where, following investigation, the case facts remain indeterminate. In the vast majority, it is hoped that the results can be used to elicit a

---

[3] The American Polygraph Association web page (polygraph.org) claims that the ". . . scientific evidence supports the high validity of polygraph examinations" and refers to findings from an article prepared for them by Forensic Research Incorporated (1997). This article reports that "researchers conducted 12 studies of the validity of field examinations, following 2,174 field examinations, providing an average accuracy of 98%" (p. 215).

confession, thereby resolving a case that might otherwise linger as unsolved or unprosecutable.

This process begins with the polygrapher's efforts to convince the examinee that polygraphs are virtually infallible. Although a suspect may doubt such claims, a skilled examiner would at least be able to convince the suspect that the examiner has complete confidence in the test outcome. At the conclusion of the test, many examinees will be confronted with the examiner's belief that their truthfulness is in doubt. At this point, using the test outcome as "evidence" that the suspect is lying, the examiner initiates an interrogation that begins with attempts to get the suspect to speculate how such an outcome is possible and ends with an effort to coax incriminating admissions or a confession from the examinee.

Confronted with the examiner's suspicion that they are untruthful, many examinees confess. When this occurs, the examiner has learned that the verdict was correct. If the examinee does not confess, in the absence of new evidence it is unlikely that the guilt or innocence of the suspect will ever be resolved. If the failed suspect was innocent, the test would be in error, but the examiner would not uncover this fact. On the other hand, when a suspect passes a CQT, there will be no attempt to obtain a confession. If the suspect was guilty, this error would go undetected. *This situation, where the failed polygraphs of guilty persons are occasionally accompanied by confessions, coupled with the fact that failed polygraphs of innocent subjects and passed polygraphs of guilty suspects are almost never discovered to be errors, leads examiners to the natural conclusion that they are virtually infallible.* This explains why polygraph examiners have repeatedly told me that if I practiced in the field like they do, I would be as convinced as they are that errors are rare.

Expert Opinion on the Scientific Basis of Polygraph Testing

Although there is consensus among experts regarding the structure of the CQT and its underlying assumptions, there is no agreement regarding the likelihood that these assumptions reflect important weaknesses undermining accuracy. The only way to determine if these weaknesses represent a serious threat to validity is to examine the scientific literature on accuracy. A comprehensive review of this literature is beyond the scope of this chapter. However, such reviews have been carried out repeatedly by both scientists who support polygraph testing and those critical of the field (Ben-Shakar, 2002; Honts, Raskin, & Kircher, 2005; Iacono & Lykken, 2005; Iacono & Patrick, 2006; Lykken, 1998; Raskin & Honts, 2002). In addition, surveys of scientific opinion regarding the validity of polygraph testing have been repeatedly undertaken (Amato & Honts, 1993; Gallup Organization, 1984; Iacono & Lykken, 1997). A review of these publications reveals almost no common ground between proponents and critics (this is starkly illustrated in the exchanges between Iacono and Lykken, 2005, and Honts et al., 2005). They do not agree what body of research is relevant to the accuracy debate, what constitute adequate criteria for the evaluation of a validity study, or how the results of existing studies should be interpreted. Proponents argue accuracy exceeding 90% while critics argue indeterminate validity and accuracy approaching chance for innocent subjects. Independent reviews conducted by scientists with no stake in the practice of polygraphy have also been undertaken (Fiedler, Schmod, & Stahl, 2002; National Research Council, 2003; Oksol & O'Donohue, 2003). Although these reviews have been highly critical of polygraph testing, they have had no palpable impact on its use in forensic settings. In this section, I will focus on a few key reports to illustrate the nature of the current dispute on polygraph testing.

One such study was carried out in collaboration with the Royal Canadian Mounted Police (RCMP) by Patrick and Iacono (Patrick & Iacono, 1991). This investigation was a field study that employed real-life cases. It stands in contrast to laboratory investigations where college students might receive course credit for participating in a mock crime followed by their taking a polygraph test. With laboratory studies, subjects are assigned to guilty and innocent conditions, so ground truth is unambiguous. However, failing a laboratory polygraph has none of the consequences associated with real-life failure, such as public embarrassment, job loss, and criminal prosecution, so using the results of laboratory studies to estimate accuracy in the field is difficult if not impossible. Although field studies circumvent this problem, establishing ground truth is a challenge. The most commonly accepted method for accomplishing this objective is to rely on confessions to identify the guilty and confirm as innocent cosuspects in the same case.

In the typical confession study, the cases are selected for inclusion if they included a polygraph test corroborated by confession. In the best of these studies, the polygraph charts are examined by skilled blind evaluators who have no knowledge of either the case facts or the details regarding test administration. The results of this chart rescoring are then compared to ground truth. The problem with this design is that under these circumstances, ground truth (i.e., the confession) and the polygraph test results are not independent. Polygraph chart scoring is highly reliable, so if the original examiner decided that the relevant questions produced stronger reactions than the control questions (i.e., deception was indicated), it should be no surprise that the blind evaluator reached the same conclusion. However, because the original examiner used the deceptive charts to interrogate the subject and elicit the confession, the confession will always be a product of a failed chart. Blind chart rescoring does not eliminate this confound, the result of which is to inflate estimates of accuracy.

The Patrick and Iacono (1991) study was designed to remedy this problem by obtaining ground truth information that was not conditioned on a failed polygraph test. They did this by first identifying the complete set of RCMP criminal cases from a major metropolitan area that included a polygraph test during a five-year period. Ignoring the outcome of the polygraph tests, they then went to the police investigative files to examine evidence that was collected subsequent to the polygraph test to see if anyone had confessed to these crimes. They found confessions from individuals who, although arrested for a different crime, never took a polygraph test but admitted committing the crime investigated with the polygraph test. They also identified cases where a reported crime was found not to have occurred, e.g., items reported stolen were found to be misplaced. By taking this step, they were able to establish a ground truth criterion that was not directly dependent on the outcome of the polygraph test. They then compared the verdicts from blindly rescored polygraph charts to this criterion. In all but one of these cases, the evidence recovered from the police files established as innocent those who had previously taken a CQT. Blind chart rescoring revealed that only slightly more than half (57%) of these innocent individuals passed their polygraphs. Because chance accuracy is 50%, this finding showed that the CQT improved only marginally over chance. This finding is perhaps not unexpected given the likelihood that CQT control questions would provide an inadequate control for an emotional but honest denial of the relevant question. Because Patrick and Iacono found only one case where follow-up police work confirmed the guilt of a person who took a polygraph, it was not possible to use the same method to estimate the accuracy for guilty subjects in this study.

Nevertheless, to tie this investigation in with other confession studies, they also identified cases where the confession followed a failed test and examined the results of blind scoring in light of these "nonindependent" confessions. Not surprisingly, when the criterion and polygraph outcome were confounded, the polygraph was 98% "accurate" for guilty subjects. The German Supreme Court took the findings from this study to heart when it used them in part to justify the exclusion of polygraph tests from the German legal system (BGH, 1998).

When considering how expert disagreement might nevertheless advance insight into the validity of polygraph testing beyond what can be gleaned from common knowledge, it is interesting to take stock of how polygraph proponents have interpreted the Patrick and Iacono results. Proponent's citations to this study ignore the problem of criterion contamination. Instead, the results are cited in such a way as to support claims of high accuracy. For instance, the American Polygraph Association cites the 98% figure given above for nonindependent confessions (Forensic Research Incorporated, 1997). The topmost scientist-proponents of polygraphy, Raskin, Honts, and colleagues (Honts, Raskin, & Kircher, 2002; Raskin & Honts, 2002) have argued that the pertinent comparison made in Patrick and Iacono that would indicate how the CQT functions in the field is that based on how often the opinion of the original examiner matched the confession. They assert "independent evaluators rarely testify in legal proceedings, nor do they make decisions in most applied settings. It is usually the original examiner who makes the decision on how to proceed in an actual case and provides court testimony. Thus, accuracy rates based on the decisions of independent evaluators may not be the true figure of merit for legal proceedings . . ." (p. 33, Raskin & Honts, 2002). They go on to note that the accuracy of the original examiners in this study was 100% for the guilty subjects. However, their conclusion ignores that the criterion contamination problem is even more pronounced when the results of the original examiner are relied on than when the blind evaluators' results are used. It was the original examiner who scored the polygraph test deceptive and then extracted the confession. Of course the original examiner's verdict will match the confession criterion 100% of the time – there is little possibility for any other result! Left unknown is how many times the original examiner failed an innocent subject who did not confess, or how many times a guilty person was passed.

Another approach to evaluating how scientific opinion has advanced the debate on polygraph validity is to consider the comprehensive review of this topic that was carried out by the National Research Council (NRC) of the National Academy of Sciences (National Research Council, 2003). The NRC was asked to undertake this study by the U.S. Department of Energy which had recently expanded its use of polygraph tests in nuclear weapons laboratories following a concern that one of its weapon scientists, Wen Ho Lee, was spying for the Chinese (a charge that was never proved; see Greenberg, 2002). A panel of 14 distinguished scholars with diverse backgrounds in psychophysiology, psychology, statistics, law, and medicine was constituted to conduct this review. The panel conducted the most far reaching and thorough evaluation of polygraph testing ever undertaken. Spanning almost two years, their work included public hearings, visits to polygraph facilities, and access to unpublished government reports, including classified material. Security screening was a primary concern of the panel, but because there is little available research on this topic the research that the panel had to evaluate was derived disproportionately from CQT studies, so their conclusions apply to forensic applications of polygraph testing.

The report provided a scathing indictment of polygraph testing. The NRC panel noted that the theoretical rationale for the CQT was weak, that research in this area was of generally low quality (e.g., the majority of studies they had to rely on were not published in scientific peer review journals), and there was little evidence of accumulated knowledge that had strengthened the scientific underpinnings of polygraph testing. The panel did not find the accuracy claims of the polygraph profession to be credible: "What is remarkable, given the large body of relevant research, is that claims about the accuracy of the polygraph made today parallel those made throughout the history of the polygraph: practitioners have always claimed extremely high levels of accuracy, and these claims have rarely been reflected in empirical research" (NRC, 2003, p. 107); ". . . almost a century of research in scientific psychology and physiology provides little basis for the expectation that a polygraph test could have extremely high accuracy" (p. 212). Accuracy cannot be established because "the evidence does not allow any precise quantitative estimate of polygraph accuracy or provide confidence that accuracy is stable across personality types, sociodemographic groups, psychological and medical conditions, examiner and examinee expectancies, or ways of administering the test and selecting questions" (p. 214).

Despite this clear indictment of polygraph testing, this report has had little effect on the practice of polygraphy, including no discernible impact on the most significant purveyor of polygraph testing, the federal government (Malakoff, 2003). There are several possible reasons for this lack of effect. The panel did not conclude that the CQT is invalid. The report states that for those untrained in countermeasures, "specific incident polygraph tests for event-specific investigations can discriminate lying from truth telling at rates well above chance, though well below perfection" (p. 214). This statement derived from the fact that none of the 57 minimally adequate studies the panel relied on generated near chance or near perfect accuracy, an outcome that suggests true accuracy falls somewhere between these extremes. This NRC conclusion is noted by proponents who find it consistent with their contention that the CQT may have better than 90% accuracy. Of course, it is also consistent with critics' claims that accuracy is substantially lower. Also, it does not contradict the NRC's main conclusion that it is not possible to estimate accurately polygraph hit rates. The panel was clear to qualify this conclusion by noting that it only holds for those untrained in countermeasures. However, no information is available on the prevalence of countermeasure use, and the NRC noted that countermeasures are "perhaps the most serious potential problem with the practical use of the polygraph" (p. 139).

Importantly, the report did not challenge strongly claims regarding the utility of polygraph testing. Rather, the authors concluded that polygraph tests may be useful when they "elicit admissions and confessions" (p. 214). Historically, the utility of polygraph testing has always been used to justify use and foster the impression that polygraph tests must be accurate.

As I have noted previously (Iacono, 1991), a polygraph test could have no better than chance accuracy and still have utility. If one used a "lie detector" that was no more accurate than a coin toss to adjudicate guilt, half of all guilty individuals would be accurately identified as liars. Confronted with the results of this lie detector by a skilled interrogator, guilty individuals would on occasion confess, demonstrating the utility of the lie detector. In the absence of knowledge that this device worked by chance, those using this technique could naturally be expected to come to believe in its validity.

Conclusions

As a form of evidence, polygraph tests are perhaps unique in several important respects. Polygraph testing, which has been in existence since the 1920s, has been largely ignored by scientists. Not surprisingly, there is little quality scientific research and the practice of polygraphy is essentially uninformed by science. Scientists not involved in polygraph testing, but with the expertise to evaluate it, have repeatedly concluded that it has at best a weak scientific basis and that the accuracy claims of the polygraph profession are unfounded. Against this backdrop, one could reasonably expect these tests to be banned or have fallen into disuse.

To the contrary, polygraph testing is flourishing. Practicing examiners, including those with scientific credentials who provide expert testimony on polygraph admissibility, believe the CQT is highly accurate. The primary force behind the continued use of polygraph tests is the U.S. federal government. Government examiners from agencies like the FBI, Secret Service, and Drug Enforcement Administration give thousands of CQTs annually. The government runs the Defense Academy for Credibility Assessment (DACA) which trains examiners for all federal and many state and local government agencies involved in law enforcement. DACA, administered by polygraph professionals, has long held that polygraph tests should be admitted as evidence in court.

These government policies reflect the value of the confession-inducing utility of polygraph tests. Confessions reinforce belief in the near infallibility of polygraphs, and this belief is used to support and amplify their application. The polygraph profession has a vested interest in preserving the extant common knowledge understanding of polygraph use to ensure that people continue to confess in the face of failed tests. This common knowledge is perpetuated by highly visible government officials (e.g., the FBI and CIA directors) publicly arguing the importance of polygraph programs for law enforcement and national security protection.

Had this chapter been written in the 1970s, it could have made the same points. The description of the CQT and the problems with its underlying assumptions have not changed. Although citations to specific studies would be different, the conclusions drawn from them would be the same for experts on both sides of this issue. The number of papers that bear on the issue of polygraph accuracy has grown substantially, but the quality of the work has changed little, and the resulting increment in new knowledge is negligible. The existing evidence does not show that polygraphs have no validity, just that the claims of high validity are unfounded and unlikely to be true.

The critical question, "Exactly how accurate is the CQT?" cannot be answered. Under the circumstances, a thoughtful lay person, armed with a description and analysis of the psychological underpinnings of the CQT, has as much relevant information to appraise the CQT as does the knowledgeable scientist. The trier of fact thus will not benefit from a courtroom debate featuring dueling experts. This field has matured little; it is difficult to see what benefit derives from the rehashing of expert speculations in the absence of significant new findings.

For this state of affairs to change, scientists need to take an active interest in the development of alternative, scientifically credible methods for assessing lying. For instance, Vrij, Fisher, Mann, and Leal (2006) noted that because lying taxes cognitive resources, it should be possible to develop techniques that tap into the extra effort required to lie during an interview. Recent developments in the cognitive sciences allow for the measurement of dynamic brain processes when people are lying or trying to conceal information about their involvement in a crime (i.e., "guilty knowledge;" Lykken, 1998). These advances have led to the development of event-related brain potential (Farwell & Smith, 2001) and functional magnetic resonance imaging technology (Kozel et al., 2005; Langleben et al., 2005) that can be used to identify deception or guilty knowledge in individual subjects (for reviews, see Iacono, 2007; Iacono & Patrick, 2006). These methods have received considerable media attention, and are already being marketed by companies with corporate names like "Brain Wave Science," "Cephos," and "No Lie fMRI." This rush to application is unfortunate because despite the technological sophistication of these procedures, their use in real-life cases is not well supported by the handful of studies carried out to date. I hope that those developing these techniques will learn from the mistakes that have plagued polygraph research throughout its history and launch the type of far-ranging, programmatic investigation needed to justify and qualify their use.

REFERENCES

Amato, S. L., & Honts, C. R. (1993). What do psychophysiologists think about polygraph tests? A survey of the membership of SPR. *Psychophysiology, 31*, S22.

www.antipolygraph.org.

Ben-Shakar, G. (2002). A critical review of the control questions test (CQT). In M. Kleiner (Ed.), *Handbook of polygraph testing* (pp. 103–126). San Diego: Academic Press.

BGH, Urteil vom 17.12.98; 1 StR 156/98.

Daubert v. Merrell Dow Pharmaceuticals, Inc., 509 U.S. 579 (1993).

Farwell, L. A., & Smith, S. S. (2001). Using brain MERMER testing to detect knowledge despite efforts to conceal. *Journal of Forensic Sciences, 46*, 1–9.

Fiedler, K., Schmod, J., & Stahl, T. (2002). What is the current truth about polygraph lie detection? *Basic & Applied Social Psychology, 24*, 313–324.

Forensic Research Incorporated (1997). The validity and reliability of polygraph testing. *Polygraph, 26*, 215–239.

Frye v. United States, 293 F. 1013 (D.C. Circuit, 1923).

Gallup Organization (1984). Survey of members of the American Society for Psychophysiological Research concerning their opinion of polygraph test interpretation. *Polygraph, 13*, 153–165.

Greenberg, D. S. (2002). Polygraph fails scientific review in the USA. *Lancet, 60*(9342), 1309.

Honts, C. R., Hodes, R. L., & Raskin, D. C. (1985). Effects of physical countermeasures on the physiological detection of deception. *Journal of Applied Psychology, 70*, 177–187.

Honts, C. R., Raskin, D., & Kircher, J. (1994). Mental and physical countermeasures reduce the accuracy of polygraph tests. *Journal of Applied Psychology, 79*, 252–259.

Honts, C. R., Raskin, D., & Kircher, J. (2002). The scientific status of research on polygraph techniques: The case for polygraph tests. In D. L. Faigman, D. H. Kaye, M. J. Saks & J. Sanders (Eds.), *Modern scientific evidence: The law and science of expert testimony* (Vol. 2, pp. 446–483). St. Paul, MN: West Publishing.

Honts, C. R., Raskin, D. C., & Kircher, J. C. (2005). The case for polygraph tests. In D. L. Faigman, D. H. Kaye, M. J. Saks & J. Sanders (Eds.), *Modern scientific evidence: The law and science of expert testimony* (Vol. 4, pp. 571–605). Eagan, MN: West.

Iacono, W. G. (1991). Can we determine the accuracy of polygraph tests? In J. R. Jennings, P. K. Ackles, & M. G. H. Coles (Eds.), *Advances in psychophysiology* (pp. 201–207). London: Jessica Kingsley Publishers.

Iacono, W. G. (2007). Detection of deception. In J. Cacioppo, L. Tassinary, & G. Berntson (Eds.), *Handbook of psychophysiology* (3rd ed, pp. 688–703). New York: Cambridge University Press.

Iacono, W. G., & Lykken, D. T. (1997). The validity of the lie detector: Two surveys of scientific opinion. *Journal of Applied Psychology, 82*, 426–433.

Iacono, W. G., & Lykken, D. T. (2005). The case against polygraph tests. In D. L. Faigman, D. H. Kaye, M. J. Saks, & J. Sanders (Eds.), *Modern scientific evidence: The law and science of expert testimony* (Vol. 4, pp. 605–655). Eagan, MN: West.

Iacono, W. G., & Patrick, C. J. (2006). Polygraph ("lie detector") testing: Current status and emerging trends. In I. B. Weiner & A. K. Hess (Eds.), *The handbook of forensic psychology* (pp. 552–588). Hoboken, NJ: John Wiley & Sons.

Kozel, F. A., Johnson, K. A., Mu, Q., Grenesko, E. L., Laken, S. J., & George, M. S. (2005). Detecting deception using functional magnetic resonance imaging. *Biological Psychiatry, 58*, 605–613.

Langleben, D. D., Loughead, J. W., Bilker, W. B., Ruparel, K., Childress, A. R., Busch, S. I., et al. (2005). Telling truth from lie in individual subjects with fast event-related fMRI. *Human Brain Mapping, 26*, 262–272.

Lykken, D. T. (1974). Psychology and the lie detector industry. *American Psychologist, 29,* 725–739.

Lykken, D. T. (1998). *A tremor in the blood: Uses and abuses of the lie detector* (2nd ed.). New York: Plenum.

Malakoff, D. (2003). Polygraph testing. DOE says fewer workers will face the machine. *Science, 301,* 1456.

Marston, W. M. (1917). Systolic blood pressure symptoms of deception. *Journal of Experimental Psychology, 2,* 117–163.

National Research Council (2003). *The polygraph and lie detection.* Washington, DC: National Academies Press.

NM Supreme Court, 96P.3d 291 (2004).

Oksol, E. M., & O'Donohue, W. T. (2003). A critical analysis of the polygraph. In W. T. O'Donohue & E. R. Levensky (Eds.), *Handbook of forensic psychology: Resource for mental health and legal professionals.* San Diego, CA: Academic Press.

Patrick, C. J., & Iacono, W. G. (1991). Validity of the control question polygraph test: The problem of sampling bias. *Journal of Applied Psychology, 76,* 229–238.

www.polygraph.com.

Raskin, D. (1986). The polygraph in 1986: Scientific, professional and legal issues surrounding applications and acceptance of polygraph evidence. *Utah Law Review, 1,* 29–74.

Raskin, D. C., & Honts, C. R. (2002). The comparison question test. In M. Kleiner (Ed.), *Handbook of polygraph testing* (pp. 1–47). San Diego: Academic Press.

Reid, J. E. (1947). A revised questioning technique in lie-detection tests. *Journal of Criminal Law and Criminology, 37,* 542–547.

Vrij, A., Fisher, R., Mann, S., & Leal, S. (2006). Detecting deception by manipulating cognitive load. *Trends in Cognitive Science, 10,* 141–142.

12

Social Science and the Evolving Standards of Death Penalty Law

Phoebe C. Ellsworth and Samuel R. Gross

Introduction

Unlike many of the topics covered in this book, death penalty litigation involves a wide variety of empirical issues. The Eighth Amendment of the U.S. Constitution provides that "Excessive bail shall not be required, nor excessive fines imposed, nor cruel and unusual punishment inflicted." But what *is* a "cruel and unusual punishment?" It could be a punishment that is *morally unacceptable* to the American people, like cutting off noses or hands. Following the other clauses of the amendment, it could be a punishment that is *excessive*, in that a lesser penalty would achieve the same ends. For example, if a death sentence served no penological purpose that was not served just as well by life imprisonment, the death penalty might be seen as excessive. Or the death penalty could be cruel and unusual *in practice* if it is rarely imposed and if the decision to take or spare the criminal's life is unprincipled. We would like to believe that the people who are executed are those who have committed the most monstrous crimes. If instead there is no rational means of differentiating the few who are sentenced to die from other killers, except perhaps for impermissible criteria like race or poverty, that could be cruel and unusual. All of these definitions have been proposed, and each has produced various lines of empirical research that have played a role in death penalty litigation.

The constitutionality of the death penalty, and of the procedures that are used to impose it, are questions of *law*. Although much of the research involves juries and the public at large, on these issues the ultimate fact finders and evaluators of the research are judges, usually Supreme Court justices, and it is their "common knowledge" and their ability to evaluate the research that matters. The evidence comes to them summarized in briefs written by the parties or by "friends of the court" – *amici curiae*. These amici may include professional organizations such as the American Psychological Association, or ad hoc groups of social scientists. The justices may evaluate the quality of the research, but initially they also decide whether the research is even relevant to the constitutional question before them, as they understand it.

It would be impossible in a chapter of this length to provide a detailed description of all the varieties of empirical research related to the death penalty, the ways in which they have been presented to the courts, and the courts' responses to them. Instead, this chapter provides a general framework for classifying and understanding the kinds of empirical questions that have been raised and their constitutional implications, the kinds of data that have been presented to the courts, and the courts' response.

It is important to remember that public policy on the death penalty does not just involve knowledge; it also involves values. Over the last 40 years capital punishment has been an emotionally charged issue in the United States, central to people's ideological self-image (Ellsworth & Ross, 1983; Ellsworth & Gross, 1994; Gross, 1998). Most of the important cases on capital punishment were decided during this period, and all of the cases that involved empirical research. The values of the Supreme Court – like those of the public at large – were decidedly pro-death penalty. As a result their evaluations of the evidence may have been less objective than their evaluation of social science evidence on less emotionally charged topics.

Public Acceptance of Capital Punishment: "Evolving Standards of Decency"

The most direct definition of a cruel and unusual punishment is a punishment that is uncommon and morally unacceptable to the public. No one, not even the strict constructionists on the Court, believes that all of the punishments commonly used in the late eighteenth century, when the Constitution was drafted, would be acceptable under the Eighth Amendment today. Mutilation and flogging were abandoned long ago. Instead, the Supreme Court has held that the Eighth Amendment "draws its meaning from the evolving standards of decency that mark the progress of a maturing society" (*Trop v. Dulles*, 1958). The implication is that there is a trend toward a penal system that is more enlightened and humane, and that some punishments that once seemed normal may eventually come to be seen as barbarous. The empirical questions are whether such a trend exists and whether we have evolved to a point where the death penalty is no longer tolerable in our society.

In Europe, this trend is clear. Since the Second World War every European country has abolished capital punishment. By the turn of the twenty-first century the policy of the European Union was that "there is no case where capital punishment can be justified under the international human rights standard" (Zimring, 2003, p. 27), and no nation that retained the death penalty was permitted to be a member. The European governments' standards of decency seem to have evolved more rapidly than those of their citizens. In most European countries the death penalty was abolished despite public support, and it was only later that popular opinion fell in line with official policy.

In the United States the primary responsibility for criminal justice rests with the states. Neither Congress nor the president has any obvious authority to abolish the death penalty at the state level. The Supreme Court could do so, however, because the Fourteenth Amendment requires states to provide "due process of law" in all criminal cases, and due process has been interpreted to include the Eighth Amendment prohibition of cruel and unusual punishment. In considering whether executions violate that prohibition, the Supreme Court has looked to the ethical standards of contemporary society.

Public support for the death penalty in the United States fell steadily from the early 1950s until the mid-1960s, when opponents were at least as numerous as proponents. The number of executions also declined during this period, from over 100 in 1951 to nearly zero in the mid- to late 1960s, followed by a judicial moratorium on executions that lasted from 1967 until 1976. In 1972, in *Furman v. Georgia*, the Supreme Court held that all death penalty laws, *as administered* at the time, were unconstitutional. But the Court left open the possibility that a fairer, less arbitrary system of capital punishment might pass constitutional muster. In 1966 public support for the death penalty reached its lowest point, with only 47% of Americans favoring it (Ellsworth & Gross, 1994); after that, the trend reversed, and support for the death penalty increased sharply between 1966 and 1982, and moderately between 1982 and the mid-1990s, when one poll (Gallup, 1994) found that 80% of Americans favored the death penalty. Since then, support has declined to around 65% in 2005. By 1976, when the Supreme Court reconsidered the constitutionality of the death penalty in *Gregg v. Georgia*, support for the death penalty had already risen to 66% (NORC, 1976), and the Court concluded that "a large proportion of American society continues to regard death as an appropriate and necessary criminal sanction" (*Gregg v. Georgia*, 1976, p. 878), and thus that capital punishment was not cruel and unusual by contemporary standards.

In general, the Supreme Court's opinions have tracked the empirical data on public opinion towards the death penalty fairly well. The death penalty was abolished not long after public support reached an all-time low, and was reinstated following the dramatic increase in support through the mid-1970's (*Gregg v. Georgia*, 1976). This is not to say that the Court analyzed the public opinion poll data carefully, or that the justices actually based their decisions on the empirical research. Their "empirical evidence" was broader and less systematic. Occasionally the opinions refer to a public opinion poll or a scholarly article, but they rely more heavily on state referenda, new legislation, and patterns of jury verdicts. On the whole, the Court has been right about where America stands in the progress of a maturing society.

This is not surprising. The results of public opinion polls on the death penalty are widely publicized, easy to understand, obviously related to the constitutional question at issue, and rarely disputed. Death penalty attitudes are relatively immune to the kinds of changes in question wording and order that raise doubts about the validity of surveys on some other topics (Schuman & Presser, 1981; Schwarz, Groves, & Schuman, 1998; Ellsworth & Gross, 1994; Gross & Ellsworth, 2003). There is quite a bit of research on death penalty attitudes that is more complex than the simple favor–oppose polls, research exploring the bases of people's attitudes, regional and demographic differences, and the reasons for attitude *change*. Few Justices have paid attention to this more nuanced research, but it is not clear that there is any reason that they should. All of the polls since the death penalty was reinstated show that a majority of Americans favor it. After 1995 this majority fell to 65%. It hovers around 50%, if respondents are explicitly given the choice between death and life in prison without parole, but it has not yet fallen to a level that could plausibly be called public rejection, and the Court has not considered the possibility of abolishing the death penalty since 1976.

The Court *has* attended to differences in public support of the death penalty for different kinds of capital defendant. Just a year after the death penalty was reinstated in *Gregg*, the Court held that the penalty of death was disproportionate and excessive for rapists, and therefore unconstitutional, and justified their decision with evidence that the public no longer felt that the death penalty was appropriate for the crime of rape (*Coker v. Georgia*, 1977). (The Court mostly cited legislative decisions and jury verdicts, rather than opinion polls, and completely ignored the powerful empirical evidence of racial bias in executions for rape.)

In the late 1990s, after a 15-year plateau of general enthusiasm for the death penalty, support dropped significantly, from 75% or higher to about 65% (Gross & Ellsworth, 2003; Death Penalty Information Center). Correspondingly, after a short lag, the Supreme Court has begun to restrict the use of the death penalty. In two recent cases, the Court relied heavily on changes in public attitudes. In *Atkins v. Virginia* (2002) the Court held that the execution of people who are mentally retarded is unconstitutional, relying primarily on the fact that a majority of state legislatures had outlawed the practice; but also citing briefs by the APA and other professional organizations, as well as national opinion polls, to reach the conclusion that the "legislative judgment reflects a much broader social and professional consensus" (*Atkins v. Virginia*, 2002, FN 21). This is an accurate reflection of the research on public opinion. Even when levels of overall support were at their highest, only about 25% of the population favored the death penalty for mentally retarded killers. For example in 1988, when 71% of the population favored execution of murderers and 51% favored the execution of rapists, only 21% favored the death penalty for mentally retarded defendants (Gross & Ellsworth, 2003). By 2002 support was down to 13% (Gallup, 2002).

In the second case, *Roper v. Simmons* (2005), the Court held that it was unconstitutional to execute people for crimes they committed before the age of 18. The opinion closely follows the holding in *Atkins*, using evolving standards of decency as the rationale, and relying primarily on state legislative changes for evidence, although the movement to abolish capital punishment for defendants under 18 was more sluggish than it was for mentally retarded defendants. The Court used social science data not for the proposition that the public has come to repudiate the execution of juveniles, but for evidence that the juvenile mind is not the same as the adult mind: It is less aware of responsibility, less able to resist peer pressure, and more susceptible to further development. The Court also emphasized the rejection of the death penalty for juveniles by every other nation in the world (except Somalia, which had no functioning government.)

On the surface, the *Roper* opinion looks like the *Atkins* opinion bolstered by two additional lines of supporting evidence. A cynic might conclude that these two new lines of evidence were trotted out because the core argument – that the American public rejects the death penalty for young offenders – is somewhat weaker than the parallel argument in *Atkins*. The legislative evidence is less compelling, and public opinion surveys – which the Court does not mention in *Roper* – are less overwhelmingly one sided. In 1989, when the Court held in *Stanford v. Kentucky* that the execution of 16- and 17-year-olds was acceptable to Americans, 57% of the public favored that position (Time\CNN\Yankelovich, 1989). In 1994 61% favored it (Gallup, 1994). By 2001, with overall support for the death penalty declining, support for juvenile executions dropped to about 36% (NORC, 2001 [34%]; Princeton Survey Research Associates, 2001 [38%]), and remained at that level (Princeton Survey Research Associates, 2003 [35%], and 2005 [37%]). Still, while rejection of the death penalty for juvenile defendants is more recent and less overwhelming than for retarded defendants, the Court's decision accurately tracks changes in public opinion.

Excessiveness of Capital Punishment: The Question of Deterrence

The argument that the death penalty is excessive has two prongs. The simpler one is that it is grossly disproportionate to the crime for which it was imposed. This was the specific legal ground the Court relied on in *Coker v. Georgia* (1977) to outlaw the death penalty for rape. Evidence of public rejection of death as a punishment for rape (and other nonhomicidal crimes) was used to support the claim that the death penalty was excessive because it was categorically disproportionate to the crime. The Court has never entertained the argument that death is a disproportionate punishment for murder. But it did consider a second type of excessiveness in murder cases: that the death penalty is excessive because it serves no legitimate purpose that is not equally well served by life imprisonment. In *Furman* (1972) some of the justices in the majority took the position that death sentences as rare and unpredictable as the ones before the Court served no useful retributive purpose. The main question, however, was the marginal deterrence of capital punishment: Do executions deter homicide more effectively than imprisonment for life?

When *Furman* was decided the main source of systematic evidence on the deterrent effect of the death penalty was the seminal work of Thorsten Sellin (1967). Sellin conducted a series of comparisons of homicide rates in the United States between 1920 and 1955: Between states that had the death penalty and neighboring states that did not; within states that had had the death penalty and abolished it, and then sometimes restored it; and between states that abolished or restored the death penalty and neighboring states that did not. None of these comparisons indicated that the death penalty lowered the homicide rate. Justice Marshall, in his concurring opinion in *Furman*, discussed this evidence in detail in support of his position that the death penalty is inherently unconstitutional.

In *Gregg* in 1976 the Court was presented with a new study, by Isaac Ehrlich, that analyzed the relationship between executions and homicide rates in the United States as a whole, by year, from 1933 through 1969. Using econometric models and multiple regression analyses, Ehrlich claimed to find that each execution reduced the homicide rate to the extent of saving eight lives (1975). By the time *Gregg* got to the Court, Ehrlich's study had been subjected to extensive and withering criticism (see Blumstein, Cohen & Nagen, 1978; Dike, 1982; Lempert, 1981, for reviews). Among other problems, critics pointed out that he had not controlled for the severity of the alternative, noncapital sanctions for murder; and that the effect he found disappears entirely if the years from 1965 through 1969 are removed from the analysis – a period in which a very low rate of executions coincided with the beginning of a long-term rise in homicide rates. The plurality of the Court in the decisive opinion in *Gregg* did not attempt to address any of these methodological questions. Instead, it wrote the issue of deterrence out of the legal debate over the constitutionality of capital punishment. It noted that there were conflicting studies – which was literally true, ignoring the value of those studies – and concluded that "there is no convincing empirical evidence either supporting or refuting" the claim that the death penalty is a unique deterrent, and that this is "a complex factual issue the resolution of which properly rests with the legislatures" (*Gregg*, 1976, p. 186).

Having kicked the issue over to legislatures, the Supreme Court has never revisited the question of deterrence. Nor is it likely to. In *Furman* there was an active debate over the appropriateness of retribution as a justification for capital punishment (or punishment in general). For example, Justice Powell, writing for the four pro-death penalty dissenters, quoted an earlier Supreme Court statement that "Retribution is no longer the dominant objective of the criminal law" and explained: "It is clear, however, that the Court did not reject retribution altogether" (*Furman*, 1972, p. 452). In *Gregg*, four years later, the Court explicitly upheld retribution as a justification for the death penalty because a legislature could legitimately conclude "that certain crimes are themselves so grievous an affront to humanity that the only adequate response may be the penalty of death" (*Gregg*,

1976, p. 184). So deterrence is no longer a necessary argument for the punishment. The Court's position here tracks public opinion. In the past forty years retribution has become accepted and popular in the United States as justification for punishment in general (Ellsworth & Gross, 1994), and it has overtaken deterrence and become the dominant reason people give for supporting for the death penalty. At the same time, a strong majority of the public has come to believe that the death penalty does not deter homicide better than life imprisonment (Gross & Ellsworth, 2003).

Academic debate over the deterrent effect of capital punishment continued after *Gregg*. In 1978 the National Academy issued a report reviewing the evidence in support of a deterrent effect of capital punishment – basically, the Ehrlich study – and found it unpersuasive (Blumstein et al., 1978). In the 20 years that followed there were periodic new studies on the issue, most of which found no deterrent effect (Bailey, 1998; Sorenson, Wrinkle, Brewer, & Marquart, 1999). In the past several years there has been a spate of new econometric studies of deterrence and the death penalty, most of which claim to find a deterrent effect, but not all. As with Ehrlich's, these studies have been reviewed and heavily criticized. Independent researchers have demonstrated that the findings of deterrence are unstable and depend on arbitrary methodological choices (Berk, 2005; Donohue and Wolfers, 2006), and have concluded that, as the National Academy found 28 years earlier, "We can be sure that the death penalty does not cause or eliminate large numbers of homicides, but we learn little else from the data" (Donohue & Wolfers, 2006, p. 844). The new claims of a deterrent effect – whatever their worth – are not likely to figure directly in court decisions one way or the other, but might be used in policy debates to bolster support for capital punishment now that it is in decline.

Arbitrariness and Discrimination: Capital Punishment in Practice

In 1972, when the Supreme Court held that the death penalty as then administered was unconstitutional (*Furman v. Georgia*, 1972), neither deterrence nor contemporary standards figured importantly in the decision. *Furman* is a particularly difficult case to interpret, because it was a 5 to 4 decision in which each Justice wrote a separate opinion. Brennan and Marshall, the two Justices who were categorically opposed to capital punishment, discussed both of these issues, but the only issue that was common to the five majority Justices was that the death penalty statutes of the time resulted in decisions that were at best arbitrary, and possibly discriminatory against racial minorities, particularly African Americans. Those who were executed were not the ones who had committed the most awful murders, but a haphazard, unlucky selection – "like being struck by lightning" in the words of Justice Stewart (*Furman*, 1972, p. 309) – or, worse, a systematic selection of people without money, friends, or white skin. As Justice Douglas put it, "one searches our chronicles in vain for the execution of any member of the affluent strata of this society" (*Furman*, 1972, pp. 251–252).

Jury instructions

At the time of the *Furman* decision, capital juries were typically given no instructions at all on how to decide who should be executed and who should not. They were simply sent into the jury room and told to decide whether the defendant was guilty, and, if so, whether the penalty should be life or death.

By the time the *Furman* decision was handed down, public support for the death penalty was on the rise. Most states responded quickly and enacted new death penalty statutes designed to ensure that the unfettered jury discretion of the past would be suitably directed so that death sentences would be calibrated to the seriousness of the crime. In 1976, in *Gregg v. Georgia* and its companion cases, the Supreme Court declared that the death penalty was constitutional if states provided a bifurcated trial, in which the penalty was decided in a separate proceeding after guilt had been decided; there were specific instructions limiting the aggravating factors that could be considered in deciding for the death penalty, and requiring that the jury balance these against any mitigating factors. The idea was that these "guided discretion" statutes would eliminate the arbitrariness and possible discrimination that had existed in the pre-*Furman* days. As the plurality opinion stated, "No longer can a jury wantonly or freakishly impose the death sentence; it is always circumscribed by the legislative guidelines" (*Gregg*, 1976, pp. 206–207).

If the Court had hoped to settle the issue once and for all in *Gregg*, it certainly failed. Since then, capital cases have been a constant item on the Court's agenda, and there is no sign that the number of cases is diminishing. Most of these cases have concerned the administration of the death penalty and the effectiveness of the post-*Gregg* laws in eliminating arbitrariness and discrimination.

This is not surprising. Decisions about the appropriate penalty – particularly when the choice is life or death – inevitably implicate values and moral principles more deeply than decisions about guilt or innocence. In most states the list of aggravating factors that the jury is supposed to consider include vague value-laden considerations – such as whether the murder was especially heinous, atrocious, and cruel – and sometimes considerations that invite race or class bias, such as whether the defendant would be dangerous or a threat to society in the future. One of the fundamental arguments for trial by jury is that the jury represents the "conscience of the community," the values of the public, rather than the views of the government or an elite ruling class. Efforts to circumscribe community morality by formulaic rules may be incompatible not only with the purpose of the jury but with human psychology itself. In addition to the motivational and emotional difficulties of deciding good and evil according to a prescribed recipe, the cognitive challenge is substantial. Most researchers agree that jurors have a very hard time understanding legal instructions in general (Ellsworth & Reifman, 2000; Lieberman & Sales, 1997), and the instructions that they are given at the penalty phase of a capital trial are especially difficult (Diamond & Levi, 1996; Eisenberg & Wells, 1993; Haney & Lynch, 1994, 1997). Even before *Furman*, in *McGautha v. California* (1971) Justice Harlan foresaw this dilemma: "To identify before the fact those characteristics of criminal homicides and their perpetrators which call for the death penalty, and to express these characteristics in language which can be fairly understood and applied by the sentencing authority, appear to be tasks which are beyond present human ability" (*McGautha*, 1971, p. 204). The Court in *Furman* ignored this dire warning, and proceeded on the assumption that legislatures could somehow square the circle. Psychological research, unfortunately, seems to have confirmed Justice Harlan's pessimistic assessment. It has certainly shown that efforts to date have not been successful.

The guidelines that jurors are supposed to apply in deciding between life and death are opaque. They include terms such as "aggravating circumstances" and "mitigating circumstances" that are unfamiliar or, worse yet, have different meanings in everyday discourse than they do in law (Haney & Lynch, 1994, 1997). In addition, many juries have difficulty understanding the rules for balancing aggravating and mitigating factors to reach a decision – what they should do if they find that aggravating factors outweigh mitigating factors, that mitigating factors outweigh aggravating, or that they are equally strong; and whether they must agree unanimously that an aggravating or mitigating factor is present. Haney and Lynch (1997) found that 41% of jurors incorrectly believed that if the mitigating factors equaled the aggravating factors, they could still vote for death, and 27% believed that they could vote for death even if the mitigating factors outweighed the aggravating factors. More alarming, 41% of the jurors they studied thought that when the aggravating factors outweighed the mitigating factors the law *required* them to vote for death. This is not true. The law never requires a jury to vote for death, but apparently jurors believe that it does.

The Supreme Court has been remarkably oblivious to the research on this issue, basically subscribing to the legal fiction that if the jury is given the legally correct instructions, the jury understands the law. The case of *Weeks v. Angelone* (2000) is a vivid example. In that case the prosecutor argued that there were two applicable aggregating circumstances: that Weeks would "constitute a continuing serious threat to society," and that his crime was "outrageously or wantonly vile, horrible, or inhumane . . ." The jury was instructed: "If you find from the evidence that the Commonwealth has proved beyond a reasonable doubt, either of the two alternatives, and as to that alternative you are unanimous, then you may fix the punishment of the defendant at death; or, if you believe from all the evidence that the death penalty is not justified, then you shall fix the punishment of the defendant at life imprisonment" (*Weeks*, 2000, p. 229). The jury had a written copy of the instructions, but apparently had trouble figuring out what they meant. After deliberating for 4½ hours, they asked the judge: "If we believe that Lonnie Weeks Jr., is guilty of at least one of the alternatives, then is it our duty as a jury to issue the death penalty? Or must we decide (even though he is guilty of one of the alternatives) whether or not to issue the death penalty, or one of the life sentences? What is the Rule? Please clarify" (p. 241).

The judge could have answered the question by saying: "You are not required to give the death penalty even if you find one of the aggravating circumstances; it is up to you to decide between life and death." Instead he simply referred them to the paragraph in the instructions describing their choices, the very paragraph they said they did not understand. The jury, in tears, sentenced Weeks to death. Weeks appealed on the grounds that the jury had not understood that a life sentence was permissible. In this case, as in others (e.g., *Buchanan v. Angelone*, 1998) the consensus of the social science research was shared by the jurors themselves. They did not understand the instructions; they knew it; they said so; they asked for help – and they did not get any.

The Supreme Court was not impressed. The majority held that "A jury is presumed to follow the instructions [citations omitted]. Similarly, a jury is presumed to understand a judge's answers to its questions" (p. 234). No social science research was mentioned. Did the Court really believe that the jury understood the judge's answer? Or did it maintain the legal fiction of understanding, because the problem of juror misunderstanding was surely not unique to Weeks's case but had troublesome implications for many other capital and noncapital cases? Either way, it is clear that unintelligible instructions are no safeguard against arbitrary decisions.

An empirical study of people's understanding of capital jury instructions was presented to a federal trial court in the case of *United States ex rel Free v. McGinnis* (1993). The judge held that the instructions failed to provide jurors with a "clear understanding of how they are to go about deciding whether the defendant lives or dies" (p. 1129). The study, conducted by Hans Zeisel (described in Diamond & Levi, 1996), tested prospective jurors in a Chicago courthouse with 16 questions about the legal instructions for weighing aggravating and mitigating factors, and found that a majority of the respondents gave the correct answer on only three of the questions. The Seventh Circuit Court of Appeals reversed and reinstated Free's death sentence. However, unlike most courts, which simply affirm the legal presumption that jurors understand and follow the instructions, Judge Posner, writing for the majority in *Free*, said that empirical evidence that jurors misunderstand the instructions on capital sentencing *could* be grounds for a constitutional reversal. The data from Zeisel's study, however, were not persuasive, primarily because Zeisel had not shown that any alternative, rewritten instructions would have been more comprehensible to the jurors. A concurring judge also faulted the study for not including jury deliberations. In response, Diamond and Levi (1996) conducted a follow-up study in which they found that: (1) rewritten instructions were understood significantly better than the Illinois pattern instructions; and (2) deliberation generally did not increase the jurors' ability to understand the instructions.

Diamond and Levi's data were not available to the Court when they reinstated Free's death sentence, and Free was executed in 1995. But the court's opinion in *Free* is an unusual and encouraging departure from the common judicial practice of altogether ignoring empirical data on juries' ability to understand the legal instructions. No matter how well crafted a set of guidelines might be in theory, if the jury cannot understand them, then in practice life or death decisions will be arbitrary.

Predicting dangerousness

So far we have been discussing the instructions governing the *process* by which jurors are to weigh the aggravating and mitigating factors in deciding between life and death. There are also problems with the factors themselves. Most states give jurors a list of aggravating factors and instruct them that they must find that one or more were present in order for the defendant to be eligible for the death penalty. Some of the factors are straightforward and unproblematic: for example, that the victim was a police officer. Many states include at least one factor that seems to allow the same unbridled discretion that was held unconstitutional in *Furman* (1972), allowing the jury to consider whether the murder was heinous, outrageous, wantonly cruel, vile, or depraved. Social science has generally had little to say about the validity of these specific factors, except for one. In several states the jury is asked to consider whether the defendant is likely to be a continuing threat to society, to commit violent crimes in the future. If so, the death penalty is warranted. The constitutionality of this factor was considered in the case of *Barefoot v. Estelle* (1983), in which the American Psychiatric Association filed a brief as a Friend of the Court. The APA pointed to a strong consensus among social scientists that not even experts can predict future dangerousness with any accuracy, and argued that future dangerousness should not be permissible as an aggravating factor because it was impossible to predict, and that expert psychological testimony of future dangerousness should be prohibited, because the data indicated that such predictions were usually wrong. In other words, the APA argued that its own members could not be trusted on this issue.

Nonetheless the Supreme Court held that the factor was constitutionally acceptable, and that expert psychologists and psychiatrists should be allowed to testify and to predict whether or not the defendant would pose a continuing threat to society. Astonishingly, the majority found the psychiatric evidence satisfactory because "Neither petitioner nor the [American Psychiatric Association] suggest that psychiatrists are *always wrong* with respect to the future dangerousness, only most of the time" (*Barefoot v. Estelle*, 1983, p. 901; emphasis added).[1] In *Barefoot* the court accepted a form of social science "evidence" that was strongly repudiated by the scientific community. The

---

[1]   Of course, if predictions of dangerousness *were* "always wrong" they would be a perfect (negative) predictor of future behavior – which would be a strong argument for admitting them.

"common sense" of the Justices seems to be that predicting the violent potential of capital defendants is sufficiently important for capital sentencing that if a legislature wants juries to do it, they must be allowed to, even when the acknowledged experts on the issue say it cannot be done.

A more cynical view is that drawing jurors' attention to future dangerousness is one of the most effective methods of getting them to return a verdict of death. Research suggests that one of the strongest justifications for the death penalty in the minds of the public in general and of capital jurors in particular is that it guarantees that the defendant will never kill again (Bowers & Steiner, 1999; Eisenberg & Wells, 1993; Gross, 1998). The "common knowledge" of prosecutors, courts, and legislatures is consistent with this research, and because they favor death sentences, they may want to reinforce the image of the dangerous killer out on the streets and eager to kill again. Unfortunately, this strategy is fundamentally misleading. In almost every state a capital defendant who is sentenced to life imprisonment is ineligible for parole, will die in prison, and is no danger to private citizens. But sometimes this information is kept from the jury, leaving them to believe that if he is not executed the murderer will be released – perhaps in 20 years, perhaps in 10, maybe sooner (Bowers & Steiner, 1999; Eisenberg & Wells, 1993). In *Simmons v. South Carolina* (1994) the Supreme Court held that when a capital defendant's "future dangerousness is at issue, and state law prohibits the defendant's release on parole, due process requires that the sentencing jury be informed that the defendant is parole ineligible" (p. 154). South Carolina attempted to evade this rule in a subsequent case (*Kelly v. South Carolina*, 2002), arguing that their evidence that Kelly was a "butcher" was relevant to character, not to dangerousness, but lost again in the Supreme Court. Judges seem to understand that evidence of future dangerousness is powerfully persuasive to juries, but although the Supreme Court has attempted to limit the influence of future dangerousness in cases in which it is fundamentally misleading, it has not reconsidered its position on the overall appropriateness of such evidence.

Racial discrimination

Broad, vague legal standards and juror misunderstanding of the law not only lead to decisions that are arbitrary, but also provide an opportunity for racial prejudice. As early as the mid-1960s, Marvin Wolfgang conducted a study that showed that across the South death sentences for rape were about 18 times more likely when the defendant was Black and the victim was White than in other racial combinations (*Maxwell v. Bishop*, 1970; Wolfgang & Reidel 1973). Uneasiness about racial discrimination has haunted the death penalty ever since. For the most part it has lurked in the background, appearing in concurring and dissenting opinions, but never squarely addressed – until the case of *McCleskey v. Kemp* in 1987. The issue in *McCleskey* was discrimination in the entire process that led to death sentences – not just jury discrimination, but discrimination in the decisions to arrest, to go forward with the prosecution, and to try the case as a capital case.

By 1987 several studies had examined whether the new guided discretion statutes enacted after *Gregg* had managed to eliminate racial discrimination in capital sentencing. All showed that defendants who killed White victims were much more likely to receive the death penalty than those who killed Black victims. There was some evidence that Black *defendants* were more likely to be sentenced to death than White defendants, but it is less powerful and less consistent, and the effect often disappears when the studies control for legitimate aggravating factors such as killing a stranger or committing the murder in the course of another felony. The race of the victim, however, showed up as an independent factor even in the best-controlled studies. Regardless of other factors, killing a White person is more likely to result in a death sentence than killing a Black person.

McCleskey was a Georgia case, and the centerpiece of the case was a comprehensive landmark study of Georgia's homicide prosecutions (Baldus, Pulaski, and Woodworth, 1983). In this study David Baldus and his colleagues analyzed data on more than 400 variables in over 1,000 Georgia homicide cases and found that nothing but race could explain the discrimination against defendants who killed White victims. The study also found that Blacks who killed Whites were more likely to be sentenced to death than Whites who killed Whites in some subsets of the cases. Similar patterns were found in less comprehensive studies in Florida (Radelet, 1981; Radelet & Pierce, 1985), South Carolina (Jacoby & Paternoster, 1982), and eight other states (Gross & Mauro, 1984), and in many studies across the country in the years since *McCleskey*.

The Supreme Court rejected the claim of discrimination in *McCleskey* by 5 to 4, with Justice Powell writing for the majority. Powell begins by assuming the accuracy of Baldus's findings, but, all the same, goes on to say that: "At most the Baldus study indicates a disparity that appears to correlate with race" (*McCleskey*, 1987, p. 312), and "we decline to assume that what is unexplained is invidious" (p. 313). In fact, Baldus and his colleagues had found a powerful correlation between capital sentencing and race of victim that could not be explained by any combination of other variables that they considered, or that was offered by any other researcher or interested party. Powell's central argument, however, is that – at least in this context[2] – statistical evidence is inherently "insufficient to support an inference that any of the [individual] decisionmakers in McCleskey's case acted with discriminatory purpose" (p. 297). That holding created an essentially insuperable barrier to proof of racial discrimination in capital sentencing.

Years later, after he had retired, Justice Powell told his biographer that his decision in *McCleskey* was the only one in his career that he truly regretted, that his understanding of statistics "ranges from limited to zero," and that he had come to believe that the death penalty ought to be abolished (Jeffries, 1994, p. 451). Given the importance of the issue of racial discrimination, abolition would have been a likely consequence if the Court had sided with McCleskey. In 1987 this was not an acceptable outcome to Justice Powell or his colleagues in the majority on the Supreme Court.

Death qualification

Death qualification is the practice of excluding all citizens who adamantly oppose the death penalty from serving as jurors in capital cases. Thus in capital cases, unlike all other cases, the jury is made up exclusively of people who would be willing to sentence a person to death. The empirical question is whether such a "death-qualified" jury is more than usually likely to decide that the defendant is guilty.

As with race bias, the common knowledge of prosecutors and judges is that the answer is yes. Jurors who favor the death penalty tend to favor the arguments of the prosecution, and prosecutors have admitted to using death qualification in order to increase the likelihood of conviction (Oberer, 1961). As with race bias, the empirical data coincide perfectly with legal intuition: Death-qualified jurors are more favorable to the prosecution and more likely to vote for guilt than the citizens who are excluded from capital juries. Conceptually, this creates a problem of discrimination of a different sort than the

---

[2] In other contexts, such as discrimination in employment in and in the composition of juries, the Court has accepted statistical evidence as proof of discrimination (Gross & Mauro, 1989, pp. 173–191.)

one we have just considered. The issue is not discrimination between different categories of capital defendants, but against capital defendants by comparison to other criminal defendants.

In 1968, when the issue first came before the Supreme Court (*Witherspoon v. Illinois*), there was little research, and the Court held that the evidence was insufficient to demonstrate that death-qualified juries were biased towards conviction. However, the Court acknowledged that the question was an empirical one, and that they might be persuaded in the future by a stronger empirical record. By the time the issue came back to the Supreme Court in 1986, in the case *Lockhart v McCree*, the evidence consisted of 15 empirical studies, conducted over a 30-year period, using samples from different regions and demographic groups, and multiple methods: attitude, surveys, simulations, and interviews with actual jurors. All of the research converged on the conclusion that death-qualified jurors were more favorable to the prosecution and more likely to vote guilty than the citizens who were excluded, and that jury deliberation did not erase the bias (Ellsworth, 1988). As in *McCleskey*, the Court was faced with a substantial, consistent, and highly persuasive body of research that pointed to a conclusion opposite to the one the majority wanted to reach.

Justice Rehnquist, writing for the majority, first criticized the research, and then declared that even if the studies proved what they claimed, death qualification would still be constitutional. The critique was fairly extensive. Rehnquist examined the 15 studies one by one, finding a flaw in each and discarding it from the set, until only one study was left (Cowan, Thompson, & Ellsworth, 1984) – and "Surely," he concluded, "a constitutional decision should not be based on a lone study" (*Lockhart*, 1986, p. 173). Although the APA amicus brief, the lower court cases, and Justice Marshall's dissent clearly described the concept of convergent validity, the majority managed to overlook it. As in *McCleskey*, the majority opinion also rejected McCree's claim because he had failed to demonstrate that the particular jury that had tried him included jurors who were biased towards guilt. Rehnquist's general position is that if a jury contains 12 impartial individuals, it is an impartial jury, even if large segments of the population are excluded from serving. In effect, the Court decided that the constitutionality of death-qualification was not an empirical question not all, despite the holding in *Witherspoon*: "We do not ultimately base our decision today on the invalidity of the lower courts' 'factual' findings" (*Lockhart*, 1986, p. 1762, n.3). In capital cases it is constitutional to decide guilt or innocence with juries that are biased toward guilt.

Conclusion: Retribution, Innocence, and Public Opinion

In *Lockhart v McCree* (1986) the Court held that empirical research was not relevant to the constitutionality of death qualification. In *McCleskey v. Kemp* (1987) the Court held that statistical data could not prove race discrimination in capital sentencing. Many people – members of the public and members of the judiciary – question whether empirical research is relevant to the constitutionality of capital punishment at all. For many supporters and opponents of the death penalty the issue is a moral one, not an empirical one. Supporters believe that death is appropriate as a form of retribution: just punishment for heinous murderers, a life for a life (Ellsworth & Gross, 1994). Opponents believe just as strongly that it is morally wrong for the State to kill. The empirical research we have reviewed in this chapter has been evaluated in the contexts of these moral principles. Over the past 35 years – the period when the constitutionality of various aspects of the death penalty has been at issue – moral beliefs about the death penalty have been intense and passionate. The Supreme Court of course was aware of the public's fervent support for the death penalty during most of this period, support that was compatible with the Court majority's own ideological commitment to the constitutionality of capital punishment. In this context, dealing with the empirical data on public opinion and evolving standards of decency was smooth sailing: The public favored the death penalty, the Court favored it, and the Court's decisions matched the data.

On the other issues, the empirical research revealed serious problems in the actual practice of capital punishment in America, in particular the continuing existence of the arbitrariness and discrimination that were supposedly eliminated by the guided discretion standards endorsed in *Gregg v. Georgia* (1976). Challenges to the death penalty have relied heavily on social science data, and the empirical arguments have been exceptionally sophisticated and thorough, particularly on the issues of racial discrimination and death qualification. The Court's attempts to evade research with implications that they did not like has contributed to what Gross and Mauro (1989) called "an expanding swamp of uncertain rules and confusing opinions" (p. 7).

This is not a matter of judicial "common knowledge", but of values and ideology. Most lawyers and judges know that death-qualification produces juries that favor the prosecution, and that the criminal justice system is not color-blind. Nor is it a matter of a general reluctance to consider social science data. In other contexts involving race, such as employment, education, and the use of peremptory challenges, the Court has found discrimination based on weaker data than those presented in *McCleskey*. In other cases involving the fairness of the jury, such as the cases on jury size, they have relied on weaker evidence than that presented in *Lockhart*. They have generally avoided considering the research that shows that juries do not understand the legal standards for sentencing a person to death, but have allowed the jury to hear inaccurate and misleading expert testimony on future dangerousness. The Court's use of social science evidence is related less to its compatibility with scientific standards than to its compatibility with a decision already reached. The death penalty is morally justified, and data that threaten this premise are circumvented.

There is a growing uneasiness, however. The moral principle of just retribution only makes sense if the people we are executing are heinous murderers – sane, intellectually competent people who choose evil over good. Doubts that our system of capital punishment has been effective in singling out these morally depraved killers are reflected in the recent Supreme Court decisions outlawing the execution of mentally retarded defendants and juveniles.

In the past decade, however, a much more important challenge has emerged. Until recently, most people believed that the safeguards built into our system of capital punishment – trial by jury, a seemingly endless series of appeals, executive clemency – were so complete that the possibility of executing someone by mistake was negligible. If anything, people believed that these protections, particularly the appellate process, were greater than necessary and should be curtailed. The near infallibility of the system was common knowledge. That view has fundamentally changed.

Between 1973 and January 2007, 122 convicted capital defendants have been exonerated and released from death row in the United States (Death Penalty Information Center). In 2006 new investigations produced strong evidence that several executed defendants were innocent (Shaw, 2006). In addition, hundreds of innocent noncapital defendants have been released in the past two decades, mostly rape defendants who were cleared by DNA evidence (Gross, Jacoby, Matheson, Montgomery, & Patil, 2005). The problem of false convictions in general – and false capital convictions in particular – has received widespread attention in the news media, and has been the subject of many popular books, television shows, and movies. It has generated a growing movement to reform police investigative procedures. It led to a moratorium on executions in Illinois in 1999, and a more recent one in

New Jersey in 2006. It is the most important development in the American criminal justice system in the past 25 years.

The Supreme Court might someday consider a direct challenge to the death penalty on the grounds that it leads to executions of innocent people. One lower court did hold the death unconstitutional on that basis, but it was reversed on appeal (*United States v. Quinones*, 2002). More likely the issue will affect the Court indirectly.

Concerns about the execution of innocent people have already weakened public support for capital punishment. This is the engine that drove down support in the late 1990s. Most Americans already believe, abstractly, that innocent defendants have been put to death in recent years (Gross & Ellsworth, 2003). If specific false executions are proven by DNA, or other incontrovertible evidence, support will drop further. If the public comes to oppose the death penalty, legislatures and courts will follow suit, as they did in the case of the execution of the mentally retarded. The "evolving standards of decency" standard puts public acceptance at the center of the constitutional debate over capital punishment. For years the public enthusiastically accepted capital punishment, and the Supreme Court's decisions were consistently pro-death penalty; recently, public support has weakened, and the Court has ruled against the death penalty for particular kinds of defendants. In the future, if a majority of the American public comes to oppose the death penalty altogether, it will be history.

REFERENCES

Atkins v. Virginia, 536 U.S. 304 (2002).
Bailey, W. C. (1998). Deterrence, brutalization, and the death penalty: Another examination of Oklahoma return to capital punishment. *Criminology, 36,* 711–748.
Baldus, D. C., Pulaski, C. A., & Woodworth, G. (1983). Comparative review of death sentences: An empirical study of the Georgia experience. *Journal of Criminal Law and Criminology, 74,* 661–753.
Barefoot v. Estelle, 463 U.S. 880 (1983).
Berk, R. (2005). New claims about executions and general deterrence: Déjà vu all over again? *Journal of Empirical Legal Studies, 2,* 303–325.
Blumstein, A. J., Cohen, J., & Nagen, D. (Eds.) (1978). Deterrence and incapacitation: Estimating the effects of criminal sanctions on crime rates. *Panel on Research on Deterrent and Incapacitative Effects, Committee on Research on Law Enforcement and Criminal Justice, Assembly of Behavioral and Social Sciences, National Research Council.* Washington, DC: National Academy of Sciences.

Bowers, W. J., & Steiner, B. D. (1999). Death by default: An empirical demonstration of false and forced choices in capital sentencing, *Texas Law Review, 77,* 605–717.

Buchanan v. Angelone, 522 U.S. 269 (1998).

Coker v. Georgia, 433 U.S. 584 (1977).

Cowan, C., Thompson, W., & Ellsworth, P. C. (1984). The effects of death qualification on jurors predisposition to convict and on the quality of deliberation. *Law and Human Behavior, 8,* 53–79.

Death Penalty Information Center, www.deathpenaltyinfo.org.

Diamond, S. S., & Levi, J. N. (1996). Improving decisions on death by revising and testing jury instructions. *Judicature, 79,* 224–232.

Dike, S. (1982). *Capital punishment in the United States: A consideration of the evidence.* New York: National Council on Crime and Delinquency.

Donohue, J. J., & Wolfers, J. (2006). Uses and abuses of empirical evidence in the death penalty debate. *Stanford Law Review, 58,* 791–846.

Ehrlich, I. (1975). The deterrent effect of capital punishment: A question of life and death. *American Economic Review, 65,* 397–417.

Eisenberg, T., & Wells, M. T. (1993). Deadly confusion: Juror instructions in capital cases. *Cornel Law Review, 79,* 1–17.

Ellsworth, P. C. (1988). Unpleasant facts: The Supreme Court's response to empirical research on capital punishment. In K. C. Haas & J. Inciardi (Eds.), *Adjudicating death: Moral and legal perspectives on capital punishment.* New York: Sage.

Ellsworth, P. C., & Gross, S. R. (1994). Hardening of the attitudes: Americans' views on the death penalty. *Journal of Social Issues, 50,* 19–52.

Ellsworth, P. C., & Reifman, A. (2000). Juror comprehension and public policy. *Psychology, Public Policy, and Law, 6,* 788–821.

Ellsworth, P. C., & Ross, L. D. (1983). Public opinion and the death penalty: A close examination of the views of abolitionists and retentionists. *Crime and Delinquency* (January), 116–169.

Furman v. Georgia, 408 U.S. 238 (1972).

Gallup Poll (1994, September).

Gallup Poll (2002, May 6).

Gregg v. Georgia, 428 U.S. 153 (1976).

Gross, S. R. (1998). Update: American public opinion on the death penalty – It's getting personal. *Cornell Law Review, 83,* 1448–1475.

Gross, S. R., & Ellsworth, P. C. (2003). Second thoughts: Americans' views on the death penalty at the turn of the century. In S. P. Garvey (Ed.), *Beyond repair? America's death penalty* (pp. 7–57). Durham, NC: Duke University Press.

Gross, S. R., & Mauro, R. (1984). Patterns of death: An analysis of racial disparities in capital sentencing and homicide victimization. *Stanford Law Review, 37,* 27–153.

Gross, S. R., & Mauro, R. (1989). *Death and discrimination: Racial disparities in capital sentencing.* Boston: Northeastern University Press.

Gross, S. R., Jacoby, K., Matheson, D. J., Montgomery, N., & Patil, S. (2005). Exonerations in the United States 1989 through 2003. *Journal of Criminal Law and Criminology, 95,* 523–560.

Haney, C., & Lynch, M. (1994). Comprehending life and death matters: A preliminary study of California's capital penalty instructions. *Law and Human Behavior, 18,* 411–436.

Haney, C., & Lynch, M. (1997). Clarifying life and death matters: An analysis of instructional comprehension and penalty phase closing arguments. *Law and Human Behavior, 21,* 575–595.

Jacoby, J. E., & Paternoster, R. (1982). Sentencing disparity and jury packing: Further challenges to the death penalty, *Journal of Criminal Law and Criminology, 73,* 379–387.

Jeffries, J. C., Jr. (1994). *Justice Lewis F. Powell, Jr.: A biography.* New York: Fordham University Press.

Kelly v. South Carolina, 534 U.S. 246 (2002).

Lempert, R. O. (1981). Desert and deterrence: An assessment of the moral bases of the case for capital punishment. *Michigan Law Review, 79,* 1177–1231.

Lieberman, J. D., & Sales, B. D. (1997). What social science teaches us about the jury instruction process. *Psychology, Public Policy, and Law, 3,* 589–644.

Lockhart v. McCree, 476 U.S. 162 (1986).

Maxwell v. Bishop, 398 U.S. 262 (1970).

McCleskey v Kemp, 481 U.S. 279 (1987).

McGautha v. California, 402 U.S. 183 (1971).

NORC General Social Survey, April, 1976.

NORC National Gun Policy Survey, May, 2001.

Oberer, W. E. (1961). Does disqualification of jurors for scruples against capital punishment constitute denial of fair trial on the issue of guilt? *University of Texas Law Review, 39,* 545–573.

Princeton Survey Research Associates, May, 2001.

Princeton Survey Research Associates, April, 2003.

Princeton Survey Research Associates, May, 2005.

Radelet, M. (1981). Racial characteristics and the imposition of the death penalty. *American Sociological Review, 46,* 918–970.

Radelet, M., & Pierce, G. L. (1985). Race and prosecutorial discretion in homicide cases. *Law and Society Review, 19,* 587–621.

Roper v. Simmons, 112 S. W. 3d 397, affirmed (2005).

Schuman, H., & Presser, S. (1981). *Questions and answers in attitude surveys.* San Diego: Academic Press.

Schwarz, N., Groves, R., & Schuman, H. (1998). Survey Methods. In D. Gilbert, S. Fiske, & G. Lindzey (Eds.), *Handbook of social psychology* (4th ed., Vol. 1, pp. 143–179). New York: McGraw-Hill.

Sellin, T. (1967). *Capital punishment.* New York: Harper & Row.

Shaw, T. (2006). Wrong on wrongful executions. *The Washington Post,* July 2, p. 134.

Simmons v. South Carolina, 512 U.S. 154 (1994).

Sorenson, J., Wrinkle, R., Brewer, V., & Marquart, J. (1999). Capital punishment and deterrence: Examining the effect of executions on murder in Texas. *Crime and Delinquency, 45,* 481–530.

Stanford v. Kentucky, 492 U.S. 361 (1989).

Time/CNN/Yankelovich Poll, June, 1989.

Trop v. Dulles, 356 U.S. 86 (1958).

United States ex rel Free v. McGinnis, 818 F. Supp. 1098 [N. D. Ill.] (1993).

United States v. Quinones, 313 F. 3d 49 (2002).

Weeks v. Angelone, 528 U.S. 225 (2000).

Witherspoon v. Illinois, 391 U. S. 510 (1968).

Wolfgang, M. E., & Reidel, M. (1973). Rape, judicial discretion, and the death penalty. *Annals of the American Academy of Political and Social Science, 407,* 119–133.

Zimring, F. E. (2003). *The contradictions of American capital punishment.* New York: Oxford University Press.

13

Pretrial Publicity: Effects, Remedies, and Judicial Knowledge

Margaret Bull Kovera and Sarah M. Greathouse

"The extent and intensity of the publicity in this case is of unprecedented proportions in Northern California," said attorney Mark Geragos about the media attention focused on his client, Scott Peterson (CNN. com, 2003). At the time, Peterson stood accused of killing his young wife, Laci, and their unborn child, Conner. Scott claimed to have gone fishing early Christmas Eve morning and that when he returned from his trip Laci was nowhere to be found. Over four months later, the bodies of Laci and little Conner washed up on the shore of San Francisco Bay, not far from the site where Scott reported he had been fishing that Christmas Eve.

There is no question that the publicity surrounding this case was intense and widespread. While Laci was missing, the massive search effort and the televised pleas from her mother begging for information about Laci's whereabouts, attracted concentrated media attention to the case. After the bodies were recovered and the trial neared, the judge – in an attempt to quell prejudicial information about the defense in the media – issued a gag order, restricting the attorneys, potential witnesses, the police, and court personnel from disclosing any information about the case to the press. The judge was not the only trial principal who was concerned about the risk of a tainted jury pool because of the pervasive media attention to the case. The defense argued that the trial be moved out of Modesto, where the community members were particularly incensed by the death of Laci and the reports of Scott's behavior. The prosecution fought this change of venue motion. They questioned whether there was any county where the jurors would have escaped the prejudicial effects of the media and argued that juror bias could be uncovered using traditional questioning in voir dire, the jury selection process (CNN.com, 2004). Ultimately, the judge ruled with the defense and moved the trial to San Mateo County.

Although the Peterson case has some unique features, it is not the case that pretrial publicity (PTP) is a rare phenomenon. With some frequency, the media report prejudicial case-relevant information (i.e., information that may not be admissible at trial but could cause a potential juror to prejudge the guilt of a defendant). Content analyses of 14 newspapers across the country revealed that 27% of the reports on criminal trials described the defendant in a prejudicial manner (Imrich, Mullin, & Linz, 1995). A recent search in the legal database, Lexis-Nexis, for cases involving PTP issues revealed that between 1994 and 2004 over 7,000 defendants claimed that owing to negative PTP, they could not receive a fair trial (Chrzanowski, 2005). This figure has dramatically increased since the 1980s, when a similar search identified 3,000 defendant complaints of prejudicial PTP (Minow & Cate, 2001). Of course, some cases elicit tremendous media attention, resulting in massive amounts of PTP; for example, almost 1,000 stories about Timothy McVeigh and the bombing of the Murrow Federal Building in Oklahoma City appeared in the local paper in the nine months following the bombing (Studebaker & Penrod, 1997; Studebaker, Robbennolt, Pathak-Sharma, & Penrod, 2000).

Since the 1960s the courts have recognized the potential biasing effect of PTP (*Irvin v. Dowd*, 1961; *Rideau v. Louisiana*, 1963; *Sheppard v. Maxwell*, 1966). In these cases the Court addressed the conflict between the First Amendment to the United States Constitution, which guarantees the right to free speech, and the Sixth Amendment, which guarantees the defendant's right to a fair and speedy trial. Although the Supreme Court has protected the right to free speech in some cases involving PTP (*Nebraska Press Association v. Stuart*, 1976; *Richmond Newspapers, Inc. v. Virginia*, 1980), rulings in cases such as *Irvin v. Dowd* (1961) demonstrate the Court's awareness of the media's influence on potential jurors' opinions and the bias it creates before evidence is presented at trial.

There exist many types of information that, when publicized by the media, may bias a potential juror against a defendant, making it impossible for that defendant to receive a fair trial. What is less clear is what should be done to protect a defendant's right to a fair trial. The simplest method of preventing unfair influence of the media on the potential jurors in upcoming trials would be to restrict the ability of the media to present information about defendants or the crimes they have been accused of committing through judicial gag orders; however, the First Amendment guarantees that the press have the freedom to print information that is of interest to the community. The difficult question is how best to balance the defendant's Sixth Amendment right to a fair trial by an impartial jury and the freedom of the press guaranteed by the First Amendment (Fulero, 2002; Linz & Penrod, 1992).

In an attempt to answer this question, it is important to understand the extent and nature of PTP, the effects that this publicity has on jury decisions, and the potential effectiveness of available remedies for the effects of PTP on jury decisions. Toward that end, we will examine the effects of PTP on juror decisions, discussing the roles of moderators of PTP effects such as PTP content, affective tone, study method, and potential remedies (e.g., voir dire and jury selection, judicial instruction, delaying a trial, and changes of venue). Finally, we will consider the way in which PTP scholarship may be used in court to support pretrial motions for the application of remedies and whether the information that might be presented to judges in these motions provides more than can be known through common sense.

The Effects of PTP

The American Bar Association (2000) recognized the potential for prejudicial impact when the press publicizes certain types of information about a defendant and established categories of information that attorneys should avoid divulging pretrial. These categories include, among others: (a) the defendant's prior criminal record; (b) information about the defendant's character or reputation; (c) any confession or admission against interest produced by the defendant (or the refusal to provide information); (d) whether the defendant has or has not submitted to any examination or test; and (e) any opinion about the defendant's guilt or about the sufficiency of the evidence against the defendant. In general, these categories cover information that might lead a juror to infer the guilt of the defendant but that are inadmissible at trial because of the questionable reliability of the evidence. Ethical guidelines bind attorneys from conveying any of this potentially prejudicial information if they know that there is a substantial likelihood that it would prejudice an upcoming trial.

Does knowledge of these classes of information influence the way jurors evaluate defendants and the evidence against them? Overall, psychological studies testing the effects of PTP on juror judgments indicate that PTP has a negative influence on both pretrial and posttrial judgments of defendant guilt (Studebaker and Penrod, 1997; 2005).

Early psychological research manipulated the type of PTP to which jurors were exposed (e.g. whether the defendant had a prior record or the defendant confessed to the crime) and measured perceptions of guilt (DeLuca, 1979; Hvistendahl, 1979). Those jurors who were exposed to negative PTP were more likely to judge the defendant as guilty. As the number of different types of PTP experienced by jurors increased, so did jurors' ratings of defendant guilt (DeLuca, 1979). Similarly, a meta-analysis of the PTP literature showed that the effect size for studies in which the PTP consisted of multiple categories of prejudicial information was larger than the effect for studies in which jurors were exposed to only one type of PTP (Steblay, Besirevic, Fulero, & Jimenez-Lorente, 1999). Even general PTP that is topically related to a case but does not include prejudicial information about the defendant of that case can result in an increased likelihood that the defendant will be convicted (Greene & Loftus, 1984; Greene & Wade, 1988; Kovera, 2002).

The prejudicial effects of PTP are rather robust. PTP not only affects guilty verdicts in criminal trials; similar effects have been found in research using civil cases, with PTP containing prejudicial information against the defendant in personal injury cases increasing the probability that the defendant would be found liable (Bornstein, Whisenhunt, & Nemeth, 2002). In addition, to generalizing across case type, PTP effects not only influence pretrial judgments of defendant guilt but also withstand the presentation of evidence to affect posttrial judgments (Chrzanowski, 2005; Otto, Penrod & Dexter, 1994). A meta-analysis of 23 PTP studies containing 44 tests of whether PTP affects juror judgments and a total of 5,755 participants concluded that there was a small to moderate PTP effect across these studies ($r = .16$) and that it would take 2,755 studies that failed to find a relationship between PTP exposure and juror judgments to change the conclusion that PTP affects juror judgments (Steblay et al., 1999).

Methods used to study PTP effects

Investigations of PTP effects have generally followed one of three forms: field studies of PTP effects in real cases using survey methods; experimental studies of PTP effects conducted in laboratories using trial simulation methods (Studebaker & Penrod, 2005); and meta-analyses of the entire body of research on PTP. Each method has its strengths and weaknesses, both for understanding PTP effects and for their relevance to courts' decisions about whether to provide remedies for PTP effects.

In the field studies, researchers contact community members from the venue in which a case is being tried and ask them questions about the extent of their exposure to media about the case, the information that they recall or recognize about the case, and their perception of the likelihood of the defendant's guilt. Similar questions are also asked of community members in other venues to which the case may be moved. Researchers then compare both the extent of the PTP exposure and the perceptions of defendant guilt for the different venues, and also examine the correlations between the magnitude of PTP exposure (as reported by respondents) and respondents' pretrial judgments of defendant guilt. Although this survey method has the advantage of looking at the effects of real PTP on those who are exposed to it through natural means, there are drawbacks to this method as well. Because no evidence is presented to respondents, it is unclear whether their pretrial biases would survive voir dire, the presentation of evidence, or deliberation.

In contrast, experimental studies are typically conducted in a laboratory, with researchers carefully manipulating the nature and extent of the PTP exposure jurors receive. Typically, although not always (e.g., Ogloff & Vidmar, 1994), participants in experimental studies then view a trial stimulus, after which they judge the guilt of the defendant. Deliberations may or may not be part of the experimental procedure. Researchers then examine the effects of these manipulations on the verdicts rendered by the mock jurors. The major advantage of these experimental simulation methods is that researchers can draw causal conclusions about the effects of PTP on mock-juror judgments. Yet these studies can be criticized because they are often conducted with undergraduate student participants and with relatively artificial PTP exposure and trial stimuli.

The most ambitious examination of PTP effects used a combination of survey and experimental methods, exposing mock jurors attending universities across the country and mock jurors attending college in the trial venue to varying levels of real PTP about a gang rape case (Chrzanowski, 2005). In the experimental study, researchers manipulated the slant of the PTP so that participants in the remote condition were either exposed to publicity that favored the prosecution, the defense, or was neutral. Additionally, students living in the area in which the trial was held were placed in a natural exposure condition; researchers categorized these participants based on the amount of naturally occurring PTP they reported experiencing. All participants were presented with trial evidence over a series of six sessions and were asked to provide judgments of guilt after each session.

Both naturally occurring and experimentally manipulated PTP had similar effects on mock jurors' pretrial and posttrial judgments of the defendants' guilt.

One objection that has been raised regarding both the survey and experimental data on PTP effects that is not resolved by the Chrzanowski study is that none of the survey studies and very few of the experimental studies allow jurors to deliberate before rendering judgments. The courts often rely on deliberation to remove any potential bias, including bias caused by PTP. It is assumed that an individual will be reluctant to publicly state any biases they possess because of inadmissible PTP and therefore such information will not be discussed during deliberation nor will the jury use it to make a judgment. If the information is raised, then the other jurors presumably will correct the juror offering the inadmissible PTP to support an argument. In one study that included an examination of jury deliberations in the study of PTP (Kramer, Kerr, & Carroll, 1990), very few of the taped deliberations included a discussion of the PTP. When PTP was mentioned, other jury members reminded the group that such information is prohibited from discussion. However, deliberations did not counteract the PTP effects, as differences were still observed between juries that were exposed to PTP and those that were not. Furthermore, when the type of publicity jurors were exposed to was emotional, deliberations seemed to increase the negative effects of PTP rather than diminish them. Other research suggests that deliberation only minimizes the biasing effects of PTP when the likelihood of convicting the defendant is high even in the absence of PTP; when the evidence is more ambiguous, deliberation serves to exacerbate PTP effects (Kerr, Niedermeier, & Kaplan, 1999).

The Steblay et al. meta-analysis (1999) provides some insights into whether study method moderates PTP effects on juror judgments. According to the meta-analysis, survey studies resulted in larger PTP effects than did experimental studies. However, the meta-analysis also showed greater PTP effects for community members than for college students. Because the survey studies' participants were always community members, it is not clear whether the sample or the method is driving this pattern of effects.

Remedies for PTP Effects

At the same time that the American Bar Association (2000) recognized the harm that could come from providing the media with certain pieces of information about a defendant and provided guidelines for information that should not be divulged, it also suggested numerous methods to counteract existing prejudicial PTP, including voir dire, judicial admonitions, continuances, jury sequestration, and change of venue. The Supreme Court has also expressed concern about prejudicial PTP and has charged judges to take measures to ensure that excessive media coverage does not interfere with the defendant's right to a fair trial (*Irvin v. Dowd*, 1961; *Rideau v. Louisiana*, 1963; *Sheppard v. Maxwell*, 1966). In the majority of these cases, the Court has focused on the conditions necessary to warrant a change of venue. For example, in *Rideau v. Louisiana* (1963), the Court determined that a change of venue motion was necessary when the substance, quality, and distribution of the PTP created an inherently prejudicial atmosphere. In *Sheppard v. Maxwell* (1966), the Supreme Court offered several more solutions to combat the effects of PTP including continuances, extended voir dire/rehabilitation, sequestered juries, and judicial instructions. Although common sense dictates that each of these potential remedies should eliminate the effects of PTP on juror judgments, there is not much empirical evidence to support these common-sense notions.

Voir dire

One of the methods judges most often employ to combat the effects of negative PTP is voir dire, the legal proceeding in which attorneys and/or judges question potential jurors (also known as the venire) about any biases they may hold that would prevent them from hearing the case fairly. When there has been PTP about a defendant or the case, the judge has the option of allowing extended questioning during voir dire to determine if any members of the venire express bias due to PTP. In addition, the attorneys may use voir dire to educate jurors about the perils of PTP, to admonish jurors to set aside any information that they learned before the trial, and to elicit commitments from jurors that they will ignore the PTP when making decisions.

Although voir dire may seem like an effective means to encourage jurors to ignore PTP and to weed out jurors who cannot set aside prior knowledge about the case, empirical research has identified several issues that prevent its effectiveness. First, attorneys may not be particularly effective at jury selection. In one study of felony voir dire, the attitudinal composition of 12-person juries chosen by attorneys was compared both to 12 individuals randomly selected from the venire and the first 12 jurors to be called for service. There were no differences in attitudinal composition between the attorney-selected juries and the randomly chosen juries (Johnson & Haney, 1994). Although this study did not directly examine attorney's abilities to identify jurors who are biased by PTP, it does raise questions about the ability of attorneys to conduct the voir dire process in a way that identifies bias.

An additional problem inherent in relying on voir dire to reveal potential PTP biases is the use of jurors' self-report used to glean such information. Although psychologists are cognizant of the problems inherent in relying on self-report, the courts often rely on venire members' self-reports of their own biases without question. Research surveying both community members in the jurisdiction of a highly publicized trial and community members of a remote, nonexposed community found that although the jurisdiction members were more likely to possess beliefs about the defendant's guilt, there were no differences between populations in their reported ability to keep an open mind if they were called to serve as jurors in the case (Moran & Cutler, 1991; Simon & Eimermann, 1971).

These findings suggest that respondents may lack the awareness that PTP will influence their perceptions of defendants. Social psychological research suggests that individuals lack the ability to tap into the cognitive processes driving their responses and fail to make a causal connection between the original stimulus (such as PTP) and their responses (Nisbett & Wilson, 1977). Moreover, people believe themselves able to disregard previously presented information (Pronin, Gilovich, & Ross, 2004); however, other research indicates that individuals are unable to follow instructions to disregard information in their judgments after the misinformation has been presented (Wyer & Budesheim, 1987; Wyer & Unverzagt, 1985). By extension, although people previously exposed to PTP may report an ability to be neutral during voir dire, they are unlikely to disregard the previous information and lack the introspective ability to recognize their use of PTP in their judgments.

In addition to lacking the awareness of PTP effects on their judgments, jurors' self-reports of bias may be influenced by social desirability concerns. During a gang rape case in California in 2005 that contained a great deal of local media coverage, the presiding judge was concerned about the potential biasing effect of the media coverage and allowed a large number of community members, 250, to comprise the venire (Chrzanowski, 2005). All members of the venire completed an informational questionnaire that assessed their knowledge of the case, as well as their ability to hear the case fairly. A telephone survey was also conducted in the local county, and community members were questioned about their knowledge of the case and their ability to hear the case fairly. Large differences were observed between the community members in the telephone survey and venire members who reported having heard about the case. Of those community members in the telephone survey who reported hearing about the case, 70% reported an inability to hear the case fairly. In contrast, of those venire members who reported prior knowledge of the case, 10% stated in court that they could not hear the case fairly. Perhaps because jurors are told that it is their duty to put aside bias, jurors are more willing to report that they can in court because they do not wish to displease the court. Jurors may also believe jury service to be a civil duty and are reluctant to express opinions that will prevent them from participating in the process. In the media frenzy often surrounding high profile cases, it is also possible that potential jurors wish to benefit from high profile cases by achieving media attention in posttrial interviews or financial gain through book deals. Whatever the reason, the data indicate that in the courtroom jurors are significantly more likely to deny bias due to PTP.

Furthermore, potential jurors who stated that their prior knowledge about a case would not affect their ability to be fair and impartial were, in fact, affected by their prior knowledge when making decisions about the case (Sue, Smith, & Pedroza, 1975). Mock jurors were presented with either neutral or negative PTP before reading a trial summary of a case and were later asked to report whether the PTP exposure affected their opinions of guilt. Of those jurors who were reportedly uninfluenced by the PTP, there were still significant differences in verdicts between publicity exposure conditions. Those jurors who were exposed to negative PTP still rendered more guilty verdicts than jurors who were exposed to neutral PTP (Sue et al., 1975).

There is mounting evidence that when jurors are asked during voir dire whether their future trial decisions will be influenced by the PTP they have seen, they will claim that they can remain unbiased even when it is likely that their trial judgments will be affected. This lack of awareness would make it difficult for attorneys and judges to identify those who may be biased. But it is still possible that voir dire could be used as a vehicle for encouraging jurors to set aside their biases. The only valid study to have examined the effectiveness of voir dire as a combatant to PTP is not very promising (Dexter, Cutler, & Moran, 1992). In addition to manipulating PTP exposure, one study manipulated whether participants were exposed to a standard voir dire, or an extended voir dire process designed to counteract the influence of PTP

by educating the jurors about its effects, making the jurors feel accountable for their decision, and asking the jurors to report any influence
PTP may have had on them (Dexter et al., 1992). Participants who
were exposed to PTP were more punitive than those who were not,
regardless of whether they had been exposed to extended voir dire,
suggesting that this safeguard may be ineffective. Other research that
has attempted to explore this issue has failed to obtain an effect of
PTP in the conditions without a remedy (Freedman, Martin, & Mota,
1998), making it impossible to evaluate whether the remedy is successful. In sum, a significant body of research suggests that voir dire
may not be an effective means of identifying jurors who are biased or
an effective means of reducing pretrial bias. However, judges possess
a strong belief in their ability to rehabilitate biased jurors (i.e., convince self-admitted biased jurors to reverse their opinions or put aside
their biases so that they may serve as impartial jurors), and because
extended voir dire may be one of the least radical and least costly
available methods, it may be particularly attractive to judges.

Judicial instruction

Another potential remedy for PTP effects is judicial instruction to
jurors on their duty to avoid being influenced by PTP. These instructions often address the importance of disregarding any information
the jurors may have previously heard about the case and solely relying
on evidence presented during trial. Although jurors generally do not
follow judicial instructions to disregard inadmissible evidence (Steblay,
Hosch, Culhane, & McWethy, 2006), these instructions are somewhat more effective when paired with a rationale for why the information should be disregarded. Perhaps jurors would be better able to
understand the rationale behind disregarding prejudicial PTP if they
were provided with a rationale in the instructions for putting aside
their bias.

Although early research on judicial instructions seemed to indicate
that admonitions by the judge were successful in reducing the effect
of PTP (Kline & Jess, 1966; Simon 1966), methodological issues
within the research, such as lack of control groups and cueing participants to the hypotheses of the study, require caution in interpreting
the results. Methodologically sound research has yet to find an effect
of judicial instructions on reducing the negative effect of PTP (Sue,
Smith, & Gilbert, 1974; Fein, McCloskey, & Tomlinson, 1997). In
one study judicial instructions were ineffective at reducing the negative
effects of both factual and emotional PTP (Kramer et al., 1990).

Another study found that judicial instructions did not remedy PTP effects in civil cases either (Bornstein et al., 2002).

Continuance

A judge may decide to remedy PTP effects by delaying the start of the trial, hoping that the PTP will die down in the intervening time period. This remedy is known as a continuance. Very little research exists on the effectiveness of continuances in combating the effects of PTP. The courts assume that if the PTP has resulted with pervasive bias within the community at present, the passage of time may decrease the bias in the venire's pretrial judgments. The few research studies that have been conducted indicate that the passage of time does decrease certain types of pretrial information. Specifically, the effects of factual PTP are reduced over time; however, the influence of emotional PTP remains strong despite the passage of time between media exposure and trial judgment (Kramer et al., 1990; Davis, 1986).

The amount of time between the PTP and the trial in these studies ranged from only 7 to 12 days. Continuances are often longer than this short period of time, and so it is possible that the effects of emotional PTP would be reduced over a more extended period of time. Contrary to the previous research, results from the Steblay et al. meta-analysis (1999) indicate that the effects of negative PTP increase when the period of time between the publicity exposure and the trial exceeds seven days. It is not clear what to make of these different findings. The few experimental manipulations of time delay between PTP exposure and trial judgment show little remedy. The meta-analysis suggests that longer delays increase PTP effects. It is possible that these findings from the meta-analysis are correct and that sleeper effects (e.g., the tendency to be more influenced by unreliable information over time as the memory for the unreliable source becomes detached from the memory of the information) may account for the increasing influence of PTP over time. A recent meta-analysis of sleeper effect research indicates that persuasion for a message increased over time when the information presented was particularly impactful, as well as when the individuals received the discounting message and cue after the initial message and when motivation was high (Kumkale & Albarracin, 2004). These moderators of the sleeper effect are all present in PTP situations. The meta-analytic test of delay in PTP studies included not only studies that manipulate delay but also those that do not (including in the short delay conditions studies that had only short delays, and including in the long delay conditions those studies that only had long delays). It is possible, therefore, that other characteristics in the meta-analyzed studies may have systematically varied with delay (e.g., studies with longer delays also had other factors present that would increase the influence of PTP). It will take further empirical tests, including manipulations that include much longer delays, to resolve this difference between the meta-analytic and experimental findings.

Change of venue

According to the Federal Rules of Criminal Procedure, a change of venue motion may be granted, "if the court is satisfied that there exists in the district where the prosecution is pending so great a prejudice against the defendant that the defendant cannot obtain a fair and impartial trial at any place fixed by law for holding court in that district" (Federal Rule of Criminal Procedure 21[a]). The motion for a change of venue may be supported by evidence from a public opinion survey about the case conducted in the current venue and, for comparison, at least one other community that is presumed to be less saturated with PTP. Reports based on these surveys may include comparisons between a large number of local and distant community members' case-relevant opinions (Nietzel & Dillehay, 1983). This information can assist the judge in definitively determining the level at which PTP in the current jurisdiction has influenced community members' pretrial impartiality.

Content analysis of media coverage is another method that may be used to objectively establish the level of prejudicial information available to different communities (Studebaker et al., 2000). Content analyses of local media coverage concerning the trial may also provide information about the extent of PTP in the current venue, as well as the type of PTP (e.g., emotional vs. factual, proprosecution vs. prodefense), which can then be compared to the pervasiveness and content of media coverage in other geographical areas. If the level of prejudicial PTP is high and it can be established that it is significantly lower in other areas, the content analysis may provide objective support for a change of venue, as well.

Of the suggested methods to remedy the negative effects of PTP, empirical research suggests a change of venue to be the most promising. When community members' opinions in counties where a highly publicized trial is to be conducted are compared to community members' responses in other nearby counties, it is generally the case that communities members exposed to PTP are more likely to be favorable to the prosecution and possess negative perceptions of the defendant than are those community members with less exposure (Constantini & King, 1980/1981; Nietzel & Dillehay, 1983; Moran & Cutler, 1991; Simon & Eimerman, 1971; Vidmar & Judson, 1981).

One argument against using change of venue to remedy PTP effects is that, especially in extremely high profile cases, it might be impossible to find a venue with a venire that has not been tainted by PTP. Although for defendants such as Timothy McVeigh, O. J. Simpson, and Scott Peterson it may seem unlikely that there would be a location that remained untouched by the PTP surrounding their cases, recent content analytic studies demonstrate that even in cases as high profile as the Oklahoma City bombing case, this supposition proves untrue. In the months after the bombing, there were 939 articles (over 100 on the front page) about the incident with 307 pictures among the pages of the primary newspaper in Oklahoma City, the *Daily Oklahoman*. The *Denver Post*, the major paper in Denver to where the McVeigh trial was moved, published fewer than 200 articles, with only 24 on the front page and only 9 photos (Studebaker et al., 2000). Similar results were obtained in a content analysis of the Lizzie Grubman case, in which a woman well known in New York society circles was tried for injuring several people when backing up her SUV outside a nightclub (Penrod, Groscup, & O'Neil, 2002). Although the New York City area papers carried over 500 articles about the incident in the six months following the accident, fewer than 10 articles appeared in the Albany newspaper, only 150 miles away. Thus, it is likely that for most cases, courts can identify an alternative venue with little or at least reduced PTP.

PTP Research in Court

When motions are filed seeking remedies to prejudicial PTP, either side may call an expert on PTP to testify about the evidence either supporting or refuting the need for remedy. In this capacity, the expert can inform the court of empirical research on the influence of PTP on juror judgments. The testimony may also address the similarity between the conditions under which the research was conducted and the actual PTP released in that particular case (Studebaker et al., 2000). In their description of the available empirical PTP research, experts may also be able to inform the court of research on the effectiveness of common remedies, including results that indicate the inefficacy of some methods such as extended voir dire and judicial instruction.

Studebaker et al. (2000) advocated that providing information on three types of information – experimental studies of the PTP effect; public opinion surveys conducted with the community from the current venue and other nearby venues; and content analyses of the relative amounts of media coverage in the different venues – would allow psychologists to better inform the court. Presenting these three types of information provides the court with the necessary information about the amount and nature of the PTP surrounding the case, how the types of PTP in this case are similar or different from types of PTP that experiments have shown to influence jurors' perceptions of guilt, and how media coverage in the community has affected perceptions of defendant culpability (Studebaker et al., 2000).

It is important to note that the role of a PTP expert is different from the role of many other psychologists called to serve as experts in court. PTP experts will often testify about research they were hired to conduct specifically for the case in which they are testifying (also known as social fact evidence; Monahan & Walker, 1988) in addition to relevant social framework evidence about the influence of PTP on juror behavior. In other areas, however, an expert might be called to discuss previously conducted research that is relevant to one or more of the issues in dispute in the case (termed social framework evidence by Monahan & Walker, 1988). Another difference is that issues relevant to PTP (such as whether remedies are necessary) are considered before the jurors for a case are even chosen. Rather than testifying during trial to educate jurors about the psychological research that is case relevant, PTP experts generally testify before the judge in support of pretrial motions regarding the need for change of venue or a continuance. Therefore, in the case of PTP, the triers of fact will not be lay people, but rather judges who may believe themselves well informed of relevant issues, including the effects of PTP on juror judgments. However, the judges' common-sense notions of human behavior may not be consistent with psycholegal research findings (Posey & Dahl, 2002).

For example, one survey of judges indicated that judges are satisfied with the suggested methods for remedying PTP (Carroll et al., 1986). In response to the survey, judges reported their beliefs that jurors have the ability to be impartial and set aside previously learned information. The data from several studies suggest that their common-sense notions are incorrect. Jurors appear to be unaware that PTP has influenced their pretrial judgments (Constantini & King, 1980/81; Kerr, 1989; Kerr, Kramer, Carroll, & Alfini, 1991; Moran & Cutler, 1991; Ogloff & Vidmar, 1994: Simon & Eimermann, 1971; Sue et al., 1975).

In the same survey, judges reported a strong belief in the effectiveness of voir dire to combat PTP, but also reported that judicial instructions, continuances, and additional preemptory challenges may be effective remedies (Carroll et al., 1986). Despite empirical evidence that the commonly employed methods to remedy prejudicial publicity fall short of their intended effects, the courts continue to rely on their common-sense notions about juror behavior (e.g., jurors accurately report their own bias) to choose remedies. Although judges readily employ methods such as an extended voir dire, they are reluctant to employ a change of venue (Carroll et al., 1986). Moreover, cases are commonplace in which it was established that overwhelming pretrial bias was present but the judge refused to move the trial to another jurisdiction. For example, in *Mu'min v. Virginia* (1991), 8 of the 12 seated jurors admitted to pretrial media exposure, and in the more recent Enron scandal over 80% of community members in a telephone survey admitted that they held pretrial perceptions of guilt, yet the judges were reluctant to move the trial. Thus, judges are reluctant, perhaps because of expense and inconvenience, to use the one remedy that empirical research suggests is effective at curbing the influence of PTP on juror judgments.

Conclusions

A substantial body of research suggests that PTP influences jurors' pretrial inferences of a defendant's guilt and their posttrial judgments (Steblay et al., 1999). Although there are fewer studies competently testing the effectiveness of judicial remedies for PTP effects, the studies that have been conducted suggest that several of these remedies (e.g., voir dire, judicial instruction) are ineffective. It is possible that future research testing longer delays between PTP exposure and trial will demonstrate the effectiveness of a continuance in remedying PTP effects, but the current findings with shorter delays suggest otherwise. Only one remedy, change of venue, appears capable of providing defendants with fair trials in cases with extensive PTP.

Judges lack understanding of PTP effects on juror bias, and the extent to which they believe the opinions that the jurors form pretrial will persist beyond voir dire are often based on common-sense notions about human behavior. These common-sense notions about jurors' awareness of their own bias, jurors' abilities to set their biases aside when instructed, and the efficacy of many potential PTP remedies are often at odds with psycholegal research and underestimate the vulnerabilities of the decision-making processes when damaging and extensive information against the defendant is presented pretrial (Chrzanowski, 2005). There is little empirical research that provides support for the remedies most often favored by judges, and according to some practicing in the field, it seems as if judges are reluctant to factor the psycholegal research on effective and ineffective remedies into their change of venue decisions (Posey & Dahl, 2002). To date, there remains little research on the whether data offered by experts are considered by the judge, but anecdotal evidence (Posey & Dahl, 2002) and our own survey of recent cases involving change of venue motions failed to find a single judicial decision that mentioned psycholegal research in support of their decision.

If judges remain reluctant to order changes of venue despite their status as the only empirically supported remedy to PTP effects, it will be necessary to identify new remedies. If psychologists wish to be at the forefront of suggesting empirically supported remedies, it would be helpful if they would first turn to identifying the psychological mechanisms behind PTP effects, an effort that has largely been ignored (cf., Hope, Memon, & McGeorge, 2004; Kovera, 2002). They could then suggest remedies that counter the psychological mechanisms behind the insidious effects of prejudicial PTP.

REFERENCES

American Bar Association (2000). *Model rules of professional conduct,* 2003 ed.

Bornstein, B. H., Whisenhunt, B. L., & Nemeth, R. J. (2002). Pretrial publicity and civil cases: A two-way street? *Law & Human Behavior, 21,* 3–17.

Carroll, J. S., Kerr, N. L., Alfini, J. J., Weaver, F.W., MacCoun, R. J., & Feldman, V. (1986). Free press and fair trial: The role of behavioral research. *Law and Human Behavior, 10,* 187–201.

Chrzanowski, L. M. (2005). *Rape? Truth? And the media: Laboratory and field assessments of pretrial publicity in a real case.* Unpublished doctoral dissertation, City University of New York.

CNN.com (December 15. 2003). Change of venue sought in trial of Scott Peterson. www.cnn.com/2003/LAW/12/15/peterson.case/index.html. Retrieved April 17, 2006.

CNN.com (February 14, 2004). Prosecutors oppose venue change for Scott Peterson. www.cnn.com/2004/LAW/01/02/peterson.venue/index.html. Retrieved April 21, 2006.

Constantini, E., & King, J. (1980/1981). The partial juror: Correlates and causes of prejudgment. *Law and Society Review, 15,* 9–40.

Davis, R.W. (1986). Pretrial publicity, the timing of the trial, and mock jurors' decision processes. *Journal of Applied Social Psychology, 16,* 590–607.

DeLuca, A. J. (1979). *Tipping the scales of justice: The effect of pretrial publicity.* Unpublished master's thesis, Iowa State University, Ames.

Dexter, H. R., Cutler, B. L., & Moran, G. (1992). A test of voir dire as a remedy for the prejudicial effects of pretrial publicity. *Journal of Applied Social Psychology, 22,* 819–832.

Federal Rules of Criminal Procedure, 21(a).

Fein, S., McCloskey, A. L., & Tomlinson, T. M. (1997). Can the jury disregard that information? The use of suspicion to reduce the prejudicial effects of pretrial publicity and inadmissible testimony. *Personality and Social Psychology Bulletin, 23,* 1215–1226.

Freedman, J. L., Martin, C. K., & Mota, V. L. (1998). Pretrial publicity; Effects of admonitions and expressing pretrial opinions. *Legal and Criminological Psychology, 3,* 255–270.

Fulero, S. M. (2002). Empirical and legal perspectives on the impact of pretrial publicity: effects and remedies. *Law and Human Behavior, 26,* 1–2.

Greene, E., & Loftus, E. F. (1984). What's new in the news? The influence of well-publicized news events on psychological research and courtroom trials. *Basic and Applied Social Psychology, 5,* 211–221.

Greene, E., & Wade, R. (1988). Of private talk and public print: General pre-trial publicity and juror decision-making. *Applied Cognitive Psychology, 2,* 123–135.

Hope, L., Memon, A., & McGeorge, P. (2004). Understanding pretrial publicity: Predecisional distortion of evidence by mock jurors. *Journal of Experimental Psychology: Applied, 10,* 111–119.

Hvistendahl, J. K. (1979). The effect of placement of biasing information. *Journalism Quarterly, 56,* 863–865.

Imrich, D., Mullin, C., & Linz, D. (1995). Measuring the extent of prejudicial pretrial publicity in major American newpapers: A content analysis. *Journal of Communication, 43,* 93–117.

Irvin v. Dowd, 366 U.S. 717 (1961).

Johnson, C., & Haney, C. (1994). Felony voir dire: An exploratory study of its content and effect. *Law and Human Behavior, 18,* 487–506.

Kerr, N. L. (1989). The effects of pretrial publicity on jurors' values. *American Courts,* 190.

Kerr, N. L., Kramer, G. P., Carroll, J. S., & Alfini, J. J. (1991). On the effectiveness of voir dire in criminal cases with prejudicial pretrial publicity: An empirical study. *American University Law Review, 40,* 665–701.

Kerr, N. L., Niedermeier, K. E., & Kaplan, M. F. (1999). Bias in jurors vs bias in juries: New evidence from the SDS perspective. *Organizational Behavior and Human Decision Processes, 80,* 70–86.

Kline, F.G., & Jess, P.H. (1966). Prejudicial publicity: Its effects on law school mock juries. *Journalism Quarterly, 43*, 113–116.

Kovera, M. B. (2002). The effects of general pretrial publicity on juror decisions: An examination of moderators and mediating mechanisms. *Law and Human Behavior, 26*, 43–72.

Kramer G. P., Kerr, N. L., & Carroll, J. S. (1990). Pretrial publicity, judicial remedies, and jury bias. *Law and Human Behavior, 14*, 409–438.

Kumkale, G. T., & Albarracin, D. (2004). The sleeper effect in persuasion: A meta-analytic review. *Psychological Bulletin, 130*, 143–172.

Linz, D., & Penrod, S. (1992). Exploring the First and Sixth Amendments: Pretrial publicity and jury decision making. In D. K. Kagehiro & W. S. Laufer (Eds.), *Handbook of psychology and law* (pp. 1–20). New York: Springer.

Minow, N. N., & Cate, F. H. (2001). Who is an impartial juror in an age of mass media? *American University Law Review, 40*, 631–664.

Monahan, J., & Walker, L. (1988). Social science research in law: A new paradigm. *American Psychologist, 43*, 465–72.

Moran, G., & Cutler, B. L. (1991). The prejudicial impact of pretrial publicity. *Journal of Applied Social Psychology, 21*, 345–367.

Mu'min v. Virginia, 111 S. Ct. 1899 (1991).

Nebraska Press Association v. Stuart, 427 U.S. 539 (1976).

Nietzel, M. T., & Dillehay, R. C. (1983). Psychologists as consultants for changes in venue. *Law and Human Behavior, 7*, 309–355.

Nisbett, R. E. & Wilson, T. D. (1977). Telling more than we can know: Verbal reports on mental processes. *Psychology Review, 84*, 231–259.

Ogloff, J. R. P., & Vidmar, N. (1994). The impact of pretrial publicity on jurors. A study to compare the relative effects of television and print media in a child sex abuse case. *Law and Human Behavior, 18*, 507–525.

Otto, A. L., Penrod, S., & Dexter, H. R. (1994). The biasing effects of pretrial publicity on juror judgments. *Law and Human Behavior, 18*, 453–469.

Penrod, S. D., Groscup, J. L., & O'Neil, K. (2002). Report filed on behalf of Elizabeth Grubman, November 6, 2002.

Posey, A. J., & Dahl, L. M. (2002). Beyond pretrial publicity: Legal and ethical issues associated with change of venue surveys. *Law and Human Behavior, 26*, 107–125.

Pronin, E., Gilovich, T., Ross, L. (2004). Objectivity in the eye of the beholder: Divergent perceptions of bias in self versus others. *Psychological Review, 111*, 781–799.

Richmond Newspapers, Inc. v. Virginia, 448 U.S. 555 (1980).

Rideau v. Louisiana, 373 U.S. 723 (1963).

Sheppard v. Maxwell, 384 U.S. 333, 362 (1966).

Simon, R. J. (1966). Murder, juries, and the press. *Transaction*, 64–65.

Simon, R. J., & Eimermann, R. (1971). The jury finds not guilty: Another look at media influence on the jury. *Journalism Quarterly, 66*, 427–434.

Steblay, N. M., Besirevic, J., Fulero, S. M., & Jimenez-Lorente, B. (1999). The effects of pretrial publicity on juror verdicts: A meta-analytic review. *Law and Human Behavior, 23*, 219–235.

Steblay, N. M., Hosch, H. M., Culhane, S. E., & McWethy, A. (2006). The impact on juror verdicts of judicial instruction to disregard inadmissible evidence: A meta-analysis. *Law and Human Behavior, 30*, 469–492.

Studebaker, C. A., & Penrod, S. D. (1997). Pretrial publicity: The media, the law, and common sense. *Psychology, Public Policy, and Law, 3*, 428–460.

Studebaker, C. A., & Penrod, S. D. (2005). Pretrial publicity and its influence on juror decision making. In N. Brewer & K. D. Williams (Eds.), *Psychology and law: An empirical perspective* (pp. 254–275). New York: Guilford Press.

Studebaker, C. A., Robbennolt, J. K., Pathak-Sharma, M. K., & Penrod, S. D. (2000). Assessing pretrial publicity effects: Integrating content analytic results, *Law and Human Behavior, 24*, 317–336.

Sue, S., Smith, R., & Gilbert, R. (1974). Biasing effects of pretrial publicity on judicial decisions. *Journal of Criminal Justice, 2*, 163–171.

Sue, S., Smith, R. E., & Pedroza, G. (1975). Authoritarianism, pretrial publicity and awareness of bias in simulated jurors. *Psychological Reports, 37*, 1299–1302.

Vidmar, N., & Judson, J. (1981). The use of social sciences in a change of venue application. *Canadian Bar Review, 59*, 76–102.

Wyer, R. S., & Budesheim, T. L. (1987). Person memory and judgments: The impact of information that one is told to disregard. *Journal of Personality and Social Psychology, 53*, 14–29.

Wyer, R. S., & Unverzagt, W. H. (1985). Effects of instructions to disregard information on its subsequent recall and use in making judgments. *Journal of Personality and Social Psychology, 48*, 533–549.

14

Media Violence, Aggression, and Public Policy

Craig A. Anderson and Douglas A. Gentile

Two questions have dominated public debate about media violence since the 1930s: (1) Does exposure to violent media have harmful effects on youth? (2) How should society handle this problem? Even before the explosive growth of television in the 1950s, research on potentially harmful effects of movie violence was indeed discovering such effects (e.g., Blumer & Hauser, 1933; see Wartella & Reeves, 1985, for an historical overview). The public debate still rages, despite numerous governmental and nongovernmental health organization reviews and reports, all of which have concluded that the research shows significant harmful effects (e.g., the 1954 Kefauver hearings, the 1969 National Commission on the Causes and Prevention of Violence, the 1972 Surgeon General's report *Television and Growing Up* [U.S. Surgeon General's Scientific Advisory Committee, 1972], the 1982 National Institute of Mental Health [NIMH] report *Television and Behavior*, and Eron, Gentry, & Schlegel's 1994 report for the American Psychological Association).

For example, in 1972 U.S. Surgeon General Jesse Steinfeld testified before Congress that "the overwhelming consensus and the unanimous Scientific Advisory Committee's report indicates that televised violence, indeed, does have an adverse effect on certain members of our society" (Steinfeld, 1972, p. 26). The 1982 NIMH report reinforced this conclusion, and numerous professional health organizations have taken a similar position in viewing media violence as a serious threat to public health because it stimulates aggressive and even violent behavior by youth. Six medical and public health professional organizations held a Congressional Public Health Summit on July 26, 2000. At the conclusion of the summit they issued a *Joint Statement on the Impact of Entertainment Violence on Children*. This statement noted that "entertainment violence can lead to increases in aggressive attitudes, values, and behavior, particularly in children" (Congressional Public Health Summit, 2000, p. 1). The statement also concluded that the research points "overwhelmingly to a causal connection between media violence and aggressive behavior in some children" (p. 1). The six signatory organizations were the American Academy of Pediatrics, American Academy of Child and Adolescent Psychiatry, American Medical Association, American Psychological Association, American Academy of Family Physicians, and American Psychiatric Association. The most recent comprehensive review of research on exposure to media violence was conducted by a panel of experts brought together by the U.S. Surgeon General for an upcoming report on youth violence (Anderson et al., 2003). This panel concluded that, "Research on violent television and films, video games, and music reveals unequivocal evidence that media violence increases the likelihood of aggressive and violent behavior in both immediate and long-term contexts" (Anderson et al., 2003, p. 81).

To what extent have these scientific conclusions entered into common knowledge? Not much. Given the unanimity among the many expert scientific panels, it is puzzling that the general public appears to believe that the scientific evidence is equivocal. Additional ironies abound. Although about three-quarters of American parents agree that children who watch a lot of violent TV are more aggressive than children who watch less TV (Gentile, 1999), only 13% of American households with children have *any* sort of rules about the content that may be watched (Roberts, Foehr, & Rideout, 2005). Furthermore, over half of parents agree that their children are affected by the violence they see in movies or on TV (57%) or in video games (51%), yet parents are between 6 and 11 times more likely to believe that the media have less influence on their children compared to other children than they are to believe that media have more influence on their children (Gentile, 1996; Gentile, 1999; Gentile & Walsh, 2002). The media rating systems facilitate parental control over the media their children watch/play, but parents do not seem to exercise this control. For example, in a survey of 657 4th through 12th grade students, fewer than half said that their parents understand the video game ratings and only one out of four said that a parent has *ever* stopped them from getting a game because of its rating (Walsh et al., 2005). The statistics do not change much even after removing the 52 participants who were 17 or 18 years old. One reason that parents might not use the ratings to restrict game access might be that children only play age-appropriate games, but this is not so. In this same sample of 605 9- to 16-year-olds, 7 out of 10 reported playing M-rated ("Mature") video games, and 61% owned M-rated games. Almost half said they bought M-rated games themselves, and only slightly over half said that a parent was present the last time they bought an M-rated game.

Similarly, a nationally representative sample of 7th through 12th graders found that 65% reported having played the M-rated game Grand Theft Auto (Roberts et al., 2005). Furthermore, of those who are supposedly too young to gain access to this game (12–16-year-olds), 75% of the boys and 51% of the girls reported having played this game (Joanne Cantor, personal communication, February 20, 2006). There is a large disconnect here – even if parents claim to believe the scientific evidence about the effects of media violence, that belief does not transfer into action, which suggests that the belief is not deeply held.

There are several reasons why the conclusions of numerous expert panels have not been fully understood or adopted by the general public. First, the media industries spend a lot of money on public relations experts who issue press releases, write op-ed pieces for newspapers, give interviews in which they deny that any valid research shows any negative effects of violent media, and occasionally claim positive effects. Second, the media industries routinely promote (and sometimes fund) their own "experts," often academicians without true expertise in media violence research. These "experts" denounce as poorly conducted any research that finds harmful effects, but praise the occasional study with nonsignificant findings (see Huesmann & Taylor, 2003). Third, since 1980 news media reports on media violence effects have moved in the opposite direction of the research findings. That is, as the evidence for harmful media violence effects has grown stronger, news reports about harmful effects have grown weaker (Bushman & Anderson, 2001). Fourth, and most relevant to this chapter, is the possibility that media violence researchers have been less than clear in articulating their findings and the public policy relevance of their findings to news reporters and the general public. Part of the problem is that neither the general public nor most media violence researchers understand the role of science in good public policy planning. Another part of the problem has been miscommunication between media violence researchers and the general public, a miscommunication based on differences in use of language. Still other aspects of the problem involve differences between scientific experts and the general public in their understandings of causality, expertise, and the scientific enterprise.

Science, Communication, and Public Policy Beyond Common Knowledge

Four inputs to public policy

Scientifically derived information does not and can not *automatically* translate into appropriate and effective public policy. We are not public policy experts, but we believe that there are at least four very different and important sources of information underlying the formulation of effective public policy: scientific, legal, political realities, and personal values (Gentile & Anderson, 2006). Few people understand this, and one reason so many First Amendment proponents, video gamers, and industry officials attack existing media violence research is because they do not understand these distinct sources of relevant information.

The *science facts* category refers to the relevant scientific knowledge base, consisting of relevant theory that has been created, revised, and supported by a diverse and converging set of empirical studies generated (and later summarized) by appropriate expert research scientists, in this case, truly expert media violence scientists. Though the basic meaning of this category is obvious, there are several important issues to which we will return shortly. The *legal issue* category concerns legal (e.g., constitutional) limits on potential public policies. One major legal issue in the media violence domain concerns U.S. Constitution First Amendment questions about the legality of government-imposed restrictions on access and exposure to violent materials by children and young adolescents (e.g., under the age of 21 or 18). Though the question of government restrictions lies outside our expertise, we note that there are government restrictions on children's access to pornography, and some leading First Amendment scholars have written persuasive accounts of how certain forms of government restrictions on children's access to violent media would pass all legal tests (e.g., Saunders, 2003a, b). The third category concerns *political realities*. What is likely to be popular with voters? Who has the money and clout to influence legislators and the executive and judicial branches of local, state, and federal government? The fourth category, concerning *personal values*, seems less clear than the other three. In a democracy it is perfectly legitimate and rational for an individual to oppose a potential policy that he/she believes would be good for society if it conflicts with a personal value held as more important. For example, a person who believes that exposure to media violence increases aggression and violence in youth and that reduction of aggression and violence by youth would be good for society could rationally oppose government restrictions on children's access to violent media, if that person places a higher value on having a totally open media landscape than on having a less violent society.

Science facts and theories

Public policy-makers, judges, and the general public often have a different understanding of scientific facts and theories than scientists do; most people neither know of nor understand these differences. Social scientists rarely use the word *fact*, a tacit acknowledgement that scientific findings, theories, and concepts should be open to revision in the light of new discoveries. However, public policy-makers, judges, and the general public frequently ask scientists for the "facts." Nonscientists typically also do not understand the role of good theory in science. Whereas most scientists view a good theory as one that is falsifiable, has been tested and revised repeatedly, and provides a causal understanding of the phenomenon, nonscientists oftentimes think that *theory* means an idiosyncratic guess (e.g., public debates about theories of evolution and creationism).

What nonscientists are seeking is information about what the bulk of the scientific evidence shows on a specific question, that is, "Does exposure to violent media have harmful effects on youth?", and they seek it in their own nonscientific language. When media violence researchers answer with the hedging and the convoluted language that may be appropriate at a scientific conference, they are actually misinforming their nonscientific questioner. Indeed, the legal standard for what constitutes a scientific fact is "a reasonable degree of scientific certainty," usually interpreted to mean that most true experts in the domain will agree. In our view, a reasonable degree of scientific certainty has been reached on many basic questions concerning media violence effects, in large part because true experts realize that the research domain has satisfied four criteria: (1) There is a good theoretical basis; (2) the data fit the theory; (3) different research methodologies converge on the same conclusion; and (4) there are no remaining (i.e., un-debunked) plausible alternative explanations that can account for any substantial portion of the findings, let alone all of them (Anderson & Bushman, 2002b). This does not mean that there are no unresolved issues about a host of finer theoretical and methodological points; rather, the main questions of interest have been answered about whether there are harmful effects.

Probabilistic versus necessary/sufficient causality: The risk factor approach

The major public health problems in modern society result from an accumulation of multiple causal factors, and for this reason the public health approach to understanding and dealing with those problems is the risk factor approach. In other words, modern science, especially in public health domains, is largely probabilistic. For example, most people agree that prolonged exposure to tobacco smoke causes lung cancer. Of course, not all who smoke get lung cancer, and some who do not smoke do get lung cancer. Exposure to tobacco smoke is neither a necessary nor a sufficient cause of lung cancer. Technically, smoking causes an increase in the likelihood of getting lung cancer; it is a probabilistic cause. Unfortunately, many people who seem to understand the probabilistic nature of causality in medical domains have great difficulty in the media violence domain (Anderson & Bushman, 2002b; Potter, 2003). This difficulty is not limited to non-scientists, but in fact many good social scientists have difficulty using the "C" word in writings, discussions, and presentations in part because of scientific conservatism and in part because of the probabilistic nature of modern science. But good public policy decisions require that scientists and nonscientists come to a better and more consensual understanding of probabilistic causality and get over hang-ups regarding the "C" word.

Expertise

Public policy debates involving dangers brought to light by scientific research are not new, nor are the tactics used by industries that feel threatened by such findings. One common response (e.g., by the lead industry, the tobacco industry, the media violence industries) is to find or create "experts" to dispute the findings of harm. In the public domain (e.g., newspapers, television) there are essentially no rules on what constitutes an expert. Frequently, the expert opinion of a parent of a teen who consumes high levels of media violence (or the expert opinion of the teenager him/herself) are juxtaposed with the opinions of a true media violence research expert; the consumer is presumably supposed to decide who is right, with very little information to judge who is an expert. One might expect courtroom definitions to be much clearer, but in fact all one needs is an advanced degree in an appropriate field and a claim that one has read and accurately understands the literature.[1] Interestingly, the strongest critics of media violence research findings have either a very weak or no record of significant, original media violence research (Huesmann & Taylor, 2003).

So, what criteria might be used to determine who is qualified to speak about the entire media violence effects domain? We do not presume to have *the* single best answer. Nonetheless, a few features seem absolutely necessary (but perhaps not sufficient), and a number of additional features would certainly strengthen an individual's claim of expertise. Minimal features include:

a.   a doctorate in an appropriate empirical science;
b.   multiple publications in top-ranked, peer-reviewed journals, based on original empirical data gathered to examine media violence effects;
c.   an understanding of the strengths and weaknesses of all of the major research designs (i.e., experimental, cross-sectional correlation, longitudinal); and
d.   a demonstrated willingness and ability to accept and integrate findings from all major research designs.

Additional desirable features include:

a.   a demonstrated understanding of and willingness and ability to use results of meta-analytic studies;
b.   a demonstrated expertise in using multiple research designs, by publications of empirical studies using different designs in top-ranked, peer-reviewed journals;
c.   demonstrated theoretical contributions to media violence issues; and
d.   a demonstrated understanding of key media violence related philosophy of science issues (e.g., internal and external validity, probabilistic causality, role of theory and theory-testing in good science, methodological triangulation in hypothesis testing).

---

[1]   Technically, this is a gross oversimplification of the rules regarding scientific expertise in the courtroom. (See *Daubert v. Merrell Dow Pharmaceuticals, Inc.*, 1993.) However, in our personal experience this captures the essence of what has happened in cases involving media violence expertise.

Individuals who possess all eight of the listed criteria do exist. Furthermore, teams of scholars can essentially pool their expertise in joint products, such as in the various summary reports mentioned earlier (e.g., Anderson et al., 2003). We turn next to the key findings from the media violence effects literatures.

Media Violence: Scientific Facts Beyond Common Knowledge

Media violence has been one of the most heavily studied areas of psychological science, with hundreds of independent studies, as well as hundreds of theoretical analyses and reviews. This research literature is sufficiently broad and deep to be able to answer most of the basic questions about whether there are effects and of what types (for reviews, see Anderson et al., 2003; Cantor, 2002; Gentile, 2003; Potter, 1999, 2003). For example, there are several types of studies that can be conducted: laboratory experiments, field experiments, cross-sectional (sometimes called correlational) studies, and longitudinal studies. Each type of study has different strengths.

Four types of media violence studies

Randomized experiments (laboratory or field) allow for the clearest tests of causality, as other potential factors are controlled either by holding them constant or by the random assignment of participants to different treatment groups. However, media violence experiments usually do not use measures of extreme forms of aggression as it would be unethical to allow participants to hit, stab, or shoot each other after watching a violent or nonviolent show. They also usually measure short-term effects. Some field experiments, however, have measured some of the more extreme forms of aggression, and have done so across a longer time span.

In a typical experimental study, researchers randomly assign participants to either a high or a low media violence exposure condition. Random assignment ensures that the two groups are approximately equal on potentially relevant but unmeasured factors. This randomization procedure provides experiments with their greater ability to yield valid causal conclusions, because there is no reason to believe that the violent and nonviolent media exposure groups are different on any relevant personal characteristics. After media violence exposure (e.g., playing a violent or nonviolent video game), the researchers might observe how the participants interact with each other, measuring physical or verbal aggression. Alternatively, researchers might measure their aggressive feelings, aggressive thoughts, attitudes, or even physiological arousal. For example, Bjorkqvist (1985) randomly assigned 5- to 6-year-old Finnish children to view either a violent or nonviolent film. Two raters (blind to experimental condition) later observed the children playing together in a room. Compared to those who had viewed the nonviolent film, children who had just watched the violent film were rated much higher on physical assault and on other types of aggression.

Cross-sectional correlational studies allow for tests of a long-term relation between media violence exposure and more extreme "real-world" measures of aggression, but they are weaker with regard to testing causality. They are useful in testing the generalizability of experimental findings, and in testing causal theoretical models, as will be discussed in a later section. In a typical cross-sectional correlational study, researchers give surveys or conduct interviews with youths or young adults, and often also with their peers, their parents, or teachers. These surveys gather information about participants' media violence exposure, their aggressive behaviors (which have ranged from verbal aggression through delinquency and even to serious violence), and often personality and demographic characteristics. Again, the consistent finding across studies of different forms of media violence is that children and adolescents with greater exposure to violent media exhibit higher amounts of aggressive behaviors than those with less exposure. These associations typically remain significant even when a host of other variables are statistically controlled. For example, Anderson and Dill (2000) assessed exposure to violent video games, and correlated it with college students' self-reported acts of aggressive delinquent behavior in the past year (e.g., hitting or threatening other students, attacking someone with the idea of seriously hurting or killing him or her, participating in gang fights, throwing objects at other people). The overall correlation between exposure to violent video games and violent behavior was substantial and significant ($r = .46$, $p < .05$). The association remained significant even in analyses that controlled for antisocial personality, gender, and total time spent playing any type of video game.

Longitudinal studies allow for tests of long-term effects, by following the same people over time. They can provide good evidence of causal direction even though they are correlational, because later events cannot affect earlier ones. They can allow statistical controls for plausible alternative explanatory factors. Furthermore, they can assess more extreme forms of aggression. However, they are very expensive and difficult to conduct. The consistent finding across longitudinal studies of TV and film is that early violent media exposure is related to later increases in aggressive thoughts and aggressive behaviors, rather than the other way around, although there is also evidence that it is a vicious circle, with each increasing the other over time (e.g., Slater, Henry, Swaim, & Anderson, 2003). To date, there is only one longitudinal study of violent video games, but it is consistent in showing that 3rd through 5th grade children change over the course of a school year to become more physically aggressive if they play a lot of violent video games at the beginning of the year (Anderson, Gentile, & Buckley, 2007).

If only one of these classes of studies yielded evidence of media violence effects, most scientists (including the present authors) would be hesitant to claim that the effect was *real*, but instead would worry about the possibility of some hidden artifacts. The strongest scientific evidence possible would be if *all* types of studies showed the same effect, regardless of differences in methods, measurements, or subject populations. Such strong evidence exists in the case of media violence studies. For recent reviews see Anderson and Bushman, 2001; Anderson et al., 2003; Anderson et al., 2004; Bushman and Huesmann, 2001; Gentile and Anderson, 2003; Gentile and Stone, 2005; Kirsh, 2006; Strasburger and Wilson, 2003.

Meta-analyses

As we have said, the strongest scientific evidence would be if *all* types of studies showed the same effect. This is what the overall body of media violence research shows. Nonetheless, some studies show no significant effect, and a very few demonstrate the opposite effect. How can scientists make sense of apparently contradictory findings? One objective approach is meta-analysis, in which all studies are combined statistically to determine whether the effect holds once all the data are combined. There have been numerous excellent meta-analyses of the media violence literature (which are summarized in Comstock & Scharrer, 2003). Figure 14.1 displays the results of a meta-analysis of 284 independent studies (including 51,597 participants) of the four types of studies of media violence effects on aggression (defined as behavior intended to harm another person). Regardless of how it is studied, there is a positive relation between media violence exposure and aggression (Anderson & Bushman, 2002a). To summarize, experimental studies (laboratory and field) conclusively demonstrate that

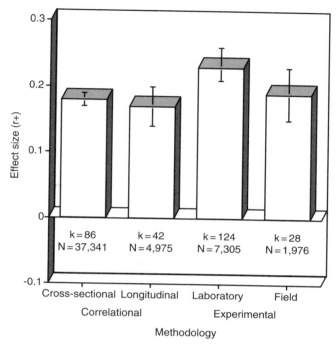

Figure 14.1   Results of meta-analyses of studies of media violence exposure and aggressive behavior. Positive effect sizes indicate that media violence exposure is positively related to increases in aggression/violence. Vertical capped bars indicate the 95% confidence intervals for the average effect size. (Based on data originally reported in Bushman & Anderson, 2001)

k = number of independent samples, N = total number of participants used in the effect size estimate, r+ = the average effect size

the link is causal. Laboratory experiments yield a slightly larger effect size than other methodologies, probably because of the greater control over irrelevant factors one has in the laboratory. Field experiments demonstrate causal effects in naturalistic settings. Cross-sectional studies demonstrate a positive link between media violence exposure and aggression in the "real world," including serious forms of aggression that cannot ethically be studied in the laboratory (e.g., physical assault). Many of the cross-sectional studies also effectively test and rule out key alterative explanations. Longitudinal studies demonstrate long-term effects of early media violence exposure on later aggressive behavior, rule out additional alternative explanations, and provide additional support for causal conclusions. As shown in figure 14.1, each type of study supports the scientific fact: Media violence exposure causes increases in aggression.

The scientific facts about media violence

So, what are the main scientific facts about media violence effects that meet the courtroom criterion of "a reasonable degree of scientific certainty?" The following list summarizes the conclusions of a number of major reviews.

1. Brief exposure to media violence:
    a. increases aggression in the immediate situation
    b. increases aggressive thoughts or cognitions in the immediate situation
    c. increases aggressive feelings in the immediate situation
    d. can cause fear, anxiety, and nightmares, especially in children, which sometimes persist for long periods of time
    e. can teach new ways to harm others.
2. Repeated exposure to media violence:
    a. increases aggression and violence across long time spans (22 years or more)
    b. desensitizes people to scenes of violent acts and consequences of such acts
    c. increases acceptance of violence as a means of solving conflicts
    d. increases aggression-supportive attitudes and beliefs, such as hostile attribution biases
    e. may be larger for younger children and adolescents.
3. Several basic psychological processes underlie media violence effects; these processes are general, that is, not specific to media violence and aggression:
    a. imitation of observed action, especially by young children
    b. observational learning of:
        i.   specific behaviors and behavioral scripts
        ii.   attitudes and beliefs about how the world works
        iii. outcome expectations about the consequences of specific behaviors
    c. priming or cueing of existing behavioral scripts, cognitions, and affect
    d. desensitization
    e. increases in physiological arousal resulting in excitation transfer and other effects.

4. There does not appear to be any identifiable group (e.g., age, sex, personality type) that is wholly immune to media violence effects.
5. Media violence effects are best viewed as one of the many risk factors that contribute to aggression and violence in modern society.
6. Media violence effects are sufficiently large, both in terms of absolute size and relative to other aggression/violence risk factors, to warrant public policy debate about possible ameliorative action.
7. Reducing exposure to media violence reduces later aggression.

Science facts and politics

Thus, science has done its job – it has provided us with factual answers. However, once these facts are established, they can be manipulated by political and societal pressures. One recent example is demonstrated by the Anderson et al. (2003) review. In 2000 the U.S. Surgeon General asked the National Institute of Mental Health to establish an expert panel of media violence researchers who would evaluate and summarize all of the relevant scientific research on media violence effects. This report was to be included as part of the Surgeon Genera's report on youth violence (U.S. Department of Health and Human Services, 2001), as a separate chapter. A panel of distinguished and experienced media violence scientists was formed, led by Dr Rowell Huesmann, one of the pioneers in this field. Once the panel's scientific review was completed, it was altered without their approval in a way that they considered to be a distortion of the science. Whether the revisions were the results of political pressure, industry pressure, ignorance or biases of the NIMH and/or Surgeon General's staff working on the report, miscommunication between the panel and the NIMH and Surgeon General's offices, or some other source is unknown (at least, to the expert panel). What is known is that the revisions made media violence effects appear less strong than the research demonstrated. The panel worked with NIMH and Surgeon General officials to find a compromise that the panel could accept as being scientifically accurate. However, when the final Surgeon General's report on youth violence was released, the chapter that the expert panel had written was altogether and inexplicably absent. A revised and updated version was eventually published in an academic journal (Anderson et al., 2003). This anecdote is germane because it illustrates that the intersection of science, public policy, and the law is not always obvious or transparent. Kennedy (2002) noted that: "These entanglements [between science and politics], although not always welcome, are an inevitable consequence of the fact that science matters" (p. 1765).

Common Challenges to the Facts

Beyond political challenges to scientifically derived facts, many scientific challenges have been raised and answered throughout the history of media violence research. Several of the most common ones are described next. Though many people are familiar with these challenges, the fact that they have been adequately answered is not common knowledge. For a more detailed discussion of these issues, see Anderson et al. (2007), Gentile (2003), Potter (2003), and Singer and Singer (2001).

Field studies, especially cross-sectional correlation and longitudinal designs, are frequently criticized as being low in internal validity. That is, they don't "prove" that variation in the independent variable caused observed differences in the dependent variable. This criticism is often highlighted with the glib phrase, "Correlation is not causation." This is an oversimplified mantra taught to introductory psychology (and other science) students. The more correct scientific understanding is that correlational studies are quite useful for testing causal theoretical models and alternative explanations. For example, one alternative explanation of the correlation between media violence exposure and aggressive behavior is that it is the amount of time spent on entertainment media in general that leads to poorer social skills and higher levels of aggression. This alternative explanation has been ruled out by numerous correlational studies in which the effect of media violence exposure on aggression remains significant even when total time spent consuming media has been statistically controlled.

Similarly, laboratory studies are frequently criticized as lacking in external validity. The claim is that they do not generalize to other (usually real-world) contexts and populations. Part of the criticism is aimed at the measures of aggressive behavior used in controlled laboratory settings, such as the intensity and duration of punishments delivered to an opponent. Both the generalization criticism and the more specific criticism of aggression measures have been empirically demonstrated to be false (e.g., Anderson & Bushman, 1997; Carlson, Marcus-Newhall, & Miller, 1989).

A third common challenge to the scientific facts is the claim that the results are mixed. It is certainly the case that not every study of media violence finds statistically significant effects. As in any research domain (e.g., smoking/cancer), the results from different studies vary somewhat. Some of this variation is due merely to the usual sampling variability, some is due to use of different methods and possibly to different populations. Studies with smaller samples will, of course, tend to show greater variability in estimated effect size. Furthermore, recent analyses of the violent video game literature have shown that studies with poorer research methods tend to yield smaller effect sizes (e.g., Anderson et al., 2004). Meta-analyses are particularly well suited to address the question of whether there is a significant overall effect of media violence on aggression, and all major meta-analyses have come to the same conclusion. Indeed, a cumulative meta-analysis by Bushman and Anderson (2001) found that by 1975 (the first year in which a sufficiently large number of studies for a meta-analysis had accumulated) the evidence of such an effect was quite clear.

A fourth, oft-repeated challenge is that the violent crime rate in the U.S. has been dropping in recent years while the use of violent media (especially violent video games) has been increasing. It is ironic that this challenge is frequently uttered by the same critics who promote the "correlation is not causation" dismissal of all correlational studies. The problem with this argument is that it assumes that media violence is the only or the most important factor driving violent crime. Media violence researchers have never made such extreme claims, and indeed they see media violence as one of a dozen or more risk factors for aggression and violence. Several other major variables have also been at work during the recent downturns in violent crime. For example, the proportion of the U.S. population that falls within the high violence age group has been declining, fewer young people are carrying handguns, there have been huge improvements in trauma care, unemployment rates have dropped, and we now have record high incarceration rates. Furthermore, the most recent data suggest that violent crime rates are again increasing despite all of these favorable changes in other risk factors.

A final common challenge is based on a common misperception of what the media violence experts have said. This challenge frequently takes the following form: "I've played violent video games for years and haven't killed anyone yet." We have heard such arguments from a wide variety of individuals, ranging from elementary school children to public policy-makers to social scientists. As noted in the Science Facts and Theories section, exposure to media violence is a risk factor for increased levels of aggression. Extreme acts of violence typically involve the convergence of multiple risk factors, and even then are fairly rare. No single risk factor by itself predicts extreme violence very well. Media violence exposure differs from most other risk factors, though, in that it can be controlled with essentially no financial cost by parents who understand the need for control, if they are given the proper tools to assist their attempts to restrict their children's access.

Summary and Conclusions

The media violence research literature is large, diverse, and consistent. True scientific experts on media violence effects have reached a consensus that, in our view, meets the criterion of a scientific fact as a conclusion held with a reasonable degree of scientific certainty. The key fact is that exposure to media violence causes an increase in the likelihood of aggressive and/or violent behavior in both short- and long-term contexts. There are, of course, disagreements about a number of more specific issues (e.g., who is most and least susceptible). Also, additional research is needed to answer a host of these more fine-grained scientific issues. But, once one understands and resolves the issues of probabilistic causality (versus the old necessary and sufficient causality criteria), and of differences in language and question-intent between the scientist role versus the legal expert role or the advisor to public policy and general public roles, then the potential of this vast body of research to have a positive impact on modern society becomes clearer and more easily accomplished.

One final domain that deserves brief mention concerns the difference between the normative or average case and the individual case of media violence effects. We (and most media violence researchers we know) are quite comfortable in discussing the probabilistic effects of media violence exposure on the likelihood of aggression and violence in large populations, that is, the normative case. However, we frequently receive calls from reporters and occasionally from defense lawyers and parents of violent crime victims and perpetrators asking about whether a specific violent crime was caused by that perpetrator's exposure to violent media. In recent years, this has usually concerned violent video games. In our view, it is very difficult to know in the individual case how much impact (if any) the media violence exposure had on the ultimate decision to behave violently. Of course, the same issue arises in many trials, both criminal and civil, involving harmful products (such as tobacco). Some lawsuits have been brought alleging that media industries should be held culpable in individual cases of violence (e.g., school shootings). It is not clear to us whether it is possible at this point in time to arrive at a definitive scientific answer to the question of how much (if at all) did exposure to a specific media violence product causally contribute to a specific violent crime.

Certainly, the broad scientific literature on media violence does provide a sound scientific context for thinking about individual cases. But this is not the same as proving that in any specific case media violence *caused* the specific violent action. Nonetheless, because violent behavior is multicausal, understanding the average increase in risk posed by media violence exposure can allow a decision-maker to reach a conclusion about the multiple causes that bear on a specific case that is consistent with the scientific research. In other words, a juror or judge might reasonably decide that media violence in general or that a specific media violence product was at least somewhat responsible for a specific act of violence, and could reasonably assign a portion of responsibility (and damage cost) to the product manufacturer and to those who exposed the perpetrator to the product, as is commonly done in product liability cases.

What is even clearer to us is that: (1) the individuals who commit violent crimes must be held responsible for their acts; (2) modern society (especially parents) must become better informed about media violence effects; and (3) the problem of media violence exposure is severe enough to warrant serious action to reduce children's and adolescents' exposure.

ACKNOWLEDGMENTS

We thank Joanne Cantor, Steve Kirsch, the book editors, and several anonymous reviewers for comments on earlier versions.

REFERENCES

Anderson, C. A., Berkowitz, L., Donnerstein, E., Huesmann, L. R., Johnson, J., Linz, D., Malamuth, N., & Wartella, E. (2003). The influence of media violence on youth. *Psychological Science in the Public Interest, 4,* 81–110.

Anderson, C. A., & Bushman, B. J. (1997). External validity of "trivial" experiments: The case of laboratory aggression. *Review of General Psychology, 1,* 19–41.

Anderson, C. A., & Bushman, B. J. (2001). Effects of violent video games on aggressive behavior, aggressive cognition, aggressive affect, physiological arousal, and prosocial behavior: A meta-analytic review of the scientific literature. *Psychological Science, 12,* 353–359.

Anderson, C. A., & Bushman, B. J. (2002a). The effects of media violence on society. *Science, 295,* 2377–2378.

Anderson, C. A., & Bushman, B. J. (2002b). Media violence and the American public revisited. *American Psychologist, 57*, 448–450.

Anderson, C. A., Carnagey, N. L., Flanagan, M., Benjamin, A. J., Eubanks, J., & Valentine, J. C. (2004). Violent video games: Specific effects of violent content on aggressive thoughts and behavior. *Advances in Experimental Social Psychology, 36*, 199–249.

Anderson, C. A., & Dill, K. E. (2000). Video games and aggressive thoughts, feelings, and behavior in the laboratory and in life. *Journal of Personality and Social Psychology, 78*, 772–790.

Anderson, C. A., Gentile, D. A., & Buckley, K. E. (2007). *Violent video game effects on children and adolescents: Theory, research, and public policy.* Oxford: Oxford University Press.

Bjorkqvist, K. (1985). *Violent films, anxiety, and aggression.* Helsinki: Finnish Society of Sciences and Letters.

Blumer, H., & Hauser, P. (1933). *Movies, delinquency, and crime.* New York: Macmillan.

Bushman, B. J., & Anderson, C. A. (2001). Media violence and the American public: Scientific facts versus media misinformation. *American Psychologist, 56*, 477–489.

Bushman, B. J., & Huesmann, L. R. (2001). Effects of televised violence on aggression. In D. Singer & J. Singer (Eds.), *Handbook of children and the media* (pp. 223–254). Thousand Oaks, CA: Sage Publications.

Cantor, J. (2002). Fright reactions to mass media. In J. Bryant and D. Zillmann (Eds.), *Media effects: Advances in theory and research* (2nd ed., pp. 287–306). Mahwah, NJ: Erlbaum.

Carlson, M., Marcus-Newhall, A., & Miller, N. (1989). Evidence for a general construct of aggression. *Personality and Social Psychology Bulletin, 15*, 377–389.

Comstock, G., & Scharrer, E. (2003). Meta-analyzing the controversy over television violence and aggression. In D. A. Gentile (Ed.), *Media violence and children* (pp. 205–226). Westport, CT: Praeger.

Congressional Public Health Summit (2000). *Joint statement on the impact of entertainment violence on children.* Retrieved December 2, 2003, from www.aap.org/advocacy/releases/jstmtevc.htm

Daubert v. Merrell Dow Pharmaceuticals, Inc., 509 U.S. 579 (1993).

Eron, L. D., Gentry, J. H., & Schlegel, P. (Eds.) (1994). *Reason to hope: A psychosocial perspective on violence and youth* (pp. 219–250). Washington, DC: American Psychological Association.

Gentile, D. A. (1996). *NIMF 1996 National survey of parent media attitudes, behaviors, and opinions.* Minneapolis, MN: National Institute on Media and the Family.

Gentile, D. A. (1999). *MediaQuotient: National survey of family media habits, knowledge, and attitudes.* Minneapolis, MN: National Institute on Media and the Family.

Gentile, D. A. (Ed.) (2003). *Media violence and children.* Westport, CT: Praeger.

Gentile, D. A., & Anderson, C.A. (2003). Violent video games: The newest media violence hazard. In D. A. Gentile (Ed.), *Media violence and children* (pp. 131–152). Westport, CT: Praeger.

Gentile, D. A., & Anderson, C. A. (2006). Violent video games: Effects on youth and public policy implications. Chapter in N. Dowd, D. G. Singer, & R. F. Wilson (Eds.), *Handbook of children, culture, and violence* (pp. 225–246). Thousand Oaks, CA: Sage.

Gentile, D. A. & Stone, W. (2005). Violent video game effects on children and adolescents: A review of the literature. *Minerva Pediatrica, 57,* 337–358.

Gentile, D. A. & Walsh, D. A. (2002). A normative study of family media habits. *Journal of Applied Developmental Psychology, 23,* 157–178.

Huesmann, L. R., & Taylor, L. D. (2003). The case against the case against media violence. In D. A. Gentile (Ed.), *Media violence and children,* (pp. 107–130). Westport, CT: Praeger.

Kefauver, E. (1954). U.S. Congress, *Juvenile Delinquency (Television Programs),* 1954.

Kennedy, D. (2002). When science and politics don't mix. *Science, 296,* 1765.

Kirsh, S. J. (2006). *Children, adolescents, and media violence: A critical look at the research.* Thousand Oaks, CA: Sage Publications, Inc.

National Commission on the Causes and Prevention of Violence (1969). *Commission statement on violence in television entertainment programs.* Washington, DC: U.S. Government Printing Office.

National Institute of Mental Health (1982). *Television and behavior: Ten years of scientific progress and implications for the eighties: Vol. 1. Summary report* (DHHS Publication No. ADM 82-1195). Washington, DC: U.S. Government Printing Office.

Potter, W. J. (1999). *On media violence.* Thousand Oaks, CA: Sage Publications.

Potter, W. J. (2003). *The 11 myths of media violence.* Thousand Oaks, CA: Sage Publications.

Roberts, D. F., Foehr, U. G., & Rideout, V. (2005). *Generation M: Media in the lives of 8- to 18-year-olds.* Menlo Park, CA: Kaiser Family Foundation.

Saunders, K. W. (2003a). Regulating youth access to violent video games: Three responses to First Amendment concerns. *2003 Michigan State Law Review, 51,* 51–114.

Saunders, K. W. (2003b). *Saving our children from the First Amendment.* New York: New York University Press.

Singer, D., & Singer, J. (Eds.) (2001). *Handbook of children and the media.* Thousand Oaks, CA: Sage Publications.

Slater, M. D., Henry, K. L., Swaim, R. C., & Anderson, L. L. (2003). Violent media content and aggressiveness in adolescents. *Communication Research, 30*(6), 713–736.

Steinfeld, J. (1972). *Statement in hearings before Subcommittee on Communications of Committee on Commerce* (U.S. Senate, Serial No. 92–52, pp. 25–27). Washington, DC: U.S. Government Printing Office.

Strasburger, V. C. & Wilson, B. J. (2003). Television violence. In D. A. Gentile (Ed.), *Media violence and children* (pp. 57–86). Westport, CT: Praeger.

U.S. Department of Health and Human Services (2001). *Youth violence: A report of the Surgeon General.* Rockville, MD: U.S. Department of Health and Human Services, Centers for Disease Control and Prevention, National Center for Injury Prevention and Control; Substance Abuse and Mental Health Services Administration, Center for Mental Health Services; and National Institutes of Health, National Institute of Mental Health.

U.S. Surgeon General's Scientific Advisory Committee on Television and Social Behavior (1972). *Television and growing up: The impact of televised violence* (DHEW Publication No. HSM 72-9086). Washington, DC: U.S. Government Printing Office.

Walsh, D. A., Gentile, D. A., Walsh, E., Bennett, N., Robideau, B., Walsh, M., Strickland, S., & McFadden D. (2005). *Tenth annual MediaWise video game report card.* Minneapolis, MN: National Institute on Media and the Family.

Wartella, E., & Reeves, B. (1985). Historical trends in research on children and the media: 1900–1960. *Journal of Communication, 35,* 118–133.

Part III

Commentaries

15

The Limits of Science in the Courtroom

David L. Faigman

Most evidence codes require that expert testimony "assist the trier of fact" in order for it to be admissible (see, e.g., Federal Rules of Evidence, 2006–2007, 702.) Much complexity lies hidden in this simple helpfulness requirement. As an initial matter, scientific expert testimony must be legally relevant and have evidentiary reliability (i.e., scientific validity) (*Daubert v. Merrell Dow Pharmaceuticals, Inc.*, 1993). Moreover, expert opinion must offer insights beyond what triers of fact could do on their own. Put another way, scientist experts are limited to testifying about what their respective field's research can validly add to fact finders' deliberations – and nothing more. This injunction, however, is not always followed. In particular, scientists frequently seek to comment not simply on the import of general research findings, but also on whether aspects of a particular case fit those findings. Scientists who can validly describe a general phenomenon, however, do not invariably have the capacity to validly determine whether an individual case is an instance of that general phenomenon.

This comment is concerned with the packaging of science for courtroom use in ways that suggest that it is more helpful than the data allow. In particular, I will address a fundamental issue that most topics in psychological science present, but researchers too often ignore. Specifically, I will consider whether general scientific research permits expert opinion about particular events. It may be, for instance, that general research indicates that certain factors are associated with eyewitness errors, particular conditions increase the likelihood of false confessions, certain physiological signs are associated with deceit, or that group stereotypes lead to discriminatory behavior, and so on. Even if research is adequate to support these general observations – which is often not the case – it does not necessarily follow that experts should be permitted to opine about a specific occurrence.

Although this comment employs many examples, I do not mean to single out any of the contributions in this book for special attention or condemnation. To the extent that this comment is a criticism, it is of the general failure of the contributors to give the subject adequate attention. In fact, many of the contributors to this book limit their view of the reach of scientific research in the courtroom to what the general research data support. I applaud this approach. In general, though, the problem of reasoning from general research to specific cases is ignored in this volume and largely overlooked in the literature (*but* see Borgida, Hunt & Kim, 2005). Even though this short comment cannot remedy this deficit, I hope to raise a few considerations that future scholars writing on the role of psychological science in court might ponder.

I have previously observed that, "while science attempts to discover the universals hiding among the particulars, trial courts attempt to discover the particulars hiding among the universals" (Faigman, 1999, p. 69). The usual practice among scientists is to study variables at the population level, and most of their methodological and statistical tools are designed for this kind of work. The trial process, in contrast, usually concerns whether a particular case is an instance of the general phenomenon. This essential difference in perspective between what scientists normally do and what the trial process is ordinarily about has yet to be studied with any degree of rigor – including by me – and page limits preclude my ability to give it more than cursory treatment here. But given the subject matter of this book – "beyond common knowledge" – this issue, which is endemic to the science and law connection, must be raised and considered, if only too briefly.

General Research and Specific Application

Clearly, scientists have the tools to study population-level data, and when those tools have been used adequately, the law should welcome their input. It is less clear that scientists have the tools that would support expert opinion regarding individual cases. If they do not, then the scope of scientific expert testimony should be limited accordingly.

Courts have become fairly well acquainted with the difficulties inherent in employing general scientific data to reach conclusions about specific cases. This recognition, however, has largely occurred in drug and toxic tort cases in which courts routinely distinguish between "general causation" and "specific causation" (Faigman, Kaye, Saks, Sanders & Cheng, 2007). Not all science is engaged in describing cause-and-effect relationships, however, so general causation and specific causation are subcategories of what I will call "general propositions" and "specific application." Sometimes general propositions in science will be stated in causative terms, but very often they will be associational, technical, or descriptive. Specific application refers to the determination as to whether a particular case is an instance, use, or example of general propositions that are supported by adequate research. It must be emphasized at the outset that the jurisprudential limits associated with the scientific model – that is, the methodological limits to reasoning from the general to the specific – arise across scientific domains, including psychology, psychiatry, the forensic identification sciences, engineering, and economics. From the judiciary's perspective, the difficulties associated with reasoning from the general to the specific are particularly noticeable in the medical causation cases. At the same time, however, some scientific domains have largely bridged the science–law divide. DNA profiling, for instance, is founded upon very sound general data, and the research permits highly specific (albeit probabilistic) statements to be made about the evidence.

Because ordinary science operates at the general level of descriptive and inferential statistics, it can readily be employed to determine general propositions. For example, consider the legal/scientific matter of whether secondhand cigarette smoke causes lung cancer. One would expect, and indeed would find, research on this question, including clinical reports, toxicological research, and epidemiological studies (Balbach & Glantz, 2007). In the courtroom, however, the ultimate question is whether the plaintiff's lung cancer was caused by secondhand exposure to cigarettes. This issue entails not only proof that secondhand smoke *could cause* lung cancer, but that *some other cause was not responsible* for the plaintiff's lung cancer.

Although the matter is not without difficulty, it is a relatively straightforward exercise to determine whether various kinds of research converge sufficiently to give scientists enough confidence to say that exposure to X causes (or is associated with) condition Y. Indeed, this is the sort of exercise that is a staple of training in science. Ideally, a community of researchers studies hypotheses using a wide range of methodological and statistical tools. For example, eyewitness researchers interested in comparing error rates of simultaneous lineups (e.g., viewing six photos at once) versus sequential lineups (e.g., viewing six photos one at a time), might employ a wide assortment of methodologies, including anecdotal reports, data from DNA exoneration cases, field studies, and laboratory experiments. If these differing methods point in the same direction, then some general conclusions might be made regarding the phenomenon of interest. (If they point in different directions, the task is complicated greatly, if not made impossible until more research is completed.) But even when the body of social science work is robust, as is the case with lineup procedures, conclusions are likely to be tentative and described in probabilistic terms. In the case of lineups, research indicates that presenting photos sequentially tends to make the procedure less sensitive, which reduces the false-positive rate, but also reduces the number of true positives obtained (Wells & Olson, 2003). This phenomenon, if it is so, is true for some population of cases and not necessarily in any one particular case.

In the courtroom, however, research on general propositions, such as whether lineup procedures affect accuracy rates or whether second-hand smoke causes lung cancer, merely addresses the threshold question, since the point in question is whether a particular case is an instance of the general phenomenon. In the lineup example, the matter concerns whether the lineup resulted in a misidentification of the defendant; in a tort case, the issue might involve whether the defendant's cigarettes proximately caused the plaintiff's cancer. This issue of specific application poses a complex and difficult cognitive exercise. Moreover, it is an exercise that varies in different empirical contexts. It is also a subject that has been virtually ignored by psychological scientists interested in the courtroom use of their data.

Reasoning from the General to the Specific

The problem of reasoning from the general to the specific has been given substantial attention in legal cases involving medical causation (Faigman et al., 2007). In a nutshell, the first task is to demonstrate that the substance *could* have caused the ailment (i.e., the validity of the general proposition), and the second task is to show that it probably did, and that other substances probably did not, cause the plaintiff's condition. In the simplest situation, general research indicates that the substance causes an ailment that is uniquely associated with that substance. For instance, asbestos has been shown to cause mesothelioma and it is the only substance known to cause it (Roggli, 2007). Since mesothelioma is a "signature disease," the only question concerns the circumstances of the individual's exposure to asbestos (i.e., was the defendant responsible?), not whether exposure caused the condition. In contrast, while secondhand smoke has been linked to lung cancer, many other substances are known to cause lung cancer. Hence, in regard to identifying the cause of a person's lung cancer, an expert must not only rule in tobacco smoke as a possible cause, but also rule out other possible causes (Balbach & Glantz, 2007).

The principal tool used to move from general research findings to statements about individual cases is "differential etiology," sometimes misleadingly referred to as differential diagnosis. Properly understood, differential *diagnosis* refers to the identification of the illness or behavioral condition that a person is experiencing. Differential *etiology* refers to the cause or causes of that condition. Hence, the determination that a person suffers from "dissociative amnesia" and not "dissociative fugue" is a diagnostic issue (American Psychiatric Association, *DSM-IV-TR*, 2000). The determination that a sexual assault at age 10 caused the diagnosed dissociative amnesia, and that it did not result from a medical condition or physical trauma, is an etiological matter. Very different skill sets are usually involved in these two determinations. Indeed, the *DSM* explicitly eschews any claim of etiological verity of its diagnostic categories (American Psychiatric Association, 2000, p. xxxiii). It is worth emphasizing, as well, that the validity of the diagnosis of dissociative amnesia is a matter of general research. The entire process of differential diagnosis and differential etiology assumes that the designated category has adequate empirical support in the first place as a general proposition. Hence, although it is logically obvious, it should be stated plainly that an expert should not be permitted to testify about a specific application of a general proposition if research does not adequately support the general proposition.

In clinical psychology, as is true in much of clinical medicine, the primary concern is diagnosis and not etiology. An oncologist might be curious about what caused his or her patient's leukemia, but the doctor's first task is to diagnose and treat the condition, not determine whether it was caused by trichloroethylene, electromagnetic fields, or something else. Similarly, a psychologist treating a person thought to suffer from either posttraumatic stress disorder (PTSD) or adjustment disorder is primarily concerned with identifying and treating the condition, not determining the true causes of that condition. In the ordinary practice of clinical medicine and clinical psychology, treatment and therapy are the principal objectives, not assessing cause. A person presenting symptoms associated with PTSD, therefore, might claim that the traumatic event was a sexual assault committed by her uncle. From the therapeutic standpoint, at least at the start, the important factor is that there was a traumatic event. Whether the patient's uncle was the cause need not be specifically resolved for diagnostic purposes. In the law, of course, *who* caused the traumatic event is the crux of the matter.

In the courtroom, therefore, differential etiology is the operative issue. Moreover, the same basic principle is implicated, whether the expert opinion comes from research-based psychological science or clinical psychology. Indeed, at least superficially, the former suffers a comparative disadvantage, since the research tradition does not ordinarily purport to offer conclusive statements about individual cases. For example, research might identify factors highly associated with false confessions, but these general propositions are some distance from what is needed to allow experts to opine regarding the truth or falsity of any particular confession. Clinicians at least have a history of applying general knowledge to individual cases, though, as noted, while this practice might be well accepted for therapeutic purposes, its validity for forensic ends is in some doubt. Whether researchers or clinicians have the wherewithal to be helpful to triers of fact in applying general research propositions to specific cases is a threshold legal matter that should depend on the reliability and validity of the differential etiology done in the respective case. It may be, that is, that in vast areas of clinical practice there is no general research foundation in the first instance; and, as stated above, if research does not support a general proposition – say, the phenomenon of repressed memories – then clinical expert testimony that a particular person has repressed certain memories of early sexual abuse cannot be sustained.

Differential Etiology

Differential etiology is a reasoning process that involves a multitude of factors, few of which are easily quantified. An expert offering an opinion regarding a specific case must first consider the strength of the evidence for the general proposition being applied in the case. If the claim is that substance X caused plaintiff's condition Y, the initial inquiry must concern the strength of the relationship between X and Y as a general proposition. For example, both secondhand smoke and firsthand smoke are associated with lung cancer, but the strength of the relationship generally is much stronger for the latter than it is for the former. The inquiry regarding strength of relationship will depend on many factors, including the statistical strength of any claims and the quality of the methods used in the research. Additionally, the general model must consider the strength of the evidence for alternative possible causes of Y and the strength of their respective relationships (and possibly interactions with other factors). Again, the quality of the research and the different methodologies employed will make comparisons difficult.

Complicating matters further regarding identification of potential causes of condition Y are the myriad possible causes that have not been studied, or have been studied inadequately. Hence, determining the contours of the general model is a dicey affair in itself, since it requires combining disparate research results and discounting those results by an unknown factor associated with additional variables not yet studied. This is just the first part of the necessary analysis if the expert wants to give an opinion about an individual case.

The second part of the analysis – specific application of general propositions that are themselves supported by adequate research – requires two abilities, neither of which is clearly within most scientists' skill sets. The first, and perhaps less problematic, is that of forensic investigator. Almost no matter what the empirical relationship, whether medical or psychological, exposure or dosage levels will be relevant to the diagnosis. The first principle of toxicology is that "the dose is the poison," since any substance in sufficient quantities could injure or kill someone (Goldstein & Carruth, 2007). Similarly, in a wide variety of psychological contexts, the exposure or dose will be the poison. For instance, degree of trauma affects diagnostic category between PTSD and adjustment disorder, level of anxiety affects eyewitness identifications, amount of lack of sleep affects false confession rates, and so on. The expert testifying to specific causation must determine exposure and dosage levels for the suspected cause (i.e., the source suspected by the client) as well as for all other known or possible causes. This task is difficult enough alone, but is enormously complicated by the significant potential for recall bias, given that the litigation will be profoundly affected by what is recalled.

The second skill set that is needed has not yet been invented or even described with precision. Somehow, the diagnostician must combine the surfeit of information concerning the multitude of factors that make up the general model, combine it with the case history information known or suspected about the individual, and offer an opinion with some level of confidence that substance or experience X was the likely cause of condition Y. In practice, this opinion is usually stated as follows: "Within a reasonable degree of medical/ psychological certainty, it is my opinion that X caused [a particular case of] Y." This expression has no empirical meaning and is simply a mantra repeated by experts for purposes of legal decision-makers who similarly have no idea what it means. But even less extreme versions of this statement – such as, "it is more likely than not true that this case is an instance of some general phenomenon" – are objectionable. Just how, for instance, would an eyewitness researcher determine that a witness was more likely than not inaccurate when the witness made a cross-racial identification of the defendant after seeing the unarmed perpetrator for five minutes under a streetlight from an unobstructed view 20 ft away from the crime? To my knowledge, there are no data that would support psychologists' ability to make such statements, however modest or innocuous they might at first appear. Experts' case-specific conclusions appear largely to be based on an admixture of an unknown combination of knowledge of the subject, experience over the years, commitment to the client or cause, intuition, and blind faith. Science it is not.

Yet the legal system, as noted above, is all about discovering "the particulars hiding among the universals." What should conscientious scientists – who have discovered "the universals hiding among the particulars" – do when asked to opine on matters beyond their expertise?

What is the Conscientious Expert to Do?

There are two basic models that might be employed to set parameters on scientists' ability to testify on matters specific to individual cases. The *limits model* and the *no-limits model*. The first would prohibit scientists from testifying to matters not supported by data. Under this approach, an expert would be required to demonstrate the validity of the general propositions that support his or her testimony and the validity of the basis for his or her opinion that this case is or is not an instance of the general phenomenon. The second, the no-limits model, would allow experts to apply valid general propositions to individual cases even though insufficient data are available to show that such opinions can be validly made. The no-limits model would leave to individual scientists the discretion as to whether to offer case-specific expert opinions.

The limits model is adopted by most of those who research and testify regarding the reliability of eyewitness identifications. In all likelihood, eyewitness experts have opinions about the accuracy of the particular identifications in the cases in which they testify. There is no subject in psychology and law that is better researched. Yet, eyewitness researchers provide only general research results and leave to the fact finder the complicated task of applying the general findings of psychology to the particular facts of the case. Their modesty is to be admired, for there are no data that indicate that eyewitness experts would be any better than triers of fact at the task of applying general research findings to the particular case at hand.

In the courts, the limits model is the basic approach followed in medical causation cases. Most courts agree that some empirical basis must be offered to support an expert's opinion that a substance known generally to be associated with a particular illness was responsible for the illness in the case at hand (Faigman et al., 2007). However, courts disagree regarding the amount of proof necessary to support such opinions. Some courts require a fairly rigorous offer of proof (e.g., *Moore v. Ashland Chemical, Inc.*, 1998), while others permit a fairly lax standard of proof (e.g., *Heller v. Shaw Industries, Inc.*, 1999).

In many legal contexts, a field's competence to offer specific application opinions can be tested, at least theoretically, in a fairly straightforward manner. In many of the forensic identification sciences, such as handwriting, firearms, and fingerprinting, proficiency rates can be readily measured. In fact, a lot of these areas are largely devoid of good research data demonstrating the general propositions of their respective fields, but purport to have extensive proof of their forensic value through proficiency testing. (DNA profiling is a particularly noteworthy exception to this observation, since it is well validated both generally and in application to specific cases.) Similarly, many areas of clinical psychology lack research bases for many of the diagnostic categories they rely upon. Examples abound, including repressed memories, battered woman syndrome, and parental alienation syndrome. The analogue to proficiency testing in clinical psychology is reliability rates among diagnosticians. Most forensic identification science and many areas of clinical psychology, therefore, present the opposite situation to that of research-based areas. They lack well-established general propositions, but claim proficiency on a case-by-case basis. In general, however, adequate proficiency and reliability studies have yet to be done in many of these fields.

Many areas of scientific psychology have substantial research traditions, but have not systematically studied their forensic capacity to offer expert opinions regarding specific cases. This research could be done and, at least at first, would probably involve research paradigms testing proficiency or reliability rates. For instance, it would be fascinating to study whether eyewitness researchers could validly identify which witnesses were accurate and which were not under a variety of experimental conditions. The same sort of research could be contemplated in other well-developed areas of scientific psychology, such as false confessions and gender stereotyping. To my knowledge, no such research has been attempted in any area of scientific psychology.

Ultimately, of course, scientific psychologists might never travel the path toward developing the technology to apply general data to specific cases. Nor should they have to do so. Well-researched areas in psychology, such as eyewitness identification, can have great relevance to legal disputes, though the matter of applying that research to the case at hand is left to the trier of fact. Scientific psychology, as well as many other disciplines, can offer substantial assistance to the courts, despite their inability to answer all of the specific questions the law asks. The bigger danger lies in a different direction. Of greater concern than scientists limiting themselves to reporting general research results is the more likely danger that scientists and their cargo-cult impersonators will seek to offer specific testimony based on data that cannot support their expert opinions.

The second option is the no-limits model. This alternative is considerably more prevalent in psychology and permits experts to forge ahead despite the absence of any foundation for believing that an expert knowledgeable about the general model is superior to the fact finder in terms of connecting the dots to a particular case.

There are two basic arguments in favor of permitting experts to testify about specific application of general research propositions. The first comes from claims of validity and the second comes from an argument of necessity. If systematic research does not support the validity of a specific application, it might still be argued that experts who are specialists regarding general research findings will have greater insights and experience with the subject than will fact finders. Experience alone, the argument goes, should permit experts to make inferences regarding whether a specific case is an instance of the general phenomenon. This contention is a version of the "I know it when I see it," or "trust me, I've been doing this for 30 years" course of reasoning. In legal parlance, it is referred to as *ipse dixit*. In *General Electric Co. v. Joiner* (1997), Chief Justice Rehnquist used *ipse dixit* in a sentence, as follows: "[N]othing in either *Daubert* or the Federal Rules of Evidence requires a district court to admit opinion evidence that is connected to existing data only by the *ipse dixit* of the expert. A court may conclude that there is simply too great an analytical gap between the data and the opinion proffered" (p. 146).

A second argument in favor of allowing experts to testify about specific application without adequate empirical foundation is based on necessity. This argument holds that the legal framework is designed around individualized adjudications, and therefore general data need to be brought down to particular cases. But while this is true, it begs the question of who should supply the intellectual analysis that would connect a particular case to the general research data. As noted, experts on eyewitness identification leave this task to the trier of fact. There is no obvious reason why other experts could not do the same. Subject areas such as the battered woman syndrome, rape trauma syndrome, gender stereotyping, posttraumatic stress disorder, and many others could potentially be presented at the general level without accompanying opinion about whether a particular case is an instance of the more general phenomenon. In the terminology of Walker and Monahan, experts would be limited to testifying about the social framework, but would be precluded from giving an opinion about the extent to which that framework applies in a particular case (Walker & Monahan, 1987).

Conclusion

This comment considers issues surrounding what appears to be a blind spot in many psychologists' approach to the juncture of science and the law. A basic difference in perspective between science and the law is that science studies individuals in order to make statements about populations, while the law studies populations in order to make statements about individuals. It does not necessarily follow that a scientist who can validly describe a general psychological phenomenon also has the wherewithal to say whether an individual case is an instance of that general phenomenon. In many respects, the matter of translating scientific research findings into helpful information for fact finders in court should be a subject of first concern for psychological science. Yet this issue has been largely ignored by psychologists.

The task of applying general research findings to specific cases is, to be sure, a monumental intellectual challenge. Hard tasks are easy to ignore, but ignoring them does not make them go away. In a sense, then, this comment is a cry for attention, imploring psychological scientists to begin considering more carefully the inferential leap they make when they bring population-level research to individual-based trial processes.

REFERENCES

American Psychiatric Association (2000). *DSM-IV-TR: Diagnostic and statistical manual of mental disorders – Text revision*, 4th ed. Washington DC: American Psychiatric Association.
Balbach, E. D. & Glantz, S. A. (2007). Tobacco: Scientific status. In Faigman, D. L., Kaye, D. H., Saks, M. J., Sanders, J., & Cheng, E.K., (Eds.), *Modern*

scientific evidence: The law and science of expert testimony, Vol. 3 (pp. 245–296). Eagan, MN: Thompson/West Publishing Co.

Borgida, E., Hunt, C., & Kim, A. (2005). On the use of gender stereotyping research in sex discrimination litigation. *Journal of Law and Policy*, *8*(2), 613–628.

Daubert v. Merrell Dow Pharmaceuticals, Inc., 509 U.S. 579 (1993).

Faigman, D. L. (1999). *Legal alchemy: The use and abuse of science in the law.* San Francisco: W.H. Freeman & Co.

Faigman, D. L., Kaye, D. H., Saks, M. J., Sanders, J., & Cheng, E.K., (2007). *Modern scientific evidence: The law and science of expert testimony.* Eagan, MN: Thompson/West Publishing Co.

Federal Rules of Evidence (2006–2007), Washington, DC: U.S. Government Printing Office.

General Electric Co. v. Joiner, 522 U.S. 136 (1997).

Goldstein, B. D. & Carruth, R. (2007). Toxicology: Scientific status. In Faigman, D. L., Kaye, D. H., Saks, M. J., Sanders, J., & Cheng, E.K., (Eds.), *Modern scientific evidence: The law and science of expert testimony*, Vol. 3 (pp. 88–109). Eagan, MN: Thompson/West Publishing Co.

Heller v. Shaw Industries, 167 F.3d 146 (3rd Cir. 1999).

Moore v. Ashland Chemical, Inc., 151 F.3d 269 (5th Cir. 1998) (en banc).

Roggli, V. (2007). Asbestos: Scientific status. In Faigman, D. L., Kaye, D. H., Saks, M. J., Sanders, J., & Cheng, E.K., (Eds.), *Modern scientific evidence: The law and science of expert testimony*, Vol. 3 (pp. 326–359). Eagan, MN: Thompson/West Publishing Co.

Walker, L. & Monahan, J. (1987). Social frameworks: A new use of social science in law. *Virginia Law Review*, *73*, 559–598.

Wells, G. L. & Olson, E. (2003). Eyewitness identification. *Annual Review of Psychology*, *54*, 277–295.

16

Research on Eyewitness Testimony and False Confessions

Margaret A. Berger

Is the law making effective use of scientific knowledge about human behavior to achieve its paramount goals? Certainly, a central objective of the criminal justice system is to avoid convicting the innocent but convicting the guilty. We know that flawed eyewitness testimony and false confessions sometimes subvert this goal. Two chapters in this book survey and evaluate social science research that bears on these two sources of error. Wells and Hasel (chapter 8) seek to identify research findings about eyewitness identifications that can be utilized by the legal system; Kassin (chapter 10) presents the state of our present scientific knowledge about what causes false confessions. My comments are directed to analyzing how the criminal justice system can make use of this research. My conclusion will be that evidentiary barriers pose problems with exposing false confessions that do not exist with regard to mistaken eyewitness identifications. We need to consider new legal approaches if we are to avoid erroneous verdicts that result when innocent persons admit to perpetrating a crime they did not commit.

The DNA exonerations have validated psychological research that relied primarily on simulations. No longer can critics claim that in a nonexperimental condition, the subjects being tested would act differently. The 200 DNA exonerations to date confirm what psychologists have long hypothesized – that under particular circumstances eyewitnesses make inaccurate identifications, and persons who are not guilty tell the police that they are (see www.innocenceproject.org/causes). In roughly 75% of the DNA exonerations, mistaken eyewitness testimony contributed to the erroneous conviction, and false confessions played a role in more than 25% of the cases. At this point in time, the research in both domains – eyewitness testimony and false confessions – appears sufficiently robust to provide valid explanations for these errors. But the field of eyewitness research – which has a long history (Wells & Hasel) – is more advanced than the false confessions field in implementing solutions. Looking at the two fields in tandem suggests that insights gained in studies of eyewitness testimony could help translate the conclusions derived from false confession research into appropriate legal responses. After a brief survey of what we know about mistaken eyewitnesses and how to guard against their false testimony, I turn to false confessions.

Eyewitness Identifications

Wells and Hasel (chapter 8) note that psychologists have been interested in this subject since the beginning of the twentieth century, although systematic research into the operation of lineups did not commence until the 1970s. According to Wells and Hasel, these 30 years of intensive research resulted in at least four reliable conclusions about conditions that cause eyewitness failures: (1) cross-racial identifications; (2) the perpetrator's possession of a weapon; (3) nonsequential lineups; and (4) giving the eyewitness postidentification feedback confirming the witness' identification. This research has had an impact on the legal system. Two different types of reforms have been advocated to respond to these well-researched causes of error. One approach, which relies on estimator variable research, such as that which led to the first two findings above, aims to present jurors with information about the causes of eyewitness error so that they can better evaluate eyewitness testimony; the other, which builds on analyses of system variables, seeks to prevent the eyewitness from making a mistaken identification. A 2006 report by the Criminal Justice Section of the American Bar Association proposes best practices that incorporate both of these approaches.

Educating jurors about factors that have a negative impact on witness accuracy is usually attempted through expert testimony. As Wells and Hasel point out in chapter 8, we know that such testimony has been admitted in virtually every jurisdiction, but we do not know how often. We are aware from reported decisions that experts continue to be excluded on the ground that jurors do not need their assistance in dealing with matters of "common knowledge" or because courts find that the underlying research is not sufficiently reliable. The research summarized by Wells and Hasel suggests that both of these objections are flawed. Even if jurors understand that witnesses may make mistaken identifications, that does not mean they have specialized knowledge about the situational factors that lead to errors, and the reliability of studies on eyewitness testimony has been confirmed by the DNA exonerations.

Other objections to admitting expert testimony rest on sounder grounds. The proffered expertise must "fit" the facts of the case. For example, an expert may not testify about factors that impair accuracy – such as cross-racial identifications – if they were not present in the case. Of course, even if the court excludes the expert, a sophisticated defense attorney may make use of research findings in cross-examining the eyewitness. Thus, if the witness testifies about a knife displayed during the crime, counsel may suggest that the witness was looking at the weapon rather than the perpetrator even though expert testimony on weapon focus was disallowed. Some judges may also be willing to instruct the jury about case particular factors that may impair identifications.

But even if expert testimony is admitted, or some other means is found to inform the jury about factors that skew eyewitness accuracy, how does a juror go about integrating this information with the rest of the evidence? After all, not every cross-racial identification is inaccurate, and not every victim accosted at knife point makes a mistaken identification. Concern about the efficacy of expert testimony has led to a shift in emphasis from estimator variables to system variables research. Considerable progress has been made in trying to prevent errors when the eyewitness is making the identification, rather than seeking to expose mistakes at trial. Prophylactic guidelines based on social science research have been developed that require prosecutors and police to adhere to policies that reduce the risk of tainted identifications. A number of jurisdictions, such as New Jersey, North Carolina, and Wisconsin have already put into effect precautions such as requiring sequential lineups or photospreads, double-blind identification procedures, and instructions to eyewitnesses advising them that the perpetrator or his photo may not be present.

False Confessions

We have no idea how many false confessions are made by persons who are innocent. In most instances, the confession will be followed by a guilty plea and the case will vanish from sight. Potentially false confessions become visible only when: (a) the confession is so riddled with inconsistencies that charges are dropped, which may not happen in a high profile case such as that of the Central Park jogger, discussed below, when prosecutors are under enormous pressures to secure a conviction; (b) the maker recants and moves to suppress or tries to raise the issue at trial; (c) a claim is raised in postconviction proceedings; or (d) in very rare instances, the real perpetrator is identified (as in the Central Park jogger case) when the guilty party comes forward and irrefutable evidence, such as DNA, confirms that he is in fact guilty. Although it is impossible to calculate a prevalence rate for false confessions, researchers have long been convinced that many false confessions are made (Drizin & Leo, 2004). The statistics from the DNA exonerations show that in over 25% of the cases the inmate cleared by DNA testing had made an obviously false confession (Scheck, Neufeld, & Dwyer, 2000; www.innocenceproject.org/).

Kassin, in chapter 10, surveys the extensive body of psychological research that explains the phenomena of false confessions. He concludes that three well-established core principles account for why persons confess to crimes they did not commit:

1. Human behavior "is influenced more by perceptions of short-term than long-term consequences," and trained police investigators know how to strategically manipulate a suspect to confess through the use of many different techniques, such as isolation, sleep deprivation, threats, and promises;
2. Individuals in custody are vulnerable to persons in authority such as police interrogators, "who bring *power, proximity*, and *number* to bear on their exchange with suspects;" and
3. Persons who are "dispositionally or situationally" vulnerable can be manipulated through the misrepresentation of evidence into believing they are guilty of a crime they did not commit.

Difficult as it may be to overcome and avoid mistaken identifications, minimizing the impact and incidence of false confessions is an even greater challenge. In the first place, although jurors may not comprehend all the subtle factors that affect eyewitness testimony (Wells & Hasel), they clearly seem aware that mistaken identifications can occur. But the notion that innocent suspects will admit to committing crimes such as murder and rape is deeply counterintuitive. Kassin admits that "few, if any, phenomena of human behavior . . . are less intuitive than that of false confessions." Not only jurors, but all the other players in any given case – judges, prosecutors, the police or witnesses – are also prone to believe that confessions are truthful. Indeed, the law generally assumes that reasonable human beings do not falsely make statements inculpating themselves. For instance, out-of-court statements that would be barred by the hearsay rule may be admitted if the statement tends to subject its maker "to criminal liability." We assume that such statements are reliable because a reasonable person would not make such a statement unless it were true (Federal Rules of Evidence 804[b][3]).

Second, the research that demonstrates the unreliability of eyewitness testimony is much less attenuated – and therefore more compelling – than research designed to show that false confessions can be induced. It is relatively simple to stage a simulation, as the TV program Dateline once did in 1995 when a young man came into my Evidence classroom and grabbed my purse, and to calculate the error rate – usually quite significant – associated with identifying the perpetrator. Some of my smartest students made mistaken identifications when shown the equivalent of a photographic show-up. Furthermore, while one cannot do live simulations of bank robberies and murders, one can create supposed events on film. Regardless of the format and objective of the simulation, the central point – that eyewitnesses make mistakes – is always present and easy for jurors to grasp. Moreover, the DNA exonerations have effectively reinforced the concept of eyewitness error. Many of the exonerations have received extensive media coverage that often includes interviews with, or other references to, the victim who made the wrong identification. Some of these mistaken victims are regularly in the limelight speaking out against the death penalty because they fear that erroneous eyewitness testimony could put a defendant on death row, as has indeed occurred.

It is much more difficult, however, to construct an experiment showing that an innocent person will admit to a criminal act. Although the crashing computer study is marvelously ingenious (Kassin), it lacks the immediacy of the eyewitness studies. To reason from mistaken identifications in a staged purse snatching to the conclusion that identical errors may be made by witnesses to far more heinous crimes does not involve a gigantic leap; these demonstrations quite effectively convey the message that witnesses to an incident frequently err in recognizing the perpetrator. But to conclude that a subject's false admission that he touched an off-limits button on a computer means that some persons will falsely confess to committing a murder requires drawing a series of complex inferences based on studies of human behavior. These are inferences that some are unwilling to make. Despite DNA exonerations of inmates who made false confessions, some members of the law enforcement community seem to find it impossible to concede that suspects who confess are not always guilty (Hirsch, 2005). Their reluctance is understandable given the counterintuitive nature of the inference, and because, as Kassin's work demonstrates, they may have participated in the process that created the false confession. It is hard to accept responsibility for sending an innocent person to prison.

One approach to saving innocent persons who have made false confessions parallels the effort with regard to false identifications – to educate jurors through the testimony of experts about relevant research findings. Expert testimony would seem the perfect vehicle for helping jurors understand counterintuitive propositions about which they are unlikely to have any background knowledge. But while the proposed approach is identical to that often used in attacking eyewitness testimony, the evidentiary setting is very different. Although we do not know how often expert testimony on eyewitness testimony is admitted, or how effective it is, we do know that when an expert is allowed to testify, the testimony usually can be structured to intersect with the evidence in the case. The person who made the identification will virtually always be a witness at the trial. Because of the constraints of the hearsay rule (Federal Rule of Evidence 801[d][1][C]) and the Confrontation Clause (*Crawford v. Washington*, 2005), evidence of an out-of court identification is generally not admissible unless the witness testifies. Consequently, the jury will be aware of case specific facts that social science research has identified as important to making a false identification. If, for instance, there was a weapon, or a prior relationship between the witness and the defendant, the eyewitness will have testified to these details on direct or on cross. Undoubtedly, the circumstances under which the witness viewed the perpetrator, and the circumstances under which the identification was made will also have been explored.

There may, of course, be disputes about some of the facts surrounding identification testimony. Eyewitnesses may, for instance, disagree about how long the event lasted or whether there was a gun, but the jury will have heard evidence bearing on the dispute. In addition, the jurors will see the victim and the defendant so that they will know whether this is a cross-racial identification case, and they will be able to match the witness' out-of-court description of the perpetrator with their perception of the defendant's appearance. Accordingly, the expert's testimony about factors that skew accurate identifications can focus on the evidence that has been presented.

The situation in false confession cases is very different. Although as an abstract principle involuntary confessions are constitutionally deficient, courts almost never find that the prosecution's resort to interrogation tactics, such as those discussed by Kassin, requires the suppression of the confession (Magid, 2001). Once the confession is admitted into evidence, the defendant's attempt to present expert testimony may be rejected by the trial court, on the basis of reliability concerns, under either a *Frye* or a *Daubert* test.

Even were the judge willing to find that the proposed expert testimony passes a reliability threshold, other problems remain. Suppose the expert wishes to explain why innocent persons make false confessions based on the three explanatory principles mentioned above (and discussed in detail in chapter 10). Each of these principles turns on how the police interrogation was conducted. When there is no evidence about how the questioning proceeded, some courts will exclude expert testimony because it does not fit the facts of the case. They are unwilling to allow a lecture by the expert about false confessions and their cause when no evidence has been introduced that any of the relevant factors were present.

Getting the relevant case specific factors before the jury raises a host of problems that do not exist in eyewitness testimony cases. The persons who have personal knowledge about what happened during the interrogation are the defendant and his interrogators. The interrogators are likely to testify that they have been trained on the proper interrogation procedures, and that they have acted accordingly. Defendants, of course, have a constitutional right not to testify and often have good reasons to exercise this right. If they testify, they can be impeached by prior crimes and bad acts to undermine their credibility (Federal Rules of Evidence 609 and 608). Many suspects who make false confessions are probably especially prone to these modes of impeachment. Their past criminal involvements may be what caused the police to view them as suspects in the first place. If the jury hears about the defendant's past via the impeachment route, it may conclude that he must be guilty in this case as well, particularly if the prior crimes and the charged crime are similar, or if the prior crime is reprehensible. This propensity inference, which is corroborated by the confession, is prohibited by rules of evidence (Federal Rule of Evidence 404), and jurors will be instructed accordingly. Nevertheless, the fear that jurors will reason in this forbidden manner, or conclude that society benefits when someone like the defendant is imprisoned even if innocent this time, keeps many defendants off the stand.

Difficulties remain even if the defendant has led an unblemished life. The same weak personality or mental deficiencies that enabled the interrogator to overpower him into making a confession may also serve him badly if he testifies and then has to undergo cross-examination about committing the crime. Sometimes, the defense seeks to have an expert testify about the defendant's mental make-up to prove that his will could have been overcome. This approach may run foul of Federal Rule of Evidence 704(b), which prohibits expert opinion about the defendant having "the mental state or condition constituting an element" of a defense.

If the defendant testifies, he will seek to explain to the jury what his questioners did that caused him to make a false confession, such as the length of the interrogation, isolation, sleep deprivation, and what the interrogators said in the way of explicit or implicit promises and threats or lies about the existence of inculpating evidence. If the interrogators testify and disagree about what occurred, the result will be a swearing contest in which defendant will have an uphill battle against the forces of good.

These problems with expert testimony have led to demands for prophylactic rules. The demand most often made is for the video-taping of all in-custody police interrogations. Videotaping, it is believed, not only reduces the types of police behavior that produce false confessions, but also enables a defendant to substantiate what occurred, making it more likely that a court would suppress a con-fession or allow an expert to testify at trial if the confession is admitted. The American Bar Association's House of Delegates adopted Resolution 8A at its 2004 midyear meeting which resolved that all law enforcement agencies should videotape the entirety of custodial interrogations of crime suspects (ABA, Criminal Justice Section, 2006). A number of jurisdictions, either by judicial opinions or legislation, have mandated the recording of in-custody police questioning.

Will videotaping suffice to alleviate the problem of false confessions? It will certainly help. Even as I was writing this comment the press reported the DNA exoneration of an inmate who had served 10 years for a murder he did not commit but to which he had confessed. He was convicted on the basis of admitting details about the crime that only the killer would have known. The freed inmate alleged that he was fed these critical details while being questioned by the homicide detective in charge of the investigation (Dwyer, 2006). A tape would have revealed what the police were doing.

But will videotaping reveal all instances of false confessions? Pro-bably not. There will still be many who will plead guilty after a false confession. Overworked, underpaid defense counsel cannot possibly investigate these cases. Furthermore, Kassin's work suggests that even if improper police techniques could be eradicated or reduced by taping confessions, there will still be false confessions. Some in custody will wish to please their questioners, others will want the questioning to cease, while still others may believe that cooperation will lead to lesser punishment. Juveniles and the mentally infirm may be particularly susceptible.

Another approach that could be used in tandem with videotaping would be to develop protocols of behavior for police interrogators. Law enforcement agencies could implement the protocols by training their personnel about prohibited conduct, and insisting on disciplinary proceedings for those who refuse to conform. Most effective of all would be for the Supreme Court (or state courts on the basis of their own constitutions) to conclude that certain enumerated conduct by a police interrogator would lead to automatic exclusion of a confession just as occurs when a suspect is not given the requisite *Miranda* warnings. But it must be conceded that the likelihood of a constitutional solution is remote at this time.

Of course, any proposal suggesting that any aspect of law enforcement conduct is out of bounds is extremely controversial. Some believe that any limitations on interrogation techniques are inappropriate because no proof exists that false confessions outnumber genuine confessions, and that the minimal risk of convicting the innocent is greatly outbalanced by the benefits that accrue (Magid, 2001). They praise confessions for clearing criminal dockets efficiently and economically, while quieting the anxieties of victims and society over unresolved crimes. They view the occasional wrong conviction as worth the price.

But even if we grant that some advantages stem from encouraging confessions, there are certain actions by law enforcement personnel that the system should not tolerate. Any code of law enforcement behavior should ban two kinds of statements by police interrogators. First, explicit threats of violence will probably, even today, render a confession involuntary. In addition, threats of violence to the suspect or his family, even if implicit, should be prohibited as behavior that is antithetical to what law enforcement is supposed to prevent. Finding that the ends justify the means in the face of such conduct undermines the moral objectives of the criminal justice system. Second, falsely telling the suspect that the police have found generally irrefutable forensic evidence, such as the suspect's DNA or fingerprints, should not be allowed. In this world of *CSI*, a falsehood like this may be powerful enough to convince innocent suspects that they must have committed the crime of which they are accused; such toying with people's minds smacks of totalitarian regimes and should not be allowed in a democratic society. Even if the suspect realizes that he is innocent, a lie about this kind of forensic evidence may convince him that he is being framed and has no chance of success at trial so that he may as well cooperate in the hope of averting a sentence of death or life imprisonment. This is a technique that impugns the integrity of police investigations.

A recent case, *United States v. Belyea* (2005), illustrates actions by law enforcement personnel that should be put on a list of prohibited conduct. Belyea was charged with possession of a stolen firearm and possession of a firearm by an unlawful user of a controlled substance. He was convicted of the latter charge only. Belyea had confessed to possessing the guns – the only direct evidence of possession. At trial he renounced his confession and sought to introduce expert testimony about false confessions. The trial court excluded his expert, essentially on the basis that "jurors know people lie." Belyea, a narcotics addict who suffered from clinical depression and behavioral problems, had been told two lies by a Special Agent from the Bureau of Alcohol, Tobacco, and Firearms: (1) that one of the stolen guns had been used in a murder and bore only one fingerprint, Belyea's; and (2) that he could be held as a material witness in a DC jail where "a skinny, white boy like [you] wouldn't last very long" (p. 527). The appellate court, in an unpublished opinion – that consequently may not be cited as binding precedent – found on appeal that the district court's refusal to allow expert testimony on the basis of a broad generalization did not amount to the required "nuanced, case-by-case analysis of whether the proposed expert testimony will assist the trier of fact" (p. 529). It noted that without the expert testimony, Belyea "could not explain that false confessions, while counter-intuitive, do in fact occur and are more likely to occur in certain circumstances, perhaps in the very circumstances of his case" (p. 529). The trial court was told to reconsider whether the expert testimony should have been admitted, and to grant a new trial if the expert was improperly excluded.

The trial court's statement that "jurors know people lie" is probably true but of little relevance or help when someone claims that his previous confession was false. Without exposure to research such as Kassin's, the jurors' "knowledge" will likely lead them to conclude that the confessor is lying *now* when he repudiates his confession. Confessions have an enormous impact. In the Central Park jogger case, the jurors brushed aside numerous significant inconsistencies in the five teenage defendants' descriptions of their alleged attack on the jogger, who barely survived after suffering serious head injuries. The incident and the subsequent trial attracted a frenzy of media attention. Thirteen years after the defendants were convicted, an imprisoned serial rapist confessed that he alone was responsible for the Central Park rape. His DNA matched the crime scene sample, he knew details about the crime that had never been publically released, and the particulars of the jogger attack, such as the strange manner in which the victim was tied up, were strikingly similar to other rapes he had committed, all of which he perpetrated by himself. Nevertheless, even after the teenagers' convictions were vacated at the request of the district attorney, a panel convened by the police commissioner concluded that the convictions were proper and that the five confessing defendants had participated in the crime (Davies, 2006).

Conclusion

In the case of eyewitness testimony we have seen progress in dealing with the circumstances that lead to mistaken identifications. We can put ourselves in the shoes of someone who is a witness to a crime. We know that people make mistakes of this kind and that we need to guard against them. There is much less empathy for someone accused of a crime such as rape or murder. We want to believe that the police have found the culprit, and in high profile cases the press often reinforces our wish by giving extensive reports on what led to the arrest. To contemplate that an arrestee who then confesses may nevertheless be innocent is obviously beyond some people's understanding, perhaps because most of us lack common knowledge about how we would react to police pressures if we were in custody. Kassin's work is so valuable because it furnishes an explanatory theory for otherwise inexplicable behavior. If we are to make progress in identifying false confessions and rectifying their consequences we need to increase public awareness about this phenomenon. Now that we know through the DNA exonerations that false confessions are real, we need to consider reforms that would promote the objectives of the criminal justice system to protect the innocent while convicting the guilty.

REFERENCES

American Bar Association, Criminal Justice Section (2006). *Achieving justice: Freeing innocent, convicting the guilty.* Washington, DC: American Bar Association.
Crawford v. Washington, 541 U.S. 36 (2005).
Daubert v. Merrell Dow Pharmaceuticals, Inc., 509 U.S. 579 (1993).

Davies, S.L. (2006). The reality of false confessions – lessons of the Central Park jogger case. *New York University Review of Law and Social Change*, *30*, 209–253.

Drizin, S. A. & Leo, R. A. (2004). The problem of false confessions in the post-DNA world. *North Carolina Law Review*, *82*, 891–1007.

Dwyer, J. (2006, May 16). Inmate to be freed as DNA tests upend murder confession. *New York Times*, B1.

Federal Rules of Evidence (2006–2007). Washington, DC: U.S. Government Printing Office.

Frye v. United States, 293 F. 1013 (D.C. Cir. 1923).

Hirsch, A. (2005). The tragedy of false confessions (and a common sense proposal). Book review of M. Edds, *An expendable man. North Dakota Law Review*, *81*, 343–350.

www.innocenceproject.org/causes (Innocence Project).

Magid, L. (2001). Deceptive police interrogation practices: How far is too far? *Michigan Law Review*, *99*, 1168–1210.

Scheck, B., Neufeld, P. & Dwyer, J. (2000). *Actual Innocence: five days to execution and other dispatches from the wrongly convicted*. New York: Doubleday.

United States v. Belyea, 159 Fed. Appx. 525 (4th Cir. 2005).

17

Commentary on Research Relevant to Sex Discrimination and Sexual Harassment

Barbara A. Gutek

Prior to The Civil Rights Act of 1991, charging parties were entitled only to remedies that would put them in the position they would have been in had they not been a victim of discrimination. But after The Civil Rights Act of 1991, they could be compensated for their pain and suffering and they could receive punitive damages whereby the employer is punished monetarily for discriminating. Thus, winning litigants could potentially walk away with a lot more money. The 1991 Act therefore increased the attractiveness of lawsuits for both employees who felt aggrieved and for law firms who would represent those employees. Not too surprisingly, this statute led to a substantial increase in litigation (Weisenfeld, 2003) and an increase in monetary benefits awarded under Title VII. Monetary awards amounted to $101.3 million in 2005 (Equal Employment Opportunity Commission [EEOC], 2006).

Although employing expert witnesses in employment litigation occurred before the Civil Rights Act of 1991, it is likely that the possibility of obtaining punitive damages has sufficiently increased the stakes as to make it attractive to plaintiffs and their attorneys to obtain expert witnesses where such expertise would inform the jury in a manner that helps the plaintiff. Once the plaintiffs hire an expert, the defense is likely to do so, too. Unless the law changes, I see no reason why the use of expert witnesses should decrease in the future. In fact, as the chapters in this volume show, attorneys have discovered many areas of psychological expertise that are relevant to specific types of litigation, so, more likely the use of experts will increase.

Experts are probably particularly likely to be sought for class actions where the stakes are high because the plaintiffs represent a whole class of people rather than merely themselves. As Landy (2005) noted: "If a lawyer represents a single individual in a discrimination case, a win and an award of $400,000 may result in a fee of $100,000 to the lawyer. If, instead, a class is certified and that class includes 500 plaintiffs, the award may be in the multimillion-dollar range and the fee for the lawyer may be in the millions of dollars" (p. 7). Not surprisingly, in my experience lawyers, not plaintiffs or defendants, are most likely to contact experts. It is in their self-interest to develop contacts with researchers whose expertise is likely to be helpful to them and their clients.

In the litigious U.S., it is perhaps not surprising that attorneys, not government entities, have realized the usefulness of social science research. I have always thought it was unfortunate that in the U.S., government has tapped only economists among social scientists to help set policy, unlike in the Nordic countries in Europe where social science is regularly used in developing policy. Reliable and valid social science research, leading to clear and consistent policies and recommendations appropriately applied in the courtroom, may, however, lead various government agencies to call on social scientists for information that can guide policy.

The Experience of Being an Expert Witness

Expert witnesses provide specialized information that would not normally be known to jurors.[1] Accustomed to generalizing their research findings to society at large, researchers working as expert witnesses are asked whether a set of research findings applies to a specific set of facts at hand that unfold in a specific order. In the areas in which I have worked, some courts disparage laboratory research even though it typically allows us to draw conclusions about causality that are rarely possible with surveys. Furthermore, laboratory research often provides results that are consistent with findings from field studies involving adult populations (Locke, 1986).[2]

---

[1]   According to the Federal Rules of Evidence, Rule 702: "If scientific, technical, or other specialized knowledge will assist the trier of fact to understand the evidence or to determine a fact in issue, a witness qualified as an expert by knowledge, skill, experience, training, or education, may testify . . ."

[2]   Borgida, Hunt, & Kim (2005) described and discussed consistent research findings from the laboratory and field with respect to the effects of self-promoting experienced by women.

In theory, expert witnesses are neutral parties, yet when researchers take on the role of expert witness, they enter an adversarial world where the players are interested in research if it supports their side. It is not surprising that many experts work predominantly for either plaintiffs or defendants, but rarely both, because their research may support one side more than the other.[3]

There are many areas of expertise that may be useful in litigation, but I will limit my comments to two related areas where I have worked as an expert on employment litigation: sex discrimination and sexual harassment. In doing so, I want to differentiate class actions from individual actions because they present slightly different challenges for the expert.

The Failure to Complain: An Example of Using Social Science Research in Individual Actions

Most sex discrimination and sexual harassment lawsuits involve an individual plaintiff who sues her or his employer. One area where individual plaintiffs in sexual harassment cases commonly retain experts is to testify about the plaintiff's failure to formally complain about sexual harassment. As law professor Theresa Beiner (2005, chapter 5) pointed out, the court often expects employees to complain. Because filing a complaint demonstrates that the behavior was unwelcome, the failure to file a complaint when the respondent considered the behavior severe enough to file a lawsuit makes the plaintiff less credible. Plaintiffs may lose and courts may sometimes dismiss cases on summary judgment because the plaintiff did not complain or did not complain soon enough. (See Wiener and Hurt, 1999, for a discussion of this issue.) A study of 81 cases filed in Illinois over a two-year period found that notifying management before filing a formal complaint increased the probability of a favorable outcome for the plaintiff alleging sexual harassment (Terpstra & Baker, 1992).

It is not only the law that expects a complaint, but people more generally expect a formal or informal complaint from someone who has been sexually harassed. But many people never complain at all. A person who never complains or does not complain until the boss fires

---

[3] I have worked on both sides in lawsuits involving sexual harassment or sex discrimination, but typically the issues differed (see Gutek & Stockdale, 2005; Gutek, 2007).

her or she quits her job leaves her behavior open to interpretation. Defense attorneys present jurors with what seems to be a logical argument: If the harassment was so bad, why would she not complain about it right away? Did she complain after she left the company because she is angry about her boss firing her or because she was harassed? Fitzgerald and Collingsworth explore the failure to complain in chapter 6. The social science research that reveals this failure to complain is an example of the way social science research provides valid information that is contrary to popular belief.

Why do people not complain? Psychological science provides the answers. For example, Kidder, LaFleur, and Wells (1995) showed that people who at some later period in time label their experience sexual harassment may not have done so at the time of the actual experience. How could someone complain about sexual harassment right after the behavior happened if they have not yet labeled it as such? Experimental research also demonstrates that people who think they would complain often do not. LaFrance and Woodzicka (2001) found that, when confronted with offensive behavior, people's response to that behavior was not consistent with what they said they would do prior to having experienced it. More specifically, they were not as assertive as they claimed they would be. Consistent with their findings, many surveys of social sexual behavior have shown that people do not always complain for very good reasons. This "underreporting" is robust, and is widely found; the results hold up across samples and the idiosyncrasies of individual studies (see, for example, Fitzgerald, Swan, & Fischer, 1995; Gutek & Koss, 1993; Livingston, 1982; Stockdale, 1998). Although virtually all of the surveys that I am aware of do not use a legal definition and thus may overestimate the extent to which victims of illegal harassment do not complain, the small percentages who do complain, the reasons they give, the negative consequences reported by many people who did complain, and consistent experimental results (LaFrance & Woodzicka, 2001) all provide convincing evidence that many people who are illegally harassed do not complain.[4]

Despite the research evidence, the U.S. Supreme Court's decisions in *Faragher v. City of Boca Raton* (1998) and *Burlington Industries v. Ellerth* (1998) place a significant burden on plaintiffs to come forward and make a formal report about harassment as soon as possible after it occurred. As Beiner (2005) wrote: "This might make sense in terms

---

[4]   There is a literature on complaining (especially in studies of consumer satisfaction) that would situate research on complaining about sexual harassment in a broader context (see Kowalski, 1996, for a review).

of giving the employer the opportunity to nip the harassment in the bud, but it does not reflect the manner in which many targets respond to sexual harassment" (p. 145).

Although complaining is what victims of harassment are expected to do and it was employers who apparently pressed for some mechanism that they could rely upon to exonerate themselves if an employee was harassed, it is not obvious to me that organizations really want their employees to complain, especially if the behavior is not likely to be illegal. In an organization aware of the current state of the law, a complaint of sexual harassment is likely to trigger an investigation, which uses time and personnel. In addition, if the matter eventually finds its way to court, the company's decision will be scrutinized and may be found inadequate or inappropriate. In short, although companies encourage people to complain, the very presence of written complaints constitutes evidence that can be used by both sides in litigation.

In addition, psychological science shows that the phenomenon of complaining is complex, not simple (Kowalski, 1996). An investigation may trigger expectations in the complainant that may not be realized and it can be traumatic for the complainant, as Fitzgerald and Collinsworth note in chapter 6. An employee who anticipates that complaining will solve her or his problem may be in for a rude awakening (see U.S. Merit Systems Protection Board, 1995). If a person complains and the behavior is judged to be not harassing, the complainant may be blamed and disparaged as a whiner, as is true of complainers in other situations (Kowalski, 1996). Similarly, if the investigator is simply unable to make a determination that harassment occurred, the complainant may be embarrassed and/or angry and she or he may also be criticized for wasting the organization's resources required of an investigation.

Psychological research shows the social costs that are associated with blaming negative outcomes on discrimination. More specifically, African American respondents who attributed a failing test grade to discrimination were perceived as complainers and were less favorably evaluated than African Americans who attributed their failure to the quality of their test answers (Kaiser & Miller, 2001). This was true regardless of the actual likelihood that discrimination occurred. Sensing that they will be disliked or their careers derailed for even mentioning that they believe they are victims of discrimination, real victims may not file a complaint.

Perhaps because the research on complaining is so compelling, defense experts may argue that in order to be useful in court, research on complaining (or research on some other area like stereotyping or a hostile work environment) would have to be done in the defendant organization because research done elsewhere is not sufficiently relevant. Placing such a restriction on research, that it must be done in the defendant organization, certainly makes it much harder to use data in court and it places a tremendous financial burden on the plaintiff (or in some cases, the defendant). Furthermore, since the research already shows that what people say they would do or think they would do if they were harassed (that is, to complain) is inconsistent with what most real victims of harassment actually do (not complain), it makes little sense for defendants to argue that research on complaining should be done in the defendant organization − and such research would simply expose the organization to learning about the occurrence of potentially illegal behavior on the premises. Furthermore, one can argue that doing research in an organization under such circumstances may yield biased responses, based on the respondents' views about the lawsuit (see also Gutek & Stockdale, 2005, for a discussion of this issue). In short, although defendants may object to research *unless* it is done in their organization, they may also object to doing any research in their organization.

In addition, since the research conducted for a specific legal proceeding is not peer-reviewed, it might be challenged on *Daubert* principles. More generally, imposing such a restriction would differentiate social science research from other areas of expertise. For example, in the case of medical claims, the expert does not have to perform surgery on the plaintiff in order to opine about the quality of care that person received or the risk associated with the surgical procedure. It simply makes no sense to assert that only research conducted in the defendant organization should be admissible in discrimination and harassment lawsuits.

Finally, an expert can discuss this research on the failure to complain in the face of illegal treatment without having to read reams of deposition testimony and other documents relevant to the case at hand. One can simply review the relevant research for the jury without drawing any conclusions about the specific case. Fitzgerald and Collinsworth (chapter 6) make the same point with respect to providing testimony on organizational climate. One can discuss the effects of a harassing climate on women's experiences without offering any opinions about the climate of the specific organization. The jury then uses the expert testimony in coming to their conclusions.

Evaluating Organizations' Practices and Measuring Sexual Harassment in Class Actions

Because class actions may involve hundreds or even thousands of employees and typically cover a number of years, as many as 10 or more in my experience (e.g., *EEOC v. The Dial Corporation*, 2002), the stakes are much higher in a class action case than in an individual case, as I noted above. They also present different challenges to the expert. In the case of charges of discrimination, the issue is not so much what happened to any individual employee, but was there a "pattern and practice" that discriminated against a particular protected group? Class actions can be more efficient than lots of individual cases if the alleged illegal behavior is endemic to the organization or built into its formal or informal policies and practices.

Experts can examine the organization's practices because research has revealed some of the organizational practices that correlate with potentially harassing social-sexual behavior, as Fitzgerald and Collinsworth discuss in chapter 6. Focusing on the organization's practices can also be useful in actions involving charges of sex discrimination in hiring, performance appraisal, and promotion. In chapter 7 Heilman and Haynes discuss research showing the practices that promote subjectivity as well as how and when subjectivity leads to biased judgments. They focus on the crucial difference between evaluations based on tangible outcomes versus evaluations based on expectations and describe the processes by which evaluations based on expectations can easily be tainted by stereotypes. Policies and practices that rely heavily on subjectivity foster biased evaluations and promotions that disadvantage women and minorities. Whole classes of workers are disadvantaged by such policies and practices.

In charges of discrimination, one can examine performance records and records of promotions to find out if there is a pattern or practice of illegal discrimination. In sexual harassment cases, the record may not be so clear. One may want to know whether the members of the class who have made charges of sexual harassment represent the tip of the iceberg or whether they are anomalies. Experts may find themselves with boxes and boxes of deposition testimony to go over in order to determine the magnitude and scope of potentially illegal behavior. In short, whereas it is possible to examine details about a single person, in a class action case there are hundreds or thousands of different employees who have worked for the company during some or all of the years that are encompassed by the class action.

Under those circumstances, exactly what is it that the expert needs to know in order to develop an opinion? Eagly and Koenig (chapter 4, p. 77) note that "to judge whether discrimination has occurred for a particular person in a particular situation, a wealth of specific facts must be known, to rule out that differential treatment was based on legitimate factors such as poor job performance." How much more needs to be done to develop valid opinions in class actions? One may find dozens of alleged examples but they may span hundreds of people and several years or even a decade or more of alleged discriminatory behavior.

In the case of sexual harassment, the law requires that the behavior be "severe" or "pervasive." One way to get at severity and pervasiveness is to survey the relevant employees. While there are pros and cons of doing research on a company that is being sued, it is a possibility (see Gutek and Stockdale, 2005, for a discussion of this point). Lots of issues need to be addressed in doing such a survey, however, such as making sure it does not come from either party or a law firm, not suggesting respondents will receive money if they have been treated illegally, and the like. In order to draw conclusions about whether or not the alleged behavior is pervasive, one needs some reliable and valid way of determining if the level of the behavior found in the survey rises to the level of illegal behavior, such as by establishing base rates for the behavior or being able to apply the law specifically to the survey results.

Various versions of the Sexual Experiences Questionnaire (SEQ) were used in several legal actions, including a case against the Dial Corporation on which I was hired by the defense. Unfortunately, the published research on the SEQ available at that time did not contain a copy of any version of the instrument.[5] Furthermore, if the published research presented any mean scores, they typically were not discussed.[6] In contrast, in the *Dial* case, the SEQ was being used to determine that a "high level of hostile and degrading sexualized

---

[5]   I attribute the failure to publish instruments in part to many of our journals which are content with "sample items" or any reference to a prior publication whether or not the instrument was actually contained in that prior publication.

[6]   In doing an earlier review of the research on sexual harassment with Robert Done (Gutek & Done, 2001), I could not determine how much sexual harassment was found in the studies using the various versions of the SEQ. In the published research, there was virtually no discussion of whether any particular sample had a "high" or "low" level of sexual harassment as measured by the SEQ.

behavior" was directed towards women. I could see no justification for saying that any level was high or low based on the published research on the SEQ in which various SEQ versions were used.[7] Evidence gained from the SEQ was dismissed in the federal trial case against Dial Corporation (*EEOC v. The Dial Corporation*, 2002; see also Gutek, Murphy, & Douma, 2004, which also discusses other problems with the SEQ.)

If we expect our instruments to be used in court, social scientists need to pay careful attention to the validity of the instrument for use in a legal setting, as well as more generally understanding what qualifies as admissible testimony (Wingate & Thornton, 2004). Sexual harassment is particularly tricky because it is a legal concept but also has a broader lay usage and if one is intending to offer opinions about the amount of sexual harassment in an organization, one needs to know exactly whether one or the other, both, or neither, is being measured. In sexual harassment research, that means also taking into account the important clause, "severe or pervasive enough to alter the conditions of employment and create an objectively hostile or intimidating work environment."[8]

Using Social Science Research to Reduce the Probability of Illegal Sex Discrimination

Besides using social psychological research directly in the courtroom, it can be used to change organizational practices that contribute to potentially illegal behavior. Thus, organizations that have been found guilty of illegal discrimination or sexual harassment can fix their problems by working with social and organizational psychologists.

Stereotyping provides a good example. If people think of stereotyping as something bad that only other people do, they are unlikely to consider the possibility that they themselves engage in stereotyping. And yet, as it has been described in this volume as well as elsewhere, stereotyping is something that we all do to some extent and it can have significant consequences. In chapter 2 Crosby and Dovidio point out that stereotyping is a mechanism by which "the slow accumulation of disadvantage by some . . . and the complementary accumulation of

---

[7]   I find that to still be the case, despite the fact that many additional studies have been published in recent years in "A" journals like the *Journal of Applied Psychology*.

[8]   Of course, there are many, many psychological measures that are reliable and valid and do not measure legal constructs.

advantage by others" (p. 23) happens. The goal is to mitigate the consequences of stereotyping. Managers and attorneys who typically defend organizations may complain that because stereotyping is common, it is not controllable. But perhaps if managers think of stereotyping a bit like they think of self-interest (which is also common), they will both appreciate the importance of stereotyping and realize ways to reduce its harmful effects.

Economists believe that people generally act in their self-interest, so no well-run organization would try to pit employees' self-interest against the interests of the company. Instead through its policies and procedures, organizations try to align the company's interests with the self-interest of its managers and other employees.[9] Similarly, organizations can set up policies and practices that mitigate the harmful effects of stereotyping because stereotyping is something that happens with great frequency. Maybe we can look forward to an enlightened future in which no well-run organization would fail to set up mechanisms to mitigate the harmful effects of stereotyping in the same way that successful organizations today create mechanisms to align the self-interest of employees with those of the company as a whole. Until such time, one such mechanism for reducing stereotypes already exists: affirmative action.

As Crosby and Dovidio point out in chapter 2, affirmative action is one mechanism for countering the slow accumulation of advantage and disadvantage (see also Konrad & Linnehan, 1999). Affirmative action does not simply make up for past offenses, it is also a mechanism that counters the negative effects of stereotypes. A woman may be hurt by stereotypes, but affirmative action provides a counterforce to the negative effect of both negative stereotypes and subjective positive female stereotypes (as reviewed by Rudman, Glick, and Phelan in chapter 5), as well as stereotypes of subgroups such as women who promote themselves (Borgida et al., 2005). In the long run, effectively implemented affirmative action may be a cheaper and fairer way of providing equal opportunity than for individuals or classes of individuals to sue individual companies, with the attending psychological and monetary costs of litigation.

Training employees about the pervasive effects of stereotyping is a logical step for employers. Employers embraced training about sexual

---

[9] Basing pay on performance is an example of aligning the organization's interests with employees' self-interests. Examples of tying pay to performance include basing executive pay on the company's stock price, basing the sales staff's pay on volume of sales, or basing faculty raises on number and impact of publications.

harassment. Why not train employees to recognize the effects of stereotypes? I would like to see employers hire social psychologists and others with appropriate expertise to teach them how potentially potent and destructive stereotyping can be as well as how to reduce the amount of stereotyping and spillover in their workplace. Employers could hire social scientists to help create a work environment that decreases the probability that sexual harassment will occur.

Adopting HR mechanisms that minimize stereotyping is another step that employers can adopt. If employees know the difference between evaluations based on tangible outcomes versus evaluations based on expectations, as Heilman and Haynes note in chapter 7, then not only would they be less likely to stereotype, they would also do better performance appraisals and other evaluations of employees.

For years, social science researchers have been making suggestions for reducing prejudice, harmful discrimination, and harassment (e.g., Pettigrew & Martin, 1987) but little of it seems to have worked its way into practice. In general, social scientists have had very little say in how organizations can or should change to reduce the probability of illegal human behavior. Employers are not accustomed to working with social psychologists and may be unaware of what they have to offer or even what it is that social psychologists do. In contrast to their lack of experience with social psychologists, managers have significant contacts with lawyers through their own legal staff and/or the law firm or firms with whom they regularly work on a variety of matters including issues involving employees. Lawyers are also attractive to employers because lawyers can presumably tell them how to avoid lawsuits as well as handle the lawsuits that do occur. So organizations mostly seek advice from lawyers, rather than other experts. These same lawyers may be leery of involving social psychologists – or any non-lawyers – in developing practices or developing policies that may be relevant in employment lawsuits for fear that a nonlawyer might recommend some action that increases the organization's exposure to legal action.[10]

That exclusive reliance on attorneys needs to change. One sign that we may be moving in the right direction is a recent book by a law professor, Theresa Beiner. Beiner's (2005) book on sexual harassment reviewed significant areas of the law and the social science research findings that are relevant to it, including the "unwelcomeness" requirement and the effect of the reasonable woman standard. She argued

---

[10]   I have been asked by a university to develop a sexual harassment policy only to have the university attorneys change it.

forcefully that the law can learn about sexual harassment from social science research and that in order to be effective at eliminating sexual harassment, the law should be reformulated to conform to what social scientists have learned about sexual harassment. To that sentiment, I can only add: the sooner, the better.

REFERENCES

Beiner, T. (2005). *Gender myths v. working realities: Using social science to reformulate sexual harassment law.* New York: New York University Press.

Borgida, E., Hunt, C., & Kim, A. (2005) On the use of gender stereotyping research in sex discrimination litigation. *Journal of Law and Policy, 13*(2), 613–618.

Burlington Industries, Inc., v. Ellerth, 524 U.S. 742 (1998).

Equal Employment Opportunity Commission (2006). www.eeoc.gov/stats/litigation.html

EEOC v. The Dial Corporation, WL 31061088, N. D. Ill., (2002, September 17).

Faragher v. City of Boca Raton, 524 U.S. 775 (1998).

Fitzgerald, L., Swan, S., & Fischer, K. (1995). Why didn't she report him? The psychological and legal implications of women's responses to sexual harassment. *Journal of Social Issues, 51*(1), 117–138.

Gutek, B. A. (2007). My experience as an expert witness in sex discrimination and sexual harassment litigation. In Crosby, F., Stockdale, M. S., & Ropp, S. A. (Eds.), *Sex discrimination in the workplace.* Boston, MA: Blackwell Publishing.

Gutek, B. A. & Done. R. (2001). Sexual harassment. In R. K. Unger (Ed.), *Handbook of the psychology of women and gender* (pp. 367–387). New York: Wiley.

Gutek, B. A. & Koss, M. P. (1993). Changed women and changed organizations: Consequences of and coping with sexual harassment. *Journal of Vocational Behavior, 42,* 28–48.

Gutek, B. A., Murphy, R. O., & Douma, B. (2004). A review and critique of the Sexual Experiences Questionnaire (SEQ), *Law and Human Behavior, 28*(4), 457–482.

Gutek, B. A., & Stockdale, M. S. (2005). Sex discrimination in employment. In F. Landy (Ed.), *Employment discrimination litigation: Behavioral, quantitative, and legal perspectives* (pp. 229–255). San Francisco, CA: Jossey-Bass.

Kaiser, C. R. & Miller, C. T. (2001). Stop complaining! The social costs of making attributions to discrimination. *Personality and Social Psychology Bulletin, 21*(2), 254–263.

Kidder, L. H., Lafleur, R. A., & Wells, C. V. (1995). Recalling harassment: Reconstructing experience. *Journal of Social Issues, 51*(1), 53–68.

Konrad, A. M., & Linnehan, F. (1999). Affirmative action: History, effects and attitudes. In G. N. Powell (Ed.), *Handbook of gender and work* (pp. 429–452). Newbury Park, CA: Sage Publications, Inc.

Kowalski, R. M. (1996). Complaints and complaining: Functions, antecedents, and consequences. *Psychological Bulletin, 119*, 179–196.

LaFrance, M., & Woodzicka, J. (2001). Real versus imagined reactions to sexual harassment. *Journal of Social Issues, 57*(1), 15–30.

Landy, F. (2005). Phases of employment litigation. In F. Landy (Ed.), *Employment discrimination litigation: Behavioral, quantitative, and legal perspectives* (pp. 3–19). San Francisco, CA: Jossey-Bass.

Livingston, J. A. (1982). Responses to sexual harassment on the job: Legal, organizational, and individual actions. *Journal of Social Issues, 38*(4), 5–22.

Locke, E. A. (Ed.) (1986). *Generalizing from laboratory to field settings.* Lexington, MA: Lexington Books.

Pettigrew, T., & Martin, J. (1987). Shaping the organizational context for black American inclusion. *Journal of Social Issues, 43*(1), 41–78.

Stockdale, M. S. (1998). The direct and moderating influences of sexual harassment pervasiveness, coping strategies, and gender on work-related outcomes. *Psychology of Women Quarterly, 22*, 521–535.

Terpstra, D. E., & Baker, D. D. (1992). Outcomes of federal court decisions on sexual harassment. *Academy of Management Journal, 35*, 181–190.

U.S. Merit Systems Protection Board (1995). Sexual harassment of federal workers: An Update. Washington, DC: U.S. Government Printing Office.

Weisenfeld, D. B. (2003). The year employment law dominated the docket: How the Supreme Court's 2001–2002 term affects employees. *Employee Rights Quarterly, 3*, 1–7.

Wiener, R. L., & Hurt, L. E. (1999). An interdisciplinary approach to understanding social sexual conduct at work. In R. Wiener & B. Gutek (Eds.), *Advances in sexual harassment research, theory and policy.* Special edition of *Psychology, Public Policy, and Law, 5*, 556–595.

Wingate, P. H., & Thornton, G. C. I. (2004). Industrial/organizational psychology and the federal judiciary: Expert witness testimony and the *Daubert* standards. *Law and Human Behavior, 28*(1), 97–114.

18

The Tenuous Bridge Between Research and Reality: The Importance of Research Design in Inferences Regarding Work Behavior

Frank J. Landy

As a commentator, I have been asked to consider the extent to which various authors of an interrelated set of chapters in this volume have succeeded in identifying: (a) research findings and implications on which most reasonable scholars could agree; and (b) how these research findings might inform a fact finder struggling with the task of understanding the behavior of various actors in the complex legal arena. So in my commentary, I will address these two points for the subset of the chapters that touch on my areas of expertise and knowledge.

Although there are many fascinating chapters in this book, there is only a subset that touch on my areas of expertise. These include chapters 7 (Heilman & Haynes), 4 (Eagly & Koenig), and 5 (Rudman, Glick, & Phelan). These chapters have several themes that are in common. They all deal with issues of gender and work and all address the potential for unfairness in various decisions made at the workplace. In addition, they all deal with the issue of gender stereotypes and the potential effects of these stereotypes on personnel decisions. Finally, they all address factors that have been proposed to mitigate the effects of gender stereotypes on personnel decisions.

Although the three chapters share some common foci, they are also unique in their approaches to the general issue of gender stereotyping. Heilman and Haynes focus on performance evaluation. Eagly and Koenig address the issue of the extent to which the "fit" between an individual and a job opening might influence a decision to hire or promote. Finally, Rudman, Glick, and Phelan deal with the issue of potential mitigators of gender stereotypes.

A great deal of the research that represents the foundation for the conclusions drawn in the chapters I reviewed has been done with undergraduate students evaluating paper (or computer) "people." This would include research on stereotyping (age, race, gender, or disability) as well as more recent research investigating implicit attitudes and automatic cognitive processing. A common paradigm involves an undergraduate student agreeing to participate in a study for course credit. The study usually involves reviewing some information about a target person then making an evaluation of some sort involving either a simulated personnel decision (hiring, promotion, termination, performance evaluation) or a broader statement about some general positive/negative valence toward the target. The results are then analyzed to determine if the evaluations demonstrate differences that favor one or another demographic subgroup. Often, the results show statistically significant differences favoring majority hypothetical targets (males, Whites, younger individuals) and the researcher uses this difference to draw inferences about how things happen outside of the laboratory. Some studies are relatively simple, such as those using the Goldberg paradigm (i.e., presenting a résumé and keeping everything constant except a demographic characteristic such as gender). Others are more complex, involving interactive simulations of work. For ease of discussion, henceforth I will refer to these studies as representative of the "artificial work" paradigm. This is in contrast to what I will refer to as a "real-world" paradigm where the design includes the analysis of data gathered from intact groups or dyads in a naturally occurring work setting. No pejorative tone should be inferred from the choice of the term "artificial." It is simply a convenient way of anchoring two ends of a design continuum.

Considerable debate has arisen regarding the extent to which results generated in this laboratory paradigm can generalize to work settings. Copus (2005) presented a detailed discussion of this issue and concluded that laboratory research – which he referred to as the stranger-to-stranger paradigm – is of limited usefulness in understanding work-related decision-making. By extension, the same argument might be made against the relevance of laboratory research findings related to gender stereotypes in forensic settings.

For purposes of the current discussion, I will make a distinction between individual-oriented research and group-oriented research. In the former paradigm, decisions and evaluations about a "target" individual are often made based on information provided about that individual (e.g., via paper descriptions or videotaped performance vignettes) without undue emphasis on group interaction or group-related information.

Thus, a hiring or promotion decision for a male "candidate" will be contrasted with a hiring or promotion decision for a female "candidate." The emphasis is on the individual and what stereotypes (e.g. descriptive, prescriptive, agentic, communal) might be activated by gender identification. In the latter paradigm, there is often interaction between the target individual and others in the form of either an intact (e.g., sports, fraternity/sorority) or nominal (e.g., laboratory-formed) group activity. It is the individual-oriented research that interests me more than the group-oriented research because in many, if not most, real work settings, the decisions of interest are not made by group members but by individuals – usually those in a superior position (e.g., a manager) to the "target" individual.

There is a substantial body of group-oriented research that addresses the potential confound represented by artificial groups as opposed to real groups. For the most part, these studies focus on the concept of ingroup versus outgroup bias. As examples consider the meta-analyses of Mullen and Hu (1989), Mullen, Brown, and Smith (1992), Mullen and Copper (1994), as well as nonmeta-analytic reviews such as Ostrom & Sedikides (1992). These studies distinguish between artificial groups (e.g., undergraduate students in a laboratory setting) and real groups (e.g., sports teams, military groups, intact social groups, and occasionally work groups). The general conclusion from these studies is that the effects of in- and outgroup bias are, if anything, more noticeable in real groups than in artificial groups. These group-oriented research findings are interesting and potentially important for applications for some settings – but not work settings.

Work-related decisions regarding issues such as promotions, performance evaluations, assignments, and compensation share some common characteristics. These include the following:

- The evaluatee is well known to the evaluator;
- the evaluator has been making decisions like this for many years and has taken both classroom and on line training in the process;
- the evaluator can interact and communicate with the evaluatee to obtain additional information;
- the evaluator's appraisal will be known to both the evaluatee and other managers; the evaluator's decision will be known to both the evaluatee and other managers;
- the evaluator depends at some level (either directly or as a member of a broader institution) on the evaluatee for successful performance;
- the evaluator observes the evaluatee's behavior on a regular basis;

- the evaluator knows a great deal about the work history, accomplishments, and performance-related attributes of the evaluatee;
- the evaluator is provided with a complex, behaviorally anchored, multidimensional instrument to use in making the evaluation.

To be sure, many of the group-oriented research studies identified in the meta-analyses I have cited above contain one or more of these features, particularly when they include data from "real" or previously intact groups. The problem is that there are very few studies that incorporate all or most of these characteristics. It is not so much that the researchers are to be faulted for not incorporating these characteristics into their designs, it is simply a recognition that the work setting is unique in many important respects and if research results are to generalize to applied settings, the research paradigm must incorporate these characteristics. It is not possible to simply "stretch" the results from one paradigm to another as an exercise in Procrustean inference.

It is tempting to substitute high powered analytic methods for rigor of design. For example, in chapter 4, Eagly and Koenig suggests that the results of research on stereotyping are more easily generalized because of "excellent methods of integrating" these results.

> These methods, known as *meta-analysis*, implement statistically justified techniques for synthesizing research studies. Studies examining prejudice in congruent and incongruent roles have been systematically integrated with these methods. This modern method of integrating research constitutes a shift away from informal, qualitative, or "narrative" reviews of studies that were common at earlier points in psychology and other fields . . . (p. 75)

Heilman and Haynes, in chapter 7, are more realistic and cautious about the value of meta-analysis in the gender stereotyping area.

> Meta-analyses, which are important in so many ways, do not really help with these problems. Meta-analyses are informative only about moderator variables that are investigated in a substantial number of studies that are reviewed. They are limited by the research that is available; if a moderator variable has not been the focus of multiple studies, it cannot be examined. (p. 147)

Eagly and Koenig cite a meta-analysis in Davidson and Burke (2000) to support their opinion that "available research . . . substantiates the conclusion that women are discriminated against when they vie for positions that are incongruent with the female gender role" (p. 72). But the Davidson and Burke meta-analysis, as Eagly and Koenig acknowledge, examines *only* studies using artificial work contexts. As Heilman and Haynes recognize, such meta-analytic evidence would have only been of value if it included a moderator variable to represent real versus simulated employment contexts. If that moderator variable was found to have no influence, then a strong case might be made for the relevance of laboratory studies for employment contexts.

Those seeking to generalize from research conducted following the artificial work paradigm justifiably point to the fact that extraneous variables can be controlled, thus allowing for greater confidence in causal inferences. But there must be a balance. By "controlling" the conditions of the research in the manner represented in these research paradigms, the researcher is denied the possibility of inferring generalizability to the work setting. There are simply too many differences, as I have described in the list above.

Certainly, field studies do not represent a panacea. The fact that certain variables *cannot* be controlled presents its own problems. Consider a recent field study conducted by Lyness and Heilman (2006) investigating performance evaluation and circumstances of promotion of men and women into line and staff management positions. They found an advantage in performance ratings for men in line positions and women in staff positions and attributed this difference to the view that women are seen as communal while men are seen as agentic. Thus, they concluded that gender interacts with job type to influence the presence or absence of stereotype effects. They conclude: "Our data strongly suggest that gender bias affects performance evaluations of managers in actual organizational settings, and illustrate the different consequences of performance evaluations for promotion of men and women in managerial roles" (p. 784). Nevertheless, several paragraphs earlier, the authors acknowledge that: ". . . we cannot rule out the possibility that the differences in performance ratings were based on real performance differences, not on biased assessments" (p. 784). In addition, there was a significant difference in organizational tenure between male and female managers and tenure was associated with performance ratings. It should also be mentioned that the observed differences were very modest. The interaction of gender and job type accounted for 1% of the variance of the ratings for managers.

Having conducted both laboratory and field research in the area of performance evaluation, I am sympathetic to the difficulties of drawing inferences without certain critical controls. Nevertheless, in an area as important and contentious as gender discrimination, the design must be adequate to support the inferences. The artificial work paradigm will not support inferences to the work setting and field studies leave potentially important confounding variables uncontrolled.

Nevertheless, to return to the issue of meta-analysis and gender stereotyping, a substantial step forward in determining whether or not we have something to add to forensic discussions of gender discrimination in employment would be to at least investigate the possible moderating effects of work setting versus laboratory in observed male–female differences in hiring, promotion, performance evaluation, compensation, leadership ratings, etc. Until we can say with some confidence that research setting does not account for results, we should proceed cautiously with our expert opinions.

The Nature of Work in the Twenty-first Century: What We Used to Know But Do Not Know Any More

Both work itself and the social context of work in the twenty-first century have been radically transformed from what they had been as recently as 1980 (Landy & Conte, 2007). The forces are obvious – global competition, downsizing, digitization, mergers and acquisitions, and the clash between westernization and multinationalization in industrialized countries. These forces have profound effects on the psychosocial environment of work. In the 1960s the sociotechnical scholars of the Tavistock Institute noted that when methods of mining coal changed from longwall to shortwall, group dynamics changed as well. Similarly, the changing nature of twenty-first century work will profoundly influence the social dynamics of work.

The astute epistemologist Donald Rumsfeld has been famously quoted with respect to what we know (". . . there are things we know we know . . . we know there are some things we do not know . . . there are also unknown unknowns – the ones we don't know we don't know"). To this litany, I would add: ". . . and some things we used to know but we do not know anymore." The rapid change in the nature of work will render a great deal of what we "knew" about work (and the social context of work) obsolete. Nevertheless, one theme of the current volume is to identify what we "know" as social scientists, and in particular, how what we "know" may be different from what the finder of fact "knows" about a given phenomenon. Good examples of such discrepancies include phenomena such as eyewitness identification and spousal abuse. So I would add a codicil and a corollary to the Rumsfeldian epistemology: The codicil is "what the finder of fact thinks he or she knows but does not really"; the corollary is "what the finder of fact thinks he or she knows that is *contradicted* by the results of empirical social science research."

There are several implications to this observation. The first is that meta-analyses that include research studies related to "work" done as recently as 1980 will be problematic since they will represent work as it used to be rather than as it is now. So even when we may try to educate the finder of fact with respect to what we know and what they do not about work-related phenomena, if what we "know" is based on the research of the 1980s, we are likely to mislead that finder of fact. The second implication is that research designs will need to incorporate these aspects of "modern" work to be of any applied value. Below, I will elaborate on three of the more important changes in work that impact the social context of that work. In particular, I will consider implications for research on processes such as stereotyping which are proposed to be the foundation for discrimination at the workplace.

The multinationalization of work

On the production floor in a Holden auto plant on the outskirts of Melbourne, Australia, 57 first languages could be spoken. Of course, the "official" language is English, but that is beside the point. Each language represents the potential of a unique national culture. The same phenomenon occurs on American factory floors. The concept of a "foreign" worker no longer has any meaning. In fact, in many U.S. organizations the native-born American worker is in a distinct minority.

The "we/they" dichotomy is a building block of many theories of bias. That might have been plausible when the we's were all native-born white males under the age of 40. But as the proponents of the tokenism argument suggest, strength lies in numbers. What happens to ingroup–outgroup mechanisms as the outgroup grows in numbers and complexity? So many things to disdain and so few hours. How will the various "tensions" play out? As an example, will gender-based differences be enhanced or diminished? Will a native-born American woman be a member of an ingroup in contrast to middle-eastern or African or Chinese men and women? Or will there be a parsing of outgroups? How will salience be determined? And how are we to interpret the leadership dynamics of the manager from a high power distance culture, e.g., Japan (Hofstede, 1980; 2001), who eschews participation from subordinates? Or how are we to contrast the behavior of the Swedish manager toward female subordinates with his or her American counterpart? Is the examination of stereotypic behavior to occur at an ipsative or a normative level?

We can be sure of one thing – work will grow more culturally diverse. As a result, the construct of national culture – and its fellow traveler, national personality – will play an increasingly important role in the interpretation of behavior in the workplace. Hofstede and his colleagues have been conducting field and survey research in this area since 1971 (Hofstede, 2001) and have developed high-credibility instruments for assessing culture. Similarly, the work of the GLOBE researchers on leadership encompasses over 50 nations and has been ongoing since 1990 (House, Javidian, & Dorfman, 2001). There could not be a better time for collaboration between those studying the effect of culture in the workplace and those interested in social cognition in the workplace.

Teams

In virtually every workplace, to one degree or another, teamwork has replaced solitary work. This is the result of multiple forces including downsizing (which has decimated middle-level management ranks), the introduction of new methods of manufacturing (such as Total Quality Manufacturing and Six Sigma systems), and expanded theories of work motivation and performance that emphasize organizational citizenship behavior.

There are several implications of the emergence of "team." The most obvious is that individual contributions are more difficult to identify, if individual contributions even have any meaning in the modern workplace. To be sure, there are still some "solo contributors" but they are rapidly dwindling. Even sales and marketing reps now are part of a team including technical reps, account executives, and administrative assistants, all serving a single customer. How then do we disentangle group behavior and accomplishments from individual behavior and accomplishments? Heilman and Haynes (2005) found that in laboratory teams, men tend to be given more credit for successful team performance. More importantly, for the theories such as stereotyping, what happens when interdependencies among group members increase? Does the very emergence of the "team" of interdependent contributors axiomatically diminish or cancel stereotyping tendencies? There is experimental laboratory-based research that suggests that such interdependencies will result in stereotype mitigation (Fiske, 2000) but it is not clear that these results will transfer easily to the work setting. At the very least, relevant research designs need to incorporate truly interdependent work groups with real accountabilities to each other when examining the presence of stereotyping and in- or outgroup bias.

Virtual work and telecommuting

More and more work is being done away from a central work location. Organizations realize substantial economic and operational efficiencies from virtual work so there is little doubt that it will grow in frequency (Cascio, 2000). It is being done on the phone, or more commonly, on the computer (or Blackberry). This has been labeled virtual work. The "virtualness" of work varies from a complete absence of face-to-face interactions through a mix of face-to-face and distant interactions (Martins, Gilson, & Maynard, 2004). This degree of virtualness becomes a new variable in the social psychology of work, and associated processes such as stereotyping and implicit associations. Researchers need to investigate the effect of this type of work context.

This work context is unique in several ways. The actors are not strangers to one another, there are clear interdependencies (e.g., team member to team member, subordinate to supervisor), and there are frequent opportunities to interact (often several times per day – both scheduled and unscheduled). Although one can imagine that in the absence of face-to-face contact, stereotyping and implicit association tendencies might be enhanced, some preliminary research suggests that communications media such as email and the internet can actually be used to build interpersonal trust, commitment, and feelings of ingroup membership (Thompson & Nadler, 2002; Tyler, 2002). Similarly, one might imagine that the virtual nature of the work actually increases perceived interdependencies thus mitigating the effect of stereotypes, as has been suggested by Fiske (2000). As virtual work continues to grow, there should be ample opportunity to examine the interaction of variables such as individuation, interdependency, etc., on stereotyping. One particularly interesting aspect of the interaction might be the *speed* with which stereotypes might be mitigated by virtual work, particularly in the absence of frequent face-to-face interaction. It is also likely that the role of the virtual team leader will be extremely important in moderating biases. While the skill set of the virtual leader may not need to be very different from the skill set of the more traditional leader, the *level* of both agentic and communal skills may need to be much higher (Bell & Kozlowski, 2002; Hertel, Konradt, & Orlikowski, 2004).

Culture, teams, and virtual work designs are only three of the characteristics of modern work that likely impact the social dynamics at issue in the chapters I have considered in this volume. There are other changes in work that are equally important for research design. To name a few, work has become less "observable" and more latent or cognitive; work is less stable in both a career sense and in a task sense.

Work performance has been effectively parsed into citizenship behavior, task performance, adaptability performance, and counterproductive work performance (Landy & Conte, 2007). The concept of an unparsed view of work may be too primitive a view of work behavior to tell us anything about the subtle social dynamics of evaluation or personnel decision-making. Research designs including field samples will need to move beyond "composite" or overall performance ratings (such as those used in Lyness & Heilman, 2006). Just as Lyness and Heilman (2006) suggest that job type (line vs. staff) interacts with gender to activate descriptive stereotypes, one might also suggest that "performance type" interacts with gender to activate stereotypes. As an example, one might expect female managers to receive lower ratings on leadership and decision-making and higher ratings on interpersonal skills and team behavior than their male counterparts if gender stereotypes were operating. We are at a stage now in the deconstruction of work performance where such investigations are feasible.

Conclusion

I am both concerned and excited about the research lines described in the three chapters I chose to examine in this volume. I am concerned because most of the extant research is based on paradigms that are far removed from the world of work that I know. I am excited because the questions being posed by these researchers are important. I share the enthusiasm of these researchers for finding out *when* and *why* gender biases occur, and equally importantly, what the effects of these biases are in the workplace.

It is reasonable to assume that many twenty-first century workplaces and workers are not free of the shackles of "-isms" such as racism, sexism, and ageism. I applaud the motives of the authors of the chapters I have examined. Social scientists should be partners in policy formulation and change. But, to the extent to which social scientists depend on scientific knowledge bases to get their seat at the table, they must fairly represent the limits of that research. In my opinion, a great deal of time has been spent on "available" research paradigms rather than relevant ones. I encourage researchers who seek to investigate social-cognitive phenomena such as stereotyping and implicit cognition related to demographic characteristics to get out of the laboratory and into the field, to understand more clearly the industrial "behavior" they attempt to mimic in the laboratory.

There is an old story about an unfortunate soul who lost a wallet on a dark street at night, and went to an adjacent street to look for it because there was a streetlight on in the adjacent street and that made the search easier. Needless to say, no wallet was found. I have the same feeling about the research cited in the chapters I reviewed. I do not think there is much hope of unraveling the complexity of work-related behavior in artificial research settings.

REFERENCES

Bell, B. S., & Kozlowski, S. W. J. (2002). A typology of virtual teams: Implications for effective leadership. *Group and Organization Management, 27,* 12–49.

Cascio, W. F. (2000). Managing a virtual workplace. *Academy of Management Executive, 14,* 81–90.

Copus, D. (2005) Avoiding junk science: A lawyer's view. In F. J. Landy (Ed.), *Employment discrimination litigation: Behavioral, quantitative, and legal perspectives* (pp. 450–462). San Francisco: Jossey-Bass.

Davidson, H. K., & Burke, M. J. (2000). Sex discrimination in simulated employment contexts: A meta-analytic investigation. *Journal of Vocational Behavior, 56,* 225–248.

Fiske, S. J. (2000). Interdependence and the reduction of prejudice. In S. Oskamp (Ed.), *Reducing prejudice and discrimination. The Claremont Symposium on Applied Social Psychology* (pp. 115–135). Mahwah, NJ: Erlbaum and Associates.

Heilman, M. J., & Haynes, M. C. (2005). No credit where credit was due: Attributional rationalization of women's success in male–female teams. *Journal of Applied Psychology, 90,* 905–916.

Hertel, G., Konradt, U., & Orlikowsi, B. (2004). Managing distance by interdependence: Goal setting, task interdependence, and team-based rewards in virtual teams. *European Journal of Work and Organizational Psychology, 13,* 1–28.

Hofstede, G. (1980). *Culture's consequences: International differences in work-related values.* Beverly Hills, CA: Sage.

Hofstede, G. (2001). *Culture's consequences: Comparing values, behaviors, institutions, and organizations across nations.* Thousand Oaks, CA: Sage

House, R. J., Javidian, M., & Dorfman, P. (2001). Project GLOBE: An introduction. *Applied Psychology: An International Review, 50*(4), 489–505.

Landy, F. J., & Conte, J. M. (2007). *Work in the 21ˢᵗ century: An introduction to industrial and organizational psychology* (2nd ed.). Boston, MA: Blackwell.

Lyness, K. S., & Heilman, M. E. (2006). When fit is fundamental: Performance evaluations and promotions of upper-level female and male managers. *Journal of Applied Psychology, 91,* 777–785.

Martins, L. L., Gilson, L. L., & Maynard, M. T. (2004). Virtual teams: What do we know and where do we go from here? *Journal of Management, 30,* 805–835.

Mullen, B., Brown, R., & Smith, C. (1992). Ingroup bias as a function of salience, relevance, and status: An integration. *European Journal of Social Psychology, 22,* 103–122.

Mullen, B., & Copper, C. (1994). The relation between group cohesiveness and performance: An integration. *Psychological Bulletin, 115,* 210–227.

Mullen, B., & Hu, L. (1989) Perceptions of ingroup and outgroup variability: Two meta-analytic integrations. *Basic and Applied Social Psychology, 10,* 233–252.

Ostrom, T., & Sedikides, C. (1992). Out-group homogeneity effects in natural and minimal groups. *Psychological Bulletin, 112,* 536–552.

Thompson, L., & Nadler, J. (2002). Negotiating via internet technology: Theory and application. *Journal of Social Issues, 58,* 109–124.

Tyler, T. R. (2002). Is the internet changing social life? It seems the more things change, the more they stay the same. *Journal of Social Issues, 58,* 195–205.

19

Psychological Contributions to Evaluating Witness Testimony

Shari Seidman Diamond

The legal system depends heavily on witness testimony. Victims, bystanders, and perpetrators themselves may assist police in identifying the person responsible for the crime and provide details on how the crime occurred. Without information from a witness, the legal system may not even know that a crime has taken place. Yet witnesses and even wrongly accused suspects can provide false incriminating evidence. DNA has provided stunning confirmation for what psychologists have shown in a myriad of studies: Even honest and confident eyewitnesses can be wrong (Wells & Hasel, chapter 8); even innocent suspects may "confess" to offenses they did not commit (Kassin, chapter 10); and even nonvictims may report, and honestly believe, they were victims of crimes that never occurred (Loftus, Garry & Hayne, chapter 9).

Long before the biological sciences developed knowledge about DNA that could be applied to forensic settings (National Research Council, 1992; 1996), cognitive and social psychologists were studying perception, memory, and social influence, compiling an impressive body of research reflected in the writings of such scholars as Elizabeth Loftus, Gary Wells, and Saul Kassin. This body of psychological research reveals that perception is selective and imperfect. It also has shown that recall is a constructive as well as reconstructive process, reflecting images almost immediately altered by pre- and postevent experiences, adjusted over time, and influenced by the circumstances used to elicit them. Although psychologists cannot specify how often witnesses make false identifications, psychological research has shown how various factors affect eyewitness accuracy. Some of these factors are "estimator variables" that the legal system cannot alter (Wells, 1978). For example, a large body of research has shown that estimator variables such as same versus cross-race identification (Meissner &

Brigham, 2001) and presence or absence of a weapon (Steblay, 1992) affect the accuracy of eyewitness identifications. Other factors shown to influence the probability of a false identification, like the instructions given to a witness during a lineup, are "system variables" that the justice system can control. In particular, research by psychologists has demonstrated how lineup procedures can reduce (or increase) the likelihood that victims and bystanders will identify an innocent suspect and then confidently testify that the suspect is the perpetrator.

Experts on these issues provide the legal system with two forms of assistance: corrective and preventative. Corrective assistance is supplied when an attorney in a specific case seeks advice about the conditions that, when applied to a particular witness, may make it more or less likely that the identification by the eyewitness is accurate. An expert providing corrective expertise may describe the effects of both estimator and system variables. In contrast, preventative expert advice focuses on the criminal justice system as a whole, concentrating on system variables to show how procedures can be designed to increase eyewitness accuracy and reduce the need for corrective assistance. Nonetheless, when the legal system fails to put in place these appropriate safeguards, attorneys may need to turn to experts for corrective assistance.

The court faced with an expert offering advice about eyewitness identification must decide whether to permit the expert to testify. Despite the general reluctance of courts to allow expert testimony that impinges on judgments about witness credibility by the trier of fact, courts in recent years have shown some receptivity to expert testimony on the factors that affect the accuracy of eyewitness identification (e.g., *U.S. v. Norwood*, 1996; *U.S. v. Hines*, 1999). These courts have recognized that lay persons may fail to appreciate what psychological research has shown about the factors that influence the accuracy of perception and memory.

When courts have refused to admit the proffered testimony on eyewitness identification, they have done so largely on the grounds that it will not assist the trier of fact because the evidence is a matter of common sense (e.g., *State v. McKinney*, 2002). That objection is surprising, because it can be easily rebutted. Surveys comparing experts and lay persons reveal substantial gaps between what lay persons believe and research scientists accept as proven about the factors that influence eyewitness accuracy. As Wells and Hasel (chapter 8) demonstrate, not only lay persons, but courts as well, may often require expert assistance in evaluating the factors that influence the accuracy of eyewitness testimony.

Only a few courts have grappled with the specific post-*Daubert* era issues focusing on the "evidentiary reliability" of the research (the phrase that courts use to refer to validity; *Daubert v. Merrell Dow Pharmaceuticals, Inc.*, 1993); the same applies to the question of whether results from a research literature that has depended heavily on laboratory experimentation, much of it with student samples, can be extrapolated to actual crime events. Concern about extrapolation may increase in the near future, however, at least with respect to lineups, in light of a report on an Illinois field test on lineup identifications issued in 2006 that purportedly failed to replicate findings from laboratory research. Using the example of the Illinois field test, I discuss how reluctance to squarely grapple with the extrapolation issue can unreasonably threaten court acceptance of grounded scientific research.

It is always relevant to raise questions about extrapolation from the laboratory to the field. A good field replication of research generated in the laboratory is unambiguously a valuable product. Nonetheless, the difficulty of conducting tightly controlled field research should not be underestimated, and a badly designed or poorly implemented field test can be misleading. When its flaws are sufficiently severe and the results are inconsistent with laboratory findings, such a field test should not undercut or receive greater weight than well-designed laboratory-based research conducted under better-controlled conditions. That is the story that unfolded in Illinois.

Preventative Expertise on Eyewitness Testimony

In the wake of DNA evidence revealing disturbing cases of convictions based on inaccurate eyewitness testimony, some jurisdictions across the United States have turned to psychological research for guidance in maximizing the dependability of evidence from eyewitnesses. Indeed, eyewitness testimony has been widely recognized as producing one of the most successful collaborations between psychology and the legal system (e.g., Doyle, 2005). In 1998, then Attorney General Janet Reno created a working group of police, prosecutors, defense attorneys, and eyewitness scientists to write guidelines for the collection and preservation of eyewitness testimony. The resulting guide (U.S. Department of Justice, 1999) included a section on lineups that reflected many (Wells et al., 2000), though not all (e.g., videotaping lineups; Kassin, 1998), of the insights obtained from decades of eyewitness research. For example, it recommended instructing the witness that the lineup might not include the perpetrator, based on research showing that witnesses are more accurate when they are provided with that information. Since the 1999 guide was published, several jurisdictions have implemented changes in the way eyewitnesses and lineups are handled, in some instances collecting data to track the results after the implementation of the changes (Klobucher & Caligiuri, 2005).

One innovation in lineups that has garnered substantial recent interest is the sequential lineup, in which the witness views a series of individuals, including a suspect, one at a time. In the traditional simultaneous lineup, the witness views the entire set of lineup participants at the same time. According to psychological research, a witness faced with a simultaneous lineup tends to engage in a process of relative judgment, evaluating which member of the lineup most resembles the witness's recollection of the perpetrator. In contrast, a sequential procedure which shows the witness a series of potential candidates one at a time encourages the witness to compare each candidate with the recalled mental image of the perpetrator. The result is that when the lineup contains a falsely accused suspect rather than the perpetrator, a witness is less likely to make a false identification in response to a sequential lineup than in response to a simultaneous lineup (Steblay, Dysart, Fulero, & Lindsay, 2001). Some theorists suggest that the reduction in false identifications with sequential lineups occurs, at least in part, because the witness applies a more stringent standard before making an identification (McQuiston-Surrett, Malpass, & Tredoux, 2006). Indeed, there is evidence that sequential lineups may produce a drop in accurate as well as inaccurate identifications (Steblay et al., 2001; McQuiston-Surrett et al., 2006).

Several jurisdictions, including New Jersey and Hennepin County in Minnesota, have responded to concerns about false identifications and to the research on lineups showing an increased likelihood of false identifications with simultaneous lineups by implementing sequential lineup procedures. Illinois took a different path. In 2003, in the wake of a series of exonerations that helped to persuade then Governor George Ryan to commute the death sentences of 167 prisoners on death row, the Illinois legislature passed a death penalty reform bill. It called for a test of the use of sequential lineups to evaluate whether they could improve the accuracy of witness lineups. The study promised to provide evidence on the question of whether the laboratory research indicating the superiority of sequential lineups for avoiding false identifications could be extrapolated to the field.

Table 19.1   Results reported from Illinois (data from Mecklenburg, 2006, table 3a, p. 38)

Witness decision	Simultaneous (319)	Sequential (229)
Suspect ID	59.9%	45.0%
Filler ID	2.8%	9.2%
No ID	37.6%	47.2%

The report from the Illinois field study was released on March 17, 2006 and received national attention. On April 19, 2006 the *New York Times* reported the results on p. 1 (Zernike, 2006). The study purportedly showed that witnesses performed better in simultaneous than in sequential lineups – they were both more likely to identify the suspect and less likely to err by identifying one of the filler members of the lineup. Table 19.1 shows the primary table of results presented in the report (Mecklenburg, 2006).

The results appeared to contradict the findings from laboratory research, most importantly calling into question claims that sequential lineups would offer greater protection from false identifications. Witnesses responding to sequential lineups appeared more, not less, likely to select innocent fillers than those responding to simultaneous lineups. This description of the study, however, omits some crucial pieces of the story. In fact, the surprising results can be easily explained by major errors in the research design and implementation of the lineup procedures, described below. The unfortunate result is a fundamentally flawed test that ultimately provides no probative information on the influence of sequential versus simultaneous lineups on the relative accuracy of identifications.

The Illinois field test faced two crucial obstacles, the first representing a challenge in any field test of lineups and the second, a fatal confound, unnecessarily introduced by the research design implemented in the Illinois pilot test. The first obstacle is that the outcome measure of interest – the accuracy of the identification – is always problematic once the researcher leaves the laboratory. In a laboratory setting, witnesses respond to a staged offense in which the actual perpetrator is determined by the experimenter, the experimenter controls whether or not the perpetrator is present in the lineup, and if the witness makes an identification, the experimenter knows whether the witness is correct or incorrect. In the field setting, no one knows whether the suspect is the perpetrator. Indeed, the lineup tests should be providing evidence not only of the perception and memory of the witness but

also on the question of whether or not the lineup includes the perpetrator. The only unambiguous response by a witness to a lineup that
can occur in a field setting is a mistaken identification of one of the
fillers as the perpetrator. How then would we interpret any pattern of
differences obtained from two different lineup procedures? It depends
on the likelihood that the suspect in the lineup is the perpetrator. The
lineup data alone cannot provide this information. Although a detective may be confident that the suspect is the perpetrator, the lineup is
conducted to provide a test of that belief.

It is not possible to completely overcome this obstacle in the
field, but it is possible to test its impact. Other researchers have
collected information on extrinsic evidence of guilt, comparing
the pattern of results obtained from lineups when there is strong
extrinsic evidence with the results when extrinsic evidence does not
exist (e.g., Wright & McDaid, 1996). The Illinois field test included
little additional information on the cases that would have enabled
researchers to conduct such analyses. Thus, we are left with suspect
identifications that could assist in prosecuting a guilty person if
the suspect was the perpetrator, but would provide dangerous fodder
for incriminating an innocent person if the suspect was not the
culprit.

Even more fundamentally misleading, and specific to the Illinois
test, the cause of any difference in the results of the simultaneous and
sequential lineups is totally ambiguous because of the two versions of
the lineup used in the test. Prior laboratory research indicated that
the sequential lineup, when appropriately done, would reduce false
identifications and even overcome weaknesses in the choice of fillers
in the lineup. It also suggested that the sequential lineup was particularly subject to influence, whether inadvertent or intentional, from
the administrator (Phillips, McAuliff, Kovera, & Cutler, 1999) who
would control, for example, the pacing of the display of lineup
members. As a result, the Illinois investigators sensibly required that
the sequential lineups be administered in a double-blind fashion, so
that neither the administrator nor the witness would know the identity of the suspect. But the field test failed when it chose to compare
the double-blind sequential lineup to the traditional administrator-
aware simultaneous lineup. The administrators of the sequential
lineups never knew the identity of the suspect, but the administrators
in the simultaneous lineups always did – the classic instance of a
complete confound. As a result, any differences between the results
from the two procedures could be due either to the simultaneous
versus sequential difference *or* to the aware versus blind administrator

difference *or* to some combination of both. The crucial omission, the 2000 lb gorilla *not* in the study, was a condition using a double-blind simultaneous lineup.

A substantial history of research in psychology documents the influence of experimenter effects in a variety of settings (Harris & Rosenthal, 1985); more recent laboratory research on lineups has demonstrated the effect of administrator contact on lineup outcomes (Haw & Fisher, 2004). Moreover, the results in table 19.1 are completely consistent with the pattern that would be expected if administrators had influenced witness choices in the simultaneous lineups in the Illinois field test. Witnesses who viewed the simultaneous lineup, in which the suspect's identity was known to the administrator, were more likely to select the suspect than to refrain from making an identification, and they were less likely to choose (indeed, strikingly and surprisingly almost *never* chose) a filler member of the lineup. Thus, the bald comparison data from the field test provides a classic example of what the law would deem "not relevant" to the proposition that eyewitness identifications based on simultaneous lineups are better than, worse than, or no different from identifications based on sequential lineups. The field test provided no probative evidence on this issue.

It remains to be seen how much these results will affect the future evolution of witness identification in the legal system, in light of the substantial publicity that the study generated. In the short run, the Illinois field test represents a missed opportunity with potentially damaging fallout inside and outside of court if the study is interpreted as raising serious questions about the findings from psychological research on eyewitness identification. It also offers a case study in problems associated with translating even a careful and theoretically grounded body of laboratory research into a field test. *Daubert* and the Federal Rules of Evidence call on courts to address questions about extrapolation, the "fit" between the research that provides the grounding for expert testimony and the facts of the case at hand. What the Illinois field test demonstrates is that poorly designed field tests may detract from, rather than add to, what laboratory investigations can reveal.

A Lost Opportunity

What can (or could) such a field test tell us? If a blind simultaneous condition had been included in the study, we would know whether the almost nonexistent filler choices with aware simultaneous lineups were the result of influence, however inadvertent, from the aware administrator on the witness. We would also learn whether the higher suspect choice was due to administrator cues. In addition, if the study had focused more on process information, the investigators could have systematically identified and reported on the type and frequency of various problems encountered in arranging for blind administrators, including the annoyance that witnesses expressed when they were asked to wait until a blind administrator was available.[1] It could also have investigated the circumstances under which investigators used live versus photo lineups. That process information might have helped to explain the fact that live displays produced higher rates of suspect identification than did photo displays in Chicago and lower rates in Evanston.[2] As it is, the study apparently did not collect any information on the characteristics of the lineup fillers, apart from the number of fillers and suspects in the lineup. Moreover, because only the sequential lineups required double-blind administration, some of the cases which originally were assigned to a sequential lineup condition were actually handled using a simultaneous lineup when a blind administrator could not be located. It is unlikely that this occurred on a random basis (e.g., blind administrators would presumably be more difficult to locate at 3 a.m. or when personnel were particularly busy). According to the report (see table 19.1 above), the test produced 90 more simultaneous than blind sequential lineups. It is not clear how many of these were originally assigned to the blind sequential condition, but the difference undermines the assumption that the two sets of cases were comparable in all ways other than the lineup procedure used for the identification.[3]

An easy response to the Illinois field test is that the field is a messy place. That might also account for the inexplicable failure to replicate the well-documented effect of weapon presence in the Illinois study.[4]

[1]   Personnel were required to write down why the change was made, but the report contains no data on how often or the circumstances under which this occurred.
[2]   The third jurisdiction in the field test, Joliet, used only photo displays for all lineups.
[3]   There are other reasons as well to be concerned about the comparability of the two sets of cases at two of the three research sites. At these two sites, the cases originally assigned to sequential versus simultaneous lineups were obtained from different geographic areas so they may have differed in unknown ways. At the third (and smallest) site the type of lineup used was determined by whether the case number ended in an odd or even number.
[4]   According to one consultant (Malpass), but not the other (Ebbesen), the test also failed to find evidence of the well-documented cross-race identification effect.

It would be reasonable to simply dismiss the Illinois results on sequential lineups. We should not, however, also conclude that the questions about sequential lineups have all been answered. Although the sequential versus simultaneous lineup comparison has generated substantial research, most of it pointing to superiority for the sequential lineup, some important questions remain. What happens when the witness is permitted to view the sequential lineup a second time? Does the second viewing after seeing all of the members of the lineup transform the lineup to a relative judgment task like the one that occurs with a simultaneous lineup? Does it matter where the suspect is placed in the order of the sequential lineup (McQuiston-Surrett et al., 2006)? What are the consequences of photo versus live lineups when, unlike in the Illinois field test, everything else is held constant? What about the effect of video versus live versus photo displays of sequential versus simultaneous lineups? What is the size of the effect of administrator awareness in the lineup context?

Field research from Minnesota provides an interesting contrast and demonstrates what might be learned when well-documented field investigations are combined with laboratory backup. Consulting with psychologist Nancy Steblay, and at the behest of innovative State's Attorney Amy Klobuchar, Hennepin County (Minnesota) implemented a trial field test for blind sequential lineups. When the study reported 8% filler choices, the question arose as to whether the lineups were simply too easy. If most of the fillers were readily identifiable as inappropriate choices, they would functionally reduce the size of the lineup, making it easier for a witness to avoid selecting a filler. Using a mock witness paradigm – that is, applying laboratory procedures to test the hypothesis that the lineup construction rather than the memory of the eyewitness produced the identification – the researchers were able to evaluate the fairness of the lineups. A sample of mock witnesses viewed the lineup after receiving only the description of the perpetrator given by the real witness. Steblay reports that the mock witnesses did not avoid the fillers, as they would have if the fillers had not been plausible choices (Steblay, 2006). We have no way of knowing in the Illinois study whether the fillers selected for the sequential lineups were more or less plausible choices than those selected for the administrator aware simultaneous lineups.

Why do field testing? For two reasons. First, lessons worth learning emerge even from problematic field tests. For example, the Illinois field test identified a potential cost of blind administrators that had not emerged, and would not emerge, in a laboratory setting. The investigators reported that some witnesses were reluctant or unwilling to wait for law enforcement to find an unaware administrator to conduct the lineup. That cost should be recognized and addressed.[5] One promising approach is a further evolution of lineups that avoids or at least reduces the influence of administrators and would provide precisely the form of documentation that would make it possible for the parties to evaluate the fairness of the lineup: adopting a video system of the display of the lineup. By permitting the witness to control the video presentation of a series of individuals, it would reduce the potential impact of much of the inadvertent influence that an administrator would have on the witness. Moreover, the choices of fillers could be expanded through an ability to draw from a large database of candidates, selected by inserting the factors in the description of the perpetrator (a computer program is already used in some cases to assist in composing a photo lineup; Kemp, Pike, & Brace, 2001). In this way, the procedure would not only provide, more easily, an unbiased test of the witness's memory, it should also make it easier to construct an appropriate lineup. In addition, if the choice made by the witness were also computerized, it would be possible to record directly how much time the witness spent looking at each, providing a measure that some research shows is associated with accuracy. With the reduced cost of video and computer equipment, what may have seemed inconceivable a few years ago is now clearly an idea worth pursuing – accompanied by research that fairly tests its impact in a field setting.

A second rationale for further field testing is its persuasive value. Law enforcement bodies, particularly in the wake of the Illinois pilot project, may be unwilling to change their procedures and courts may be less willing to admit expert testimony on problems associated with simultaneous lineups in the absence of further field testing. Not surprisingly, courts and other nonscientists are more inclined to trust results obtained in settings field rather than in laboratory. All other things being equal, this is a reasonable reaction. But all other things are seldom equal. In particular, we rarely know ground truth in the field for questions about lineups and polygraph testing. More broadly, causal inferences from field tests are well grounded only when the design, implementation, and measurement of the study approximate conditions that can be controlled in the laboratory. That does not mean that laboratory studies are immune from criticism. Researchers in the laboratory often fail to replicate critical attributes of the phenomenon being studied or measured (for a more complete discussion, see Diamond, 1997). The familiar call is for multiple research strategies that produce convergent

---

[5]   It is worth noting that such difficulties did not arise in the Minnesota pilot test (Klobuchar, Steblay, & Caligiuri, 2006).

results. The harder problem is what to do and what conclusions to draw when results do not converge between laboratory and field tests. A meta-analysis can test for consistency across studies, but if field versus laboratory setting is a moderator variable that makes an effect appear or disappear, only a meta-analysis that grapples with the quality of the research can tell us which result better describes the relationship of interest.

Courts increasingly struggle with the issue of "fit" in the form of extrapolation in dealing with both psychological and nonpsychological forms of scientific evidence. The issue emerged as crucial in *Daubert* and its progeny. For example, courts must decide whether claims based on well-designed laboratory-based toxicology experiments on animals provide a sufficient basis to permit a case to go to a jury. They must also determine what to do when a human epidemiological study, however flawed, finds results that differ from those obtained in animal studies addressing the same question. The tendency to prefer epidemiological (field) evidence may be a reasonable heuristic – but when the field study is deeply flawed, the preference is unwarranted. What is required is a detailed analysis of the strengths and weaknesses of each piece of evidence. Psychologists faced with a similar challenge to their research findings from the laboratory must work with courts and other decision-makers in the legal system both to design high quality field tests and to understand the theoretical and methodological strengths (and weaknesses) of results from the laboratory. Psychologists must recognize and address both the allure and the real value of field research, studying both process and outcomes not from a distance, as in the Illinois study, but on the ground.

Psychological research on perception, memory, and social influence have contributed substantially to the education of decision-makers in the legal system and have provided the basis for the increasing acceptance of expert advice from psychological researchers on eyewitness testimony. Yet flawed field studies can undermine the progress of understanding between psychology and law. The response, of course, is critique and more data. It is not hard to see why persuading courts of the value of expert advice, even in this well-studied research area, will continue to call for patience and persistence.

REFERENCES

Daubert v. Merrell Dow Pharmaceuticals, Inc., 509 U.S. 579 (1993).

Diamond, S. S. (1997). Illuminations and shadows from jury simulations, *Law and Human Behavior*, *21*, 561–571.

Doyle, J. M. (2005). *True witness*. New York: Palgrave Macmillan.

Harris, M. J., & Rosenthal, M. (1985). Mediation of interpersonal expectancy effects: 31 Meta-analyses. *Psychological Bulletin 97*, 363–386.

Haw, R. M., & Fisher, R. P. (2004). Effects of administrator–witness contact on eyewitness identification accuracy, *Journal of Applied Psychology*, *89*, 1106–1112.

Kassin, S. M. (1998). Eyewitness identification procedures: The fifth rule, *Law and Human Behavior*, *22*, 649–653.

Kemp, R. J., Pike, G. E., & Brace, N. A. (2001). Video-based identification procedures: Combining best practice and practical requirements when designing identification systems, *Psychology, Public Policy, & Law*, *7*, 802–808.

Klobucher, A., & Caligiuri, H. L. (2005). Protecting the innocent/convicting the guilty: Hennepin County's pilot project in blind sequential eyewitness identification, *William Mitchell Law Review*, *32*, 1–26.

Klobucher, A., Steblay, N., & Caligiuri, H. L. (2006). Improving eyewitness identifications: Hennepin County's blind sequential lineup pilot project, *The Cardozo Public Law, Policy, and Ethics Journal*, *4*, 381–413.

McQuiston-Surrett, D., Malpass, R. S., & Tredoux, C. G. (2006). Sequential vs. simultaneous lineups: A review of methods, data, and theory. *Psychology, Public Policy, & Law*, *12*, 137–169.

Mecklenburg, S. H. (2006, March). *Report to the legislature of the state of Illinois: The Illinois pilot program on sequential double-blind identification procedures.* www.chicagopolice.org/IL%20Pilot%20on%20Eyewitness%20ID.pdf.

Meissner, C. A., & Brigham, J. C. (2001). Thirty years of investigating the own-race bias in memory for faces. *Psychology, Public Policy, & Law*, *7*, 3–35.

National Research Council (1992). *DNA technology in forensic science.* Washington, DC: National Academies Press.

National Research Council (1996). *The evaluation of forensic DNA evidence.* Washington, DC: National Academies Press.

Phillips, M. R., McAuliff, B. D., Kovera, M. B., & Cutler, B. L. (1999). Double-blind photoarrray administration as a safeguard against investigator bias. *Journal of Applied Psychology*, *84*, 940–951.

State v. McKinney, 74 S.W.3d 291 (Tenn.), cert denied, 537 U.S. 926 (2002).

Steblay, N. (1992). A meta-analytic review of the weapon-focus effect. *Law and Human Behavior*, *16*, 413–424.

Steblay, N. (2006, May 3). Observations on the Illinois lineup data. www.nacdl.org/sl_docs.nsf/freeform/eyeID_attachments/$FILE/Steblay-IL_Observations.pdf.

Steblay, N., Dysart, J., Fulero, S., & Lindsay, R. C. L. (2001). Eyewitness accuracy rates in sequential and simultaneous lineup presentation: A meta-analytic comparison, *Law and Human Behavior*, *25*, 459–473.

U.S. Department of Justice (1999). Office of Justice Programs, *Eyewitness evidence: A guide for law enforcement.* National Institute of Justice.

U.S. v. Hines, 55 F. Supp. 2d 62 (D. Mass.) (1999).

U.S. v. Norwood, 939 F. Supp. 1132 (D. N.J.); aff'd 142 F.3d 430 (3rd Cir. 1998) (1996).

Wells, G. L. (1978). Applied eyewitness testimony research: System variables and estimator variables, *Journal of Personal & Social Psychology, 36,* 1546–1557.

Wells, G. L., Malpass, R. S., Lindsay, R. C. L., Fisher, R. P., Turtle, J. W., & Fulero, S. M. (2000). From the lab to the police station: A successful application of eyewitness research, *American Psychologist, 55,* 581–598.

Wright, D. B., & McDaid, A. J. (1996). Comparing system and estimator variables: Using data from real line-ups, *Applied Cognitive Psychology, 10,* 75–84.

Zernike, K. (2006, April 19). Study fuels debate over police lineups, *New York Times*, p. 1.

Beyond Common-sense Understandings of Sex and Race Discrimination

R. Richard Banks

Introduction

A number of the chapters in this volume consider the findings of social psychological research regarding bias and discrimination with respect to race (Crosby & Dovidio, chapter 2; Banks, Eberhardt, & Ross, chapter 1) or sex (Rudman, Glick & Phelan, chapter 5; Eagly & Koenig, chapter 4; Heilman & Haynes, chapter 7; Fitzgerald & Collinsworth, chapter 6). These chapters present the findings of social psychological research in a manner accessible to judges, lawyers, policy-makers, and students. Indeed, the research presented in these chapters is useful for anyone interested in how discrimination might persist in contemporary society, notwithstanding the fact that discrimination is widely prohibited and that nearly everyone claims not to discriminate.

The findings reviewed in these chapters call for a rethinking of the reigning, common-sense understandings of sex and race discrimination. The common-sense view situates sex and race discrimination as the conscious and intentional expression of stereotypes or animus applicable to an entire group. The revision of widespread yet erroneous mental models of discrimination is important because judges may rely on such flawed models in developing and applying antidiscrimination law.[1] Social psychological researchers hope to enhance the courts' ability to detect and eliminate discrimination through refuting the

---

[1] Throughout this commentary, for the sake of convenience I refer to legal decision-makers as judges. Of course, juries also may play an important role as fact finders in many discrimination cases, and legislatures may play an important role in establishing the substantive and procedural rules that govern discrimination cases.

naïve psychological theories on which judges may rely and replacing them with a more accurate and sophisticated understanding of the factors that lead to discriminatory behavior. While experimental researchers do not suggest that laboratory studies can indicate for certain whether discrimination occurred in a specific instance, they do believe that such studies can alert decision-makers to the specific contextual factors that render discrimination more or less likely.

The social psychological research, however, is not wholly critical of prevailing, common-sense understandings. Although the research challenges erroneous understandings of the psychology of discrimination, it passively participates in erroneous understandings of the actual operation of antidiscrimination law. Increasingly, social psychologists (and legal commentators) vigorously refute the common knowledge of discrimination. Yet, the common knowledge of antidiscrimination *law* remains intact, virtually unchallenged.

The common-sense understanding of antidiscrimination law is that it prohibits decision-making on the basis of race or sex. In this account, antidiscrimination law centers on decision-making processes, and nearly always invalidates those decisions that rely on criteria such as race or sex. In fact, however, courts do not judge all race- or sex-dependent decisions as discriminatory, much less categorically prohibit them. More generally, in evaluating the permissibility of a particular practice, courts routinely take into account considerations extrinsic to the decision itself. Indeed, in many cases the declaration of a decision as prohibited discrimination is better understood as a conclusion that the consequences of the decision are unacceptable, rather than simply that the decision relied on race or sex. While social psychological researchers have largely abandoned the common-sense understanding of discrimination, they remain wedded, along with many legal scholars, to the common-sense view of the operation of antidiscrimination law.

The Common Knowledge of Discrimination

Race and sex discrimination are typically envisioned as conscious and intentional.[2] People who discriminate want to do so, the thinking goes. They do so as a result of either irrational animus or overbroad

---

[2]   In earlier eras, discriminatory practices on the basis of race and sex were for the most part overt and intentional. They were also often categorical, disadvantaging all Blacks, for example, or all women. Such discriminatory practices operated purely on the basis of status. Thus, an employer, for example, might not hire any women or any Blacks.

and unfavorable stereotypes, often openly expressed, which are directed toward an entire race or sex group. Whether stemming from stereotypes or animus, sex and race discrimination are often assumed to burden all group members, to operate in what one might term a categorical fashion.

This common way of thinking about discrimination reflects the characteristic forms of discrimination that the struggles of the civil rights era sought to overcome. De jure segregation, for example, limited the rights of all African Americans,[3] and sex discriminatory laws denied all women the right to vote, to serve on juries, and to enter certain occupations. This history provides a psychological template for current thinking about discrimination, causing people to contemplate discrimination now as it was then.

Revising the Common Knowledge of Discrimination

Recent social psychological research persuasively rebuts this commonsense understanding of discrimination. The recent research emphasizes that discrimination need not necessarily result from conscious bias and that it may burden some group members, but not others. Perhaps even more fundamentally, the social psychological research counters the tendency to divide the world up into racists and nonracists (or sexists and nonsexists). The conventional way of thinking conceptualizes discrimination as the expression of some stable trait or disposition with respect to which individuals will differ. A central message of social psychology, however, centers on the importance of context, and highlights the role of the situation in rendering discrimination more or less likely. Social psychological research redirects attention from the individual to the situation.

The role of conscious beliefs

These chapters undermine the view that discrimination is necessarily conscious and intentional. Crosby and Dovidio describe subtle forms

---

[3]   The formal symmetry of the system of de jure segregation known as Jim Crow should not obscure its role in disadvantaging non-Whites. Jim Crow laws prohibited interracial sex and marriage, and mandated racially segregated schools, neighborhoods, public accommodations, public transportation, recreational facilities, and even, restrooms and drinking fountains.

of racial discrimination that may occur without people's awareness, and even among those who genuinely believe themselves to be un-biased. Much gender discrimination, Rudman, Glick and Phelan explain, may result from stereotypes that influence reasoning and behavior in ways of which most people remain unaware. In evaluating a job applicant or employee, for example, gender stereotypes may influence what information one seeks out, how one interprets the available information, and what information one remembers about the employee. In short, a variety of factors might incline one to evaluate a woman, for example, consistent with gender stereotypes, which might make the woman applicant seem less desirable than an equally qualified male applicant.

Stereotyping

These chapters also counter the tendency to tightly couple discrimina-tion with animus or negative stereotypes. Rudman, Glick and Phelan, for example, explain that women may be treated poorly even as a result of seemingly positive stereotypes, which the authors term "paternalis-tic prejudice" (p. 91). The stereotyped perception of women as espe-cially kind and likable, for example, also depicts them as less competent than men. Moreover, women may be judged as kind and likable only insofar as they maintain a low status role. Thus, an ostensibly favorable stereotype may cause someone to treat a woman in a manner that is consistent with, or even reinforces, the woman's low professional status. An individual woman is not exempt from such stereotypes simply because she does not fit them. While stereotypes are not wholly resistant to individuating information, they may only yield when the individuating information is clear and unambiguous (Rudman, Glick & Phelan, chapter 5).

Intragroup distinctions

Recent research also counters the assumption that discrimination typically burdens an entire race or sex group. Rather, discrimination may burden some group members, but not others. Banks, Eberhardt, and Ross describe the findings of research regarding the role of racial prototypicality in the sentencing of criminal defendants. In one of the studies they describe, the researchers examined whether racial prototypicality – that is, how stereotypically Black a defendant appeared – would influence the likelihood that the defendant would be sentenced to death. Using actual data from Philadelphia regarding the sentencing of death eligible defendants, the researchers found that among murderers of White victims, 58% of the African American defendants rated as highly stereotypically Black had been sentenced to death, while only 24% of those rated as low in racial stereotypicality were sentenced to death. This stereotypicality effect remained statistically significant even after controlling for defendant attractiveness and a variety of other nonracial factors that might have influenced sentencing, including aggravating and mitigating circumstances, heinousness of crime, defendant socioeconomic status, and victim socioeconomic status.

This research suggests that in cases with White victims, sentencing juries did not categorically treat African American murderers more harshly than White murderers, so much as they made distinctions among African American murderers in deciding who deserved to die. The more stereotypically Black a defendant appeared, the more likely he was to receive a death sentence.

The importance of context

Perhaps the overriding message of these chapters is that discrimination is a matter of context. Women are more likely to be discriminated against when there is a mismatch or lack of fit between their presumed characteristics as women and the demands of many high status jobs. While women are generally viewed as empathetic, nurturing, and understanding (Rudman, Glick, & Phelan, chapter 5), many high status jobs require the agentic characteristics that are more typically associated with men. Qualities such as empathy are valued among daycare workers, but independence and leadership are valued among corporate lawyers or management consultants. Thus, common stereotypes of women disadvantage them with respect to the latter types of jobs, as their expected or prescribed roles as women conflict with the role of high achieving professional.

For both sex and race, discrimination is more likely in circumstances where a decision-maker exercises substantial discretion. As Heilman and Haynes (chapter 7) note, subjectivity in the appraisal process creates an opportunity for stereotypes to influence evaluations in a way that disadvantages women. They explain that stereotypes produce expectations that, in turn, may shape evaluations. A male supervisor's stereotype of women as ineffectual managers, for example, may lead the supervisor to expect that the woman manager he is evaluating will not be an effective manager. The supervisor may then, unintentionally, attend more closely to information that is consistent with his expectation, remember that information better, and forget or overlook information that is contrary to the expectation. The supervisor, again without intending to, may require significantly less information to confirm his initial expectation than to rebut it. Once the supervisor has enough information to justify or confirm the initial expectation, the evaluative process might cease. In contrast, if the supervisor initially encountered information contrary to the initial expectation, then the supervisor may be more likely to continue the information-gathering process rather than immediately abandon the expectation. It is easy to see, in this sort of scenario, how a common group stereotype – for example, that women are not forceful or effective group leaders – could lead to worse evaluations for a woman than for a man, even if objective indicators of their performance were identical. As Heilman and Haynes explain, "the greater the subjectivity, the more opportunity for stereotype-based expectations to influence evaluative judgments" (p. 127).

Subjective decision-making enables race discrimination as well. The lack of a clear behavioral benchmark permits a decision-maker to discriminate without appearing to do so, and without believing that he or she has done so. Adverse decisions with respect to racial minorities might be explained on the basis of considerations other than race, owing to the many characteristics that are associated with race. The availability of plausible nonracial explanations not only permits one to credibly deny that one has discriminated, but also to maintain one's image of oneself as racially unbiased (Crosby & Dovidio, chapter 2).

Just as there is a common-sense account of discrimination, there are also common-sense expectations about the responses of victims of sex discrimination. Fitzgerald and Collinsworth undermine widely held beliefs about victims of sexual harassment. Most counterintuitively perhaps, they rebut the common-sense notion that not reporting an incident as sexual harassment suggests either that it was not regarded seriously or that it was welcome (in which case it was not harassment). Victims of sexual harassment might not report, they tell us, because victims often believe, sometimes correctly, that reporting would only make things worse, in part by exacerbating feelings of embarrassment or shame. Victims might instead cope with being harassed by trying to avoid, or even appease, the harasser. Fitzgerald and Collinsworth also identify aspects of the organizational climate that may either discourage or promote sexual harassment, in part by rendering its reporting either an avenue of remedy or a means of further victimization.

The Common-sense Account of Antidiscrimination Law

While the social psychological research critiques common intuitions about discrimination, it embodies a common-sense understanding of the operation of antidiscrimination law. The common-sense understanding of antidiscrimination law is that the nondiscrimination mandate nearly categorically prohibits the decision-makers to whom it applies from basing decisions on impermissible factors such as sex or race.[4] A decision is judged discriminatory, in this account, if it relies on impermissible criteria such as race or sex,[5] and if a decision is discriminatory, it is nearly always prohibited.

This conventional account of antidiscrimination law is almost universally accepted. It is embraced by most social psychological researchers and legal scholars alike. Indeed, one might even observe that many of the chapters in this volume relating to sex or race discrimination presuppose that whether a decision relies on an impermissible factor such as race or sex is what determines whether the decision will be identified by a court as discriminatory and hence prohibited. Similarly, legal scholarship that critiques courts' identification of discrimination typically presumes that what courts are, and should be, doing is invalidating those decisions that rely on race or sex. Moreover, this common account of antidiscrimination law is reflected in the opinions of the judges who interpret and apply that law. Quite simply, it is what judges say the law requires and how they explain their own rulings. Judges have often declared that employment discrimination law, for example, prohibits decisions based on sex or race stereotypes.

Revising the Common Knowledge of Antidiscrimination Law

The common-sense account of antidiscrimination law, however, does not adequately explain courts' application of the law. To see the

---

[4] According to this conventional view, the law does not, as a general matter, circumscribe employment outcomes, but only the decision-making processes. The task for judges or other fact finders, in this view, is to identify those decisions that rely on some impermissible consideration such as sex or race.

[5] The question of whether antidiscrimination law does, or should, prohibit unintentional discrimination is not especially salient as long as the conventional image of discrimination is embraced.

difficulties with understanding the operation of antidiscrimination law solely on the basis of whether a decision relies on race or sex, consider a few examples.

First, consider a young black female – let's call her Andrea – who has a bad day. Andrea's application for a waitress job at a restaurant is rejected, as is her application to rent an available apartment. Disgruntled, she files a lawsuit against the employer and the owner of the apartment complex, in both cases alleging racial discrimination. Both the employer and the landlord introduce uncontradicted evidence that they have many African American employees and tenants, respectively. Andrea produces evidence that she was denied the job and the apartment because of how she speaks. She admits that she speaks a strong form of Black English. None of the current employees or tenants speak Black English to the extent Andrea does. Andrea argues that she was discriminated against for being a speaker of Black English, and that such adverse treatment constitutes racial discrimination in violation of the law.

Would Andrea prevail on her claims? If the court accepts her contention that she was denied the apartment because the landlord did not like to rent to speakers of Black English, she might well prevail on that claim. However, she would be less likely to prevail on her employment discrimination claim, even if the court similarly accepted the evidence that her being a Black English speaker accounted for the adverse decision. Having been treated poorly because she is a Black English speaker might entitle Andrea to prevail in one case, but not the other.

How could one explain contrary rulings in cases that seem so similar? Although different federal statutes would govern the two cases, the applicable statutes ostensibly embody the same prohibition of racial discrimination.[6] And in both cases Andrea produced persuasive evidence that her use of Black English prompted the defendant to treat her poorly. Thus, if reliance on certain decisional criteria determines the permissibility of a challenged action Andrea should either win or lose in both cases, not win one but lose the other. If being treated poorly because she is a Black English speaker counts as racial discrimination in one case, then it would in the other as well.

One might explain the different outcomes in these cases on the basis of intuitions about the likely relative weight of the interests of potential defendants and potential plaintiffs in each setting. The

---

[6]   The employment claim would be governed by the federal employment discrimination law, known as Title VII. The apartment rental case would be governed by federal Fair Housing Act. Of course, state or local antidiscrimination laws may apply as well.

court may be balancing the interests of the plaintiff against those of the defendant, and considering the sort of treatment to which potential tenants or employees should be legally entitled in each context. A court might determine, for example, that prospective tenants who are able to pay the rent and can show themselves to be financially responsible are entitled to an available apartment, unless they behave in a disruptive manner that impacts other tenants. The landlord's decision not to rent the apartment to Andrea because of her use Black English would have breached that entitlement. In contrast, in the employment context the court might reason that an employer assembling a workforce has a weightier and more legitimate interest in how employees speak than does a landlord in how tenants speak. After all, being able to speak in a certain manner, which may facilitate communication with customers and coworkers, could be considered a requirement of the position that an employer seeks to fill. For that reason the employer may be granted leeway in considering prospective employees' speech patterns.

Two points bear emphasis: (1) The cases could come out differently; and (2) the different outcomes in these two cases need not be viewed as inconsistent or indefensible. There would be an underlying logic to a court's determination that the employer should prevail, and that the landlord should lose. That logic, though, cannot be found by trying to decide whether each defendant "discriminated on the basis of race." Both defendants took Andrea's use of Black English into account. Yet, a court might well have found racial discrimination in one case but not the other. A finding of discrimination in one case but not the other would be a conclusion, a way of saying that Andrea should have been permitted to rent the apartment, but that she was not entitled to have an employer disregard her manner of speaking.

This characterization of a hypothetical court's reasoning process recasts the common-sense understanding of the operation of antidiscrimination law. The conventional understanding would be that the court ruled against the landlord, say, *because* the court found that the landlord discriminated on the basis of race. In my alternative account, one might say, instead, that the court found that the landlord discriminated on the basis of race *because* the court believed that Andrea should have been permitted to rent the apartment, that her use of Black English is not a sufficient reason to deny her that apartment. The conclusion that the landlord racially discriminated would not be the means by which the court reached its judgment in favor of Andrea, so much as a justification, a way of validating the ruling consistent with the formal requirements of the law. Similarly, a finding that the employer did not engage in racial discrimination might reflect the view that the employer should for some positions at least, be permitted to consider applicants' manner of speech. One need not wholly reject the common-sense account of antidiscrimination law in order to acknowledge its inadequacy in accounting for and justifying the actual operation of the law.[7]

This same point applies even more obviously with respect to sex discrimination. It is often assumed that antidiscrimination law prohibits decisions that are animated by sex stereotyping – that is, by judgments that a woman (or man) does or should conform to characteristics associated with women (or men). Decisions animated by sex stereotypes are thus thought to violate the nondiscrimination mandate, understood as a prohibition of the consideration of impermissible criteria such as race or sex. But, in fact, courts do not enforce any such categorical prohibition, and most of us would not want them to do so. Consider, in this regard, the most famous of all stereotyping cases, *Hopkins v. Price Waterhouse* (1989), the essential reference in any discussion of sex stereotyping and the law.

Ann Hopkins sued her employer Price Waterhouse, claiming that it discriminated against her on the basis of sex in its consideration of her for a partnership position in the firm. Hopkins was the only woman among the 88 nominees for partnership in 1982. Hopkins was denied partnership that year, and put over to the next year, at which time the firm declined to reconsider her case. Hopkins then sued. In support of her sex discrimination claim, Hopkins introduced evidence that one partner, in counseling her about how to improve her chances of being made partner, recommended that she walk, talk, and dress in a more feminine manner, and wear more makeup. Other evidence suggested that a number of the firm's partners regarded Hopkins as too manly and aggressive.

The Supreme Court upheld Hopkins' sex discrimination claim, describing gender stereotyping as a form of sex discrimination. The Court reasoned that "we are beyond the day when an employer could evaluate employees by assuming or insisting that they matched the stereotype associated with their group" (p. 251).[8] This

---

[7] There is truth, of course, in both accounts. The relationship between judgments of discrimination and unfairness is bidirectional. We are more likely to judge an outcome we think unfair as discriminatory, and we are also more likely to think that an adverse decision is unfair if it is discriminatory.

[8] What I refer to as the Court's opinion was actually an opinion of four Justices. There was no majority opinion.

language clearly states that gender stereotyping is impermissible. More specifically, the Court seems to be saying that prescriptive gender stereotypes – ideas about how women should behave – cannot be the basis of an adverse employment action. Some commentators have concluded, based on this language in the Court's opinion, that any decision premised on prescriptive sex stereotypes is prohibited by federal antidiscrimination law.

Such a reading, however, would be inconsistent both with courts' actual application of the nondiscrimination mandate and with widely held intuitions about the legitimacy of workplace rules. It is unlikely that the Supreme Court actually intended to prohibit all adverse employment actions that result from sex stereotypes. As a practical matter, lower federal courts, which are bound to apply Supreme Court precedent, have not identified all forms of prescriptive sex stereotyping as instances of sex discrimination. Consider, for example, sex specific dress codes or grooming requirements. An employer might prohibit dresses and shoulder length hair, for example, when worn by men, but not when worn by women. Such workplace rules are certainly a reflection of prescriptive gender stereotypes. The employer might honestly and straightforwardly explain that he would fire any man who comes to work in a dress because "that is not how men should conduct themselves" and that "if a man wants to work here, he should dress like a man." Now, if we understand the antidiscrimination rule, as elaborated in *Price Waterhouse*, to prohibit all prescriptive sex stereotyping, then a dress-wearing man would prevail in a sex discrimination claim. He would have a right to be free of workplace rules that reflect sex stereotypes and thus could wear his dress (certainly as long as women were also permitted to wear dresses). But, of course, dress-wearing men do not usually prevail in such cases. Moreover, a dress-wearing man would likely not receive much sympathy from friends and colleagues. Most people accept that an employer should be able to enforce a "no dresses on men" policy.

That the dress-wearing man would almost certainly lose the case suggests that the prohibition of sex discrimination in the workplace should not be understood to preclude all decision-making that reflects sex stereotypes. Sex stereotypes are integral to every workplace with sex specific grooming and dress codes. In other words, sex stereotypes are central to nearly every workplace. Permitting policies based on such sex stereotypes does not mean that we tragically fall short of our aspirations, but rather that neither judges nor regular people actually view all policies that are informed by sex stereotypes as objectionable. We not only permit sex specific dress and grooming norms, we endorse them. Even those who most adamantly oppose sex stereo-types in the abstract would probably conclude that an employer should be able to prohibit men from wearing dresses without being liable for sex discrimination.

The Supreme Court itself, in *Price Waterhouse*, offered a narrower formulation of the sex stereotyping prohibition. The Court reasoned that "An employer who objects to aggressiveness in women but whose positions require this trait places women in an intolerable and imper-missible catch-22: out of a job if they behave aggressively and out of a job if they do not" (p. 251). On this account, Ann Hopkins was wronged not so much because she was subject to sex stereotyping, but because there seemed such a slim chance that she could both conform to the gender stereotype *and* be successful at the firm.[9] Some of the firm's partners thought she should act in a more feminine manner, even as the qualities associated with advancement likely included unfeminine characteristics such as assertiveness and determination. In sum, then, the violation of the nondiscrimination mandate may have inhered in the double bind, rather than the employer's reliance on sex stereotypes per se.

If the problem is the double bind, rather than sex stereotypes per se, then knowing that an employer relied on a sex stereotype would not be enough to decide the case. In a case like *Price Waterhouse*, the court might also consider the extent of the incompatibility of such sex stereotyping and other workplace expectations, and the actual impact on the employment prospects of women. In *Price Waterhouse*, for example, a court might have legitimately accorded some substantial weight to the fact that only 1% of the firm's partners were women, and that women generally fare less well than men in such well-paying and high status professions. All of this is a way of saying that a court would be correct to evaluate the case in light of the goals of antidis-crimination law, one of which unquestionably is to integrate outsider groups such as women into elite occupations from which they have been historically excluded. Such considerations, though, go far beyond the question of whether an employer took sex into account in making an employment decision.

Not only is the consideration of an employee's sex an insufficient condition for a declaration of sex discrimination, it may not even be necessary. Consider, for example, the sort of subjective evaluation

---

[9]   Of the 662 partners at Price Waterhouse in 1982, 7 were women. In my view, this statistic suggests that while it was not impossible to reconcile the conflicting demands the catch-22 imposed, it was extremely difficult to do so.

process contemplated by Heilman and Haynes, one in which the evaluative criteria are open ended and not based on tangible or objectively verifiable outcomes. Suppose that an employer uses such a process to evaluate low-level employees, and women fare less well than men in that process. Most of the managers who perform the evaluations are men and low-level employees who are men seem to be evaluated more favorably and to receive more promotions than low-level women employees. Consistent with the research described by Heilman and Haynes, expert testimony might indicate that sex stereotyping or bias is especially likely in such a subjective evaluation process.

Suppose, though, that the employer argues that men fare better in the process than women not as a result of sex stereotypes or bias, but simply because people tend to evaluate their friends more favorably than other employees with whom they have no personal relationship. More specifically, the employer notes that the managers who perform the evaluations are, for a variety of permissible reasons, mostly men, and that these managers, again for a variety of reasons, are much more likely to be friends with lower-level male employees than with lower-level female employees. The employer asserts that the managers, who are mostly men, evaluate their buddies (usually men) more favorably than other employees with whom they have had little personal interaction, and that this fact, rather than sex per se, accounts for the wide disparity in the evaluations of men and women. Should the outcome of this case turn on the plausibility of the employer's proffered explanation?

If the nondiscrimination mandate is understood simply to prohibit sex-based decision-making attributable to the employer, then the outcome would indeed turn on the persuasiveness of the employer's alternative explanation. If it seemed likely that sex bias or stereotypes influenced the evaluation of women employees, then a court should pronounce the employer guilty of sex discrimination. But suppose there was convincing evidence that personal relationships, rather then sex stereotypes or bias, explained the differences in the evaluations of men and women – perhaps even an empirical study showing that women with personal ties to the managers were as likely as men with similar ties to be promoted. Then, if a challenged action's permissibility is simply a matter of decisional criteria, a court should absolve the employer of liability for sex discrimination.[10]

---

[10]   In this discussion, I am putting to the side the disparate impact component of employment discrimination law, which prohibits the employer from adopting practices that disproportionately burden a protected group without adequate justification.

In fact, however, the employer could be held liable irrespective of the strength of evidence that friendship rather than sex stereotypes explained the differential evaluations of men and women. From the perspective of the women employees, the process would probably seem no less unfair than if the evaluation process had been infected with stereotyped assumptions about women's management or leadership skills. One might expect a judge that views the process as unfair to women to rule in the plaintiff's favor, no matter how strong the employer's evidence that friendship patterns accounted for the observed outcomes. And if that is the case, then the court's application of the sex discrimination prohibition cannot be understood simply as an effort to rid a decision-making process of sex bias or stereotypes. (For purposes of this discussion, I have put aside the question of the precise doctrinal rubrics on which a court might rely, and instead critiqued the common tendency to equate the sex discrimination prohibition with the use of certain prohibited decisional criteria.)

The Centrality of Context in Law and Psychology

This discussion suggests that context is central not only in social psychology, but in the application of antidiscrimination law as well. A central message of the social psychological research is that discrimination is a matter of – or more specifically a product of – context. Although often explained in terms of some stable trait with respect to which individuals may differ, the likelihood of discrimination is very much a consequence of the particular circumstances and setting in which a decision is made.

Antidiscrimination law, described by courts and commentators as a search for decisions based upon impermissible criteria such as race or sex, seems much less attentive to context than does social psychology. However, as I have suggested, courts probably do, and should, consider a variety of contextual factors that bear on the question of fairness in deciding whether to conclude that an employer has violated the law.

Judicial application of the nondiscrimination mandate that incorporates a contextual analysis of unfairness may deviate both from the formal dictates of the law and from the common-sense understanding of the law. But it comports well with widespread moral intuitions, which also inform judges' application of the law. We do not categorically oppose all sex- or race-dependent decision-making, so much as we oppose those decisions whose consequences we view as unacceptable. We do not think that all instances of race- and sex-dependent decision-making are equally objectionable, or objectionable at all.

Also, we might view an employment practice as unfair – in other words, as something that should be prohibited – even if no individual makes a decision on the basis of race or sex.

Explaining the Asymmetry in Acceptance of the Common-sense Account

Why are erroneous beliefs about the operation of antidiscrimination law more enduring among social psychological researchers and legal scholars, than erroneous beliefs about discrimination? One possibility is that the combination of skepticism toward one and easy acceptance of the other enables the remediation by courts of the persistent sex and race disparities that are so troubling to many social psychological researchers and legal scholars alike.

Common knowledge understandings of discrimination are not only a reflection of historical memory, they are also a means of making sense of the world, in particular persistent sex and race disparities. If one thinks of discrimination in terms of overt practices that are intended to categorically disadvantage nearly all members of a group, then, since the "Whites only" and "no women need apply" signs have come down, there might seem to be not much sex or race discrimination in contemporary society. One simply would not see it. If discrimination lingers only as an inconsequential vestige of a bygone era, then persistent sex and race disparities – for example, that the executive suites of most corporations remain White and male – would presumably not be a consequence of current discrimination. Such disparities might then seem less objectionable. Alternatively, if one understands discrimination as subtle, unintentional, and context specific, then the possibility that race and sex disparities in contemporary society result from current discrimination would seem more plausible, and the disparities themselves less legitimate. To say that race and sex disparities reflect current discrimination is to say that such disparities should be viewed as morally unacceptable and that the courts should rectify them. An expansive view of discrimination provides a way of making that claim.

The same sort of equality-oriented sentiments may explain scholars' acceptance of the common knowledge of antidiscrimination law. The legitimacy of the courts as the agents that enforce antidiscrimination law depends partly on the perception that they neutrally apply rules. Courts must sort out the facts of a particular case, but they are not to make the sort of politically oriented value judgments that seem the province of legislatures. Judges who seek to impose their own values are derided as "activists," which is to be accused of having abandoned one's judicial role and debased the institution. Thus, neither judges nor researchers and legal scholars would be inclined to run the risk of unmasking the value judgments that invariably inform judicial application of antidiscrimination law. Doing so might also undermine the political consensus supporting judicial enforcement of the law. For a judge to say that she is ruling against an employer because the employer engaged in sex or race discrimination is to apply a norm to which everyone agrees. For the judge to say that she ruled against the employer because the employer's practice was unfair to Blacks or to women would be to step onto shakier ground.

The Role of Social Psychology in Antidiscrimination Law

If, as I have suggested, the search for a discriminatory decision is not as central to judicial decision-making as commonly thought, then the role of social psychological research, and of social science more generally, is also not as commonly understood. The findings of social psychological research do not, and should not, dictate antidiscrimination law. The law rests on many foundations and pursues many goals. Nonetheless, the research findings regarding race and sex discrimination are unquestionably important. Social psychological research might prompt courts to see discrimination where they would not otherwise find it. Or it might provide justification for a decision that the court would have wanted to reach anyway, bolstering the credibility of a controversial ruling. Whatever the mix of roles that social psychological research performs, it will undoubtedly continue to figure prominently in the development of antidiscrimination law.

REFERENCE

Hopkins v. Price Waterhouse, 490 U.S. 228 (1989).

Behavioral Realism in Law: Reframing the Discussion About Social Science's Place in Antidiscrimination Law and Policy

Linda Hamilton Krieger

In their introduction to this volume, editors Eugene Borgida and Susan Fiske describe the book's central purposes as being to identify social science research findings on which most reasonable scholars could agree and to explore whether those findings and their implications might properly educate fact finders in legal proceedings. This framing of the volume's aims tends to direct our attention to a particular problem, namely, the proper role of the social science expert witness whose testimony is offered at trial to educate jurors about some case-relevant phenomenon that social scientists study.

It is understandable that the problem of empirical social science's proper role in adjudication would be framed this way. After all, as the introduction also describes, the project grew out of a panel discussion at the American Psychological Society's 2004 annual meeting featuring substantive presentations and commentaries by, among others, four social psychologists who had previously provided trial testimony in highly contentious discrimination cases. Trials are dramatic events, and therefore highly salient. When we debate the proper role of insights from the empirical social sciences in law, our attention is naturally drawn to the drama of the trial, particularly the jury trial.

Once framed in terms of expert trial testimony, the contours of the ensuing discussion are defined largely by the dictates of Rule 702 of the Federal Rules of Evidence, which requires that expert testimony "assist the trier of fact to understand the evidence or to determine a fact in issue,"[1] and by the case law interpreting that Rule.[2] Viewed through the trial testimony frame, our thoughts about the proper relationship between law and empirical social science inexorably center on the following sorts of questions:

- Can a social science expert *ever* properly provide an opinion on an ultimate fact at issue in a case, such as whether unconstrained gender stereotyping negatively affected a particular employment decision, or does such testimony both invade the fact-finding province of the jury and overstep the bounds of what science can validly contribute to the fact-finding process?[3]
- To what extent does social science expert testimony based at least in substantial part on laboratory as opposed to field experiments bear ecological validity and therefore a "valid scientific connection"[4] to real-world events at issue in a particular case?
- If the subject of proposed social science testimony arguably lies within the realm of jurors' ordinary experience, should expert testimony on those subjects be deemed "unhelpful" and therefore inadmissible under *Daubert v. Merrell Dow Pharmaceuticals, Inc.* (1993) and the cases that follow it?[5]
- To the extent that members of the social scientific community disagree on issues like the ecological validity of controlled laboratory experiments, should those disagreements go to the weight accorded expert testimony, or should they be deemed serious enough to render such testimony inadmissible?[6]

---

[1]   Rule 702 of the Federal Rules of Evidence provides: "If scientific, technical, or other specialized knowledge will assist the trier of fact to understand the evidence or to determine a fact in issue, a witness qualified as an expert by knowledge, skill, experience, training, or education, may testify thereto in the form of an opinion or otherwise."

[2]   These cases include, most notably, *Daubert v. Merrell Dow Pharmaceuticals, Inc.* (1993) and *Kumho Tire Co. v. Carmichael* (1999).

[3]   See, e.g., *EEOC v. Morgan Stanley* (2004), 460–462, regarding the proposed expert testimony of Dr William Bielby in Title VII systemic sex discrimination case. For a thorough treatment of this problem see David L. Faigman's (1999) commentary appearing elsewhere entitled "The Limits of Science in the Courtroom."

[4]   *Daubert* (1993), 591–592.

[5]   See, e.g., *United States v. Hall* (1996; expert testimony re: false confessions admitted over objection that the subject of the expert's testimony were within the ordinary experience of lay persons); *Ray v. Miller Maester Advertising, Inc.* (2003; 334–336, expert testimony on the mechanisms through which sex stereotypes may have lead to discrimination against the plaintiff was excluded as unhelpful on the grounds that "virtually all adults in our society know about gender stereotypes"); *Kotla v. Regents of the University of California* (2004; same).

[6]   See, e.g., *EEOC* (2004), 461–462.

All of these (and many other) questions about the proper role of expert social science trial testimony in antidiscrimination litigation ultimately relate to a root question posed by David Faigman: whether science's ability to "discover the universals hiding among the particulars" can helpfully inform the trial process's effort to discover "the particulars hiding among the universals" (Faigman, 1999, p. 69). If we frame the question of social science's role in law as a question about expert trial testimony, this is, of course, the question that matters most.

But if in thinking about the proper place of empirical social science in civil rights adjudications, we focus solely on expert trial testimony, we frame the inquiry far too narrowly. Very little of the civil adjudication process occurs in the trial context. For one, fewer than 2% of civil cases even go to trial (Galanter, 2004). Most civil cases that go to judgment (as opposed to settling) are decided not at trial, but by judges in summary judgment motions or motions for judgment as a matter of law. In this group of cases, which in the discrimination context are almost always decided in the employer's favor, a judge, reviewing the evidentiary record adduced in discovery or at trial, has decided that the facts are too "one-sided" in the defendant's favor to justify sending the case to a jury. (Berger, Finkelstein, & Chang, 2005; Clermont & Schwab, 2004).

A review of the summary adjudication case law readily reveals that it is not only jurors, or judges acting as fact finders at bench trials, who bring "common knowledge" to bear on discrimination adjudications; trial level and appellate court judges deciding issues of law regularly do so as well. Reading judicial opinions in discrimination cases, a social science-trained eye can readily identify several "common-sense" psychological theories, running like rebar through the opinions' analytical foundations and, over time, giving shape to the doctrinal "universals" that will govern the adjudication of the "particulars" in future cases. If one were to compare the content of these opinions with the various contributions to this book bearing on race, age, and gender bias one would readily see that the common-sense theories informing judicial conceptions of what discrimination is, what causes it to occur, and how its presence or absence can best be determined in specific cases are often wrong. In many significant respects, the behavioral models embedded in discrimination jurisprudence have been disconfirmed by decades of empirical social science research (Krieger, 1995; Krieger & Fiske, 2006).

As I will attempt to illustrate in the discussion that follows, federal judges who preside over antidiscrimination cases would gain much from reading the discrimination-related contributions to this volume. Judges, no less than jurors, bring their lay psychological theories into the courtroom, and the "intuitive psychologist behind the bench" (Krieger, 2004; Ross, 1978) has as many shortcomings as any other. Unfortunately however, because the judge is not an expert witness, when he or she brings intuitive behavioral theories to bear in legal decision-making, there is no *Daubert* inquiry scrutinizing their validity.

Behavioral Theories in Law

Judges use theories of human behavior for many different purposes. For example, they use them when they interpret ambiguous statutory provisions that implicate perception, judgment, or choice. Consider, for example, Title VII of the Civil Rights Act of 1964,[7] which prohibits employment discrimination based on race, color, sex, national origin, or religion. When originally enacted in 1964, Title VII made it unlawful to discriminate on the basis of certain protected characteristics, but it nowhere defined what "discrimination" meant. Over time, as judges applied their common-sense notions of how discrimination influenced employment decision-making, they developed a doctrinal model that assumed that when bias influences an employment decision, it "crowds out" all other considerations. Under this doctrinal model of what discriminatory motivation is, and how it functions, courts came to understand an employer-defendant's proffered nondiscriminatory explanation for a challenged decision as necessarily being either the employer's "real" reason – excluding discrimination as a causal factor – or a "cover-up" for the "real," discriminatory motive (Krieger 1995, 2004; Krieger & Fiske, 2006).

Congress eventually acted to override this rule, when in 1991 it amended Title VII to provide that actionable discrimination occurred whenever someone's race, sex, color, national origin, or religion was a "motivating factor" in an employment decision, even if other factors played a motivating role as well.[8] Again, however, Congress did not define what it meant by a "motivating factor." Motivation can be interpreted as "actuation," that which causes someone to act in a particular way, or it can be understood as self-conscious intentionality (Krieger & Fiske, 2006). Given these equally plausible competing interpretations of ambiguous statutory text, courts continue to apply

---

[7]   42 U.S.C. §2000e, *et. seq.*
[8]   Section 703(m), Title VII of the Civil Rights Act of 1964, as amended, 42 U.S.C. §2000e-4(m).

lay psychological theories in Title VII adjudications, at the trial court level and on appeal.

So, in 1964 and again in 1991, Congress made clear that some subjective mental process was an essential element of at least some forms of Title VII liability, but it left the courts to describe precisely what that subjective mental process is and how courts should go about identifying it in individual cases. Because a subjective mental state is an essential element of most employment discrimination cases, discrimination jurisprudence necessarily reflects and reifies a particular theory of mind. Legal theories of intergroup discrimination necessarily implicate psychological theories of intergroup perception, judgment, and behavior. There is no keeping social psychology out of discrimination jurisprudence; it is simply a question of whether the social psychology embedded in discrimination jurisprudence will be ad hoc and a priori, or self-consciously informed by advances in the empirical social sciences.

Judges use intuitive behavioral theories in other ways as well. For example, whether interpreting statutes or shaping common law doctrines, judges often choose among competing legal rules with an eye toward structuring individual or organizational incentives so as to encourage desirable behaviors and discourage undesirable ones. In doing this, judges necessarily draw upon models of individual and organizational motivation and behavior as they reason about the likely consequences flowing from competing legal policy choices. Obviously, if in predicting the behavioral consequences of a particular legal rule, a judge applies a faulty theory of human or organizational behavior, the resulting legal doctrine is unlikely to function effectively to achieve the judicially desired result.

Even outside of the jury decision-making context, behavioral theories play a significant role in factual adjudication. In civil litigation, judges are given various tools for controlling and limiting the fact finding authority of juries. In exercising this control, judges interpret and make decisions about facts, and in doing so, they bring intuitive psychological theories to bear. Judges use lay psychological theories, for example, when they craft or choose between competing jury instructions on issues implicating social perception, judgment, motivation, or choice. They also use behavioral theories when, in the context of summary judgment motions or motions for judgment as a matter of law, they decide what inferences can "reasonably" be drawn from particular facts, or whether a given set of facts, combined with "reasonable" inferences, would "reasonably" support a jury's finding in the nonmoving party's favor (Krieger & Fiske, 2006).

In short, as the following examples will illustrate, judges regularly use "common-sense" psychological theories in the construction and justification of legal doctrines. Sometimes these theories enter judicial decisions as mere rhetorical flourishes, deployed to legitimate decisions made for reasons bearing no relation to the empirical validity of the theory itself. However they are introduced into legal reasoning, such theories are rarely examined in any critical way, and there exists no *Daubert*-style mechanism for systematically scrutinizing them. Nonetheless, once they are embedded in legal decisions, judges' intuitive psychological theories, however flawed or incomplete, assume the status of precedent, and as such, they become quite difficult to dislodge or revise. This is a serious problem, worthy of our concentrated, interdisciplinary attention.

Behavioral Realism in Law

The contributors to this volume were asked to identify research findings and implications on which most reasonable scholars could agree, and to consider how those findings and implications might assist fact finders in litigation. Equally important, I suggest, is the task of considering how those findings and implications might assist judges in their roles as "law finders."

Of course, some commentators have criticized the use of social science in shaping antidiscrimination doctrine (Zick, 2003; Wechsler, 1959). However, these critics tend to ignore one extremely important point – social psychology is already *in* antidiscrimination doctrine, and it was put there not by psychological scientists, but by nonscientist judges applying intuitive psychological theories. In discrimination cases as in others, judges are constantly using "intuitive" or "common-sense" psychological theories in the construction and justification of legal rules, and in their application to specific legal disputes. This is probably unavoidable, but when those theories have been disconfirmed by advances in the empirical social sciences, their continued use violates Justice Oliver Wendell Holmes' admonition that, "The first call of a theory of law is that it should fit the facts" (Holmes, 1963, p. 167).

The various contributions to this volume are useful then not only in thinking about how consensus findings from empirical social psychology might assist jurors and other adjudicative fact finders, they are useful in advancing the larger program of what has come to be known as behavioral realism in law (Krieger & Fiske, 2006; Kang & Banaji,

2006; Blasi & Jost, 2006). Behavioral realism, understood as a pre-scriptive theory of judging, stands for the proposition that as judges develop and elaborate substantive legal doctrines, they should guard against basing their analyses on inaccurate conceptions of relevant real-world phenomena (Krieger & Fiske, 2006). In the context of antidiscrimination law, behavioral realism stands for the proposition that judicial models of what discrimination is, what causes it to occur, how it can be prevented, and how its presence or absence can best be discerned in particular cases, should be periodically revisited and revised so as to remain continuous with progress in psychological science.

The discussion that follows offers two examples of how the contri-butions to this volume relating to intergroup perception and judgment might help advance the behavioral realist agenda in employment dis-crimination law. The first of these examples relates to sexual harass-ment law, specifically, to the Supreme Court's construction of an affirmative defense to claims of hostile work environment. The second concerns a judicially created legal rule called the "same actor infer-ence," which is commonly used in summary adjudications in employ-ment discrimination cases and in judicial selection of jury instructions to be used in employment discrimination trials.

Behavioral Realism and "Preventive Law:" The Case of Sexual Harassment

In choosing among competing answers to contested legal questions, judges often consider the effects they think various approaches will have in furthering the law's normative goals. Along these lines, over the past decade the United States Supreme Court has crafted legal doctrines in antidiscrimination jurisprudence with an eye toward "pre-vention," toward structuring incentives so as to encourage people and organizations to act in particular ways and to forbear from acting in others (Bisom-Rapp, 2001).

When judges craft legal rules to shape incentives and thereby further the law's normative goals, they necessarily draw upon models of indi-vidual and organizational motivation and behavior. Sometimes the models on which judges draw are simply assumed to be accurate, even though they represent testable theories that have been subjected to scrutiny – sometimes even disconfirmation – in the empirical social sciences.

In the antidiscrimination context, the legal doctrine governing employer liability for hostile work environment harassment by supervisors illustrates how judges sometimes use unexamined behavioral theories when they craft "preventive" legal doctrines. Specifically, in two cases decided in 1998, *Faragher v. City of Boca Raton* (1998) and *Burlington Industries v. Ellerth* (1998), the Supreme Court established an affirmative defense to Title VII claims of hostile work environment harassment by supervisors. The defense permits an employer to defeat an otherwise meritorious hostile work environment harassment claim if it can show that it had promulgated antiharassment policies and instituted antiharassment education and grievance procedures, and that the plaintiff had failed to use those procedures early in an escalating sequence of harassing events (Beiner, 2005; Grossman, 2003).

Writing for the *Faragher* majority, Justice Souter acknowledged that the Court's decision to establish the affirmative defense deviated from a long line of cases applying agency principles holding employers responsible for tortious conduct by their supervisory employees. Justice Souter justified this departure, however, on utilitarian grounds. By providing employers with incentives to institute antiharassment policies, education programs, and grievance procedures, and by encouraging employees to complain early in an escalating sequence of harassing events, the new affirmative defense would, Justice Souter opined, serve Title VII's "primary objective," which he described as being "not to provide redress but to avoid harm" (*Faragher*, 1998, p. 806).

The Court's reasoning in *Faragher* reflects a particular set of unstated and unexamined, but empirically testable, assumptions. First, the Court assumes that by promulgating policies against harassment and by establishing antiharassment education and grievance procedures, employers will prevent harassment from occurring, or will, at the very least, significantly decrease its incidence. Second, the Court's analysis rests on the premise that employees who are subjected to unwelcome sexualized workplace conduct will use an employer-run grievance procedure if one is provided, and that they will do so before the conduct becomes egregious.

In chapter 6 Louise Fitzgerald and Linda Collinsworth powerfully illustrate how questionable these assumptions actually are. As they and numerous other researchers and commentators have observed, little if any empirical support exists for the proposition that antiharassment policies, training programs, or internal grievance procedures actually reduce the amount of unwanted sexualized conduct, or discrimination more generally, in the workplace (Kalev, Dobbin, & Kelly, 2006;

Beiner, 2005; Grossman, 2003). Moreover, as Fitzgerald and Collinsworth describe, a great deal of empirical evidence indicates that reporting through existing internal grievance mechanisms is a relatively rare response to unwanted sexualized workplace conduct, and that women generally have reasonable justifications for their decisions not to report. In other words, in their efforts to use the *Faragher/Ellerth* affirmative defense to structure incentives and ultimately prevent harassment from occurring, the justices appear to have presumed a behavioral world that does not in fact exist.

If sexual harassment doctrine is premised on the empirical claim that antiharassment policies, training, and grievance procedures reduce harassment, or that "reasonable" women will use those procedures early in an escalating sequence of harassing events, and if these claims are as empirically shaky as Fitzgerald and Collingsworth's review article demonstrates, the justices' attempt to deploy the *Faragher/Ellerth* affirmative defense to prevent harassment from occurring will fail to achieve its policy objectives. Rather than preventing harassment from occurring, the affirmative defense will simply operate to defeat otherwise legally meritorious harassment claims.

Of course, apart from judicial attempts to engineer incentives, legal rules can be devised to serve other functions, about which empiricism has little if anything to say. So, for example, the Court might have premised the *Faragher/Ellerth* defense on the notion that it would be unfair to impose liability on an employer that was at least trying to ensure that its employees complied with the ambiguous and often conflicting sets of legal and practical considerations that sexual harassment law implicates. Or, the Court might have based the *Faragher/ Ellerth* defense on the grounds that, as a matter of judicial economy, if an employer provides an internal grievance mechanism for redressing harassment claims and if an allegedly aggrieved employee has failed to use it, she should not be allowed to seek redress from the already overburdened federal court system. Legal doctrines can be, and often are, premised on normative principles about which empirical research has little to say.

However, empiricism is indispensable to sound consequential analysis. A legal rule can effectively shape conduct through the structuring of individual or organizational incentives only if that rule is built upon accurate models of individual and organizational behavior and choice. When judges premise legal doctrines on the notion that a particular legal rule will structure individual and organizational incentives and thereby shape behavior in a particular way, they need to get the social science right. Although far from infallible, psychological science often serves as a better source of such models than "common sense" or other forms of a priori theorizing. Behavioral realism is essential to effective preventive law.

Behavioral Realism in Law: The Case of the "Same Actor Inference"

One powerful example of how judges' faulty "common-sense" psychological theories can work their way into legal rules can be found in a doctrine known as the "same actor inference," which emerged in employment discrimination cases during the 1990s. Reading the various chapters and commentaries in this volume relating to discrimination adjudications, I was struck by one point of virtually universal agreement: Situations exert a powerful effect on the expression of intergroup bias. In fact, in employment discrimination cases, one of the most common criticisms raised by defendants to counter plaintiff-side expert testimony on implicit bias is that, in reaching his or her conclusions about the defendant's decision-making process, the plaintiff's expert did not take into sufficient account situational variables that tend to reduce or amplify the expression of stereotype-based judgments (Mitchell & Tetlock, in press; Arkes & Tetlock, 2004; Faigman, this volume; Landy, this volume).

This point of agreement reflects what is perhaps the most important insight to have emerged from social psychology in the second half of the twentieth century – that situations, combined with a person's subjective construal of these situations and his or her attempt to negotiate the conflicting constraints those situations seem to impose – exert a far more powerful effect on human behavior than the "intuitive psychologist" (Ross 1978) generally assumes. In antidiscrimination jurisprudence, as elsewhere, there is a tendency to overestimate the power of stable personality traits or "tastes" (including perhaps "implicit tastes") in shaping behavior and choice, and to underestimate the power of context.

This may be a point of near universal agreement among empirical social psychologists, but someone forgot to tell the judges. Reading opinions in federal employment discrimination cases, one sees there reflected a powerful assumption that if a person is going to discriminate against members of a particular racial, national origin, or gender group, he or she can be expected to do so *consistently*, independent of situational variables.

Extending this assumption, almost every federal circuit in the United States has adopted what is commonly known as the "same actor inference" in disparate treatment discrimination cases (Krieger & Fiske, 2006). This doctrine holds that if the same person who participates in hiring an employee later participates in a decision to fire him, a "strong inference" or "presumption" of nondiscrimination arises. In many decisions, this presumption is viewed as being so psychologically compelling that it justifies summary judgment or judgment as a matter of law for the defendant – removing the case from the jury's power to render a verdict – even if other evidence of discriminatory motivation exists (Krieger & Fiske, 2006).

Curiously, the same actor inference rule derives from what might most accurately be described as a wry aside in a 1991 law review article by economists John Donohue and Peter Siegelman, who wrote: ". . . It hardly makes sense to hire workers from a group one dislikes (thereby incurring the psychological costs of associating with them), only to fire them once they are on the job" (Donohue & Siegelman, 1991, p. 1017). First the Fourth Circuit in *Proud v. Stone* (1991), and later many other circuit and district courts, seized on this intuitive theory of discriminatory behavior and crafted the same actor rule. The rule is now frequently applied in the crafting of jury instructions and even in adjudicating motions for summary judgment or judgment as a matter of law (Krieger & Fiske, 2006).

Of course, if discrimination is viewed as stemming from a "taste" or a highly stable *ex ante* trait or preference, the same actor doctrine makes some intuitive psychological sense. But as the various substantive chapters and commentaries bearing on intergroup bias included in this volume agree, this is simply not how intergroup bias – at least in its more subtle forms – generally influences (or does not influence) decisions about individual members of stereotyped groups. Situationism muddies the forensic waters significantly.

The implications of situationism for legal doctrines like the same actor inference are both obvious and powerful. Intergroup bias does not function as a stable trait or preference that expresses consistently across all situations. Whether implicit bias will result in the behavior we call "discrimination" turns not only on a social perceiver's implicit attitudes and schematic expectancies. It also turns on the particular situation in which a social perceiver finds himself, the way he construes that situation, and the way he understands the conflicting constraints on his behavior imposed by the situation. For social perceivers functioning within a tension system (Ross & Nisbett, 1991), small changes in the situational context of judgment and choice can give rise to marked behavioral inconsistency.

For example, the hiring context often makes equal employment opportunity norms and goals salient. Human resources officials with explicit equal employment opportunity compliance functions are often involved in the hiring process, and their presence, along with the sense of accountability it generates, may constrain the expression of implicit stereotypes in the hiring process. But as Heilman and Haynes' chapter on subjectivity in performance evaluation so powerfully describes, unstructured, subjective performance appraisal may conduce to far different patterns of stereotype expression. As, day by day, managers form subjective, often spontaneously generated impressions of employee behavior, EEO goals are generally not salient. Moreover, in constructing a subjective sense of employees' performance, managers are often functioning under conditions of high cognitive load. When appraisal is unstructured and subjective, spontaneously formed impressions, as opposed to systematic behavioral analysis, can easily influence the judgmental process. Under these conditions, as Rudman, Glick, and Phelan describe in chapter 5, a stereotyped employee's behavior can easily be interpreted in stereotype-reinforcing ways. In light of the relevant social science research reviewed in this volume by both contributors and critical commentators, there is actually little reason to believe that a decision-maker who has participated in the hiring of a member of a stereotyped group will in subsequent contexts necessarily keep his or her judgments free from the influence of those stereotypes.

Of course, this is not to say that in discrimination cases an employer's past behavior should be viewed as having no probative value in determining whether his or her decision was influenced by bias in a particular case. Evidence of other acts is unquestionably relevant to proof of motive or intent, and it is explicitly made admissible for this purpose under the Federal Rules of Evidence.[9] However, the courts that have endorsed and applied the same actor inference in crafting jury instructions or deciding summary judgment motions or motions for judgment as a matter of law did not simply hold that such evidence is probative and therefore admissible to disprove *discrimination vel non*. Rather, the Fourth Circuit in *Proud v. Stone*, and the many other district and circuit courts that follow its reasoning, often find the "same actor facts" *so* probative that they are viewed as relieving

---

[9]   Federal Rules of Evidence, Rule 404(b) (providing that evidence of other acts may be admissible to prove, *inter alia*, motive or intent).

the court of the need to examine any of the other evidence in the case or to submit the case to a jury for decision. In other words, in many districts and circuits, the same actor inference functions as a judicially created *presumption* that, once raised, can be rebutted only through the introduction of clear and convincing evidence of discriminatory animus (Krieger & Fiske, 2006).

The same actor inference is a judicial creation of intuitive psychology. It has no basis in the text of any antidiscrimination statute. The judges who use it in doctrinal construction, summary adjudication, or the selection of jury instructions have made no attempt to assess its empirical validity. If they did, they would find that its theoretical premises have been largely discredited by decades of social science research. The same can be said of the organizational psychology underlying the *Faragher/Ellerth* defense. The defense is unquestionably based on a set of empirically testable claims upon which the Court relied but made no effort to assess. When deciding issues of law, there is no Rule 702 for judges, no *Daubert* hearing to scrutinize the scientific bona fides of the social science theories upon which they build legal doctrines.

Conclusion: Toward a New Role for Social Science in Antidiscrimination Adjudication

The above discussion, I suggest, points to a need for more active participation by empirical social scientists as amici curiae in employment discrimination litigation, not only in high profile appeals, but also at the trial and circuit court levels, where empirically flawed doctrines like the same actor inference gain a jurisprudential foothold. It is precisely in the "law-finding" context, where courts apply intuitive psychological theories to describe what they view as the "universals" hiding within cases' "particulars," that empirical social scientists can make the biggest difference. Judges deciding issues of law need social framework "testimony" as much as fact finders do. Participating as amici at the district court level or on appeal could help shape the legal doctrine in more behaviorally realistic ways and at the same time avoid the pitfalls associated with offering opinion testimony about the presence or absence of discrimination in a particular case.

Of course, there are strategic problems with implementing such an approach. For one, the writers of amici curiae briefs earn no fees, as expert witnesses do, so the work involved would be have to be done *pro bono*. Second, the approach would require systematic advance planning and close coordination between the bar and professional social science organizations, so that amicus briefs could be planned, written, and ready to adapt and file when they are needed in the cases best calculated to make a significant impact on the development of the law.

But if we truly expect empirical social scientists to play a significant role in advancing behavioral realism in law, we will have to forge beyond expert trial testimony. Past the familiar terrain of the jury or bench trial, there is a whole juridical world out there in the nation's courtrooms, where judges are doing psychology, much of it demonstrably bad psychology, and weaving it, unscrutinized and unvalidated, into the law.

REFERENCES

Arkes, H., & Tetlock, P. E. (2004) Attributions of implicit prejudice, or "Would Jesse Jackson 'fail' the Implicit Association Test?". *Psychological Inquiry, 15*(4), 257–278.
Beiner, T. M. (2005). *Gender myths v. working realities: Using social science to reformulate sexual harassment law.* New York: New York University Press.
Berger, V., Finkelstein, M. O., & Chang, K. (2005). Summary judgment benchmarks for settling employment discrimination lawsuits. *Hofstra Labor & Employment Law Journal, 25*, 45–83.
Bisom-Rapp, S. (2001). An ounce of prevention is a poor substitute for a pound of cure: Confronting the emerging jurisprudence of education and prevention in employment discrimination law. *Berkeley Journal of Employment and Labor Law, 22*, 1–46.
Blasi, G., & Jost, J. T. (2006). System justification theory and research: Implications for law, legal advocacy, and social justice. *California Law Review, 94*, 1119–1168. Title VII of the Civil Rights Act of 1964, 42 U.S.C. Section 2000e, *et. seq.*
Burlington Industries v. Ellerth, 524 U.S. 742 (1998).
Clermont, K. M., & Schwab, S. J. (2004). How employment discrimination plaintiffs fare in federal court. *Journal of Empirical Legal Studies, 1*, 429–458.
Daubert v. Merrell Dow Pharmaceuticals, Inc., 509 U.S. 579 (1993).
Donohue, J. J., & Siegelman, P. B. (1991). The changing nature of employment discrimination litigation. *Stanford Law Review, 43*, 1017–1033.
EEOC v. Morgan Stanley, 324 F. Supp. 2d 451, 460–462 (S.D.N.Y.) (2004).
Faigman, D. L. (1999). *Legal alchemy: The use and misuse of science in the law.* New York: St Martin's Press.
Faragher v. City of Boca Raton, 524 U.S. 775 (1998).

Federal Rules of Evidence (2006–2007). Washington, DC: U.S. Government Printing Office.

Galanter, M. (2004). The vanishing trial: An examination of trials and related matters, *Journal of Empirical Legal Studies*, *1*(3), 459–570.

Grossman, J. L. (2003). The culture of compliance: The final triumph of form over substance in sexual harassment law. *Harvard Women's Law Journal*, *26*, 3–75.

Holmes, O. W. (1963). *The common law*. Cambridge, MA: Belknap Press.

Kalev, A., Dobbin, F., & Kelly, E. (2006). Best practices or best guesses? Assessing the efficacy of corporate affirmative action and diversity policies. American Sociological Review, *71*, 589–617.

Kang, J., & Banaji, M. R. (2006). Fair measures: A behavioral realist revision of "affirmative action." *California Law Review*, *94*, 1063–1118.

Kotla v. Regents of the University of California, 8 Cal. Rptr. 3d 898 (Cal. Ct. App. 2004).

Krieger, L. H. (1995). The content of our categories: A cognitive bias approach to discrimination and equal employment opportunity. *Stanford Law Review*, *47*, 1161–1248.

Krieger, L. H. (2004). The intuitive psychologist behind the bench: Models of discrimination in social psychology and employment discrimination law. *Journal of Social Issues*, *60*, 835–848.

Krieger, L. H., & Fiske, S. T. (2006). Behavioral realism in employment discrimination law: Implicit bias and disparate treatment. *California Law Review*, *94*, 997–1062.

Kumho Tire Co. v. Carmichael, 526 U.S. 137 (1999).

Mitchell, P. G., & Tetlock, P. E. (in press). Anti-discrimination law and the perils of mind reading. *The Ohio State University Law Review*.

Proud v. Stone, 945 F.2d 796, 797 (4th Cir. 1991).

Ray v. Miller Maester Advertising, Inc., 664 N.W. 2d 355, 334–336 (Minn. Ct. of Appeals, 2003).

Ross, L. (1978). The intuitive psychologist and his shortcomings: Distortion in the attribution process. In L. Berkowitz (Ed.), *Cognitive theories in social psychology* (pp. 337–384). New York: Academic Press.

Ross, L., & Nisbett, R. E. (1991). *The person and the situation: Perspectives of social psychology*. New York: McGraw-Hill.

United States v. Hall, 93 F.3d 1337, 1343–1344 (1996).

Wechsler, H. (1959). Toward neutral principles of constitutional law. *Harvard Law Review*, *73*, 1–35.

Zick, T. (2003). Constitutional empiricism: Quasi-neutral principles and constitutional truths. *North Carolina Law Review*, *82*, 115–221.

Index